Discover The Book.org

D0736050

The Joy of a Word Filled Family

The Joy of a Word Filled Family

DR. JOHN S. BARNETT

To order a copy of this book write us at:
BFM Books/TBC, 5838 South Sheridan, Tulsa, OK 74145
or simply email us at:
books@wordfilledfamily.org

The Joy of a Word Filled Family | © 2004 by John S. Barnett

Published by Müllerhaus Publishing
2251 East Skelly Drive | Suite 103 | Tulsa, OK 74115

All rights reserved. No part of this publication may be reproduced, stored
in a retrieval system or transmitted in any form by any means, electronic,
mechanical, photocopy, recording or otherwise, without the prior permission
of the publisher, except as provided by USA copyright law.

Cover and Interior Design by Douglas Miller
Müllerhaus Publishing Arts, Inc. | *mullerhauspubarts.com*

ISBN 1-933561-02-5

Library of Congress Control Number: 2005921212

Second printing, 2005 | Printed in the United States of America

All Scripture quotations in this book, except those noted otherwise, are from
the New King James Version of the Bible. Used by permission.

The Bible version used in this publication is THE NEW KING JAMES
VERSION. Copyright 1979, 1980, 1982, Thomas Nelson, Inc., Publishers.

References marked NASB are from The New American Standard Bible,
copyright 1960, 1962, 1963, 1968, 1971, 1972, 1973, 1975, and 1977
by the Lockman Foundation and are used by permission.

References marked NIV are from The Holy Bible: New International Version, copyright
1973, 1978, 1984 by the International Bible Society. All rights reserved. Used by permission
of Zondervan Publishing House. The "NIV" and "New International Version" trademarks
are registered in the United States Patent and Trademark Office by International Bible
Society. Use of either trademark requires the permission of International Bible Society.

9   8   7   6   5   4   3

DEDICATION

THIS BOOK IS LOVINGLY DEDICATED to the one person in all the world I would love to spend every moment with—**my beloved Bonnie**, the wife of my youth, who lives out Christ each day. The law of kindness upon her lips has shaped the lives of our eight precious children, growing up around our table. As her grateful husband, I praise her here "in the gates" (Proverbs 31:31) for all the wonderful ways she portrays Christ to me and our family—I thank my God upon every remembrance of you, my sweetheart!

SPECIAL THANKS

To THE EDIT TEAM: Bonnie who typed day and night, edited countless versions, sat and captured all of my thoughts onto paper—and stayed with me through the long wait to finally get all of this into a book; Doreen Claggett for working on this with us from the earliest days by all her prayers and editing; Duke and Ann Weir for inspiring and encouraging us to actually sit down and write a book—we could not have done it without them; and to our army of faithful volunteers who edited, typed, transcribed, and helped this book through all its stages: Renee Gilligan, Julie Wright, Susan Randall, Doris Clatfelter, Terri Maltsberger, Travis Jones, Randy and Kay Watson, and Brian and Susanna Fitzgerald. And finally, many thanks to the precious elders and saints at Tulsa Bible Church who so responsively listened, so fervently prayed, and so graciously received these words as my weekly exhortations from the pulpit.

CONTENTS

A Summary of Topics for Discussion Groups, Bible Studies, and Sunday School Classes

Foreword
by John MacArthur

IT IS CLEAR THAT THE family as an institution is in serious trouble. In the 1960s, popular society openly declared war on the historic ideals of home and family. Rebellion was suddenly canonized as a virtue; divorce was destigmatized; and the role of the stay-at-home mother began to be caricatured as mindless and menial. Since then, society has rapidly and recklessly adopted new values, educational philosophies, and even government regulations that are hostile to the family. The popular media (including movies, music, talk radio, television, and even the news media) have aggressively tried to normalize whatever is aberrant and celebrate whatever is dysfunctional in modern culture while demeaning the very notion of strong, close-knit families. Our society's tolerance of abortion, homosexuality, pornography, and other evils have only further undermined the moral basis of family life.

Naturally, families are rapidly disintegrating. This is a serious threat to all civilization, because the nuclear family (consisting of father, mother, and children) is the most basic social unit and therefore the very foundation of society itself. Destroy the bonds that hold families together, and the community at large unravels. It is happening before our very eyes.

Of course, most church leaders and Christian lay people understand that the disintegration of the family is one of the greatest challenges the church faces in our generation. Scores of evangelical media ministries, Christian publishers, parachurch organizations, and parenting programs exist whose main purpose is to counteract the cultural trends that threaten the family. Some hope to solve the problem by political and legislative means. Others think the best way to influence the culture is through art, media, and education. Still others seem to believe careful training in parenting techniques is what moms and dads need most—methods of discipline, systems for teaching kids responsibility, and detailed child-rearing programs to help clueless parents.

All those things are fine and helpful in proper measure. But in this insightful book, Dr. John Barnett reminds us that the best and most important way Christians should be seeking to counter the trends of a family-hostile society is by making the Word of God the center and the focus of our own family life. The most profound and lasting impact we can make on society starts with the strengthening of our own families, and the only lasting and effective way to do that is to give the Word of God its rightful place at the center of the family.

After all, when God outlined His plan for the families of Israel, this was the whole gist of His design for parenting and home life. The Word of God was supposed to be central in every aspect of the family. It was meant to be the main subject of parental instruction and familial conversation during all times of work, travel, and leisure. The Word of God was even to be worn like jewelry and engraved on the doorposts of the house:

"These words which I command you today shall be in your heart. You shall teach them diligently to your children, and shall talk of them when you sit in your house, when you walk by the way, when you lie down, and when you rise up. You shall bind them as a sign on your hand, and they shall be as frontlets between your eyes. You shall write them on the doorposts of your house and on your gates" (DEUTERONOMY 6:6-9).

Building a Word-centered family is therefore the very heart and soul of the responsibility God Himself has given parents, and it is a duty every parent should embrace gladly and eagerly.

Dr. Barnett gives a careful and thorough explanation of what it means to have a Word-centered family and how parents can achieve that goal. He knows whereof he speaks. He and his wife Bonnie have been practicing these principles for some twenty years, raising a model family with eight children who now range from adulthood to adolescence. All of them are faithful to Christ, and they know and love His Word.

As the title of this book suggests, raising a Word-centered family is a joy, not a drudgery. That is the way God designed it to be. *"Behold, children [are] a heritage from the LORD, … Happy [is] the man who has his quiver full of them …"* (PSALM 127:3, 5). *"The father of the righteous will greatly rejoice, And he who begets a wise child will delight in him"* (PROVERBS 23:24).

For parents who are confounded and frustrated by the seemingly complex and often frustrating tasks related to leading a family, here is a much-needed resource that will help you clarify and simplify your priorities as a parent. May it be used of God to produce a generation of parents, and many generations of children whose lives and families are anchored in the Word of God, which is the only truth that lives and abides forever.

John MacArthur

"Unless the LORD builds the house, They labor in vain who build it .... Behold, children [are] a heritage from the LORD, The fruit of the womb [is] a reward. Happy [is] the man who has his quiver full of them ...."

— *Psalm 127:1a, 3, 5a*

Introduction

GOD WROTE THE FIRST BOOK on the family over 3,500 years ago through Moses—words which could be called "The Magna Carta of the Biblical Home." With 600,000 families fresh out of Egypt's idolatry to guide and nurture in the Word of the Lord, the need was great. Amazingly, the plan was simple: it can be called "The Word-Filled Family"! What specifically did the Lord ask Moses to convey to His people? He gave the key to motivating the families of Israel to keep following their God:

> "And these words which I command you today **shall be in your heart**. You shall **teach them** diligently to your children, and shall **talk of them** when you sit in your house, when you walk by the way, when you lie down, and when you rise up. You shall **bind them** as a sign on your hand, and **they shall be** as frontlets between your eyes" (DEUTERONOMY 6:6-8, Emphasis added).

What was the single most important detail of God's words to Moses? It was His call to have Word-filled marriages, families, and homes! This call is restated by Paul in the New Testament—and I believe it represents the marching orders from the God of heaven to us, His creatures. Obedience to His call is the only key that will unlock the door to a peaceful marriage, a happy family, and a joy-filled home. Yet, strange as it may seem, this very concept is foreign to most of God's people in this generation.

What happens when God's Word is ignored, neglected, or otherwise unheeded? A trip to a shopping mall, a local family department store, or sports event will alert you. We have around us a generation of frustrated and frazzled parents who don't know how to handle their children. Growing up among us is the next generation—one that is usually distracted, often spoiled, and somewhat undisciplined. The sights and sounds of disrespect, selfishness, and boiling egos are everywhere.

Sadly, the odor of selfish living is common in the one place where this type of behavior should be pleasantly absent—Christ's church. So, along with the voices of those from every generation who have held a passion for God and His Word, I raise my voice to call the family, the home, and most of all—Christ's saints—back to the Word-filled life!

Why is parenting so hard? Because we fail in so many ways! See chapter 10 for a complete guide to how to go on through failure, with our God of New Beginnings. But why do we fail? Because until heaven, we are all imperfect. I am an imperfect husband. I married an imperfect wife. We have an imperfect marriage that has produced imperfect children—which we have raised imperfectly. However, we have a Perfect Father in heaven, who has given His flawless Word as a guide to light the pathway for us to follow His plan. That plan is to have a Word-filled way of life. And that is what we have found in God's Word.

What is a Word-filled family? It is a group of individuals—beginning with Dad and Mom—who start pursuing a Word-filled life! The Apostle Paul well summarized this powerful truth and crucial need when he wrote: *"Let the word of Christ dwell in you richly ..."* (COLOSSIANS 3:16a).

- **"Let"** means "allow, invite, welcome, give yourself over to."
- **"The Word of Christ"** can be a word, a verse, a chapter, or a Book.
- **"Dwell in you richly"** so beautifully means "to overflow like a bathtub; to spill forth like a fountain; to drench and soak like a heavy rain; to permeate like water into a soft absorbent cloth."
- **"In you"** means in your mind, in your thoughts, in your life, in your plans, in your world—your marriage, your family, your home, and your job.

When we "allow, invite, welcome, and give ourselves over to" a verse, a chapter, or a Book, a portion of the very Word of Christ spills forth into our lives, drenching us—absorbing into our souls and changing every aspect of our lives—our marriage, home, life, and all! **That is the Word-filled life!** (It is also the Spirit-filled life, as Ephesians 5:18 affirms.) And that way of living is the foundation of this book.

When we have a Word-filled life it means that we are: inviting God to speak; seeking His guidance; seeking divine help, godly wisdom, supernatural involvement; and cooperating with the Holy Spirit. This amounts to plugging in the power for life, using the map God has provided, following the directions in His Book, and listening to the instructions He has left us for daily living. A Word-filled life is inviting God to speak; welcoming His help; seeking His input; wanting His advice; getting His help; showing we honor Him; partnering with God in parenting; and **unleashing Him into every corner of our lives.**

This reminds us that our marriages and families will grow either our way (without His Word), or God's way (with His Spirit-empowered Scriptures). We must start each day seeking to be emptied of self, with His Word read, our God sought, and His Spirit invited—to work in us so that Christ is honored.

What are the results of such a life and home? This book is arranged around the answers to that question. God's Word tells us these four wonderful truths for those who allow the Scriptures to permeate their lives.

- Part One: There is **no greater reward** than a Word-filled life (1 Thessalonians 2:19-20).
- Part Two: There is **no greater partnership** than a Word-filled marriage (1 Peter 3:1-7).

- Part Three: There is **no greater joy** than a
  Word-filled family (3 John 4).
- Part Four: There is **no greater power** than a
  Word-filled prayer life (James 4:2b).

My authority for writing this book on the family is not personal experience—even though I am a pastor, the husband of a fantastic and beautiful wife, and the father of eight wonderful children. Because experiences always differ, they must never be the foundation for what we believe. Rather, my authority is the God of the Word, and the scriptural instructions He has provided for having a marriage as He designed it to be, building a family, and shaping a godly, joy-filled home.

This entire book represents a challenge to get serious with the Lord, to unreservedly surrender to Christ and His Word—for His sake, and that of His precious heritage (Psalm 127:3). You will find in doing so no greater joy than to see your children walk in truth (3 John 4)!

If you'll stay with me, between the covers of this book you will be both instructed and challenged with the Scriptures. And, by God's grace, you will be drawn to desire a Word-filled life as a man or a woman, a Word-filled marriage as a husband or wife, a Word-filled family as a father or mother, and a Word-filled prayer life as a couple in oneness of heart and mind. It is my deepest prayer that you will choose to renew, restart, or begin for the first time, letting the Word of God utterly fill your life!

Sola Fide—only by faith can we enter into Christ.

Sola Gratia—only by grace can we continue walking with Him.

Sola Scriptura—only by the Word-filled life can we become all that God wants us to be!

John Barnett
Tulsa, Oklahoma
April 2004

"For what is our hope, or joy, or crown of rejoicing? Are not even ye in the presence of our Lord Jesus Christ at his coming? For ye are our glory and joy."

— *1 Thessalonians 2:19-20, kjv*

Word-filled living is living the best life possible. *When we have a Word-filled life it means that we are: inviting God to speak; seeking His guidance; seeking divine help, godly wisdom, supernatural involvement; and co-operating with the Holy Spirit. This amounts to plugging in the power for life, using the map God has provided, following the directions in His Book, and listening to the instructions He has left us for daily living. A Word-filled life is inviting God to speak; welcoming His help; seeking His input; wanting His advice; showing we honor Him; partnering with God in parenting; and* **unleashing Him into every corner of our lives.**

PART ONE

A Word Filled Life

There Is *No* Greater Reward

1

"Then Jesus said to those … who believed Him,
'If you abide in My word, you are My disciples indeed.
And you shall know the truth, and the truth shall
make you free.'"

— *John 8:31-32*

The Word
Filled Walk

JUNE OF 2004: THE DEATH and burial of our fortieth president brought forth a national resurrection of discussions about the greatness of Ronald Reagan's life. Perhaps the single greatest event he was remembered for was breaking down the "Iron Curtain" walls of Communism and opening freedom to so many. The Iron Curtain enslaved millions largely because of the incredible dedication of the few. Those devoted followers of Communism's atheistic philosophy were able to conquer much of the world in one generation.

One man in 1903, with a handful of followers, began Communism. His name was Vladimir Lenin (1870–1924). He overthrew the Russian government in 1917 with only 40,000 Communist Party members. His movement became the fastest growing system in the history of the world, and by the 1950s his followers controlled about 62 percent of the world's population—and brutally held on to their power.

Communism triumphed largely because of the complete devotion of its followers. This dedication was typified in an actual letter written by a young communist to his fiancée, breaking off their engagement. The girl's pastor sent the letter to Billy Graham, who referred to it in a crusade message a number of years ago. Listen to what this young communist wrote:

> *There is one thing, which I am in dead earnest about, and that is the communist cause. It is my life, my business, my religion, my hobby, my sweetheart, my wife, my mistress, and my bread and meat. I work at it in the daytime and dream of it at night. Its hold on me grows, not lessens, as time goes on; therefore, I cannot carry on a friendship, a love affair, or even a conversation without relating it to this force which both drives and guides my life. I evaluate people, looks, ideas, and actions according to how they affect the communist cause, and by their attitude toward it. I've already been in jail because of my ideals, and if necessary, I'm ready to go before a firing squad.*[a]

a. William MacDonald,
True Discipleship
(Kansas City, KS: Walterick
Publishers, 1975), p. 33.

That is total dedication. Even without divine help, God's grace, the Spirit's power, or Christ's love, look at the intense devotion humans can produce. Can you imagine what God does when He finds this level of dedication in our hearts, minds, and wills as His children? Turn with me to the life of another man to answer that question. It was 1917—while Lenin was master to his deeply devoted revolutionaries, God was at work in the heart of one of His servants, drawing him to deeply devote himself to Jesus. This man was being mastered by the Master of heaven and earth at the very same time Lenin was starting his destructive revolution. This man wrote down a prayer of consecration to Jesus as Master and King.

The words of his prayer became this hymn, written when the author was 51; unable to finish the career he wanted, weak and sickly, unemployed, he tried to make ends meet selling things door to door.

"LIVING FOR JESUS"

*Living for Jesus a life that is true, Striving to please
Him in all that I do; Yielding allegiance, glad-hearted
and free, This is the pathway of blessing for me.*

Living for Jesus who died in my place, Bearing on Calv'ry
my sin and disgrace; Such love constrains me to answer
His call, Follow His leading and give Him my all.

Living for Jesus wherever I am, Doing each duty
in His holy name; Willing to suffer affliction and
loss, Deeming each trial a part of my cross.

Living for Jesus through earth's little while, My dearest trea-
sure, the light of His smile; Seeking the lost ones He died
to redeem, Bringing the weary to find rest in Him.

Chorus: *O Jesus, Lord and Savior, I give myself to Thee,*
For Thou in Thy atonement, Didst give Thyself for me. I
own no other Master, My heart shall be Thy throne: My
life I give, henceforth to live, O Christ, for Thee alone.

Where did such a confession come from? A first-century saint? No, just from a man who was too weak and sick to do what he wanted to do in life. He had to leave full-time vocational ministry and do a door-to-door sales job just to stay alive and eat. His name was Thomas Obadiah Chisholm. Born in a humble log cabin in Franklin, Kentucky, on July 29, 1866, without the benefit of high school or college, he began his career as a schoolteacher at the age of sixteen in the same country schoolhouse where he had received his elementary training.

Because of a weak body, poor health, and limited finances—Tom spent most of his long life indoors seated at a writing table. Writing, however, was always his first love, and he wrote more than 1,200 poems, of which 800 were published. "Living for Jesus" captures the devotion of a life given to Jesus.

How do we cultivate that level of dedication to Jesus? Mark 4:20 tells us that Jesus calls this "accepting" the Word. That means welcoming His Word into our hearts and lives—His Word and His way we embrace as our own. What does a heart look like that accepts the Word? How is a life lived that welcomes as its own Jesus Christ the Word of God? The Gospels capture six elements from the very lips of Jesus. Listen to Him. Accept His Word. Desire this depth of devotion, and welcome Him by giving yourself to Him.

Jesus Wants to Have *All* of Us

WE CAN TRACE CHRIST'S CALL to commitment in the Gospels. He states we can't be His disciples unless we desire to evidence these characteristics. Here are some ways that we evidence Christ as our Master and that we are His followers. Notice that He wants our hearts, bodies, wills, eyes, actions, and lives.

Word-filled hearts are opened completely in love for Christ— that means *we love Him most*.

"If anyone comes to Me and does not hate his father and mother, wife and children, brothers and sisters, yes, and his own life also, he cannot be My disciple" (LUKE 14:26).

The word "hate" in this verse essentially has to do with a comparison of loves. Simply put, our love for God is to be so great that, in comparison, love for even the dearest of friends should seem as hatred. This is based upon His first and greatest commandment: *"You shall love the LORD your God with all your heart, with all your soul, and with all your mind."*[a]

a. Matthew 22:37-38

We will continually be confronted, both in the good times and the bad, with whether we are going to obey Christ and His Word—or buckle under to pressures to compromise our faith and "go with the crowd." Each opportunity to serve God represents this test: who do we love most? If we do not give Christ the preeminence He deserves, He says that we are not worthy of Him.[b]

b. Colossians 1:18
   Matthew 10:37

Loving God with an unrivaled love means that we will esteem nothing—family, friends, possessions, job, fame, power, pleasures, and especially ourselves—of more worth to us than He is. In so doing, we demonstrate His "worthship" to us by choosing to do things His way, and not our own. This is the essence of true worship. By losing our lives in that manner for Christ's sake, we will find them.[c]

c. Matthew 16:25

Chisholm's declaration of this truth is in stanza 2B of this hymn: *"Such love constrains me to answer His call, Follow His leading and give*

Him my all." If you haven't opened your **heart** like this to Him—I urge you to stop and do so now.

Word-filled **bodies** are offered completely to Christ— that means *we die to self.*

"Whoever does not bear his cross and come after Me cannot be My disciple" (LUKE 14:27).

This verse is related to Luke 14:26 in that to "bear [our] cross" means loving Christ enough to voluntarily crucify our self daily. In Mark 8:34 Christ states, *"Whoever desires to come after Me, let him deny himself, and take up his cross, and follow Me."* That word "deny" has the strongest meaning possible—"to utterly deny; to totally separate from." Taking up our cross by denying self is imperative because it's impossible to serve two masters.[a] The following testimony by George Mueller beautifully describes the heart of such a life.

"There was a day when I died, utterly died to George Mueller; ... to his opinions, preferences, tastes, and will; died to the world, its approval or censure; died to the approval or blame of even my brethren and friends. Since then I have studied to show myself approved only unto God."[b]

Here's a powerful idea: Read Mueller's testimony aloud to your wife. Tell her you are making this your personal goal. What an encouragement and joy this will be to your wife. Dying to self is a prerequisite to living for Christ. Paul wrote of this when he said, *"I am crucified with Christ; it is no longer I who live, but Christ lives in me; and the life which I now live in the flesh I live by faith in the Son of God."*[c] In spite of the cost of death to self, and whatever personal suffering that may bring, a dedicated disciple will follow after Christ, wherever He chooses to lead.

Our will is pitted against God's when we do not bear the cross of self-denial—and that is prideful. Pride is the root of all sin because self competes with God for control and glory. Humility, in contrast, is the root of all virtue because humility denies self and says, "Not my will, but Yours be done!" Such humility produces deep and abiding joy[d] as

a. Matthew 6:24

b. Mrs. Charles E. Cowman, *Springs in the Valley* (Grand Rapids, MI: Zondervan, 1939), p. 13.

c. Galatians 2:20

d. Matthew 26:39 John 15:10-11

the result of knowing—and truly pleasing—Almighty God, our Savior and Lord. Living a life that is uncompromising when it comes to bearing the cross of self-denial is a mark of a true disciple. Chisholm's declaration of this truth is in stanza 1B: *"Yielding allegiance, glad-hearted and free, This is the pathway of blessing for me."* Have you given your **body** anew and afresh to Him today?

Word-filled **wills** are surrendered unreservedly to Christ— that means *we want to obey Him.*

"Whoever of you does not forsake all that he has cannot be My disciple" (LUKE 14:33).

Because Christ purchased us with His blood, we belong wholly to Him.[a] In light of this, He expects us to acknowledge His rightful ownership by not holding back anything for ourselves.

Christ as our Master has the right of disposal of all our possessions.[b] Christ is the Owner; as His stewards, we are only employees. Consider the testimonies of such godly disciples as Martin Luther, John Wesley, and David Livingstone. Martin Luther once said, "I have held many things in my hands and I have lost them all. But whatever I have placed in God's hands, that I still possess." "I value all things," said Wesley, "only by the price they shall gain in eternity." Similarly, Livingstone stated, "I place no value on anything I possess except in relation to the Kingdom of God." These men truly forsook everything for the cause of Christ—and their lives speak to this day!

Christ says to us likewise, "Out of love for Me, forsake all you own—and your life will be truly blessed!" We should be so captivated with the Lord that we invest all we have for Him, letting nothing take higher priority than obedience and worship of Christ. A life given unreservedly back to God as a love offering is what stewardship is all about. Stewardship is not only about money, it is about life itself. Time and life are far greater treasures than money and possessions. First and foremost, God wants us—unreservedly! Chisholm's declaration of this truth is in the last half of the chorus: *"I own no other Master, My heart shall be Thy throne: My life I give, henceforth to live, O Christ, for*

a. 1 Corinthians 6:19-20

b. Matthew 19:21

Thee alone." Bow your heart. Yield your **will**. Use these words to surrender anew to Him.

**Word-filled eyes are focused eagerly on the Scriptures—
that means *we hunger to see Him in His Word.***

*"Then Jesus said to those Jews who believed Him, 'If you abide in
My Word, you are My disciples indeed. And you shall know the
truth, and the truth shall make you free' "* (JOHN 8:31-32).

Note that Jesus is addressing those who "believed Him"; belief in
Christ as personal Savior and Lord is the first step of discipleship.[a]   a. John 3:16-18
Abiding in His Word bears witness that we have true life in Christ. In
Greek, "abide" (*meno*) in verse 31 primarily means "to stay." We show
that His love is in us[b] by staying in His Word, becoming not only a "hear-   b. James 1:22-25
er" but also a "doer" of the Word. It is as we know Truth experientially,   John 15:10-11
that we too, like the psalmist, ought to cry out to our awesome Lord:

*"Oh, how I love Your law! It [is] my meditation all the day. ... I
have restrained my feet from every evil way, that I may keep Your
word. I have not departed from Your judgments, For You Yourself
have taught me. How sweet are Your words to my taste, [Sweeter]
than honey to my mouth! Through Your precepts I get understanding; Therefore I hate every false way"* (PSALM 119:97, 101-104).

Oh, that each of us would have this same passion for God and His
Word! It's inconceivable that the majority of Christians today, in light
of the rich treasures to be had, have not read the Bible through even
once—especially since it takes an average reader only 15 minutes
daily. If you haven't already been doing so, I challenge you to begin
reading the Bible through no less than once a year. Beyond reading the Word faithfully, we should also do word studies to pursue a
theme of interest; read commentaries; do Bible studies; memorize
Scripture; and meditate upon it daily.

If all we do is hear the Word preached, we're like a person trying to
grasp a softball with just our little finger. Adding hearing plus faithful
reading is better, and adding study is better still. However, we cannot
get much of a hold on the ball with only three fingers. We need all four

fingers and an opposing thumb to firmly grasp a softball. So we need to **hear, read, study, memorize,** and **meditate** upon God's Word in order to firmly grasp the Scriptures.

We will never become mature disciples without having an unbounded passion to read, study, and obey His precious Word. This is what will inspire us to truly love Christ and others as He has commanded; all relationships are centered in fulfilling these two loves.[a] Chisholm's declaration of this truth is in stanza 4A: *"Living for Jesus through earth's little while, My dearest treasure, the light of His smile."* You can see the light of His smile reflected in His Word each time you choose to fix your eyes upon it.

a. Matthew 22:37-40

Word-filled **actions** are focused selflessly on love for others— that means *we love with Christ's love.*

"A new commandment I give to you, that you love one another; as I have loved you, that you also love one another. By this all will know that you are My disciples, if you have love for one another" (JOHN 13:34-35).

The commandment to love was not new, but the manner of love to be shown was now taking on a new dimension—to love as Christ has loved. What type of love had His disciples experienced[b] from Christ up to that point? Matthew Henry writes:

b. John 13.12-17

> *He spoke kindly to them, concerned himself heartily for them, and for their welfare, instructed, counseled, and comforted them, prayed with them and for them, vindicated them when they were accused, took their part when they were run down, and publicly owned them to be dearer to him than his mother, or sister, or brother. He reproved them for what was amiss, and yet compassionately bore with their failings, excused them, made the best of them, and passed by many an oversight. Thus he had loved them, and just now washed their feet; and thus they must love one another, and love to the end.[c]*

c. Matthew Henry, *Matthew Henry's Commentary, Vol. V. - Matthew to John* (McLean, VA: MacDonald Publishing Company, 1974), p.1104.

And love to the end Christ did—all the way to Calvary—a final example of what it means to love "as He has loved us." He loved us unconditionally, and that is the way He wants us to love one another: *"Greater love has no one than this, than to lay down one's life for his friends."*[a]

a. John 15:13

Our homes are the basic testing grounds for learning how to love Christ's way. It is much easier to fool others who don't know about all our weaknesses, but it is the day-to-day relationships within our families that reveal our true character.

Personal relationships should not be guided by whether we feel like loving at any particular moment. Loving as Christ loves involves commitment: with a voluntary act of our will, we choose, by God's grace, to always act in the best interest of others, regardless of their response to us.[b]

b. Romans 13:10

Our wives and children need to see Calvary love compelling us to live sacrificially for Christ's sake and theirs.[c] This is how the world will distinguish us from Satan's crowd; they will know we are clearly Christ's disciples. Chisholm's declaration of this truth is in stanza 4B: *"Seeking the lost ones He died to redeem, Bringing the weary to find rest in Him."* Intentional investment of **selfless actions** in others is what we need to echo from our hearts to God in prayer—and then do so!

c. 2 Corinthians 5:14-15

Word-filled lives are spent intentionally on fruit bearing for God's glory—that means *we walk in the Spirit*.

"If you abide in Me, and My words abide in you, you will ask what you desire, and it shall be done for you. By this My Father is glorified, that you bear much fruit; so you will be My disciples" (JOHN 15:7-8).

The ultimate goal of discipleship is this: *"Be imitators of God as dear children. And walk in love, as Christ also has loved us and given Himself for us, an offering and a sacrifice to God for a sweet-smelling aroma."*[d]

d. Ephesians 5:1-2

Discipleship is an ongoing, lifelong process by which the Holy Spirit uses the Word of God, to conform the child of God, into the image of God, for the glory of God. And in so doing, He produces in us the fruit of God: love, joy, peace, longsuffering, kindness, goodness, faithfulness, gentleness, and self-control.[e] That fruit is manifested in a Word-filled disciple's life as:

e. Galatians 5:22

- Love, joy, and peace that flows from a Word-filled heart given in total love for Christ—**saying** I will love Him most.
- Self-control in a Word-filled body offered completely—**saying** I will die to self.
- Faithfulness demonstrated by a Word-filled will in unreserved surrender of all to Christ—**saying** I will obey.
- Goodness reflected by Word-filled eyes focused eagerly on God's Word—**saying** I will hunger for God's Word.
- Gentleness and kindness lived out in Word-filled actions focused selflessly on love for others—**saying** I will love with Christ's love.

Chisholm's declaration of this truth is in the first half of the chorus: *"O Jesus, Lord and Savior, I give myself to Thee, For Thou in Thy atonement, Didst give Thyself for me."*

None of us are able, in and of ourselves, to fulfill this blessed calling.[a] But the good news is that Christ isn't after ability—but availability. It is for that reason that He tells us to surrender ourselves unreservedly to Him, and then trust Him to do whatever it takes to produce great fruitfulness, *"for it is God who works in [us] both to will and to do for His good pleasure."*[b] It is with dedicated spirits, coupled with progressive fruit in our lives, that we may then honestly say to our families: *"Imitate me, just as I also [imitate] Christ."*[c]

a. John 15:5

b. Romans 12:1-2
Philippians 2:13

c. 1 Corinthians 11:1

APPLICATION:

Why not take a few moments and read again through this hymn of consecration? And after reading each stanza, pray them to the Lord. Ask Him to receive your life at this moment, afresh and anew, to be lived for Him.

"LIVING FOR JESUS"

Living for Jesus a life that is true, Striving to please
Him in all that I do; Yielding allegiance, glad-hearted
and free, This is the pathway of blessing for me.

Living for Jesus who died in my place, Bearing on Calv'ry
my sin and disgrace; Such love constrains me to answer
His call, Follow His leading and give Him my all.

Living for Jesus wherever I am, Doing each duty
in His holy name; Willing to suffer affliction and
loss, Deeming each trial a part of my cross.

Living for Jesus through earth's little while, My dearest
treasure, the light of His smile; Seeking the lost ones He
died to redeem, Bringing the weary to find rest in Him.

Chorus: O Jesus, Lord and Savior, I give myself to Thee;
For Thou in Thy atonement, Didst give Thyself for me. I
own no other Master, My heart shall be Thy throne: My
life I give, henceforth to live, O Christ, for Thee alone.

STUDY GUIDE QUESTIONS

1. **In Luke 14:26, Jesus says that if we don't "hate" our loved ones—and even our own lives—we can't be His disciple.** How do you reconcile that with His command to "love one another" in John 13:34-35?

2. **Is it possible to bear the cross of self-denial** (Luke 14:27) **and yet still cling to our pride?**
   How would you define pride?
   How would you define humility?
   Can you think of a biblical example of each from your own life?

3. **Why does Christ tell us to "forsake all"** (Luke 14:33) **in order to be His disciple?**

4. **Why is abiding in God's Word** (John 8:31-32) **so very important?**
   In order to firmly grasp scriptural truths, what five habits are
       vital to establish in our lives? We need to _____,
       _____, _____, _____,
   and _____ upon God's Word.

5. Give an example of what it means to love "as He has loved us"
(John 13:34-35).

> Are your relationships guided more by "feelings" or a
> "commitment" to act in the best interest of others?

6. Explain how abiding in Christ and His Word (John 15:7-8) is
directly related to having a powerful prayer life.

> What is God's ultimate discipleship goal for us?

7. How does your life compare with the six characteristics of a
disciple as described in chapter 1?

> In areas that are still weak, prayerfully list steps you believe Christ
> would have you take to become more committed to Him.

2

"And God [is] able to make all grace abound toward you, that you, always having all sufficiency in all [things], may have an abundance for every good work."

—2 Corinthians 9:8

Women Energized by Hope

THE BIBLE OFTEN RECORDS THE lives of women. There are 2,930 individuals named in Scripture—327 are women, and nearly all of them are wives and mothers. We know more specific good things about women from God's Word than from any other ancient document.

None of the women—of all the women of the Bible—are more special than the five who actually open the pages of the New Testament. Who are they? They are the five precious wives and mothers tucked away in the genealogy of Jesus Christ. Why would God place them there in that usually "men only" genealogical section? You will see, as you read this chapter, encouraging applications these women offer as a testimony from their lives:

- Their lives give **hope** to those who have failed, and feel that it is impossible to ever go on and please God.

- Their lives give **comfort** to those who ache with pain from wounds, sorrows, and hurts that God has allowed to invade their lives.
- Their lives are an incredible source of **strength** to those who have a long struggle ahead. Knowing that God helped them, sustained them, and kept them going fosters confidence that no struggle will ever exceed His grace and power to uphold.

Five Word-Filled Women

HAVE YOU EVER STUDIED THE women with whom God chose to surround Christ's coming to earth? I am talking about the highly unusual presence of five special women included in His genealogy in Matthew 1. It is interesting that no women are listed in any of the genealogical records of the Old and New Testaments except for Matthew's. Matthew 1:1-16 lists five special mothers in the line awaiting the coming of the Promised One. Women weren't highly regarded in ancient times; they lived in a man's world. This fact made life very difficult for them. God profiles these five courageous and gifted women because they were a part of God's team. Their lives were part of God's plan to bring a ray of light to herald the sunrise on the night of sin that had come into our world. Through their line, the promised Savior was going to be supernaturally born!

What is so absolutely amazing about these five? They were all women with a mark against them. When we think of Tamar, what do we think of? Incest. What is the first thing that comes to mind when I mention Rahab? Harlotry. How about Ruth? She was from the cursed, incestuously-conceived nation called Moab. And Bathsheba? Her name is synonymous with adultery! As for Mary, she's virtuous to us, but in her day she was haunted for her lifetime with a shadow of being—an unwed mother!

Each of these women was stained either by her own sin, the sins of another, or the scandalous plots of others. Additionally, not only were they marked by some kind of stain in their lives, but also most were unqualified. Do you know why? Jesus Christ was to be a Jew, and He was—but at least three, if not four of these women, weren't even Jews. God chose to reach outside of His covenant people: Mary was a Jew, and possibly Tamar; Bathsheba was Hittite; Ruth was Moabite; and Rahab was Canaanite. Only one word can adequately describe what God did in their cases—**grace**!

When we talk about these women who were energized by hope in the remainder of this chapter, we will be looking at women who were His beautiful portraits of grace—women who were defrauded, defiled, despised, defeated, or determined—yet, all were given a part in God's grand and glorious plan!

If you are like most mothers, there have probably been times in your parenting when you have felt ready to quit! Whenever that type of emotional tidal wave happens to sweep over you, remember these five incredible mothers who overcame great obstacles to shine through the centuries like the rare and precious jewels they are in God's sight! Now then, let's meet each of these special women individually.

Be a Word-Filled Woman of Hope

1. LIKE TAMAR—NO PAIN IS TOO GREAT

Thirty-eight centuries ago, in Genesis 38, we are introduced to Tamar. Whenever you think of her, think of a woman "*defrauded.*" One of Judah's sons had married her, but was personally struck dead by God because he was a wicked sinner, a rebellious man. Judah promised, as was the custom, that he would get her a new husband. Tamar put on her widow's raiment and waited, and waited, but she was forgotten. Judah had taken care of everything else except for her. Tamar was lied to and overlooked, and she finally took the law into her own hands. Posing as a harlot, she had an incestuous affair with her own father-in-law. A child born out of wedlock resulted. God never condoned what she did; He just described it. Tamar was defrauded of many things:

- She was defrauded of a normal life.
- She was defrauded of a happy marriage.
- She was defrauded of a good name.
- She was defrauded of a sterling reputation.

Tamar was robbed of all these normal expectations by one thing— sin. She was a woman who was defrauded by losing her husband. She was overlooked by her husband's father. She then allowed sin to cause her to take matters into her own hands through an illicit union. But, in spite of all that, God compassionately looked down at her and said, "I have a plan for Tamar! She is a woman of hope—a woman who portrays My plan—a wicked sinner, forgiven!" She was allowed to be part of the line that would bring the Redeemer to humanity— Christ, the One who perfectly portrays God's grace! God graciously placed Tamar in Christ's family tree, as recorded in Matthew 1:3: *"Judah begot Perez and Zerah by Tamar ...."*

Do you have the pain of being wronged or defrauded by someone who promised love, and then deserted you? Then through your pain listen to the voice of Jesus as He whispers to you, like He did to Paul, *"My grace is sufficient for you. My strength is made perfect in [your] weakness."*[a] Believe the truth and go on; let God fill you with the comfort and strength of His Word!

a. 2 Corinthians 12:9

2. LIKE RAHAB—NO PAST IS TOO BAD

If we were to identify Rahab with one word, the word that best describes her is *"defiled."* Her life story is introduced in the second chapter of Joshua. In 1406 B.C., fifteen centuries before Christ, the children of Israel faced the walls of Jericho. A woman was on those walls—a very smart businesswoman. She was in two ancient businesses that were often interchanged: (1) inn keeping, and (2) harlotry. She not only provided lodging, but also gave men a sinful substitute for what God ordained in marriage. In every sense, Rahab was defiled:

- She was a sexual sinner.
- She was a member of the cursed Canaanite race.
- She was a doomed city-dweller.
- She was literally sitting on a "time bomb" because God's judgment was about to cause the walls to fall.

However, in His mercy, God said, "I'm going to destroy everyone and everything in Jericho except for that tiny section of the wall—and that little family huddled together at the inn there." Can you imagine what it must have been like on that day of destruction? To see the 60-foot-high walls crumble and fall around you while your portion of the wall stood firm? To witness the Hebrew army march in, slice and demolish every living thing in its path? To watch the city in which you've lived and worked all of your life suddenly go up in flames?

Nevertheless, Rahab, through faith, heeded God's warning through the spies: "Stay inside of your house; hang a red cord out your *window* and you will be saved!" So that day, in Joshua 2, God reached down and plucked Rahab with her family out of the inferno of His destruction on Jericho.

Have you ever met anyone like Rahab? She was terminally defiled; in every sense her destruction was looming. Her story is one of the most beautiful pictures of how God saves lost people. You see, Rahab was part of a doomed race, and so are we. Did you know that the human race itself is doomed? Every one of us has a terminal illness. Some people know the name of it; the rest of us just don't know what is going to "get us" yet. But one thing is for certain: death will happen sooner or later. We are all going to die, and the germ that will kill us is called sin. No one gave it to us; we received it by inheritance from our forefather, Adam, who had fallen into sin. Every one of us is guilty of sin; each of us faces His judgment.[a] We are all in a world that God is going to destroy,[b] but, by God's grace, we can be eternally saved![c]

a. Romans 3:23; 6:23
b. Revelation 21:1-8
c. Ephesians 2:8-9

Rahab's life is quite a portrait of salvation by God's grace. He needed no spy report; He graciously wanted Rahab, and put this defiled woman in His plan. She was in the line of special mothers who would bring Christ to portray God's marvelous grace to the world, as recorded in Matthew 1:5: *"Salmon begot Boaz by Rahab."*

If your past is less than sterling (and whose isn't?), always remember that this too is God's offer of grace. What do I mean? Listen to the voice of Jesus as He spoke to a Rahab in the New Testament, who wept about her sinful past, at His feet: *"Her sins, which are many, are forgiven, for she loved much. But to whom little is forgiven, [the same] loves little."*[d] A stained past "forgiven" is the opportunity to "love much"—a wonderful, loving Savior who forgives much!

d. Luke 7:47

3. Like Ruth—No Problem Is Too Big

It is in the second part of Matthew 1:5 that we see another special mother in Christ's lineage—Ruth—who could be described as having been *"despised."* Yet, her life represents such a beautiful portrait of grace that God devoted a full Book to tell about it. Ruth's story began way back in Genesis 19. Ruth's distant forefather—Abraham's nephew, Lot—in the midst of a drunken orgy with his two unscrupulous daughters, sired Ruth's race. It is noteworthy that in Scripture God doesn't cut out any of the facts because they capture lessons He wants us to learn. He has always condemned drunkenness, and the various evils that accompany it. It should come as no surprise that the sins, which produced the tribe of Moabites, would lead to a people under God's judgment.

These people whom God had cursed because of their wickedness were protected until Deuteronomy 23. Because the Moabites were from such a defiled and despised race, God announced that no Moabite could enter God's assembly for ten generations.[a] Therefore, though Ruth had done nothing personally to deserve it, she was despised by the Jewish people. Remember all the strikes against her?

- She was of the wrong race.
- She was out of the wrong family.
- She was tainted by a bad past.
- She was hounded by someone else's sin.
- She was scarred by a family scandal.
- She was plagued by the darkness of a stain.

Additionally, after a short marriage, Ruth's husband died; and a famine was all around them. God tells, in the Book of Ruth, one of the sweetest Old Testament stories of grace that has ever been written! What did He write? He reported how He graciously reached down and took a woman from a cursed race, a despised people, and said, "You come into My family!" Thus a man named Boaz took Ruth to be his wife, and she then, upon that marriage, became a woman of hope. Like Tamar and Rahab, Ruth was one through whom Christ would come—one through whom God gloriously portrayed His grace, as recorded in Matthew 1:5: *"Boaz begot Obed by Ruth ...."*

a. Deuteronomy 23:3-4

Adversity reveals who we really are. Its fires burn away only what is temporary, and leave behind what is permanent. What are your trials revealing? Peter said that God's grace accepted in trials purifies us, and we become precious like costly gold.[a] Give those big problems to the Lord, allow Him to refine you and do something you could never plan or imagine—and then He will get all the glory!

a. 1 Peter 1:3-8

4. LIKE BATHSHEBA—NO STAIN IS TOO DEEP

The story of the fourth woman of hope is told in 2 Samuel 1 and 12. Bathsheba was in the wrong place at the wrong time—in all these areas we could call her "*defeated*":

- She was unwise at best.
- She was immodest in her display.
- She responded to David's interest in her, even though she was another man's wife, and he was another woman's husband.
- She muffled her heart's warning as God's conviction was upon her conscience.
- She stifled the virtuous vows that she had made of lifelong loyalty to Uriah.
- She ignored the fact that God had given her a wonderful husband.
- She yielded herself to passion, and the sin that would follow.

What did Bathsheba reap from all that defeat? Her husband, Uriah, was murderously slain, and the baby she had conceived by David choked out his life in death. Bathsheba and David—the grieving, sorrowing mother and the murderous, adulterous father—faced great sadness. And, after Nathan spoke to David about his sin, the world would forever know that Bathsheba was a defeated woman. Her sin became monumental for all time. Numerous movies have even been made about her illicit romance, which was both public and shameful.

Some people may think: *Oh, I can do that, and no one will ever find out. We can cover our tracks!* But the Scriptures say that whatever you sow, you will reap; and whatever you whisper in secret will be shouted from the rooftops.[b]

b. Matthew 10:27; Galatians 6:7-8

What did God do about Bathsheba? He graciously lifted her out of her pit of defeat. In doing so, God was saying, "Here's a woman who is unworthy, who is a sinner. Though she's done many things wrong, I'm going to let her be one through whom I will bring Christ into this world." God also poured out His grace upon David and Solomon, from whom we've received a great deal of our Scripture. Through them, we learn about what it means to live wisely—to be someone after God's own heart. And, according to His perfect plan, Bathsheba became a beautiful portrait of His grace, as we find in Matthew 1:6: *"David the king begot Solomon by her who had been the wife of Uriah."*

Jesus loves to forgive and cleanse. He is waiting today, as He was in Revelation 2-3, for us to hear His voice, repent of our sin, and let Him wash us clean. Revelation 1:5 says that Jesus wants us to know Him as the One who *"loved us, and washed us* [KJV] *and freed us* [NIV] *from our sins."* No stain of the past, no sin of our youth, no failure in our home or marriage is too deep for the God of the Second Chance. No failures are permanent with Him. Take your burdens to the Lord right now, and start over. The Christian life is a continual offer from God—new beginnings. Bow before Jesus and start over as a woman of God, a wife for God, and a godly mother—right now.

5. LIKE MARY—NO TASK IS TOO GREAT

The word that best describes our final woman of hope is *"determined."* What is interesting about Mary is that we have heard a lot about her that is not true, and we know very little about her from what the Bible records. In fact, books and books have been written about Mary, none of which contain facts from the Bible. What is in the Bible?

We know this to be truth: Mary was born a sinner. There is nothing in Scripture which says Mary was anything else other than a very normal sinner. She came to faith in the true God by acknowledging that she was lost without Him.[a] She quoted from the Old Testament, talking about the fact that God lifted her up out of the ash heap, out of the dung hill.[b] Mary, who wanted to know God's Word and obey it, even as a young woman became quiet and determined. She kept on following and obeying the Lord—even through all this:

- She fell in love, and was engaged.
- She was visited by an angel.
- She received an unusual commission.
- She supernaturally conceived a child.

a. Luke 1:47

b. I Samuel 2:7-8; Luke 1:52

- She faced possible stoning because that
  was the penalty for fornication.
- She was scorned by others and falsely accused.
- After Christ's birth, Mary patiently endured public shame for one-
  third of a century—through the entire life and ministry of Christ.
- She was even "put in her place" by Jesus.
- She was continually saddened by her unbelieving sons.
- She never gave up; she determinedly
  pressed on in faith for God's glory!

All that Mary was experiencing fit perfectly with God's gracious plan: He had chosen her to be the "Mother of the Promise." She bore Christ. She partook of grace. She rejoiced and said, "Oh, God, my Savior!"[a] She ultimately became the one through whom "The Promise" arrived: *"And Jacob begot Joseph the husband of Mary, of whom was born Jesus who is called Christ."*[b]

a. Luke 1:47

b. Matthew 1:16

The lesson for us today is to decide *now* that we are in this for the duration. We see our husband and children not just as they are, but how they will be by God's grace. We do what we are called to do, staying in close personal touch with the Lord—and persist. Mary is never mentioned again after Acts 1, yet she was so used of the Lord. Keep on keeping on—whether you are noticed or ignored, loved or rejected, needed or abused—and determine by God's grace to persist no matter how great and overwhelming the challenge may seem.

Experiencing God's Fathomless Grace

NONE OF THESE FIVE SPECIAL women deserved to be a woman of hope. None of them deserved for God to use them. All of them were women with a mark against them, and most were unqualified to serve in such a manner. Yet, God lifted up each of these special ladies as an example of His fathomless grace! Through their life experiences, women for all time can learn that:

- No pain is too great to be healed.
- No past is too bad to be forgiven.

- No problem is too big to be solved through Christ.
- No stain is too deep to be cleansed through Christ's blood.
- No task is too great for God's enablement.

Have you personally ever been defiled by sin? Defeated? Defrauded? Despised? The good news is that *"God [is] able to make all grace abound toward you, that you, always having all sufficiency in all [things], may have abundance for every good work."*[a] Regardless of your present circumstances, there is hope in Christ for the future! By God's grace, you can partake of "The Promise." You can trust Him, your Savior, to wash away whatever sin has been dragging you down—as far as the east is from the west[b]—so that He can look upon you in the righteousness of Christ!

a. 2 Corinthians 9:8

b. Psalm 103

Will you, then, as each of these five special mothers did, determine that by His grace you too will be energized by hope? What do I mean by that? Every child you bear, Mother, is marked by sin. All of them are already defiled. All of them, because they are sinners, are already defrauded out of the inheritance God wanted to give them. Every one of them is despised. Every one is defeated at birth by sin. But today, like the "Mothers of the Promise," you can point your children to Christ; your life can be a portrait of God's grace to them—a portrait of hope!

Will it be easy? No. Will it be worth it? Absolutely! And as long as you trust Christ to be your strength, you will never walk alone, for:

"He Giveth More Grace"
He giveth more grace when the burdens grow greater,
He sendeth more strength when the labors increase;
To added affliction He addeth His mercy,
To multiplied trials, His multiplied peace.

When [you] have exhausted [your] store of endurance,
When [your] strength has failed ere the day is half done,
When [you] reach the end of [your] hoarded resources,
[Your] Father's full giving is only begun.
His love has no limit; His grace has no measure,
His power has no boundary known unto men;
For out of His infinite riches in Jesus,
He giveth, and giveth, and giveth again!
                    *— **Annie Johnson Flint***

Today and onward, you who determine by His grace to obey, can join the special women of hope. Regardless of what your past may have been, you, too, can be a godly mother who points your children, and other lost souls—to "The Promise"—God's Supernatural Conqueror of the Curse! That is the highest calling anyone could ever have!

STUDY GUIDE QUESTIONS

1. **Tamar** (Genesis 38:6-30) **was "defrauded," which means that she was "injured by the withholding of what is due."** Even though she took matters into her own hands, God was faithful. Perez, the firstborn of her twins, was placed into the messianic line. Read Romans 8:28. How does that apply to Tamar? How might her story have relevance in your own life?

2. **Rahab** (Joshua 2:1-21; 5:13-15; 6:1-2, 6-7, 15-17, 23-25) **was "defiled," which means that she was "depraved; rendered impure; rendered defective and void."** Yet, God beautifully honored her faith. Read Romans 3:23, 6:23, and Ephesians 2:8-9. Now read Revelation 21:1-8. To be part of Christ's eternal bride who will experience "no more death, sorrow, crying, or pain," Romans 3:23, 6:23, and Ephesians 2:8-9 must be a reality in your life. Do you know that your "stained past" has been forgiven? Are you being blessed by the daily opportunity to love the Christ who has forgiven much (Luke 7:47)?

3. **Through no fault of her own, Ruth was "despised"— "condemned; disdained; abhorred."** Yet, in spite of numerous trials, her faith triumphed and became "more precious than gold." (For a great blessing, read the Book of Ruth!) Now read 1 Peter 1:3-8. Have you been "tested by fire"? What have such "testings" revealed about your character?

4. Bathsheba (2 Samuel 11 and 12:15-25) **was "defeated"; she was "vanquished; effectually resisted; overthrown; frustrated; disappointed; rendered null or inoperative" for a season in her life.** Though she reaped terrible consequences for her sins, God poured out His wonderful grace upon her, and she became one of the five "mothers of the Promise." Is there something in your life that makes you feel unworthy? Read, memorize, and meditate upon Philippians 3:12-14. Then pray that passage back to the Lord.

5. Although Luke 1:26-55 does not portray Mary's full story, verses 46-55 do convey that her heart and mind were saturated with the Old Testament Scriptures. She was therefore "determined"—having "a firm or fixed purpose" in life to serve the Lord. Like Mary, regardless of the circumstances, we need to "keep on keeping on" for Christ. Read, memorize, and meditate upon Romans 8:37-39. Then in gratitude pray that passage back to the Lord.

3

"Let the word of Christ dwell in you richly in all wisdom, teaching and admonishing one another in psalms and hymns and spiritual songs, singing with grace in your hearts to the Lord. And [whatever] you do in word or deed, [do] all in the name of the Lord Jesus, giving thanks to God the Father through Him."

—Colossians 3:16-17

The Disciplines of a Word Filled Man

O<small>UR FIRST</small> C<small>HRISTMAS WITH A</small> child was a lesson we'll never forget. We lived in a tiny apartment in Los Angeles. We had very little money and lots of time. So we decided to not buy the preassembled tricycle for our little boy; we would put it together ourselves.

A day later the shiny red bike stood by the tree awaiting Christmas morning. Then came the moment of truth. Our son, squealing with delight, crawled over, pulled himself up, and soon was sitting on the seat with our help and support. It was then we noticed the wobble. Something wasn't quite right. Turning the peddles made the whole tricycle twist in a slight wobble. We had put it together—but not correctly.

The next few years—as each succeeding child received the hand-me-down bike—it never stopped the wobble. And every wobble and squeak for all these years has reminded us that the only hope we have to succeed in pleasing God as we sojourn in this world is to follow His directions. How do we keep from putting our life together our way so that it won't wobble? What has been the continuous plan that the Lord has set forth? From Deuteronomy 6 to Colossians 3, from the fourteenth century B.C. to the first century A.D., from Moses to Paul—God has sought for His children to have the Word-filled life.

Have you ever longed to be able to say, like the Apostle Paul, *"Imitate me, just as I also [imitate] Christ"?* [a] That is exactly what God desires for each of His children, for we are to be holy, as God is holy.[b]

a. 1 Corinthians 11:1

b. 1 Peter 1:16

How is such victorious living possible in light of the world and its deadening forces of darkness pitted against us making it as men of God? The Apostle Paul lived in a period many considered as the most horrible time there ever was, yet he had God's Word guiding his life. What was it like in Paul's day? How did he manage to live so triumphantly?

Word-Filled Living Works in an Ungodly World

SOMETIME IN A.D. 64, PAUL was probably chained in a damp, subterranean dungeon of the Mamertine Prison, which was only a stone's throw from the epicenter of the world—the Roman Forum. Outside crowds could be heard surging to the games and great festivals at the Circus Maximus. Mighty legions returned from victory after victory with dazzling displays of plunder and captives.

Seated on the throne was one of the most blatant, openly professed, and lustful homosexual men of all time—Nero. Yet the Apostle Paul said:

> *"Let every soul be subject to the governing authorities. For there is no authority except from God, and the authorities that exist are appointed by God. Therefore whoever resists the authority resists the ordinance of God, and those who resist will bring judgment on themselves"* (ROMANS 13:1-2).

Now fast forward to today. There may be a president, a governor, or a mayor who openly opposes God and His Word, yet, as a God- appointed leader, in light of Romans 13, we must still be subject to him!

The Apostle Peter, who would die a few months later under the hand of Nero, said the same thing: *"Submit yourselves to every ordinance of man for the Lord's sake ...."*[a] Therefore, as long as a government decree was not clearly against God's Word, both apostles were saying, "Obey that human institution, but beware of exposure to the tarnishing effects of the culture of the Roman Empire."

a. 1 Peter 2:13a

Paul occupied himself in prison by writing his last book. Outside was the daily background of muted cries from wicked and bloodthirsty men anticipating what new pleasures the degenerate Nero would offer at the Roman Forum. Paul's spirit was in tune with the Holy Spirit. He breathed through Paul the eternal, flawless, inspired Word of God. Although Paul is writing to his son in the faith, Timothy, warning him as a man of God, the list of sinful descriptions in the third chapter of 2 Timothy especially applies to our era. Looking down the course of time, the apostle says this:

> *"But realize this, that in the last days difficult times will come* [even worse than Paul's day]. *For men will be lovers of self, lovers of money, boastful, arrogant, revilers, disobedient to parents, ungrateful, unholy, unloving, irreconcilable, malicious gossips, without self-control, brutal, haters of good, treacherous, reckless, conceited, lovers of pleasure rather than lovers of God, holding to a form of godliness although they have denied its power. Avoid such men as these"* (2 TIMOTHY 3:1-5, NASB).

Looking Into the Word

PAUL LIVED IN THE MIDST of a tumultuous period. While facing this uncertain world, Paul manifested an unreserved surrender to the living and written Word of God. He experientially knew that greater is He who is in us than he who is in the world.[b] Therefore, he exhorted Timothy to carefully note his example of faithful endurance in doctrine, manner of life, purpose, faith, longsuffering, love, perseverance, persecutions, and afflictions.[c]

b. 1 John 4:4; 5:4-5

c. 2 Timothy 3:10-11

If we remain steadfast in the faith, continuing in God's unchanging truths, we too will be triumphant in our walk with God![d] We will be forever grounded in the knowledge of His eternal and priceless

d. 2 Timothy 3:12-14

Truth. We will be complete in Christ and equipped to do His work:

> *"All Scripture [is] given by inspiration of God, and [is] profitable for doctrine* [Old and New Testament teachings], *for reproof* [to point out error], *for correction* [to repent of error], *for instruction in righteousness* [to train in godly behavior], *that the man of God may be complete, thoroughly equipped for every good work"* (2 TIMOTHY 3:16-17).

Like countless others down through the centuries, the Apostle Paul discovered the secret to becoming a godly man; he thus could honestly tell others to imitate him, just as He imitated Christ.[a] The secret is so simple. It is right there in the answer to these questions: *"LORD, who may abide in Your tabernacle? Who may dwell in Your holy hill?"*[b]

a. 1 Corinthians 11:1

b. Psalm 15:1

Every week in his hometown synagogue while the Apostle Paul was growing up in Tarsus, the Jews read according to the fifth century B.C. schedule the Old Testament giant, Ezra, had set down. Ezra—who copied the scrolls of the Old Testament into the biblical Hebrew we have today—left an enduring legacy. He founded the Jewish synagogues, and as a part of that system for spiritual renewal, he built in the systematic reading of the Tannach (Hebrew Old Testament). What is fascinating about that bit of history is that they still follow that schedule. So we actually know what is read on what week in their religious year. All that is to say Paul heard Psalm 15 very regularly in the readings at every synagogue he ever attended.

Filling Yourself With the Word

PSALM 15 IS TO MEN what Proverbs 31 should be to women. There is in Psalm 15 a wonderful, changeless portrait of those blessed ones who may dwell in God's presence. The Spirit of God gives us, through David, in verses 2-5, a marvelous description of a godly man—one who longs to be holy, as God is holy. The following six traits identify the disciplines we should prayerfully cultivate in our lives. As you read, "allow, invite, welcome, and give yourself over to" each verse. Then bow before the Lord, and let the very Word of Christ spill forth into your life, drenching you—absorbing into your soul and changing every aspect of your life—your marriage, home, life, and all! Here are some of the disciplines we should cultivate.

1. LIVES COMMITTED TO PERSONAL INTEGRITY.

A godly man is first described as one *"who walks uprightly, And works righteousness"* (PSALM 15:2).

His walk exemplifies integrity. In other words, he is what he looks like; he is what he says he is. Many Christians have problems with either spiritual anorexia or bulimia. Anorexic Christians are so busy that they claim to have no time to read the Bible. Bulimic Christians typically binge on the Word Sundays, but promptly purge such feedings by later ignoring God's message. That is the spiritual condition of so many people. Godliness is characterized by internalizing—being a doer of the Word, and not just a hearer.[a] A godly walk is guided by integrity, and displays works of righteousness.

a. James 1:22-25

2. TONGUES BRIDLED BY INTERNALIZED TRUTH.

David goes on to say that one who is godly *"does not backbite with his tongue"* (PSALM 15:3).

Not only does he walk with integrity and work righteousness, but truth is what he speaks inside and out. He doesn't slander with his tongue because he's not a malicious gossip, as Paul talked about in 2 Timothy 3.

Awhile ago, I was riding with my children in the car when one of them said, "Did you hear about …?" I replied, "No, but before you tell me, who did you hear that from? Do you know for a fact that is true?" The response was, "No, they just said it was." I explained, "That is slander because you don't know for sure whether or not it is true. And you are going to tell me that person is bad because someone else said so, and you've never even talked to the person?"

We need to model the confession that we sometimes don't have first-hand knowledge of a situation, and so we choose to remain silent lest we falsely accuse another. Children need to be taught this truth from a very early age: *"If anyone among you thinks he is religious, and does not bridle his tongue but deceives his own heart, this*

a. James 1:26

one's religion is useless."[a] A good rule of thumb is this: If you're not part of the problem, or part of the solution, you shouldn't discuss the problem in the first place, because that is slander.

Proverbs 6:16 reports seven things which God considers an abomination. Sowing evil reports about others is right next to the gross immoralities of licentious living. A godly man will not only internalize truth, walk with integrity, and work righteousness, but he will also speak truth in his heart and to others; he won't slander with his tongue.

3. HEARTS GOVERNED BY LOVE FROM ABOVE.

In the middle of Psalm 15:3, David says that a godly man *"does [not do] evil to his neighbor, Nor does he take up a reproach against his friend."* This is what we as New Testament believers are to invite God to do in our lives. Ask Him to make this verse real in your daily experience.

James 3:17 states, *"But the wisdom that is from above is first pure, then peaceable, gentle, willing to yield, full of mercy and good fruits, without partiality and without hypocrisy."*

Such a man will be characterized by living the truth. When a friend listens to and receives an accusation against another, it can be devastating. One who lives by the Truth will not do such a hurtful thing. The church has been hurt most by Christians who take up reproaches against each other—fighting, dividing, and speaking evil. Christ said, *"If a house is divided against itself, that house cannot stand."*[b] How can the house of God survive with such evil in its midst? A godly man will commit to not doing evil to his neighbor, and to not taking up a reproach against others. This is a huge commitment—but with God it is possible.

b. Mark 3:25

4. THOUGHTS CAPTIVATED BY GOD ABOVE.

David goes on to describe a godly man as one *"In whose eyes a vile person is despised, but he honors those who fear the LORD"* (PSALM 15:4A-B).

A godly man will respect the truth so much that he has the right heroes. Do you know why I'm very careful about what posters my children put up in our house? I don't want them to have heroes

who are reprobates—those whose lives are not governed by God.[a] a. Psalm 101
Should you have a hero who is a reprobate? No, even if that person
happens to be the greatest in your favorite music or sport.

The *USA Today* once featured a phenomenal bowler, a man
whose bowling average was 203. He laid claim to having had
twenty-five straight perfect-score games of 300. I found that to be
amazing—until I discovered that he bowls on a 15-foot-long alley!
He stands right in front of the pins, and then throws the ball. On
the surface, he looked like a great bowler, but whenever he plays by
the same rules as other bowlers, he's only average. Before viewing
others as real heroes, and thinking that they're "the best," find out
whose rules they're playing by. Are they playing by the rules that
count—God's rules? A godly man will respect truth so much that
he chooses God's kind of heroes.

Not only is a reprobate despised in his eyes, but he *"honors those
who fear the Lord ...."*[b] The upright and godly become chosen heroes. b. Psalm 15:4b
Rather than wasting time, money, energy, and emotion on the world's
heroes by striving to impress his peers, a godly man chooses to honor
time-tested men and women of faith—those in his school, work place,
or church who genuinely love and follow Christ. In doing so, this
practice also establishes righteous role models for his children.

5. PROMISES GUARDED BY TRUTH WITHIN.

David says that a godly man *"swears to his own hurt and does not
change"* (PSALM 15:4C).

In Matthew 10, as Christ's apostles went out, He instructed them
to accept the first offer of hospitality whenever they went into a new
town. Why did He say that? Before they preached initially, no one
knew who they were. Usually, the lowliest people would extend an
invitation to eat with them. (They'd simply add a little extra water to
the stew!) However, once the apostles preached their first message,
the affluent suddenly said, "Come on up here on the hill—where we
live!" What were the apostles to do? Christ expected them to keep
their commitment to the first people who invited them. A godly
man won't change his decision based upon how it will help him.
God's way is to swear to our own hurt; make the decision that's right,
and never change it for external reasons.

6. GOALS LIVED FOR
LIFE BEYOND TODAY.

David went on to say that a godly man *"does not put out his money at usury* [interest], *Nor does he take a bribe against the innocent"* (PSALM 15:5).

> **He can't be bought.** *In Israel, interest was customarily charged to foreigners, but never to fellow Israelites. People in Israel didn't borrow money unless they were in need. They didn't have long term loans; they inherited land; they would save, buy, and then construct. But when they were in desperate need, they would borrow. At such times, Israelites were not to take advantage of another person's plight. A godly man won't take advantage of someone who is hurting. He can't be bought; he can't be swayed from what is right. A godly man would thus resist this type of offer: "If you let this go through in spite of the fact that it's not up to specifications, we'll reward you handsomely!" Or, he'd refuse to compromise, in spite of possible repercussions, when asked to do something shady like this example: "Just let that report go through, even though it's not totally honest. After all, we don't want the people at corporate headquarters to get mad at us!" A godly man can't be bought; he doesn't take a bribe against the innocent; he won't let the unsuspecting be taken advantage of because it would benefit him. That is internalized truth. He also avoids the inward bribes of rationalizing away human greed, as in this example: "If I use cheaper materials, I'll make more profit and it will be years before my patients or customers would ever find out."*

Just as Paul predicted, we are indeed facing perilous times that can easily neutralize us spiritually. The apostle clearly identified traits of Satan's crowd—those ungodly ones who will be prevalent in the last days. He forewarned us to avoid exposure to their cultural cancers. In contrast, David just as clearly identified characteristics of a godly man who may abide in the Lord's presence—one who internalizes the truth, speaks the truth, lives the truth, and won't compromise the truth. A Psalm 15 man respects truth wherever he sees it. God's Word becomes his measuring stick. He is unsullied in his walk with the Lord, for every detail of his life is submitted to the scrutiny of God's Word. That is holiness, and that is God's ideal for each of us!

Guard the Little Things

IN LIGHT OF THE SIMPLICITY of becoming a godly man, why is it that many still stumble and fall? Why don't we have more who are characterized by godliness? Where are the Psalm 15 leaders who are setting the example for the rest of us? Why aren't there more men who are willing to stand unflinchingly for the truth?

I believe the answer to these questions lies in the following biblical principle: *"He who [is] faithful in [what is] least is faithful also in much; and he who is unjust in [what is] least is unjust also in much"* (LUKE 16:10). This verse is a transferable principle of faithfulness that applies to every area of life. You will see many examples throughout this book as you read on. It is usually not the big things in life that lead us astray; it is the little things, the seemingly insignificant compromises that can tarnish and neutralize our reputations, and thus our effectiveness for Christ.

While working my way through seminary in the early 1980s, I was hired as a butler by a very prominent neurosurgeon. My first assignment was to survey and maintain the Silver Room. As I entered the room, I saw sterling silver stacked from floor to ceiling in special cases, or carefully wrapped in plastic. (Some of it dated back to the time of Paul Revere!) The instruction to me was simple: "Check to make sure that none of this silver has been exposed to any contaminants." Why is that so important? Finger prints left alone, or air seeping in from even tiny holes, will cause beautiful and intricate silver to tarnish. If even the tiniest black spot is ignored long enough, it will eventually pit and blight the usefulness of the silverware. Similarly, ignoring so-called tiny sins can multiply those "black spots"—those blights on our lives—until God's design for us has likewise been distorted. It ended up taking me several weeks to roll back the damage that the tarnishing had caused on their silver.

God is vitally interested in you and me having character that draws us to His presence. Usually, we don't stumble and fall all at once from a lack of integrity; we unmindfully slip here a little, there a little—like those little warning lights we sometimes ignore on our car's instrument panel: CHECK ENGINE, OIL PRESSURE, DOOR AJAR and FASTEN SEAT BELT. Here are two examples of little things which should be considered as big warning lights.

Little Thing #1: *Authority*
Do you really obey the laws God placed over your life?

___

Earlier in this chapter we saw that the apostles instructed believers to be subject to every ordinance of man for the Lord's sake.[a] We are to be subject to all the rules of the government under which we live.[b] Did you know that applies even to seemingly small matters such as our driving practices? The first "warning light" isn't a very big deal to some, but it is to the Lord. How we drive is indicative of our true character, and thus can also reflect our view of God.

A rationalizing, impatient, and proud person might say, "Everybody else goes as fast as they want, I will too. I'm not legalistic. I'm not going to do just the speed limit!" The Bible says to obey those who rule over you; therefore, a godly man should desire to even obey speed limits. If we're not willing to obey in the least little thing, we're not likely to obey in the bigger temptations. Gradually, we will become desensitized.

Have you ever experienced this situation? While on a family outing, speeding along with everyone else, in the distance you suddenly spot the nearly hidden form of a police car, and then you slow down. What will you have just taught your family? Your children will have learned that it is only wrong to speed if you get caught; your wife will have observed that you'll do whatever you want, as long as the price isn't too high; and you'll have convinced yourself that it is all right to rationalize.

One might offer this excuse: "But I'm at work; I drive a truck and I've got to get there on time!" I used to drive a delivery truck, so I know what it is like to have to meet a demanding schedule. But being on time does not make it right to disobey God. Neither does being on time make it right to buy a police radar detector to put on the dash—to now pay money to get away with breaking the law. What would you do if someone gave you an access code that enabled you to get away with not paying cable fees? If you were given a method to circumvent your phone company's computer to avoid paying for telephone calls, would you use it? Once we sell our integrity for a price, we prostitute truth in our lives.

I remember so clearly the place and time of day when I stopped wrestling with the Lord, and finally said, "From now on, I'm going to seek by your grace to be subject to every ordinance of man for the Lord's sake—just like Paul commanded me in Romans 13!" Do you know what I discovered? That small test of obedience proved to be a great boon to my spiritual life. It helped me clearly see that we can get caught up so fast in the current of life that we don't want anyone to get ahead of us—financially, academically, athletically, or even on the road. There is something refreshing about going the speed limit and having everyone passing us (except for the 85-year-old lady in the old broken down car!). There is something neat about seeing all those red tail lights passing by and not having to be alarmed when a policeman suddenly pops out of nowhere. Having a clear conscience is really wonderful!

Little Thing #2: *Devotion*
Do you really feed on God's Word daily?

Are you spending quality time with God every day? Does e-mail get your first attention each day—or the manna of God's Word delivered fresh from your Bible? Does the latest online news grip your attention—or the Ancient of Days? Did you watch the news this week but fail to read the Word of God for an equivalent amount of time? If you're exposed to what you get on the news for even a half hour, don't you need to be renewed at least that much?

We can never meditate on what we haven't read; nor can we meditate upon what we have not downloaded by memorization. When was the last time you memorized a Bible verse? As God's leader in your home, you should be the one who sets the example by memorizing the Word. You should be the one your children "catch" praying in your house. If you don't yet have a goal, may I suggest a list I've used all of my ministry life. It is called "Verses Every Believer Should Know," and can be found at Appendix A in the back of this book. (This is also such a broad and important subject that we will cover meditation more fully in upcoming chapters.)

What I want you to fully understand is this: A godly man is one who walks with integrity, works righteousness, honors truth, and doesn't rationalize unholy decisions and behavior. Such a man is not impatient; nor does he simply do his own thing. He refuses to say in his heart: *Everyone else is doing it, so it's okay for me to do it too!* Instead, deep down, a man who desires to be holy, as God is holy, commits to this thinking: *By God's grace, I will do what is right—regardless of the cost!* And that is what God says is the portrait of someone who may abide in His presence!

We must always be vigilant by watching out for even the little things that can trip up our walk with the Lord. God wants Psalm 15 men—men who manifest an unreserved surrender to God's living and written Word. How about it? Have you made such a commitment? It takes a Psalm 15 man to be a successful husband and father!

WARNING: This *Will* Harm Your Mind

I HAVE BEEN TEACHING GOD'S Word for over 30 years. I have watched those I teach over these years struggle with "the great neutralizer." When they go home from a Bible study, fellowship, class, or worship service, they sit down in front of the single most powerful mind-altering device on the planet—and within half an hour have forgotten almost everything they had just learned. What is that mind-altering device? The visual images and powerful messages of television and movies!

Professor Neil Postman, author of *Amusing Ourselves to Death*, reports that between the ages of six and eighteen, the average child spends some 15,000 to 16,000 hours in front of the TV, whereas he spends only 13,000 hours in school. Postman says that during the first 20 years of an American child's life, he will see over one million commercials, at the rate of about 1,000 per week![a]

The results of television's effects are infamous. Children who frequently watch TV have the following: shortened attention span, reduced linguistic power, a limited capacity for

a. Neil Postman,
Amusing Ourselves to Death
(USA: Viking Penguin Inc.,
1985), pp. 104-105.

abstraction, and a blur of adulthood and childhood. Thus they can't think about God; they can't talk about God; they can't dream about heaven; and they can't grow in Christ. What a negative impact! Is the "electronic babysitter" worth that price?

And what affect does indiscriminate TV watching have upon adults? One word—desensitization. Our culture keeps testing the waters and bringing new immoral depths to the screens of America. All the while, those watching are becoming desensitized. When that happens, we are headed away from growing godly families. If your family is being exposed to constant deadly spiritual viruses on TV, consider this ominous checklist:

- **Watch godlessness** — it will callous you.
- **Watch sensuality** — it will defile you.
- **Watch violence** — it will desensitize you.
- **Watch evil** — it will distance you.
- **Watch worldliness** — it will discourage you.
- **Watch Satan's mind** — you will forfeit Christ's!

We cannot escape the "GIGO" principle—Garbage In: Garbage Out! Let me affirm and repeat what one pastor from Chicago wrote:

I am aware of the wise warnings against using words like "all," "every," and "always" in what I say. Absolutizing one's pronouncements is dangerous. But I'm going to do it anyway. Here it is: It is impossible for any Christian who spends the bulk of his evenings, month after month, week upon week, day in and day out watching the major TV networks or contemporary videos to have a Christian mind. This is always true of all Christians in every situation! A biblical mental program cannot coexist with worldly programming.[b]

b. R. Kent Hughes, *Disciplines of a Godly Man* (Wheaton, IL: Crossway Publishers, 2001), pp. 71-82.

What Is Shaping Your Mind?

LET ME BE BLUNT: YOU can't truthfully say that you are committed to Christ unless you are actually pursuing the mind of Christ. God has a will for your mind: *"And do not be conformed to this world, but be transformed by the renewing of your mind, that you may prove what is that good and acceptable and perfect will of God"* (ROMANS 12:2). You must first saturate your mind with the Word to be an effective discipler: *"Let the word of Christ dwell in you richly in all wisdom, teaching and admonishing one another in psalms and hymns and spiritual songs, singing with grace in your hearts to the Lord"* (COLOSSIANS 3:16).

Pray for wisdom, and seek God's direction for how to promote your family's growth in Christ's mind. Do not let another day go by without praying for your children's minds. Plan for their purity; expose them to the right things. Read the Bible to your children, and discuss it, so they also learn how to draw practical life applications from God's Word. It is by your walk with the Lord that you demonstrate that you love the Holy Scriptures yourself. Beloved, this calls for stopping the indiscriminate and endless watching of TV and videos, and starting systematic, prayerful reading and studying of God's Word.

We all have the time to do what is right—we simply have to make it a priority. Today, let us each choose to cultivate the mind God has willed us to have!

APPLICATION: HOW CAN WE REVERSE THE LOSS OF A WORD-FILLED MIND?

The only way to cultivate a Word-filled life is by obedience to God's command that we mortify our lusts. To mortify means "to throttle sin and crush it in our lives, sapping it of its strength, rooting it out, and depriving it of its influence." Mortification involves the cultivation of new habits of godliness, combined with the elimination of old sinful habits from our behavior.

In *The Vanishing Conscience*, John MacArthur wrote one of the most helpful presentations I've found on this subject. His seventh chapter,[a] "Hacking Agag to Pieces," is wonderful. MacArthur listed eight practical action items to begin the mortification process. Let me share an adaptation of his steps for your edification in this vital realm of sanctification:

a. John MacArthur, *The Vanishing Conscience* (Dallas, TX: Word, 1994), pp. 145-166.

> 1. **Stop the Sinning** (1 PETER 2:11). If there are specific areas you know right now are sin, you must repent of them. **Stop now!**

2. Starve the Flesh (ROMANS 13:14). Cut all supply routes. If there are magazines, videos, and so on, that are less than Christlike, destroy them. If there are avenues that defile, such as TV, cable and ungodly internet access, get rid of them. Do whatever it takes to starve the evil desires of your flesh, and those of your family. **Put on Christ!**

3. Look Unto Jesus (COLOSSIANS 3:1-2). This is a daily, purposeful, and planned focus on pleasing the Lord in all things. Start your day crying out for Christ's help. **Look on things above!**

4. Saturate With the Word (JOSHUA 1:8). After you read and ponder, work on memorizing key Scriptures that can help you have greater victory over sin, and then regularly meditate upon those verses. (See Appendix A for suggestions.) **Meditate day and night!**

5. Stay in Constant Contact (1 THESSALONIANS 5:17). Prayer is the best, greatest, and most powerful way to touch your family's lives! (See Appendix B for "*How to Develop a Prayer Journal*.") **Pray without ceasing!**

6. Stay Wary of Sin's Power (MATTHEW 26:41). As Jesus said in Matthew 26:41, a Psalm 15 man is constantly vigilant—watching out for Satan's advances! Never trust the flesh. Resist the devil, and he will flee from you! **Watch and pray!**

7. Make Little Choices (1 TIMOTHY 4:7). This is a daily pattern of saying no to specific temptations, and saying yes to the Holy Spirit as He prompts you. One small choice is to turn your monitor so those behind you can see what you are viewing. If you struggle with images online this is a great accountability step. **Discipline yourself!**

8. Walk in the Spirit (GALATIANS 5:16). Let the Word of God fill your life, and then pass it on to your family! **Walk daily!**

Those biblical commands are meant for each of us, as Christians, to obey. They are not something to simply pray about, and then get around to doing one day. No, they are for us to actively grab hold of and obey—right now!

STUDY GUIDE QUESTIONS

1. Read Psalm 15. Without referring to chapter 3, in your own words, list six characteristics that best describe a Psalm 15 man.
    How does your life line up with that description?

2. Read James 1:21-27. In what ways might that passage parallel Psalm 15?

3. Read Romans 13:1-2 and 1 Peter 2:13-17. From these passages, would a Psalm 15 man—a Word-filled man—willingly submit himself to the authorities God has placed over him?
    Scripture gives one exception in which a man is released from God's requirement to obey civil authorities. To find the answer, read Exodus 1:17; Daniel 3:16-18; 6:7,10; Acts 4:19-20; 5:28-29. What is that exception?

4. Read 2 Corinthians 10:3-5. How does that passage apply to the practice of indiscriminate and endless watching of TV and videos?

5. As described in Colossians 3:16-17, what is the key to being a Word-filled man? Read, memorize, and meditate upon this passage. Ask the Lord to ever-increasingly make this the testimony of your life.

4

"Charm [is] deceitful and beauty [is] passing, But a woman [who] fears the LORD, she shall be praised."
— *Proverbs 31:30*

The World's Most Beautiful Women

THE OTHER DAY, WHILE STANDING in one of those endless lines at the supermarket, my eyes caught the following headline on a newspaper: "World's Most Beautiful Woman Hospitalized." Quickly whipping out my cell phone, I called my wife, Bonnie. Immediately as she answered the phone, I knew it was a false story …

Actually, the headline was about actress Elizabeth Taylor—married countless times, unhappy, overweight, and in ill health. The world probably has no better candidate for their "Most Beautiful" role, but God does. In this chapter, I will introduce *God's* choice for this prestigious honor.

Three thousand years ago, Solomon, the wisest man who ever lived, sat down to write. The God of the Universe breathed a twenty-two verse acrostic poem through him—each verse beginning with a succeeding letter of the Hebrew alphabet. Solomon penned the finest tribute ever to the most beautiful woman in God's Word!

Why would God write a poem about a virtuous wife and mother

and use every letter of the Hebrew alphabet to do so? It was almost as if Solomon were saying that such a rare woman exhausts the supply of language to describe her. Every letter that can possibly be used is mustered to try to capture the wonders of what she does in sacrifice for others. Yet, mere words fail to fully measure her worth, for words alone cannot capture all she is, all she does, and all we owe to her.

The Proverbs 31:10-31 woman epitomized virtue as she faithfully fulfilled the two roles God designed for her—devoted wife and mother. Were she alive today, this unique lady would joyfully and wholeheartedly sing "Take My Life, and Let It Be": (Emphasis added.)

Take my life *and let it be*
Consecrated, Lord, to Thee;
Take my hands *and let them move*
At the impulse of Thy love,
At the impulse of Thy love.

Take my feet *and let them be*
Swift and beautiful for Thee;
Take my voice *and let me sing*
Always, only, for My King,
Always, only, for my King.

Take my lips *and let them be*
Filled with messages for Thee;
Take my silver *and my gold,*
Not a mite would I withhold,
Not a mite would I withhold.

Take my love, *my God, I pour*
At Thy feet its treasure store;
Take myself *and I will be*
Ever, only, all for Thee,
Ever, only, all for Thee.

— Francis R. Havergal

A Biography of an Incredible Woman

WHO WAS THE WOMAN GOD so highly extolled in Proverbs 31? For hundreds of years (long before we had the entire Bible), the sages—the ancient Jewish rabbis—believed Solomon wrote that passage to his mother Bathsheba as a reflection on his great-great-grandmother, Ruth. That provides an even more beautiful perspective of the Proverbs 31 woman when we think about all that happened to her, as recorded in the eighth Book of the Bible, the Book of Ruth.

Do you remember what a difficult start in life Ruth faced? Ruth's distant forefather was Abraham's nephew, Lot, who lived in the depraved city of Sodom.[a] She was from a family sired in the midst of a drunken orgy when Lot's two unscrupulous daughters tricked him into fathering their firstborn children.[b] That sin produced the Moabites, a tribe of people forever under God's judgment. Because of God's curse, Ruth had to live with the fact that no Moabite could enter God's assembly to the tenth generation.[c] Even though she never did anything to personally deserve it, as a Moabitess, she was a despised woman.

Think of it! Ruth was of the *wrong race*. Ruth was of the *wrong family*. Ruth was *tainted by the past*. Ruth was *hounded by someone else's sin*. Ruth was *scarred by a family scandal*. Ruth was *plagued by a dark stain*.

After a short and sad marriage, she was widowed during a time of great famine. So, we are not talking about a woman who had everything together, but, amazingly, by God's grace she lived as if she did. He gave her favor in the eyes of Boaz who, recognizing that she was a virtuous woman, acquired her to be his wife.[d] From her life's testimony, God wrote one of the sweetest Old Testament stories of grace.

Now, then, what is it in this lady's life that so magnifies the Lord? What elements has God put into His timeless portrait of a virtuous woman?

a. Genesis 19

b. Genesis 19:36

c. Deuteronomy 23:3-4

d. Ruth 3:11; 4:9-10

What God Looks for in a Woman

SPIRITUAL AND PRACTICAL WISDOM PLUS moral virtues mark the character of the Proverbs 31:10-31 woman. The twenty-two verses are set forth as the prayer of every mother for the future wife of her son. Although they reflect the customs of the Old World, the principles apply to women even to this day. Note that when God describes what is important to Him, His description is powerful.

1. He wants her to see that her character is priceless to God: *"Who can find a virtuous wife? For her worth [is] far above rubies" (v. 10).*

Proverbs 31:10-11

10 *Who can find a virtuous wife? For her worth is far above rubies.*

11 *The heart of her husband safely trusts her; So he will have no lack of gain.*

Rubies spoke of rarity and costliness in the ancient world. They were the most valued of all the gems, and, therefore, the most desired for displaying wealth. However, in God's sight, the value of a virtuous woman—a godly wife and biblical mother—far exceeds that of any earthly commodity.

When God puts a high price tag on something, we need to take notice. Why would He think she is so valuable? God says in Proverbs 18:22, *"He [who] finds a wife, finds a good [thing], And obtains favor from the LORD."* That word favor is the word "grace" in Hebrew. The woman who lives this way, with this mindset, choosing to conform her life around what is valuable to God, is a gracious woman in His sight—a woman of inestimable, incalculable value to Him. Because she is so rare, her worth to God is priceless!

2. He wants her husband to trust her completely: *"The heart of her husband safely trusts her; So he will have no lack of gain" (v. 11).*

Not only is her worth to God inestimable, but she has won her husband's full confidence. It is by choosing God's goals, and His ways, that the wife becomes one in whom her husband can place his absolute trust. Because of this, he will have no lack of gain in any realm—in his home, family, marriage, private life, or public life. He can feel safe in every sphere because he has faith in her godly character.

When a marriage is as God intended, both the man and woman are completed in every way.[a] That is how God designed it to be.

a. Genesis 2:18-25

When a husband has the wife of God's choosing, as she manifests the Lord's grace spoken of in Proverbs 18:22 he can rejoice in her completing all the dimensions of his life.

3. He wants her life devoted to serving: *"She does him good and not evil All the days of her life" (v. 12).*

This is powerful! Her husband is greatly blessed because his wife's life is dedicated to serving not only his needs, but also the needs of others. I believe that is where her priceless worth comes from because *"even the Son of Man did not come to be served, but to serve."*[a] Jesus said that the greatest person is the one with a servant's heart.[b] Even in Old Testament times, this amazing woman discovered this wondrous truth.

a. Mark 10:45

b. Mark 10:42-44

Outsiders are commonly hired to staff the service industries in Israel today. Affluent, the highly successful business people don't want to do service jobs. This is part of our western culture as well. When you look at who mows the lawns and who cleans the houses, it is certainly not the "movers and shakers" of the world. It is common to think that the greatest thing is being in charge, not serving. The Lord's church holds a totally opposite world view: the greatest jobs in the church are the servant jobs. And, as in this Proverbs 31 poem, the greatest jobs in the home are the serving jobs.

Proverbs 31:12-13
12 *She does him good and not evil All the days of her life.*

13 *She seeks wool and flax, And willingly works with her hands.*

The virtuous woman's life is dedicated to serving others: her husband, her children, the community, the poor, her business interests, and her many other outreaches. She has learned the reality Christ spoke of: the servant of all is the greatest of all. This is the key to God's grace making her life have an endless impact on others, because she serves them so well.

4. He wants her body focused on ministry: Starting in verse 13, the elements of the virtuous woman's character are all woven together—like the threads of a delicate tapestry.

One of the unique stops for travelers in Turkey is always the Persian rug factories. There, sitting before large looms, women work for long hours, month after month hand weaving the countless fibers of exquisite and expensive carpets. Each color is woven, cut, and beaten tight—hour after hour. Often a day is measured in tenths of an inch of work, and thousands of threads. The beauty of the front is seen in the complexity of the back side where the labor can be viewed in the myriads of threads. And that is illustrative of Proverbs 31 in that the intertwined threads of the virtuous woman's life make the delicate tapestry of her life of great worth to God.

What are those threads? We see them beautifully woven throughout verses 13-26. It is by God's grace, and as a ministry to the Lord, that the virtuous woman sacrificially uses her body members to do priceless service for the Lord; and as we look at ways she ministers to others, note that God makes no mention of her hair, or smooth skin, or how much she weighs, or what she wears. *All her beauty* is described without any outward physical element attached to it because God focuses on hearts (1 Samuel 16:7). Maybe this is because she is to do everything she can to please her husband—to be beautiful for the one man God has chosen for her to complete. Dear sister, is your God-given body focused on pleasing your husband? Have you gotten to the place where you can honestly and openly ask your husband what would help you to even more beautifully serve him? That would bring great glory to the One who created you to complete one man for life!

5. He wants her hands offered for others: *"She … willingly works with her hands. … She stretches out her hands to the distaff, and her hand holds the spindle. She extends her hand to the poor, Yes, she reaches out her hands to the needy. … Give her of the fruit of her hands …"* (vv. 13B, 19-20, 31A).

Starting in verse 13, God describes the virtuous woman as having hands that are given to serving others. If you want to see a beautiful part of a woman, look at what her hands are doing.

When our first child was 2 days old, he was rushed to a children's hospital. I will never forget the picture of little Johnny in that incubator with all the tubes, IVs, and everything else. When we finally got him back from the ICU he surely was precious. That made us really ponder where we would leave him even momentarily. It was a big moment the day we finally decided to put him into the church nursery. There at the counter a precious old saintly woman greeted us, and as she extended her hands toward Johnny, we saw the most precious crinkly-skinned face and eyes that radiated a life of ministry and service for others. We later found out

Proverbs 31:13-26

13 *She seeks wool and flax, And willingly works with her hands.*

14 *She is like the merchant ships, She brings her food from afar.*

15 *She also rises while it is yet night, And provides food for her household, And a portion for her maidservants.*

16 *She considers a field and buys it; From her profits she plants a vineyard.*

17 *She girds herself with strength, And strengthens her arms.*

18 *She perceives that her merchandise is good, And her lamp does not go out by night.*

19 *She stretches out her hands to the distaff, And her hand holds the spindle.*

20 *She extends her hand to the poor, Yes, she reaches out her hands to the needy.*

21 *She is not afraid of snow for her household, For all her household is clothed with scarlet.*

22 *She makes tapestry for herself; Her clothing is fine linen and purple.*

23 *Her husband is known in the gates, When he sits among the elders of the land.*

24 *She makes linen garments and sells them, And supplies sashes for the merchants.*

25 *Strength and honor are her clothing; She shall rejoice in time to come.*

26 *She opens her mouth with wisdom. And on her tongue [is] the law of kindness.*

that she had served in that nursery for 40 years by holding many precious babies of concerned parents just like us. Are your hands devoted tools for serving others?

6. He wants her arms extended in service: *"She girds herself with strength, And strengthens her arms"* (v. 17A).

The virtuous woman's ministry doesn't stop with her hands; her arms are also used for serving others. Sometimes her arms are carrying children; sometimes they are handing out necessities to the poor and needy; sometimes they are full of products to sell; and sometimes they are loaded with the scarlet clothes she's made for her children. Through all these ministries, her arms are strengthened for serving. How much more noble that is than mere beauty that is fleeting!

7. He wants her mouth dispensing godly wisdom: *"She opens her mouth with wisdom ..."* (v. 26A).

So her hands are beautiful because they serve; her arms are beautiful because they serve; and her mouth is beautiful because it is also used to serve others. Titus 2:1-7 calls us to use our mouths to teach, exhort, and encourage others. Is that what you have as your goal?

The virtuous woman's mouth is included as beautiful because it is given over to serving others, too. When she speaks, it is with wisdom. Where does wisdom come from? It comes from above—from the Lord.[a] God says, *"Let the word of Christ dwell in you richly in all wisdom ...."*[b] That speaks of the fullness of the Spirit, and when we are full of God's Spirit, what comes out of our mouths? The Word of God!

8. He wants her tongue controlled by kindness: *"On her tongue is the law of kindness"* (v. 26B).

The virtuous woman's tongue is harnessed by the Spirit of God, and is therefore bound by kindness for God's glory! God's woman is completely under God's control. Thus she serves others, not herself.

God, in contrast, says that *"If anyone among you thinks [she] is religious, and does not bridle [her] tongue but deceives [her] own heart, this one's religion [is] useless."*[c] That three-ounce-wonder called the tongue must be harnessed because God says it is an unruly evil.[d] The virtuous woman will *"[Let her] speech always [be] with*

Proverbs 31:27-31

27 *She watches over the ways of her household, And does not eat the bread of idleness.*

28 *Her children rise up and call her blessed; Her husband also, and he praises her:*

29 *"Many daughters have done well, But you excel them all."*

30 *Charm is deceitful and beauty is passing, But a woman who fears the LORD, she shall be praised.*

31 *Give her of the fruit of her hands, And let her own works praise her in the gates.*

a. James 1:5; 3:17

b. Colossians 3:16

c. James 1:26

d. James 3:1-18

grace ...." [a] A woman who uses her tongue for ministry will speak blessings to others!

9. He wants her household to be her priority: *"She also rises while it is yet night, And provides food for her household"* (v. 15).

The virtuous woman even sacrifices sleep for her home, for her family. God, who is inspiring this passage, is basically saying: "I'm measuring this woman by how much she ministers to her family—not by her focus on herself, not by her focus on her career, not by her focus on personal gratification. No, I'm honoring her for making her family her priority."

When Paul was writing to Timothy, women were excelling in the theatre, in hunting, and in all types of athletics and sports. Women had more options and many chose not to marry as the Roman society became more affluent. Actually, to see a woman marry, bear children, and manage her home was often a mockery in the first-century culture. This, however, has always been important to God. He emphasizes that theme in this verse: *"Admonish the young women to love their husbands, to love their children, to be discreet, chaste, homemakers, good, obedient to their own husbands, that the word of God may not be blasphemed"* (TITUS 2:4-5).

Consider one more New Testament word to women: *"I desire that [the] younger [widows] marry, bear children, manage the house, give no opportunity to the adversary to speak reproachfully"* (1 TIMOTHY 5:14). The context of this verse is referring to younger women. God wants them to marry, bear children, and manage their homes well. Instead of trying to make a mark on Broadway, Wall Street, or any other venture, a young woman should make her mark on her home. God says, "I'm the One who's passing out the rewards. I'm the One who's passing out the crowns, and if you want to know what I honor, it is not what the world honors!"

Scripture says that this woman has given her household her highest priority. First and foremost, her ministry must be to her husband, and then to her children, because God says that is what is important to Him.

10. He wants her children to be her sacred trust from God: *"Her children rise up and call her blessed; Her husband [also], and he praises her"* (v. 28).

Her children are her sacred trust from God, and when she invests in them, she receives and reaps a harvest of praise and blessing. Is there anything sweeter than the simplicity and honesty of a child's voice expressing precious words of love and adoration and thanksgiving! There is nothing no card, no honor, no medal, no trophy the world could ever give—that can match children rising up and blessing their mother! The godly woman's children are her sacred trust from Him, and when she does well, she will also reap a harvest of praise and blessing from their earthly father!

Look at how the New Testament reflects this. Because the entire Bible is written by the same Author, it is consistent in what is said from cover to cover. First Timothy 2:15 says that *"she will be saved in childbearing if they continue in faith, love, and holiness, with self-control."* The Apostle Paul is saying that even though the woman was deceived and led the human race into sin,[a] through childbearing she can be freed from the reproach of that blame by growing a godly heritage—children who continue in faith and love and holiness, with self-control. Such is the anticipated result of:

a. 1 Timothy 2:14

- Training her children by trusting God in faith.
- Training her children in love, with the law of kindness on her tongue.
- Training her children in holiness by seeking
  and separating herself unto God.
- Training her children in self-control by being
  under the control of God's Spirit.

Beginning in her children's most formative years (birth to six), the virtuous woman has the responsibility and opportunity to imprint upon each little life the code of godliness. If she does this faithfully out of devotion to the Lord, she is blessed.

A Special Note to Husbands: One precious way to encourage your Word-filled wife is to allow your children to bless her. We have trained our children in the biblical grace of giving a blessing. The celebration of Mother's Day, for example, starts with a hand-made card from each child (even the teenaged boys) that expresses love. Then we give Bonnie her breakfast in bed, accompanied by flowers picked with loving hands, and even a candle. The cards are read, prayers offered, and that portion of the blessing is over. Then at lunch we pick it up again. I, as the leader, start out and verbally bless my wife along these lines: "Honey, I thank the Lord that you are such a loving and sacrificial wife. I see the law of kindness on your lips when you train the children. And I am so grateful that I get to share my life with you."

After I give Bonnie my blessing, each of the children (as we rehearsed in the car the day before) shares just one way that they see Mom as a wonderful mother. Next, I read from Proverbs 31 and pray. Even as simple as that is, it will bless your wife, and train your children to think about and share a verbal blessing. Oh, how many wives would give almost anything to hear their husbands or children ever bless them! Men, lead the way—and harvest a crop of blessings for her!

11. He wants her family to produce enduring praise: *"Give her of the fruit of her hands, And let her own works praise her in the gates"* (v. 31).

In this verse we have the last key to this woman's value in God's sight. He expresses that value through the words "in the gates." What does that mean? According to the customs of the Old World, the gates were the public forum of every town. Remember that Boaz made the legal transaction to marry Ruth in the city gates. This is where legal contracts were ratified, disputes resolved, big announcements pronounced, and where rulers sat to give judgment. But today, the term "in the gates" generally applies to the whole world. So, what God is saying is that the whole world will take note of anyone who lives like the Proverbs 31 woman—one who:

- Values her worth to God as more important than anything else.
- Inspires confidence so that her husband trusts her completely.
- Devotes her life to serving others.
- Focuses her body on ministry for the Lord rather than fleeting physical beauty.
- Makes her household her highest priority.
- Considers her children as her sacred trust.
- Offers her life to others in love, and thus receives enduring praises from her family.

The Proverbs 31 woman is an awesome role model! Her loving service to her husband, children, and others is exemplary. But as we end this examination of the virtuous woman's life, don't lose sight of the most important point of this passage: God does not want our primary focus to be on all of her good works—no matter how wonderful they are. Our focus must be upon the reason she was able to accomplish so much—her personal consecration and reverential worship of God Almighty. God says, "*Charm is deceitful and beauty is passing, But a woman who fears the LORD, she shall be praised.*"[a] Because God Himself is the Word-filled woman's goal, good works are merely an outflow of that intimate relationship, as is so beautifully expressed in this poem:

My goal is God Himself, not joy, nor peace,
Nor even blessing, but Himself, my God;
"Tis His to lead me there, not mine, but His—
"At any cost, dear Lord, by any road!"

So faith bounds forward to its goal in God,
And love can trust Her Lord to lead her there;
Upheld by Him, my soul is following hard
Till God hath full fulfilled my deepest prayer.

No matter if the way be sometimes dark,
No matter though the cost be oft-times great,
He knoweth how I best shall reach the mark,
The way that leads to Him must needs be straight.

One thing I know, I cannot say Him nay;
One thing I do, I press towards my Lord;
My God my glory here, from day to day,
And in the glory there my great Reward.[b]

Consecrating yourself totally to the Lord, regardless of the cost, is not easy. However, in doing so, you will discover what Dr. J. Hudson Taylor, the founder of the China Inland Mission, discovered—a wondrously glad surprise. "No Moriah, no Calvary: on the contrary, a King! When the heart submits, then Jesus reigns. And when Jesus reigns, there is rest."[c]

a. Proverbs 31:30

b. Mrs. Charles E. Cowman, *Streams in the Desert* (Los Angeles, CA: Cowman Publications, Inc., 1950), p. 55.

c. J. Hudson Taylor, *Union and Communion* (Minneapolis, MN: Bethany House Publishers, n.d.), p. 22.

That type relationship with Christ releases the power to love and serve your husband, children, and others—as God desires. This then is the essence of the virtuous woman whose excellent character permeates her whole life as she obeys the living and written Word of God! That is the key which unlocks joy, deep and abiding joy, because it is the most precious of sacrifices in His sight! Does He deserve any less?

STUDY GUIDE QUESTIONS

1. The praiseworthy character of the Proverbs 31 woman—her inestimable worth to God; the confidence of her husband; her servant's heart, godly wisdom, kindness; and the way she cared for her household—was a manifestation of her personal consecration and reverential worship of God Almighty: "A woman who fears the LORD, she shall be praised" (v. 30). A woman who "fears the LORD" will have such a "dreadful, exceeding reverence" of Him that she lives her life in loving obedience to His commands (John 14:15). The Book of Proverbs has much to say about the "fear of the Lord." After you read each verse below, complete the following as applicable:

> **The fear of the Lord is...**
> Proverbs 1:7 –
> Proverbs 8:13 –
> Proverbs 9:10-11 –
> Proverbs 10:27 –
> Proverbs 14:26-27 –
> Proverbs 15:16 –
> Proverbs 15:33 –
> Proverbs 16:6-7 –
> Proverbs 19:23 –
> Proverbs 22:4 –
> Proverbs 23:17-18 –

2. **Solomon, the wisest man who ever lived, is believed to have authored Proverbs 31:10-31 as a reflection on his great-great-grandmother, Ruth.** Toward the end of his life, he wrote the Book of Ecclesiastes as a reflection on the futility of pursuing joy and fulfillment apart from the living God. Solomon concluded that fearing God and keeping His commandments is really what life is all about, for we must each ultimately give account to Him for our actions. In keeping with Solomon's conclusion in Ecclesiastes 12:13-14, read, memorize, and meditate upon Psalm 139:23-24. To be a praiseworthy woman, make this passage a regular part of your prayer life, just as it was for Solomon's father, David—a man after God's own heart.

5

"For what is [my] hope, or joy, or crown of rejoicing? [Is it] not even you in the presence of our Lord Jesus Christ at His coming? For you are [my] glory and joy. … I have no greater joy than to hear that my children walk in truth."

— 1 Thessalonians 2:19-20
3 John 4

Ending Well

THE GREATEST JOY, THE GREATEST rewards, the greatest part-nership, and the greatest power possible are the result of a Word-filled life, a Word-filled marriage, a Word-filled family, and Word-filled prayers. If you have been drawn to desire this for yourself and your family—as has been my prayer while writing this book—I praise God for your commitment to let the Word of God utterly fill your life! And I pray that He will enable you to *"be strong in the Lord and in the power of His might."* I urge you to continually *"put on the whole armor of God, that you may be able to stand against the wiles of the devil"* (EPHESIANS 6:10-11).

Your commitment to a Word-filled life, marriage, and family is likely to be met with opposition. You see, we have an adversary who walks about *"like a roaring lion, seeking whom he may devour"* (1 PETER 5:8). The devil, whose name means "slanderer," is our mortal enemy. He and his demon army are always distracting believers with temptation, discouraging them with persecution, and defiling them

a. Psalm 22:13
   Ezekiel 22:25
b. Job 1
   2 Corinthians 4:3,4
   Revelation 12

c. 2 Corinthians 11:14

d. 1 Peter 5:8
   Ephesians 6:10-12

with the flesh.[a] Satan sows discord among the saints, and accuses us to God.[b] His goal is always to neutralize God's power through us by doubt, defeat, and despair.

One of Satan's favorite tactics is to transform himself into an "angel of light"[c] so that his victims are oblivious to the dangers. For that reason, God warns us to be sober and vigilant—to be alert to the devil's schemes.[d] The following illustration typifies one subtle way he and his forces try to lead Christian families astray.

Are We Too Busy?

SATAN CALLED A WORLDWIDE CONVENTION of demons. In his opening address he said:

"We can't keep Christians from going to church. We can't keep them from reading their Bibles and we can't even keep them from forming an intimate relationship with their Savior. Once they gain that connection with Jesus, our power over them is broken. So let them go to their churches; let them have their covered dish dinners, but steal their time, so they don't have time to focus on Him. This is what I want you to do," said the devil, "distract them from gaining hold of their Savior and maintaining that vital connection throughout their day!"

"How shall we do this?" his demons shouted!

"Keep them busy in the nonessentials of life and invent innumerable schemes to occupy their minds," he answered. "Tempt them to spend, spend, spend, and borrow, borrow, borrow. Persuade the wives to go to work for long hours and the husbands to work six or seven days each week, ten to twelve hours a day, so they can afford their empty lifestyles. Keep them from spending time with their children and as their families fragment, soon, their homes will offer no escape from the pressures of work!

"Over-stimulate their minds so that they cannot hear God's still, small voice. Entice them to play the radio, tape, or CD whenever they drive…and to keep the TV, VCR/DVD, MP3s, CDs and their PCs going constantly in their home. Then see to it that every store and restaurant in the world plays non-biblical music constantly. This will jam their minds and break that union with Christ.

"Next, encourage them to upgrade their TVs by adding cable so they can have endless distractions and temptations 24/7 in the center of their homes. Then make them think that to keep their kids happy they need to buy all the latest irresistible full color, nonstop action TV and computer games; this will increase their kids' addiction to these 'electronic babysitters.' Also get them online via the World Wide Web. Get them so entangled in that web that they all (moms, dads, and children) would rather sit alone staring at a screen than sitting together and talking. Then lure them into the dark corners of the internet where lurk the strongest demons of lust, materialism, and evil. This way, we'll get husbands to be discouraged because they are unable to stop looking at pictures of which they are ashamed. And we will also get the young boys and girls to lose their mental innocence and start on a lifelong journey of overexposure to everything.

"But even that is not enough. We must fill their coffee tables and days with magazines and newspapers. Invade their driving moments with billboards. Flood their mailboxes with junk mail, mail order catalogs, sweepstakes, and every kind of newsletter and promotional offering free products, services, and false hopes. Keep skinny, beautiful models on the magazines and TV so their husbands will believe that outward beauty is what's important, and they'll become dissatisfied with their wives. Keep the wives too tired to love their husbands at night. Give them headaches too! If they don't give their husbands the love they need, their husbands will begin to look elsewhere. That will fragment their families quickly!

"Give them Santa Claus to distract them from teaching their children the real meaning of Christmas. Give them an Easter Bunny so they won't talk about Christ's resurrection and power over sin and death. Even in their recreation, let them be excessive ... have them return from their recreation exhausted. Keep them too busy to go out in nature and reflect on God's creation. Send them to amusement parks, sporting events, plays, concerts, and movies instead.

"Keep them busy, busy, and busy! And when they meet for spiritual fellowship, have them leave with troubled consciences. Crowd their lives with so many good causes that they have no time to seek power from Jesus. Soon they will be working in their own strength, sacrificing their health and family for the good of the cause.

"Yes, we will do all that so all that is left in life is to be so busy, so full of activity—that there is no time left to reflect on life as God intended it to be rather than as it has become."

"It will work! It will work!"

It was quite a plan! The demons went eagerly to their assignments causing Christians everywhere to:

• Have little time for their God or their families.
• Have no time to tell others about the power of Jesus to change lives.

I guess the question is this: Has the devil been successful at his scheme? You be the judge![a]

Dear brother or sister in Christ, it would be rare to have not experienced Satan's yoke in one form or another. Perhaps your own conscience was pricked as you read through his list of tricks. You may even be thinking: *What can God do with me since I have so obviously failed Him?* As a pastor I hear that type of question often. Is there an answer for believers who are less than perfect? Yes! Even though failure for the lost is permanent—it stays with them forever—failure for a believer is only a temporary condition. The Lord offers the reality that He is the God of New Beginnings, the God of Second Chances for us who are forgiven. We serve a Lord who is so gracious that His strength is made perfect in our weakness.[b] In fact, one might summarize the blessed life we have in Christ as "a series of new beginnings." Learn from Mark that God can and will use you.

a. Alvin Reed,
Radically Unchurched
(Grand Rapids: Kregel, 2002),
pp. 65-66; portions of this
wonderful illustration were
expanded or adapted to
modernize its language.

b. 2 Corinthians 12:9

Mark Demonstrates—
Failures are Never Permanent for Believers

MARK, THE WRITER OF THE New Testament's second Gospel, is one of the most powerful examples in Scripture of someone who openly failed God and still experienced great "new beginnings." He is a testimony to what God can do with a person we would deem a failure—someone who quit by abandoning their calling. Yet, his life went on to glorify the God of heaven who has mercy on those of us who fail, and know it, and flee to Him. And He lets us, too, have another new beginning!

There has been, and always will be, only one Perfect Servant—the Lord Jesus Christ. His perfect servanthood is the focus of the Book of Mark. All the rest of the countless men, women, boys, and girls God has used throughout the centuries have been imperfect! That knowledge is comforting to me, because the longer I live the more painfully aware I am of my own imperfections, failures, shortcomings, and sins. Isn't that true of us all? Let's face it: we are all going to fail God at one time or another. No one is exempt; and as an encouragement to rise above those times that tend to drag us down, we are going to examine the life of Mark, a New Testament saint who was known for his failures, but rose above them by experiencing the incredible grace of God.

The Gospel by Mark represents the clearest answer in all of God's Word to this question: *What can God do with a failure?* This Gospel begins with the words of Mark—inspired by God—capturing the experiences of Peter. Church history, in fact, declares almost universally that John Mark was the servant who took care of Peter in his last days. During that time, he captured Peter's experiences on paper, under the oversight of the Holy Spirit, to produce the second Gospel. We will begin by examining the human writer of this Gospel, Mark.

John Mark's Failure

To BEST UNDERSTAND MARK IS to see him in the context of when God called him to do a great work for Him: *"But the word of God grew and multiplied. And Barnabas and Saul returned from Jerusalem when they had fulfilled [their] ministry, and they also took with them John whose surname was Mark"* (ACTS 12:24-25).

We have a record of the call and commission of Barnabas and Saul for the first missionary journey in Acts 13:

"As they ministered to the Lord and fasted, the Holy Spirit said, 'Now separate to Me Barnabas and Saul for the work to which I have called them.' Then, having fasted and prayed, and laid hands on them, they sent them away" (ACTS 13:2-3).

a. This is now modern-day Turkey, which has more Roman ruins than Italy, more Greek ruins than Greece, and more Christian sites than the Holy Land.

Barnabas, as the leader (a great spiritual giant of the Jerusalem church) recruited his nephew, John Mark, to accompany them as they penetrated the Roman Empire for the first time.[a] Barnabas and Paul planned to go up to Antioch to get people saved so that they, in turn, would take the light of the Gospel to the end of the earth.

b. Acts 11:26

Antioch, a huge, ancient Roman city that was now the thriving new center of Christianity, is where the term "Christian" was inaugurated.[b] It was from that church that God raised up evangelists, prophets, and now missionaries. This was the new wave of the future: missionaries sent out from the "mother church" to far off places, but supported by the Body of Christ back home. Young John Mark was eager and ready to go on this historic trip, especially with Paul—the greatest man in the entire Roman Empire—a man who caused even rulers to tremble before him. And what a trip it was!

1. Mark got to walk, talk, sleep, eat, and share every day with Paul and Barnabas. Can you imagine sitting on a boat or traveling the ancient Roman roads with Paul beside you explaining the Scriptures? Paul's cultural and biblical commentaries on the cities they saw, the temples that towered over them, and the pagan altars that dotted the landscape as they journeyed must have been amazing. It would have been similar to a seminary education for John Mark. Just that experience alone would last a lifetime.

2. Mark got to witness the power of God first hand. The missionary team set sail from Seleucia for Cyprus; at Salamis *"they preached the word of God in the synagogues of the Jews. They also had John as their assistant"* (ACTS 13:5). Mark's eyes probably got bigger and bigger while traveling with these two giants of the faith, who were afraid of nothing. He was privileged to be in the center of all that God was doing, like the awesome confrontation in Acts 13:6-11:

> *"Now when they had gone through the island to Paphos, they found a certain sorcerer, a false prophet, a Jew whose name [was] Bar-Jesus, who was with the proconsul, Sergius Paulus, an intelligent man. This man called for Barnabas and Saul and sought to hear the word of God. But Elymas the sorcerer (for so his name is translated) withstood them, seeking to turn the proconsul away from the faith"* (vv. 6-8).

John Mark, on that beautiful island, witnessed the power of God when Paul confronted a Satanic medium who was trying to influence the provincial Roman governor, Sergius Paulus. Mark probably stood behind Barnabas and Paul, wondering how these men would handle this occultic figure who was harassing them. I doubt if he could have predicted what happened next:

> *"Then Saul, who also [is called] Paul, filled with the Holy Spirit, looked intently at him and said, 'O full of all deceit and all fraud, [you] son of the devil, [you] enemy of all righteousness, will you not cease perverting the straight ways of the Lord? And now, indeed, the hand of the Lord [is] upon you, and you shall be blind, not seeing the sun for a time.' And immediately a dark mist fell on him, and he went around seeking someone to lead him by the hand"* (vv. 9-11).

3. Mark got to witness the discipling of the governor: *"Then the proconsul believed, when he saw what had been done, being astonished at the teaching of the Lord"* (v. 12).

Afterwards, Paul (the now recognized leader) and his team set sail for Perga, which was located at the beginning of one of the marvels of the ancient world—the super highway that cut through the Sicilian gates and went to the upper plateau of central Asia Minor. Countless thousands of people were scattered in ultra-modern cities all along these Roman roads. Paul had his eyes set on getting to the heart of the Roman Empire. They settled in Perga for a little while, and then prepared to set off on a walk up the mighty Roman road to the heights of Pisidia. But something sad happened.

4. Mark bailed out, and went home: *"John [Mark], departing from them, returned to Jerusalem"* (v. 13).

His decision to leave is hard to understand because he had everything going for him. He walked among the giants; experienced God's power first hand; was led to the Lord by Peter; was discipled by Barnabas; and met every famous person in Christendom in Jerusalem. But in spite of all these privileges, he still quit. Perhaps Mark felt it was too tough, or too uncomfortable, or too dangerous. All we really know is that he quit; he left, and literally went back to his mama, back to safety, back to comfort—back to home.

The missionary team continued on, however, and the results were staggering. Paul's first recorded sermon stirred hearts, and multitudes responded. That period was probably the most crucial event since Pentecost as the Gospel cut a path across the Roman roads to light up dark pagan cities. Numerous men and women were born again; many new churches were formed as a result. And Acts 13 became the greatest chapter in church history—but John Mark missed it all!

5. Mark's quitting split the greatest evangelistic team in history: *"Then after some days Paul said to Barnabas, 'Let us now go back and visit our brethren in every city where we have preached the word of the Lord, [and see] how they are doing.'* **Now Barnabas was determined** *to take with them John called Mark.* **But Paul insisted** *that they should not take with them* **the one who had departed from them in Pamphylia,** *and had not gone with them to the work"* (ACTS 15:36-38, Emphasis added).

If Paul believed something, you knew about it. When the team returned home, he gave their report and made it known that John Mark had quit the work, failing Christ. But Barnabas came alongside his nephew:

> *"Then the contention became so sharp that they parted from one another.* ***And so Barnabas took Mark and sailed to Cyprus;*** *but Paul chose Silas and departed, being commended by the brethren to the grace of God"* (ACTS 15:39-40, Emphasis added).

This was a sad chapter in church history! When word of the split spread, neither Paul nor Barnabas were criticized. Instead, Mark was branded as: Mark the Quitter, Mark the Fearful, and Mark the Failure.

John Mark's Triumph—Finishing Well

TWENTY YEARS LATER, ACCORDING TO the nearly unanimous voice of scholarship over the centuries, it was John Mark who became

Peter's personal helper. He went back to the one who had led him to Christ,[a] and became the servant who, as inspired by God's Spirit, captured the words of Peter—those beautiful and unforgettable portraits of Christ in the Gospel of Mark. Much as Luke was to Paul, John Mark was to the aged Peter, who was arrested in old Babylon and taken to Rome.

a. 1 Peter 5:13

Mark's world was a terrible time in history. Some of the most memorable pages of the history of Christ's church are the years from A.D. 60 to A.D. 70. For half those years, the hatred and evils of Nero had led to random acts of fierce persecution of Christians. Believers were killed in the arenas and the prisons across the city of Rome. Entertaining his evening dinner guests, Nero would have the followers of Jesus dipped in tar and burned alive in sticks as torches in the Imperial Gardens. For the bloodthirsty masses at the games, Christians were wrapped in animal skins and chased to death by wild beasts. It was in this deadly environment that John Mark was no longer a failure; he was restored, renewed, and vital!

Have you ever pondered how hard it must have been to be a Christian during those 10 years? Yet, in that dangerous time, Mark boldly recorded the words of Peter to the Romans proclaiming Jesus—the Servant Savior. And he did so seated next to Peter who had become the "Most Wanted" man of that day. Mark clearly demonstrated what holy boldness Christ can bring into the lives of His children.

Ten generations of Christians, starting with Mark's generation, built and inhabited the catacombs over a period of 300 years. In the early centuries of the church, the catacombs served as meeting and burial places for perhaps as many as four million Christians. This common inscription was found on walls there: "The Word of God is not bound." This hope shared by all believers was captured in Martin Luther's "A Mighty Fortress Is Our God." As Luther declared, "The body they may kill; God's truth abideth still."

Mark—branded as a fearful quitter and failure—wrote a biography of encouragement to those living through the Roman persecutions and beyond. He wove together Peter's eyewitness accounts, and the Holy Spirit's revelations, into a fabric that portrays Jesus as the One who suffered and triumphed for us. Through Christ's power, we who are His can experience triumph in suffering as well. Even when times of failure come, we can respond like Paul:

"Not that I have already attained, or am already perfected; but I press on, that I may lay hold of that for which Christ Jesus has also laid hold of me. Brethren, I do not count myself to have apprehended; but one thing [I do], forgetting those things which are behind and reaching forward to those things which are ahead, I press toward the goal for the prize of the upward call of God in Christ Jesus" (PHILIPPIANS 3:12-14).

Mark had to learn to "press on" in spite of everything, and he went on to become a marvelous portrait of God's grace. Each of us can likewise achieve wondrous things for God's glory if we will go on allowing Him to forgive us; go on allowing Him to take our weaknesses and failures and make us portraits of His grace.

People God Uses

WE CAN DRAW FOUR VERY important and encouraging lessons from Mark's life. No matter how many times you have failed your wife, your husband, your children, or your parents—God is the God of New Beginnings. He is the God of the Second Chance. Just come back to Him in repentant faith and ask Him to get you started again.

1. God wants to use ordinary people like us. I can relate to Mark—he was afraid, unsure, hesitant, and bit off more than he could chew. He was in the "big league," but not ready for it, so he quit. Ordinary people fear; ordinary people fail. And that is just the kind of people God wants to use. The question is this: Do we want to be used by the Lord? God wants to do extraordinary things with ordinary people so that He—the Lord—will get all the credit for what is done:

"For you see your calling, brethren, that not many wise according to the flesh, not many mighty, not many noble, are called. But God has chosen the foolish things of the world to put to shame the wise, and God has chosen the weak things of the world to put to shame the things which are mighty; and the base things of the world and the things which are despised God has chosen, and the things which are not, to bring to nothing the things that are, that

no flesh should glory in His presence. But of Him you are in Christ Jesus, who became for us wisdom from God—and righteousness and sanctification and redemption—that, as it is written, 'He who glories, let him glory in the Lord' " (1 CORINTHIANS 1:26-31).

2. God wants to use those who have failed. Before Mark wrote the second Gospel, he was a dropout from ministry. But the grace of God is so wonderful! He gave him a second chance with someone we would also call a failure. Peter publicly denied Jesus Christ, but likewise found God's grace to be sufficient.[a] The Lord used Mark to give us the greatest of the Four Gospels. And even Paul and Mark reconciled by the time Paul was imprisoned in Rome.[b] God loves to restore and use those who will humble themselves and come to Him.

a. John 21:15-19

b. 2 Timothy 4:11

3. God wants to use young people to serve Him. John Mark was young when the Lord called him. Even though God knew Mark would quit, He still wanted him to go on the trip as a trophy of His mercy, which endures forever. Even when we fail, He still loves us because He is a God of the Second Chance (and third, fourth, and on and on!). And He loves to use young people—in spite of their immaturities:

"Remember now your Creator in the days of your youth, before the difficult days come, and the years draw near when you say, 'I have no pleasure in them' " (ECCLESIASTES 12:1).

4. God wants to use our weaknesses to show His grace. Even though John Mark was not useful at one time in ministry, every time we read the Gospel of Mark, we are experiencing the result of God's transforming grace. History records the path of "new beginnings" for Mark:

Mark, the failed follower of Christ, becomes —
    Mark, the forgiven follower of Christ, becomes—
        Mark, the devoted disciple of Christ, becomes—
            Mark, who writes what may be called the premier
            biography of Jesus Christ, and finally becomes—
                Mark, the honored martyr for Jesus Christ.

After Nero executed Peter, it was not too many years before the Roman Empire began hunting Mark down. They chased him like a criminal until they found him, and then savagely killed him. But this time, Mark was faithful to the end! God uses ordinary people whom we might call failures. He calls young people and makes them portraits of His grace. And that is what He wants to do in each of our lives.

John Mark's triumph by God's grace should be an incredible source of encouragement to each of us!

Prayer Example: Father in Heaven, I pray that You in a very special way will empower our hearts to concentrate on the thought of who You used to write Mark's Gospel. He was an ordinary young man who was a failure, but he is a portrait of Your grace. All of us can achieve great things for Your glory if we will but go on allowing You to forgive us: go on allowing You to take our weaknesses and failures and make them portraits of Your grace. Oh Father, I pray that Mark's life would encourage us to jump into service for You—to serve You even if we are weak, even if we are afraid, even if we are troubled and turn back at times. May we experience the incredible grace that You offered Mark, and that You offer to us today. In the name of Jesus I pray. Amen.

STUDY GUIDE QUESTIONS

1. **Mark—the writer of the New Testament's second Gospel—made a commitment to God in his youth, then bailed out on what God had called him to do.** As a result, others branded him as being "fearful," a quitter," and "a failure." How might an application of Philippians 4:6-7 to his experience have made a difference in Mark's life? How does your life experience line up with that passage?

2. **Once we've made a commitment to God to pursue a Word-filled life, Word-filled marriage, and Word-filled family, like Mark, we can count on being opposed by God's adversary, and ours—Satan (1 Peter 5:8).**

Therefore, God says that we must learn to "resist [Satan], steadfast in the faith" (1 Peter 5:9a). How can we resist this strong adversary? Read Ephesians 6:10-11. What provisions has God given us to fight the good fight of faith?

3. **Mark learned how to live by Ephesians 6:10; he finished well by becoming Peter's personal servant who, as inspired by God's Spirit, captured Peter's words portraying Christ in the Gospel by Mark.** Being "strong in the Lord and the power of His might" denotes both enablement and position. How does Ephesians 6:10 reinforce what Christ said in John 15:5?

4. **Ephesians 6:11 informs us that, to be victorious, we must daily "put on the whole armor of God."** Read Ephesians 6:14-18. Note that no armor is provided for the back, as there is nothing to defend the Christian who turns his back on spiritual warfare. Only one piece of God's armor is designed for attack—the "sword of the Spirit" (v. 17). We must know the truth of God's Word so well that, through faith, Satan's fiery darts can be quenched (v. 16). In what ways does Ephesians 6:14-18 reinforce what Christ has to say in John 15:7-8?

5. **In Ephesians 6:18, God tells us that we are to be "praying always with all prayer and supplication in the Spirit."** Prayer must bind all of the other pieces of God's armor together, because it is the consistent prayer life that unleashes the power to be "strong in the Lord." In Philippians 4:6, what does God say should always accompany "prayer and supplication"? How does that verse compare with what God has to say in 1 Thessalonians 5:16-18?

6. **If we have an attitude of gratitude, what does Philippians 4:7 say will be our continual state of mind?**

"Husbands, likewise, dwell with [them] with understanding, giving honor to the wife, as to the weaker vessel, and as [being] heirs together of the grace of life, that your prayers may not be hindered."

— *1 Peter 3:7*

"It is not good for the man to be alone; I will make him a helper suitable for him."

— *Genesis 2:18, nasb*

Marriage is God's eternal portrait of Christ's love for us. *That was His plan at creation. So when we get married, we get to live out something God has designed for His glory. The following chapters are a call to enjoy heaven's joys upon earth. When Jesus describes what we as believers will experience in eternity He says it is like marriage, and salvation is like engagement (2 Corinthians 11:2; Revelation 19:7). Understanding marriage is vital. Read God's plans and live them. Here is the path we will follow:*

PART TWO

A Word Filled Marriage

There Is No Greater Partnership

6

"For this cause shall a man leave [his] father and mother, and shall cleave to his wife: and they ... shall be one flesh."

—Matthew 19:5, kjv

A Marriage God Rewards

RECENTLY, MY SWEET 5-YEAR-OLD SON climbed on my lap while I was hunched over my laptop typing. He said, "Dad, have we had 'Good Morning Prayer Time' yet?" He must have forgotten that he'd already slipped in, and put his arms around Bonnie and me, as we started our day in prayer together early that morning, like we try to do every day. While we were praying, he wrapped those chubby little arms around our shoulders, and chimed right in with a very creative and heartfelt prayer. But this time, he came to me with more on his mind, so he wanted to pray again. His prayer was short and simple:

> *"Dear God, help me never become an 'ak-o-holie'—and **never** walk around with a bottle ... but I want to be the **best servant of the Lord there ever was!**"*

I'm not sure where he heard about an "alcoholic" or a "bottle," but I suspect it was from watching a John Wayne movie or from observations during our recent trip to New York City. I was amazed that, at the tender age of five, he already had a clear mandate for his life.

Children naturally reduce life to its barest essentials; they know what really matters: love, time, food, and the Lord! Do you have a clear mandate for your own life? Do you know what your primary relationship needs to be? Do you know how God evaluates fruitfulness for Him?

What was the most important ministry we committed to publicly when we made our marriage vows? Was it parenting? Educating our children? Serving in Christ's church, missions, Sunday school, youth work, or evangelism? All of these are important to God, but did He declare that any of them are to be our primary relationship for all of life?

God's Blueprint for Marriage

AFTER COMBING GOD'S WORD FOR instructions about marriage, I found only one mandate repeatedly presented. Four times God states His mandate for marriage—once in the Old Testament and three times in the New Testament.[a] A quick analysis of the references reveals that this mandate was laid down by the Author of Marriage— once before man fell into sin, and three times afterward. This means that God's plan applies to both perfect and sinful humans. Here is God's simple and clear commission, His Genesis mandate, to husbands and wives: *"For this cause shall a man leave* [forsake] *his father and mother, and shall cleave to his wife: and they shall be one flesh"* (MATTHEW 19:5, KJV). That is His all-time blueprint for marriage!

Isn't it interesting that God knew that even a perfect man couldn't be satisfied by work alone?[b] He saw that in unfallen perfection there was still a void in His creation's life that only a corresponding helper could fill. God knew that Adam needed a ministry—to be caring at all costs for his wife. A man has to choose to walk away from even good and acceptable relationships that have consumed his time and attention, and instead take on marriage as his primary responsibility.

Adam still had to work; he was obligated to walk with God, and to maintain his private world. But in the world of humans, all other relationships—even parents—were to be secondary.

a. Genesis 2:24
Matthew 19:5
Mark 10:7-8
Ephesians 5:31

b. Genesis 2:8-18

Actually, Adam's "father" was God, so that is why the Apostle Paul would later advise not to get married if you wanted an undistracted relationship with God.[a] Why? Because once married, spouses have now agreed to a lifelong "'til death we do part" primary human relationship

Since Paul says that unhindered ministry can only be done by the unmarried, ministry outside of the home must be secondary to marriage. Thus, an honest examination of Scripture concludes that the husband's primary ministry in life is to be his wife, and the wife's primary ministry in life is to be her husband.[b] Because these are the first words of God about marriage, they are important and warrant careful consideration. Everything we do in our marriages should be tied to fulfilling the purpose God has laid down for us in His Word. Based upon God's plan then, we must learn how to make those little choices each day which will result in His power, His peace, His favor, and His blessing permeating our lives, marriages, and families.

When God created Eve for Adam, He said:

> "It is not good for the man to be alone; I will make him a helper suitable for him [literally, corresponding to]. And out of the ground the Lord formed every beast of the field and every bird of the sky .... But for Adam there was not found a helper suitable for him. So the Lord God caused a deep sleep to fall upon the man, and he slept; then He took one of the ribs and closed up the flesh at that place. And the Lord God fashioned into a woman the rib which He had taken from the man, and brought her to the man" (GENESIS 2:18-22, NASB).

God created us for marriage. Consider these important facts about the marriage relationship which emerge from that passage:

1. God made you incomplete. God created men and women to correspond to each other. We are similar yet so different. Woman is man's completer, not his copy. Computers and software all differ, but one can't function without the other; so husbands and wives are to each other—indispensable: "Nevertheless, neither [is] man independent of woman, nor woman independent of man, in the Lord. For as woman [came] from man, even so man also [comes] through woman; but all things are from God" (1 CORINTHIANS 11:11-12).

a. 1 Corinthians 7:32-33

b. Portions of this chapter reflect ideas gained from Wayne Mack's fantastic outline in *Strengthening Your Marriage* (Phillipsburg, NJ: Presbyterian and Reformed Publishing Co., 1977).

2. God wants to complete you. God made the woman to be man's helper. Without the woman, man, even in his perfect condition, was incomplete. Therefore, the LORD God said, *"It [is] not good that man should be alone; I will make him a helper comparable to him"* (GENESIS 2:18).

3. God wants to bless you. God made the woman to be a suitable helper. None of the animals could provide the kind of help man needed. Only woman could do that. If husbands fill their lives with activity and ministry, but neglect their primary marriage ministry, they are failures in God's eyes. (The same holds true for wives.) *"[He who] finds a wife finds a good [thing], And obtains favor from the LORD. … Who can find a virtuous wife? For her worth is far above jewels. The heart of her husband trusts in her; so he will have no lack of gain"* (PROVERBS 18:22; 31:10-11).

4. God has the plan. The status of a married man's walk with God is always tied to his role as a husband. At the end of his life, Peter wrote two powerful and practical letters filled with imperatives. First Peter alone has over two dozen commands; one of them says that husbands will only succeed if their marriage reflects Christ: *"Husbands, likewise,* **dwell with [them] with understanding,** *giving honor to the wife, as to the weaker vessel, and as [being] heirs together of the grace of life, that your prayers may not be hindered"* (1 PETER 3:7, Emphasis added).

5. Follow the plan and be blessed. Husbands have needs and inadequacies that are only fulfilled by a godly wife. According to the Scriptures, the wife was created to fulfill the needs and inadequacies of her husband. She was made to be her husband's unique helper. She is to do *"him good and not evil All the days of her life"* (PROVERBS 31:12).

We all regularly face situations ("God's opportunities") that present this challenge: *"Choose … whom you will serve …"* (JOSHUA 24:15A). We should in each instance honestly ask ourselves this question: *By this choice, this action (or reaction), am I serving the Lord—or myself?* All choices in our primary ministry of marriage will fall under one of the following three categories.

Choice Number One—Cut the Cord:

"For this cause shall a man leave [his] father and mother ...." ^a

a. Matthew 19:5a, KJV. See Genesis 2:24.

GOD'S MANDATE FOR MARRIAGE IS to leave our parents. "To leave parents" means that our relationship with them matures to a new level. So, if this is the first choice we must make, how should our relationship to parents change?

1. **Marriage changes our source of authority.** Our parents become our friends, and honored ones. No longer are they the authority for us to follow, but wise friends to counsel us at times. This is the essence of an adult relationship with those priceless parents of the family with whom God chose to place us. Thus we should honor them with our words and actions all our days.^b

b. Titus 3:2

2. **Marriage changes our source of communication.** Our husband or wife becomes the greatest confidant of our life. All plans, all goals, all hopes, all fears—all of life is now shared with our perfect mate who corresponds to us in God's plan, for God says, *"Husbands ... dwell with [your wives] with understanding ..."* (1 PETER 3:7A). We must never have an attitude toward our husband or wife that reflects a desire to change them into being more like what our parents want them to be. The orientation has changed; our parents should not set the direction of our life or marriage. Our partner in Christ is now the one we seek to honor, affirm, please, and serve for the glory of God. We are to be *"giving honor to the wife, as to the weaker vessel"* (1 PETER 3:7B).

3. **Marriage changes our source of affirmation.** Our helpmate is the one from whom we derive affirmation, approval, and, most of all, acceptance and affection. Our parents used to be the foundation of all we did, but now our partner for life becomes that all-encompassing friend and completer, because we are *"heirs together of the grace of life, that [our] prayers may not be hindered"* (1 PETER 3:7B). Any sin of bitterness breeds long term spiritual ill-

ness. Consider Hebrews 12:14-15: *"Pursue peace with all [people], and holiness, ... lest any root of bitterness springing up cause trouble, and by this many become defiled."* Correspondingly, as with any spiritual issue—repentance and restoration must be desired, sought, and found. A blessed marriage has no unresolved issues that are ignored and allowed to breed a "place for the devil," as Paul says in Ephesians 4:27.

Ask yourself: *Am I clearly devoted to my partner above all others?*

Choice Number Two—Cement the Relationship:

a. Matthew 19:5a, KJV. See Genesis 2:24.

"... and shall cleave to his wife ...." [a]

GOD'S BLUEPRINT FOR MARRIAGE DIRECTS husbands and wives to cleave, or, literally, cling to one another. A good marriage is based more on commitment than feeling or mere attraction.

According to Malachi 2:14 and Proverbs 2:17, marriage is an irrevocable covenant or contract to which we are bound. When two people get married, they promise to be faithful to each other regardless of what happens. Divorce is not an option in this covenant.

1. The wife promises that she will be faithful—even if the husband is afflicted with bulges, baldness, bunions, and bifocals; even if he loses his health, wealth, job, or charm; even if someone more exciting comes along.

2. The husband promises that he will be faithful—even if the wife loses her beauty and appeal; even if she is not as neat and tidy or as submissive as he would like her to be; even if she does not satisfy his sexual desires completely; even if she spends money foolishly or is a terrible cook.

3. Both the husband and wife promise to accept full responsibility for their relationship—they thus commit themselves to each other regardless of what problems arise.

God uses marriage as a portrait of joining His family. When we are saved, we are engaged to Christ.[a] All through life we await the joy of becoming His bride.[b] When a person becomes a Christian, he leaves his former way of life, his self-righteousness, his own efforts to save himself, and turns to Christ—who died in the place and stead of sinners. It is in this act of turning that he commits himself fully to Him. The very essence of saving faith is personal commitment to Christ in which a person promises to trust and serve Him completely, regardless of feelings or what problems arise.[c]

In the same manner, God's kind of marriage involves a lifelong commitment of two people to each other—clinging to one another in sickness and health, poverty and wealth, pleasure and pain, joy and sorrow, good times and bad times, agreements and disagreements.

a. 2 Corinthians 11:2

b. Revelation 19:9

c. Cf. Romans 10:9-10; Acts 16:31; Philippians 3:7-8; 1 Thessalonians 1:9-10 .

Ask yourself: *Am I cemented to my partner?*

Choice Number Three—
Share the Wonder of Two Being One:

"... and they ... shall be one flesh." [d]

d. Matthew 19:5a, KJV. See Genesis 2:24.

GOD'S BLUEPRINT FOR MARRIAGE INVOLVES the unity and intimacy of a one-flesh relationship. This is, at its most elementary level, referring to sexual relations, or a physical union between a husband and wife. Consider 1 Corinthians 6:16: *"Or do you not know that he who is joined to a harlot is one body with her? For 'the two,' He says, 'shall become one flesh.' "*

Sex is so much like a river—kept within its appointed banks, it is an unending flow of beautiful refreshment and boundless delights. Allow it to cross over the boundaries God set up and it devastates, ruins, and destroys.

Sexual relations are holy, good, and beautiful within the bounds of marriage. However, sexual activities of any kind outside of the marriage bond become distortions from God's plan, and thus sinful in His sight.[e] Read Proverbs 5:19 for an inspired description of what marriage was designed to be, as God breathed through Solomon, the wisest man who ever lived. The description is one of a man intoxicated with his

e. Study Hebrews 13:4.

wife—completely satisfied, enjoying every part of life, and always wanting to share and experience more of her love. Are you intoxicated by your wife? Do you express that you need her presence, time, attention, touch, and love in your life? Regularly express your earnest desire for her and you will reap a bountiful crop of intoxicating love!

I often tell people when Bonnie and I travel alone, "We are on our honeymoon …" They often smile, as they look at my age and I imagine them to be thinking: *That is so precious that this couple has finally found happiness in a second (or third) marriage!* After my initial pause, I add, "… and we've been married over 20 years. It is a greater honeymoon *now* than it was *then!*" Husbands and wives—that is possible! And that is what God has offered you.

However, in the broadest sense, being one flesh means that both the husband and the wife should choose to work together, as a team, in their devotion to serving Christ and meeting each other's deepest needs.

Ask yourself: *Am I enjoying the fullest joys God offers me through marriage?*

a. Genesis 2:18-25

It is to the degree that we follow God's blueprint for marriage[a] that corresponding peace and harmony will flow in our homes. Balking here causes dissonance and can affect our children's relationship with God. Daughters will fail to learn how to be godly wives; sons will never learn what it means to be God's head of the home. Thus the Lord's name will be blasphemed before the world since the marriage union is intended as a beautiful picture of Christ's love for His bride,

b. Titus 2:5
Ephesians 5:22-33

the church.[b] However, if we faithfully make marriage our primary ministry, we will reap God's blessings on this special high calling for our lives.

So, there you have it—biblical marriage *in a nutshell.* We'll further examine God's marriage mandate in upcoming chapters and then consider how this impacts successful parenting.

APPLICATION:

I encourage you before going on to the next chapter, to "allow, invite, welcome, and give yourself over to" the Truth God has revealed to you personally. Here's how:

1. Pick something that God has prompted you to see as an **area of weakness** in your marriage and ask God to strengthen you—by His grace—to clothe you with that quality; "put on"[a] as Paul commands. Prayerfully ask Him to put that attitude or action upon you.

a. Colossians 3:12-17

2. Then pick something that God has revealed as an **area of disobedience** in your marriage. Repent, turning in your heart and mind from that sin. Cry out to the Lord asking Him to help you "put off"[b] that area, and change your life to go His way.

b. Ephesians 4:17-32

3. Share these two decisions with your husband or wife. Tell him or her what you are "putting on" and "putting off" by faith.

4. Bow as a couple before the Lord and invite the very Word of Christ to spill forth into each of your lives, drenching you—absorbing into your soul and changing every aspect of your life—your marriage, home, life, and all!

STUDY GUIDE QUESTIONS

1. Based upon Genesis 2:24, Matthew 19:5, Mark 10:7-8, and Ephesians 5:31, what is God's mandate for marriage?

2. In Genesis 2:18, what does God say is His main reason for creating women? Read Proverbs 31:12, and then describe how a woman can best fulfill her purpose as a wife.

3. The status of a married man's walk with God is always tied to his role as a husband. Read 1 Peter 3:7. In light of that verse, how would the Lord evaluate the condition of your walk with Him?

4. **All choices in our primary ministry of marriage will fall under one of three categories: (1) cutting the cord with parents; (2) cementing the relationship with our life partner; and (3) sharing the wonder of two being one.**

   What does it mean to "cut the cord" with our parents?

   Read Malachi 2:14 and Proverbs 2:17. Note that marriage is an irrevocable covenant or contract to which we are bound. A good marriage is based more on commitment than feeling or attraction. Are there areas in your relationship with your life partner that still need to be cemented?

   Read Proverbs 5:18-19 for an inspired description of what marriage was designed to be. Next, read Hebrews 13:4. What does God have to say about the physical union in marriage?

5. **Based upon God's mandate for marriage, what is each spouse's primary ministry in life?** How does your life line up with His all-time blueprint for a successful marriage? In areas of weakness, what steps do you believe the Lord would have you take to improve?

7

"Husbands, love your wives, just as Christ also loved the church and gave Himself for her, that He might sanctify and cleanse her with the washing of water by the Word, that He might present her to Himself a glorious church, not having spot or wrinkle …."

— Ephesians 5:25-27b

How to Be an *Incredible* Husband

Several years ago, *the Saturday Evening Post* published an article entitled "The Seven Ages of the Married Cold." It revealed the reaction of a husband to his wife's colds during their first 7 years of marriage.[a] It went something like this:

a. John MacArthur, *The Fulfilled Family* (Panorama City, CA: Word of Grace Communications, 1985), p. 53.

- **The first year:** "Sugar dumpling, I'm really worried about my baby girl. You've got a bad sniffle, and there's no telling about these things with all this strep throat going around. I'm putting you in the hospital this afternoon for a general checkup and a good rest. I know the food's lousy, but I'll be bringing your meals in from Rossini's. I've already got it all arranged with the hospital's floor superintendent."
- **The second year:** "Listen, darling, I don't like the sound of that cough. I called Doc Miller and asked him to rush over here. Now you go to bed like a good girl, please? Just for Papa?"
- **The third year:** "Maybe you'd better lie down, honey; nothing like a little rest when you feel lousy. I'll bring you

something to eat. Have you got any canned soup?"

- **The fourth year:** "Now look, dear, be sensible. After you've fed the kids, washed the dishes, and finished the floor, you'd better lie down."
- **The fifth year:** "Why don't you take a couple of aspirin?"
- **The sixth year:** "I wish you'd just gargle or something, instead of sitting around all evening barking like a seal!"
- **The seventh year:** "For Pete's sake, stop sneezing! Are you trying to give me pneumonia?"

This decline of a marriage, as seen through the common cold, is a funny look at a not-so-funny reality. If this husband claims to be a believer, he's obviously "lost his way" in following Christ. Unless we're willing to pay the price of discipleship, we dare not say to our wives, *"Imitate me, just as I also [imitate] Christ"* (1 CORINTHIANS 11:1). Men—to be effective disciplers, we must not just *tell* our wives how to be like Christ, we must *show* them. That, my friend, is essential, if we are to disciple our wives as a beautiful service of love.

Discipling someone is to help them "learn Christ" (EPHESIANS 4:20)—not simply the doctrine of Christ, but Christ Himself, a process not merely of getting to know the Person but of so applying the knowledge as to walk differently from the rest of the worldlings. Christ's disciples were not only pupils, but adherents; hence they were spoken of as imitators of their Teacher.[a] This was manifested by adhering to, or abiding in His Word.

It is from the preceding description that we can conclude that discipling is a specific type of training that nurtures in God's Word and His ways. Christ has given us that mandate—as our wives' lovers—which means regularly washing them with the Word, just as He does His bride, so that we can one day present our wives in glorious purity to the Lord:

> *"Husbands, love your wives, just as Christ also loved the church and gave Himself for her, that He might sanctify and cleanse her with the washing of water by the Word, that He might present her to Himself a glorious church, not having spot or wrinkle or any such thing, but that she should be holy and without blemish"* (EPHESIANS 5:25-27).

a. *The New Strong's Expanded Exhaustive Concordance of the Bible* (Nashville, TN: Thomas Nelson Publishers, 2001), pp. 156 (#3129) and 154 (#3101).

How We Model Christ to Our Wives

WHAT ARE SOME WAYS CHRIST disciples us that we can use to help our wives also be conformed to the image of Christ?

1. CHRIST GUIDES US INTO TRUTH— WE MUST GUIDE OUR WIVES INTO TRUTH.

"[When] He, the Spirit of truth, has come, He will guide you into all truth; for He will not speak of His own [authority], but whatever He hears He will speak; and He will tell you things to come. He will glorify Me, for He will take of what is Mine and declare [it] to you" (JOHN 16:13-14).

It's interesting that in this passage we're told that even the Holy Spirit doesn't speak of Himself, but directs us to Christ instead. Likewise, we as husbands should continually point our wives to the Lord, for it's not *our* opinions, preferences, tastes, and wills that count—it is Christ's!

We must first discipline ourselves to hear, read, study, memorize, and meditate upon the Word regularly in order to effectively disciple. We will then know the Word sufficiently enough so that our wives can learn from us, as directed in 1 Corinthians 14:35: *"If they* [wives] *want to learn something, let them ask their own husbands at home ...."*

Many enjoy a challenging devotional along with their Bible reading. Oswald Chambers' *My Utmost for His Highest* is a classic, loved by many who are serious about their relationship with Christ. Both partners, by spending time reading to each other from his book, would greatly benefit from Chambers' passion for God and His Word.

Reading the Word aloud is another technique for joint devotions. (*The One Year Bible*—available in a standard scriptural sequence or chronological order—is a good 15-minutes-per-day tool for reading the Bible through yearly.) And as we read, we should help our wives establish clear and well-reasoned convictions so that the Lord has first place in their hearts, and they become able to humbly and carefully explain their biblical convictions to others.[a]

a. 1 Peter 3:15

a. Philippians 2:5-8

Modeling humility during Bible reading times is crucial.[a] If wives detect any hypocrisy in us, or sense that Scripture is being used as a weapon against them, those times together will lose their intended sweetness, and growth in Christ may be hampered.

We should ask the Lord to reveal practical applications that can establish specific spiritual goals for our marriages. We should be encouragers, and become excited as each partner grows in answer to

b. Psalm 86:11-12

Word-filled prayers centered on those goals.[b]

We ought, as servant-leaders, to also provide a regular uninter-

c. Matthew 6:6

rupted time for our wives to have personal devotions.[c] Early morning would be a great time so they can start their day off right. If needed, we should cheerfully care for our children by fixing and serving breakfast, then reading the Word or Bible story to them, singing

d. Psalm 34:11

together, and praying.[d] These "special times with Daddy" should be made joyful so that everyone looks forward to them. But the most important time is a regular and consistent time—that will make the impact that changes their hearts.

2. CHRIST PRAYS FOR US— WE MUST PRAY FOR OUR WIVES.

"I do not pray for these alone, but also for those who will believe in Me through their word. … [Christ] *always lives to make intercession for them"* (JOHN 17:20; HEBREWS 7:25B).

e. John 17:15-17

Christ faithfully prays that the Father will protect us from Satan and his schemes, and set us apart for God's service.[e] What a comfort! Our wives will likewise feel comforted to know that we are praying for them daily, just as Christ does.

If we are to effectively disciple, we must first discipline ourselves to spend quality time in prayer, joyfully and thankfully making our

f. 1 Thessalonians 5:16-18
Philippians 4:6

requests known to Him.[f] We must learn to be genuine listeners in order to pray for our wives knowledgeably, *"For out of the abundance of the heart the mouth speaks"* (MATTHEW 12:34C). We should regularly arrange time for private, intimate conversations to ensure they have

g. Song of Solomon 2:14

our undivided attention.[g] Wives tend to equate not being listened to with not being loved. If they think we don't really *want* to know what is in their hearts, they are likely to just stop telling us, and their hearts may close up. If we don't know what is going on in their hearts, we can't know how to intelligently pray for them, and guide them in the right direction, which can frustrate any discipling efforts.

Now and then, we should also ask our wives if there is anything we have done to hurt or trouble them. Expressing that (if they feel the question is genuine) can have a calming effect on them. Then we should pray with our wives about particular problems, for if we don't seek to understand and honor them, our prayers may be hindered.[a]

a. 1 Peter 3:7

Our prayer example can teach our wives how to pray, and to ask for the right things. When Christ's disciples asked Him to teach them how to pray, He gave them a simple, yet comprehensive model that generally includes these elements:[b]

b. Matthew 6:9-13

- God is to be acknowledged as our holy, heavenly Father, who is to be magnified and glorified throughout the earth (Matthew 6:9-10a).
- All prayer requests must be subjected to God's will, and for His ultimate glory (Matthew 6:10b).
- Daily necessities should be prayed for, even though our heavenly Father already knows our needs before we pray (Matthew 6:8, 11). We are to honor Him as the Supplier of every good and perfect gift (James 1:17).
- We should pray for forgiving spirits (Matthew 6:12). We must daily keep "clean accounts" with God and others by confessing sin and asking for forgiveness (1 John 1:9). To avoid any root of bitterness, we should quickly pursue peace with all people, especially our wives (Hebrews 12:14-15). We should also confess our faults to one another—humbly asking for, or granting, forgiveness as needed (Matthew 6:14-15; James 5:16; Ephesians 4:32).
- We should pray that God will give us power to deny ourselves, resist temptation, and deliver us from Satan's onslaughts (Matthew 6:13; Ephesians 6:12-13).

One of the awesome things about praying together is that Christ has promised to be there, right in our midst. When two of us agree on anything that we ask, it will be done for us by our Father in heaven.[c] Even when we don't know what we should pray for, the Holy Spirit will intercede for us according to God's will.[d] If we ask anything accord-

c. Matthew 18:19-20

d. Romans 8:26-27

a. 1 John 5:14-15

b. Psalm 37:4

c. See Part IV of this book for an in-depth study on the power of practicing Word-filled prayer for our families.

ing to that will, He will hear us and grant the petitions asked.[a] When aligned with God's Word, and we are delighting in Him personally,[b] prayer has tremendous power! Prayer times together with our wives can help meet their need for emotional intimacy.[c]

3. CHRIST PROVIDES ALL OUR NEEDS— WE MUST PROVIDE FOR OUR WIVES' NEEDS.

"And my God shall supply all your need according to His riches in glory by Christ Jesus" (PHILIPPIANS 4:19).

This is a wonderful promise! In Matthew 6:31-33, Christ tells us not to worry about the basic necessities of life, for He already knows we need these things and promises to provide them. We are not to worry about needs for tomorrow either, because tomorrow will take care of itself.[d] Because women, in general, feel uneasy without financial security, modeling faith in these great promises is essential as part of the discipling process.

d. Matthew 6:34

We should be good financial providers as God enables, for *"if anyone does not provide for his own, and especially for those of his household, he has denied the faith and is worse than an unbeliever"* (1 TIMOTHY 5:8). However, we must not fall into the workaholic trap of "providing the best" at our families' expense.

Marriage partners should identify actual needs versus mere wants. Christ sets a balanced example in that He promises to supply our basic necessities but also delights in giving good gifts to those who ask of Him.[e] As imitators of Christ, we should see the importance of providing adequate household and personal allowances plus periodic "just because I love you" gifts. The best gift, however, is to model how to lay up treasures in heaven, *"For where your treasure is, there your heart will be also"* (MATTHEW 6:21).

e. Philippians 4:19
Matthew 7:7-11

4. CHRIST KEEPS HIS PROMISES— WE MUST KEEP OUR PROMISES.

"Know that the LORD your God, He [is] God, the faithful God who keeps covenant and mercy for a thousand generations with those who love Him and keep His commandments; … all the promises of

God in Him [are] Yes, and in Him Amen, to the glory of God ..."
(DEUTERONOMY 7:9; 2 CORINTHIANS 1:20).

We can always count on God to never break a promise, and He expects us to do the same. Keeping promises by following through with commitments is a matter of integrity, which is part of what we learn to be as Psalm 15 men.

Remember: Psalm 15 is to men what Proverbs 31 should be to women. Proverbs 31:11a says that *"the heart of her husband safely trusts her ...."* This matter of integrity applies to both husbands and wives. If either the husband or wife lacks integrity, repentance is in order. (Breaking promises can also spill over to children by provoking them to anger.) We should faithfully follow: *"He who is faithful in [what is] least is faithful also in much; and he who is unjust in [what is] least is unjust also in much"* (LUKE 16:10).

5. CHRIST MODELS STEWARDSHIP— WE MUST MODEL STEWARDSHIP.

"And He who sent Me is with Me. The Father has not left Me alone, for I always do those things that please Him" (JOHN 8:29).

Christ sets the perfect example of stewardship in how He cares for His creation. Since we belong to Him, along with everything else, He simply gives us permission to take care of what He's given us. However, as we learned earlier, whenever He needs anything, we must be willing to give it up. So then, what are some ways husbands and wives can work together as wise stewards?

How we make financial decisions can set the tone for a healthy or destructive marriage relationship. Disagreement over money issues is one of the top reasons many spouses end up in divorce court. Therefore, we should avoid making major financial decisions without first consulting our wives. They need to know the status of family finances so that they can work with us to honor the Lord in this vital area.[a]

a. 1 Peter 3:7

When planning our family budgets, we should opt for balance. We should, in other words, be neither misers nor spendthrifts. A priority should be regular giving to the Lord—not grudgingly, or of neces-

a. 2 Corinthians 9:6-8

b. Romans 13:8

c. Read Proverbs 21:5 and see what God says about impulse buying!

sity, but because of our delight in Him.[a] A noble goal is to keep our families debt free.[b] Credit card buying can be disastrous. Therefore, we must shop wisely, deciding ahead of time on essential purchases so that impulse buying is avoided.[c]

A very important area of stewardship is the preparation of wills that follow biblical principles. This includes prayerfully selecting guardians who will love, care for, and disciple the children in the event both parents die.

Since Christ owns everything, the more carefully finances are managed, the more we will have to give back to His work: *"Give, and it will be given to you: good measure, pressed down, shaken together, and running over will be put into your bosom. For with the same measure that you use, it will be measured back to you"* (LUKE 6:38).

6. CHRIST BEARS OUR BURDENS— WE MUST BEAR OUR WIVES' BURDENS.

"Take My yoke upon you and learn from Me, for I am gentle and lowly in heart, and you will find rest for your souls. For My yoke [is] easy and My burden is light" (MATTHEW 11:29-30).

Modeling this attitude will cause our wives' hearts and spirits to leap for joy! And in today's stressed-out society, most wives long for their husbands to be servant-leaders—to come alongside and help them carry the loads they bear.

Servant-leaders lovingly oversee that the details of household management are in keeping with *"let all things be done decently and in order"* (1 CORINTHIANS 14:40). If organization doesn't come naturally, we should encourage our wives to look for mentors who can help train them in this art. Or, at the very least, we ought to provide sufficient funds for our wives to acquire some "how to" books on the subject. In the course of this growth process, we must avoid having critical spirits because our homes do not yet meet desired goals!

We ought to encourage our wives to grow not only in their relationships with Christ but also as individuals. It's important to make sure that they get some "alone time" to pursue special ministries or personal interests. However, just as *"a man's heart plans his way, But the LORD directs his steps"* (PROVERBS 16:9), so we ought to evaluate our wives' upcoming plans so that we can gently provide direction when needed.

Sometimes wives take on more than they can handle because they have trouble saying no when asked to volunteer for various ministries. We can be our wives' safety nets by protecting them from getting in over their heads. We should remind them that marriage is their primary ministry, which also involves being godly mothers to their children. If we feel, before the Lord, that taking on anything more would overburden their schedules, and thus hurt their primary ministry, we should ask them to graciously decline that new ministry. A good rule of thumb is to ask our wives not to accept any new responsibilities without first checking with us. Our desire should be to help our wives achieve balance in what is accepted, and what should be tactfully declined.

We should also ask the Lord to help us to sense when we need to sweetly assist our wives with household chores and responsibilities, and thus *"bear one another's burdens, and so fulfill the law of Christ"* (GALATIANS 6:2). This is especially true for those who have large families with young children not yet capable of helping to carry the household load!

7. CHRIST COMFORTS US— WE MUST COMFORT OUR WIVES.

"Blessed [be] the God and Father of our Lord Jesus Christ, the Father of mercies and God of all comfort, who comforts us in all our tribulation, that we may be able to comfort those who are in any trouble, with the comfort with which we ourselves are comforted by God" (2 CORINTHIANS 1:3-4).

How to effectively minister comfort is often a puzzle to husbands. Yet, as imitators of Christ, we must learn to sensitively care for our wives' emotional needs. When we agreed to take them in lifelong companionship, we were agreeing to an emotional, spiritual, and physical responsibility. One of the hardest and yet most rewarding pursuits we can have as husbands is to get to know and understand our wives. Paul calls this comforting relationship we are to have as believers *sumpatheo*, in the language of the first century. That word means "to share feelings," which is where we get the English word "sympathy."

The biggest step we can take as husbands is the step of earnestly learning to communicate—by our faces, words, body language, and time—that we really do want to understand a bit more each day of how our wives *feel*. Bonnie and I often try to do this exercise as we drive alone together, when we can just talk. I ask her to explain how and why she feels strongly about something, and then I try to explain it back to her. She can correct anything I missed. We have found this "communications game" to be a marriage builder.

It is at those times when our wives may burst into tears, or otherwise show that they are having a difficult time, that we should show genuine concern. One might say, "Honey, I love you! How can I help?" Because men are problem solvers, we might think they want us to immediately resolve whatever is wrong. Sometimes this might be true, but it is not always the case. Often, what wives want most is just to be held, to feel the security of our strong arms around them; in this manner, we are living with our wives in an understanding way.[a]

a. 1 Peter 3:7

Above all, we should encourage our wives to cast their cares on Christ, because He cares for them.[b] No husband can ever fulfill all of his wife's needs; nor can a wife totally fulfill her husband's. Therefore, our greatest ministry is to point our wives to Christ, who is the ultimate Comforter. We should lovingly remind them that He promises: *"Peace I leave with you, My peace I give to you; not as the world gives do I give to you. Let not your heart be troubled, neither let it be afraid"* (JOHN 14:27).

b. 1 Peter 5:7

A basic need for most women is security. When they feel insecure they need to be encouraged and strengthened by God's Word. When such times come, I recommend reading the fourth chapter of Philippians together, every day, for a month. Memorize verses 4, 6-9, 11b-13, and 19. In so doing, meditate upon these wonderful, potentially life-revolutionizing truths:

- We can rejoice in the Lord always!
- We can be anxious for nothing.
- In everything we can pray, with thanksgiving.
- God gives peace beyond all understanding.
- We can meditate on what is just, pure, lovely, and of a good report.
- We can learn to be content in every situation.

- We can do all things through Christ's strength!
- God can supply all our needs.

By humbly and lovingly washing our wives with the Word, we will be helping them to be *"pulling down strongholds, casting down arguments and every high thing that exalts itself against the knowledge of God, bringing every thought into captivity to the obedience of Christ"* (2 CORINTHIANS 10:4B-5). Though the battle is in the mind, the victory is Christ's![a]

a. 1 John 5:4-5

8. CHRIST LOVES CHILDREN— WE MUST LOVE OUR CHILDREN.

"Behold, children [are] a heritage from the LORD, The fruit of the womb [is] a reward. … 'Let the little children come to Me, and do not forbid them; for of such is the kingdom of God' " (PSALM 127:3; MARK 10:14).

There is no doubt about it—Christ *loves* children! One of the strongest ways to lovingly disciple wives is through the manner in which we love our children. Their hearts are so closely connected to their children's that as we are to them, we are to our wives. If we are good fathers, we have found a key to keeping our wives' hearts open to us, and thus to our discipleship of them. However, if we are bad fathers, it is like throwing away that key—perhaps never to find it again.

Child training—causing children to come under our control and respect our word so that they are more receptive to being discipled in God's Word and His ways—is a two-edged sword. Not only are our children being nurtured in the Lord, but also we are as fathers. Fathering takes a great deal of emotional and spiritual energy as we continually seek God's face for wisdom. The very nature of being Word-filled fathers teaches that we must make sacrifices. Put simply, it means limiting things like boats, off-road vehicles, fancy cars, exotic vacations, excessive sports, and indiscriminate spending. Children require sacrificial time; they take away flexibility and mobility; they diminish financial savings. However, in return, we are making one of the greatest investments possible—one that can be enjoyed both here and in the life to come! Children provide one of the only investments that will bring honor both now and forever.

Properly trained children multiply blessings. Children are a direct physical, visible, tangible blessing from the Lord. They are unique because they are our very own, plus they can become our brothers and sisters in Christ, as well as our best friends for life. Nothing is more precious as the years pass than to see our children following Christ, for, as the Apostle John said, *"I have no greater joy than to hear that my children walk in truth"* (3 JOHN 4). And in contrast, nothing is more heart wrenching than to see any of our children not follow Christ. There is a myth in the world today, that children are expensive. However, *this* is the truth: children are rich and precious treasures sent from God Himself; happy is the father who has many![a]

a. Psalm 127:3-5

In Christ-reflecting fathers, children will see Christ in His proper perspective relative to all of life. Their own worship of God will take on new meaning because they will better understand, first hand, how He gave Himself for them.

9. CHRIST CORRECTS OUT OF LOVE— WE MUST LEARN TO CORRECT IN LOVE.

"Whom the LORD loves He corrects, Just as a father the son [in whom] he delights. … If you endure chastening, God deals with you as sons; for what son is there whom a father does not chasten?" (PROVERBS 3:12; HEBREWS 12:7).

Note that God's correction of us is because He delights in us! The Lord is longsuffering and compassionate because *"as a father pities [his] children, [so] the Lord pities those who fear Him. For He knows our frame; He remembers that we [are] dust"* (PSALM 103:13-14). Therefore, He says that we are to likewise *"have fervent love for one another, 'for love will cover a multitude of sins' "* (1 PETER 4:8).

If God reveals a deficiency in our wives that needs correction, if they are to grow in Christ, we should first search our own hearts for any unconfessed sins.[b] If any exists, we should deal with that first.

b. Matthew 7:4-5

Then, if after sufficient prayer we still feel led to talk to them about a sin problem, we should follow: *"If a [wife] is overtaken in any trespass, you who [are] spiritual restore such a one in a spirit of gentleness, considering yourself lest you also be tempted"* (GALATIANS 6:1). We must be very careful that our wives never sense critical, judgmental spirits because this can close their hearts to correction.

10. CHRIST LOVES US UNCONDITIONALLY— WE NEED TO LOVE OUR WIVES UNCONDITIONALLY.

"For I am persuaded that neither death nor life, nor angels nor prin-cipalities nor powers, nor things present nor things to come, nor height nor depth, nor any other created thing, shall be able to sepa-rate us from the love of God which is in Christ Jesus our Lord" (ROMANS 8:38-39).

Amazingly, in spite of how many times we fail Him, Christ still *loves* us! Just as we love Christ because He first loved us,[a] so wives will responsively love us if we love and accept them unconditionally—in times of kindness or irritableness, in fatness or thinness, in happi-ness or sadness, in sickness or wellness. Husbands with loving spirits are irresistible!

a. 1 John 4:19

11. CHRIST DOESN'T EXPECT PERFECTION— WE NEED TO NOT EXPECT OUR WIVES TO BE PERFECT.

"Not that I have already attained, or am already perfected; but I press on, that I may lay hold of that for which Christ Jesus has also laid hold of me. Brethren, I do not count myself to have apprehended; but one thing [I do], forgetting those things which are behind …, I press toward the goal for the prize of the upward call of God in Christ Jesus" (PHILIPPIANS 3:12-14).

We should not expect perfection, as it will never be achieved this side of heaven. But God does want us to forsake every sin that can ham-per running the race of life with endurance. We must fix our eyes on Jesus, and not look back, slow down, or give up.[b] We must forget past failures, or even successes, and run in a way that we may obtain the highest prize—Christlikeness, both now and in the future.

b. Hebrews 12:1-2a

The goal of discipling our wives is to be used by God to help them conform to Christ's image, teaching them how to rely on Him to meet needs that husbands were never intended to fulfill. As we and our wives grow in the grace and knowledge of Christ, we can better serve Him together—and that is the purpose of a truly biblical marriage.

Dedicating ourselves to the cause of Christ, then lovingly leading our wives to do the same, is the most exciting and fulfilling adventure that we can ever imagine! As Word-filled fathers and mothers, we will then be visible representations of Christ in the discipling of our children—God's heritage[a]—as a service of love to them as well. What a precious privilege and blessing!

a. Psalm 127:3

APPLICATION:

An Assignment for Dads: I have seen, for 20 years now, the priceless value of expressing love to my wife and children in a way that they can feel, hold onto, and take with them through life. This is a list of ideas to try which have served well in the lives of my eight children, each of whom is confident in our love as their parents.

1. **Hold them.** We have held them, from their earliest ages, on our lap as we talk. And to this day, my sweet college student, my eldest daughter, loves to come home from class and share her day. Often she will sit on my lap as we pray. And I know that some day she will also sit on the lap of her husband, and share. Hold your children, and prepare them to share their lives with the one for whom God is preparing them.

2. **Pray with them.** Pray at meals, in the car, on your knees by their bed, when they fall and hurt themselves, when they are sick, when they are scared, before big games, before big tests, when they are sad, and when things are so wonderful that it is one of those priceless moments—just say, "Let's pray and thank the Lord for this!"

3. **Plan with them.** Set up "father times" to take them out with you for things like washing the car, getting gas, going to the bank, or stopping and buying something. If it is planned, it becomes even more special. It shows love, care, interest, and opens the little doors of their hearts. You'll find that many times, as they look out the car windows, that they will open up the dearest parts of their lives and share them. Plan those little times—and reap precious moments.

4. Follow them. I track the growth of my children in a special file in my computer—the precious things they say, the milestones of their lives, and moments I want to capture. To that list, I add my verbal snapshot of each of their birthdays. It was on one of my son's birthdays, for example, that I wrote "James at age 6" along with a detailed description of what he loved and did at that period in his life. This habit helps me to remember where each child is, and where they are headed. Patterns and life directions become so much easier to see and shape by following their lives as a "news reporter."

5. Celebrate with them. Bonnie and I celebrate not just their physical birthdays, but also their spiritual birthdays. The older they get, the more precious this time becomes as we trace with them the "hand of the Lord" moving in their hearts.

Therefore, in other words, daily say in as many ways as possible—"I love you!" If we start this when they are young, then as they grow they will rest in the assurance of their father's love. This will prevent hours of heart-wrenching "searching for the love they never got at home" that so many young men and women go through in their young adult years.

STUDY GUIDE QUESTIONS

1. **To be effective disciplers, we must not just tell our wives how to be like Christ, we must show them.** Read Ephesians 5:25-27. In your own words, describe how that passage impacts you in terms of your walk before the Lord as a husband.

2. **As we lovingly disciple our wives through the Word, has God given us any hope that this faithful practice will bear fruit?** Read Isaiah 55:10-11. Pray that passage regularly on behalf of yourself, your wife, and your children.
   List some ways that you can gently encourage and help your wife discipline herself to hear, read, study, memorize, and meditate upon the Word of God.

3. **To the degree we are filled with the written and living Word of God, and are experiencing the joy and power of Word-filled praying, we will be effective as disciplers.** When aligned with God's Word, and we are delighting in Him personally, prayer has tremendous power! Read Psalm 37:4 and 1 John 5:14-15. What confidence can we have that God will actually hear our prayers?

    List some ways that you can discipline yourself to spend quality time in Word-filled prayer—joyfully and thankfully making your requests known to Him (1 Thessalonians 5:16-18; Philippians 4:6).

4. **In this chapter we have learned that Christ disciples us with an unconditional love (Romans 8:38-39).** Read Proverbs 10:12 and 1 Peter 4:8. Why is having a "fervent love for one another" so vital in a discipling relationship?

    For a description of "fervent love," read 1 Corinthians 13:4-7. How does the love you demonstrate toward your wife (and children) compare with that description? Memorize and meditate upon 1 Corinthians 13:4-7; pray this passage regularly on behalf of yourself—and your family.

5. **We have also learned that the Lord disciples through His loving correction of us.** (See Proverbs 3:11-12 and Hebrews 12:5-6, 11.) Read Galatians 6:1-2. How can having a godly demeanor when applying Galatians 6:1-2 help to further cement the marital relationship with your wife?

8

"Whoever desires to become great among you,
let him be [a] servant ... just as the Son of Man
did not come to be served, but to serve, and to
give His life a ransom for many."

— *Matthew 20:26b, 28*

How to Love and Lead Like Jesus

SUPPOSE YOU RECEIVE WORD THAT you have a terminal illness—as you begin reflecting upon your marriage, what would your first thoughts be? Would they be full of gratitude or full of regrets for the years you've had with your wife?

Even if your thoughts had regrets, the good news is that since coming to Christ, each of us gets to die daily to the past with its failures and sins, and begin anew in the walk of the Spirit! This takes place as we open the doors of our life to God's Word. We learn that our life is but a vapor, so we should live each day as if it were our final one with our wives and children. That is how Jesus lived. He walked in confidence—"always doing the will of His father."

When the Word fills us and takes over our minds, we have the mind of Christ. Then we can think of how He responded to the situations of life. When that mind is directed toward our marriage, it influences our choices.

We should, as husbands representing Christ, want to love and lead like Jesus. Few words can describe the sheer delights of marriage lived in this manner—one day at a time—just as God designed it to be!

- A God-designed marriage is like a joyful river of intoxicating blessings (Proverbs 5:18-19). It is as a fruitful vine that delightfully grows around our lives (Psalm 128:3).
- A God-designed marriage is such a wonderful gift that, like Jacob, waiting for your bride seven years, even at the cost of hard labor, would seem but a moment (Genesis 29:20).
- A God-designed marriage is an endless subscription to regular packages of goodness and favor from the Lord (Proverbs 18:22).
- A God-designed marriage gives us a companion of our youth— to whom we make a lifelong covenant (Malachi 2:14-15).
- A God-designed marriage is one we enjoy so much that for the past 4,000 years godly men "sport" with their spouse—just like Isaac and Rebekah (Genesis 26:8).

All who are blessed in marriage can testify that what has just been described is exactly what we who follow the Lord experience. A Word-filled marriage is a no-regrets marriage, and becomes a small snapshot of the delights of heaven. Such a marriage is a living portrait of the perfect love of Jesus. No one can understand or plumb the depths of Christ's love, but this much we do know.

If I were to ask your wife how your love compares with Christ's, what would she say? How are you striving to be more like Christ in your relationship with and love for your wife? Where is your marriage headed? You will never get to your destination or goal unless you have a plan for getting there. All unattended marriages begin to slowly decline in closeness, intimacy, fruitfulness, and blessing. Therefore, it is a good idea to periodically have a refresher course in what the Lord has to say about our God-designed responsibilities as husbands.

Word-Filled Husbands Love and Lead

GOD'S WORD OPENS WITH A wedding and closes with a marriage. Jesus launches His ministry with the first sign miracle at a wedding and Paul compares God's eternal plan for the church to a godly marriage. So there is no lack of magnificence to what we are called to do and be. There are many scriptural passages that reveal the man's part in marriage.[a] Some key passages are: Genesis 3:16; Psalms 127-128; Proverbs 5:15-19; 1 Corinthians 7:3-4; Ephesians 5:23-33; Colossians 3:19; 1 Timothy 3:4-5; and 1 Peter 3:7. God clearly revealed, as I read through these passages, that the husband has two primary responsibilities to his wife.

a. Wayne Mack
Strengthening Your Marriage
(Phillipsburg, NJ: Presbyterian and Reformed Publishing Co., 1977), pp. 27-36.

1. WORD-FILLED HUSBANDS LOVE.[b]

b. See Ephesians 5:25-33.

Love is imperative. That is what the Spirit of God told Paul. Three times, in almost as many verses in Ephesians 5, Paul commands that husbands love their wives. Either they really need love, or we really have trouble loving. Either way—love is the imperative of a Word-filled husband's life. Paul says—to help us men who need guidance—to love our wives with the same attention we care for ourselves;[c] and love them with the same selflessness as Jesus shows His bride, the church.[d]

c. Ephesians 5:28, 33

d. Ephesians 5:25

We as men carefully protect and provide for the needs of our bodies. We do not deliberately do anything to harm ourselves. When we are hungry, we eat. When we are thirsty, we drink. When we are tired, we sleep. When we are in pain, we go to the doctor. When we cut ourselves, we wash the wound and bind it up. When we see an object coming toward us, we put up our hands for protection.

Suffice it to say, in other words, that we very carefully and fervently nourish and cherish ourselves. "Well," Scripture indicates, "this is the way we are to love our wives. We are to nourish them, cherish them, protect them, satisfy them, provide for them, care for them, and sacrifice for them to the same degree and extent, and in the same manner, as we do ourselves."

That is a high standard of love for a husband to keep, but there is yet a higher standard: *"Husbands, love your wives just as Christ also loved the church and gave Himself for her"* (EPHESIANS 5:25). It is not a mystery how to love like Christ loved. It is practical, plain, and simple. It is the record of the Bible. The Scriptures are the Word of Christ. In them we find countless examples of how He loved individuals. And it is with this caliber of love that we must lead our wives.

a. See Ephesians 5:23;
1 Timothy 3:4-5, 12; and
1 Corinthians 11:3.

b. Matthew 20:20-28
describes the Bible's
concept of a leader.

2. WORD-FILLED HUSBANDS LEAD.[a]

If we want to be godly leaders, and follow Christ's example, we must lead our wives with love.[b] Like Christ, we must invest the time together with our wives to explain, discuss, and work through the way that we will fill our lives as a couple, with the Word. Then we have to model that plan—not perfectly, but humbly, as fellow heirs of Christ.

Godliness is always the key. Nothing is more irresistible for a spiritual woman than a godly man. (And correspondingly, the woman clothed in a meek and quiet spirit is beautiful in God's sight—and a godly husband's.) Just as Jesus led in love, ministered with love, and expressed His love, so a godly leader must also be a passionate lover to his wife.

So how can we as husbands love our wives with that quality of love?

How to Love Your Wife With Christ's Love

JESUS WANTS US TO INTIMATELY know Him; He has promised that He is engaged to us and will soon return to marry us—all of which speaks of an intensely loving relationship. What are the elements of loving our wives like that? By God's grace, a husband who believes that his primary ministry is his marriage will faithfully strive to be like Jesus wants him to be. What are the characteristics of such a man? There are five: intimacy, romance, humility, transparency, and service.

c. Ephesians 5:28-29

1. Intimacy is his direction. A Word-filled husband will allow his wife to see and hear that he cherishes her, and delights in her as a person, just as Christ delights in His bride.[c] Part of God's blueprint for marriage is that husbands are to cleave to their wives. Cleaving means intimacy, which transcends sex; God expects husbands' lives to encompass every dimension of their beloved wives' lives—emotionally, spiritually, and physically. This requires just plain old "being around each other." Life so often becomes like a busy highway in which marital partners are always heading in different directions. We must choose to stop this "highway mania," and stay close to each other—in conversation, with eyes locked onto theirs, and most of all with our hearts listening and sharing. That is cleaving—intimacy—and that should be our direction. A

Word-filled husband allows his wife to share his life fully, for they are *"heirs together of the grace of life"* (1 PETER 3:7).

Husbands in the process of discussion should insure that there is intellectual agreement on major issues. This promotes spiritual harmony, which in turn encourages sensitive appreciation of a mate's physical and emotional responses. As the discovery of similar values is strengthened, there can be even more imparted secrets. Cherishing a wife like this leads to a lifelong delight in the one with whom he has developed a genuine understanding of goals, plans, desires, feelings, and fears.

2. Romance is his glue. A Word-filled husband understands that intimacy opens the way for the ultimate union of life with his wife. Sex is so much more than body; it is soul, spirit, heart, and mind. *Romance starts* at the kitchen sink when a husband steps up behind his wife (like the first weeks of marriage) and says with all his heart, "You are all my dreams come true!" *Romance builds* by calling our wives sometime in the day and honestly expressing that we can't stop thinking about them, and just had to hear their voice. *Romance fills* the room with the fragrance of love. It is not a stop at a fast food drive-through. *Romance flavors* life like an exquisite five-course meal which causes you to savor every bite … each course … and, at the end of the meal, you sit back and feel satisfied—completely. **Always remember that sex is beautiful and godly because the Lord designed it, commanded it, and blesses it**. The Lord even inspired Solomon to use sexual terms to help us understand the beauty of Christ's love for His bride.

If a husband has a wrong view of the marital sexual relationship, he will have an unsatisfying marriage, an unfruitful personal life, and an unfulfilled family. God points out the importance of loving a wife intimately in what is often called the "newlywed verse."

> *"When a man hath taken a new wife, he shall not go out to*
> *war or be charged with any business; he shall be free at home*
> *one year, and bring happiness to his wife whom he has taken"*
> (DEUTERONOMY 24:5).

God in the New Testament again instructs husbands (and wives) to not be neglectful in loving each other in this manner:

"The husband should fulfill his marital duty to his wife, and like-
wise the wife to her husband. The wife's body does not belong
to her alone but also to her husband. In the same way, the
husband's body does not belong to him alone but also to his wife"
(1 CORINTHIANS 7:3-4, NIV).

"Do not deprive each other except by mutual consent and for a time,
so that you may devote yourselves to prayer. Then come together
again so that Satan will not tempt you because of your lack of self-
control" (1 CORINTHIANS 7:5, NIV).

A godly marriage is like a fountain that overflows with delights.
But if that fountain is unkempt, the spring can get fouled, and the
waters polluted. So the joys of those early days of marriage can fade
fast. Therefore, never take your wife for granted. Talk to her often
of the vital role she plays in every part of your life. Share with her
often of your loving need of time with her. Write many love notes
and cards—rather than regretfully wishing someday that you wish
you'd done more. Make it a habit of saying "I love you" in some
manner every day!

3. Humility is his goal. A Word-filled husband will lead as Jesus
did, who Himself was, first and foremost, a servant. John 13:1-15
provides the same picture of leadership. Like Jesus, godly husbands
are to lead by being servants. Just as Jesus knelt and washed the feet
of His disciples, we kneel in our hearts and humbly serve our wives.
Our emblem of servant leadership is the basin and towel. And the
greatest is the one who serves the most. This principle is found in
1 Peter 5:3: *"... nor as being lords over those entrusted to you, but being*
examples to the flock ...." Nothing can destroy a marriage faster than
a husband's unyielding pride.

Why not practice saying some of these words:

"Honey, let me do the dishes."

"Why don't you go to the grocery store without the kids,
I'll watch them."

This simple, practical way of modeling humility is the very best way to love our wives (and children)!

"Let this mind be in you which was also in Christ Jesus, who… made Himself of no reputation, taking the form of a bondservant, … He humbled Himself and became obedient [to the point of] death, even the death of the cross" (PHILIPPIANS 2:5, 7A, 8).

4. Transparency becomes his habit. Word-filled husbands give their wives complete openness, communication, and vulnerability. Just as Jesus loves us to the end, so we should love our wives. Just as Jesus will never leave us or forsake us, our wives need to know, feel, and hear from us of our lifelong loyalty. One of the best ways to encourage our wives is to clearly and regularly say how much they fulfill our lives.

I tell my wife, Bonnie, in every way I can think of, just how much I need her help, her counsel, her companionship, and her presence. If she loves my time—I give her time; if she loves gifts—I give her something she'll cherish; if she loves words—I give her quiet times of talking about whatever she needs to hear. It is vital that she feels all of her needs are being met in a loving manner.

Our marriage, over the years, has truly been deepened and enriched by the hundreds of godly couples we have met, known, loved, and learned from in the ministry. Here are some of the valuable lessons they have shared with us.

Ask for help. Some husbands are like cavemen—they mumble, grunt, and go through life in a cloud of silence at home. But the way God wired wives is so that they want to be asked to help because they like to spend time with us. Therefore, we must leave the cave of silence, and let them know what we are doing. We should ask our wives to do things, even if it is something simple like holding a tool we need for a project or going somewhere together to buy this or that. In other words, as our best friends, they should be included in our lives, words, and thoughts, and in doing this, it will make our wives feel like a valuable member of the team.

Share burdens. A burden shared is cut in half; a blessing shared is doubled. God's math in marriage is perfect. We should share the load, as Galatians 6:2 directs. If we don't, we are robbing our precious wives of what God has made them to be—lifelong helpmeets. If we pray about our burdens with them, soon they will likely open up to us and share their own burdens, so that we can help them better bear them. A marriage is only complete when both partners are loving one another, fulfilling the law of love God calls us to obey.

Confess struggles. No one can protect our integrity better than our wives. We therefore ought to share our struggles with them. For example, whenever I think a woman is too friendly, I talk about it with Bonnie. She can see things as a woman I never could as a man. As husbands, we should discuss with our wives any ideas, problems, fears, or pains we're going through because they want to share real areas of our lives—to know our struggles. Such shared burdens will bind hearts together like nothing else. The vulnerability of sharing honest struggles will do far more to affirm a vital partnership with our spouses than any fancy presents or expensive toys ever could. Our wives will know that we belong to them if we share our real problems in life!

Express needs. Nothing motivates a godly wife more than knowing that her husband truly needs her. Remember—God designed women to be completers. Wives want to invest their time and strength in what will matter to their husbands in life. Nothing will warm their hearts more than to hear these words: "Honey I really need—(you fill it in)." Perhaps time to talk, time alone with them, to get away for a night, or whatever you really need. **Telling your wife how much you need her is the greatest thing you can do because she longs to meet your needs!**

5. Serving is his plan. A Word-filled husband will be his family's best servant: *"Whoever desires to become great among you, let him be [a] servant ... just as the Son of Man did not come to be served, but to serve, and to give His life a ransom for many"* (MATTHEW 20:26B, 28).

A servant has a master. Since Christ is our Master, a husband leads his wife, even as Christ leads His church.[a] Fruitful and satisfying marriages start with the attitude of Jesus. Paul explains that Christ's motivating heart of servant ministry flowed from an attitude of joyful submission. Paul asks each of us in Philippians 2:3-11 to "let" ("allow, invite, welcome") the attitude of Jesus to become ours. As we embrace the humility of Christ, we stop being absorbed by self and begin thinking of others.

a. Ephesians 5:23

When Jesus called the twelve disciples, He distilled His plan down to one word. We see this one-word key to discipling in Mark 3:14: *"that they might be **with** Him"* (Emphasis added). We need to spend personal, face to face, heart to heart time **with** those we are nurturing. Jesus was there **with** His disciples when they needed Him. We should follow His example.[b] We, as servant leaders, need to lead in person—not from afar or by extension, but in the presence of those we serve.

b. Cf. John 1:39, 43; Mark 1:17; 3:14; 4:10; 5:1, 30-31, 40; 6:1, 30-32, 35; 8:1,10, 27, 34; 9:2, 30; 10:13, 23, 46; 11:1.

If you read the Gospels closely you will see how clearly Christ's words communicated exactly what His disciples needed. He anticipated their fears; He expected their questions; and He guided their growth. Just like Jesus, we should long to "create understanding," which is the primary purpose of communication.

How to Lead Our Wives Like Jesus Led

GOD DESIGNED MEN TO LEAD, and women to respond. It is the role of men to initiate and pursue, no matter how hard it may be. Christ's example of gentle, compassionate, servant leadership is a model for all of us who want to be godly husbands and dads. There are five characteristics of Christ's leadership that each of us men should emulate: sacrifice, kindness, strength, tenderness, and praise.

1. Sacrifice is his METHOD. Matthew 20:28 says, *"The Son of Man did not come to be served, but to serve, and to give His life a ransom for many."* A Word-filled husband will love his wife by sacrificing to meet her needs. Jesus told us that because God loved, He gave. That gift was the ultimate sacrifice. Husbands are to have that type of sacrificial love as their way of life with their own wives. Authors Dr.

Gary and Barbara Rosberg report, in a survey of over 700 couples, that wives indicated their top five love needs as follows: **1.** unconditional love and acceptance, **2.** emotional intimacy and communication, **3.** spiritual intimacy, **4.** encouragement and affirmation, and **5.** companionship.[a] The Rosbergs make a very valid point:

a. Dr. Gary and Barbara Rosberg, *The 5 Love Needs of Men and Women* (Wheaton, IL: Tyndale House Publishers, Inc., 2000), p. 8.

> Human nature is strange. Something in us assumes that if we treat our spouse the way we would like him or her to treat us, we are meeting our partner's needs. But when it comes to needs, the Golden Rule *("Do unto others as you would have them do unto you")* does not always apply. Why? Because in many cases a husband's needs are different than a wife's needs.[b]

b. Ibid.

It is really true that God wired men and women differently, and this doesn't apply only to sexual needs. For that reason, establishing a routine of intimate dialogue between husband and wife is essential so that each understands how to best make his or her partner feel loved.

2. Kindness is in his TOUCH. A Word-filled husband will practice one of the simplest, yet most neglected ways of communicating love—by the tender touches of love. A Word-filled husband will give his wife tenderness, chivalry, and courtesy.

If you have never felt the touches of Jesus[c] through the pages of the Gospels—I invite you to do so. Why not take a few moments and look up these passages and see how compassionate and gentle were Christ's hands as He touched with love so many people. Jesus had a loving touch of kindness.

c. There are at least forty passages recording the touches of Jesus. Here are some in the Gospel by Mark : 1:31, 41; 5:41; 6:5; 7:33; 8:23; 9:27; 10:16.

3. Strength is in his PRESENCE. A Word-filled husband will love his wife by being there for her, protecting her, making her feel secure in his love.[d] She needs to feel that, like Christ, her husband will never leave her, or forsake her.[e] Become a student of your wife. Learn her patterns. Does she get "the blues" in the gray of winter? Know when that is happening, and surprise her with something she loves. Does she need time alone (away from the burdens of home and family) during her monthly cycle? Then send her off to a bookstore to drink tea and read her Bible, or just look at magazines and think. How about the loss of a parent in the past—do you remember and comfort

d. Ephesians 5:28

e. Matthew 28:20b
Hebrews 13:5b

her? These are just some suggestions to start a lifetime of sacrificing your time to show her she is special, loved, and your focus. Be there for her needs by studying her life because you love her so much.

1 Tenderness is on his TONGUE. A Word-filled husband will practice one of the simplest, yet most neglected ways of communicating love—by words spoken kindly, warmly, and directly to his wife. Jesus spoke with such grace that even His enemies confessed in John 7:46: *"No man ever spoke like this Man!"* Remember those words in verse 2 of C. Austin Mile's hymn "In the Garden"?

> *He speaks, and the sound of His voice*
> *Is so sweet the birds hush their singing;*
> *And the melody that He gave to me*
> *Within my heart is ringing.*
> *And He walks with me, and He talks with me,*
> *And He tells me I am His own,*
> *And the joy we share …, None other has ever known.*

Husbands, what effect do you think demonstrating that same spirit might have on our wives? Since women are so responsive, I imagine that such sweet speech would be *"[like] apples of gold In settings of silver"* to them.[a] What a beautiful service of love! His words will be seasoned with the salt of God's grace.[b] He will refuse to compare her unfavorably with others, especially other women. He will not use jokes about her, or make cutting remarks to her in front of other people. He will speak to her in a gentle and respectful way, and treat her as he would a valuable jewel. Personally, I have chosen to believe that Bonnie is the dearest friend I'll ever have on earth—and I treat her that way, think of her that way, and talk about her in that way!

a. Proverbs 25:11

b. Ephesians 5:28
Colossians 3:19
1 Corinthians 3:4-5

5. **Praise is his GIFT.** Proverbs 31:28 has always been my goal as a husband. Many people talk about the Proverbs 31 woman, but few men strive to be the Proverbs 31:28 **husband**: *"Her husband … praises her."* Shouldn't we likewise practice that grace until it becomes part of our daily life? It is so rewarding to see the long term results! Proverbs 31:28 is the only Scripture I know of that describes the way a godly husband speaks in public about his wife. Are you doing what God

says? Are you also praising your wife in front of your children? That is the way of the godly, tender servant-leader!

Danger Signs of a Man Unfilled With the Word

IT IS WHEN WE ARE without a growing relationship with our wives as was just described, and are not faithfully following Christ's Word, that we husbands commonly end up with one or several of five common danger signs that will lead to lifelong regrets.[a]

a. Robert Lewis and William Hendricks, *Rocking the Roles* (Colorado Springs, CO: NavPress, 1991), p. 156.

1. When he abdicates his God-given role: This husband is nothing but a little boy in search of a mommy, and he seems to have found one in his wife. He is thoroughly self-centered, but manages to appear to others as a loving and devoted husband.

2. When he disengages his emotions: This man may be recognized as one of the most stable and even-tempered men in his community. He is frequently asked to serve on the boards of numerous organizations because of his organized mind and methodical way of making decisions. However, in his home he is about as detached and emotionally unavailable as a man can get.

3. When he demands rather than earns: This man's idea of "head of the household" means that nothing happens without his approval. When his wife dares to question his authority or decisions, he resorts to intimidating tactics and, if that doesn't work, he goes into a blind rage.

4. When he serves his job not his family: This man never leaves work mentally or emotionally. He lives under pressure, and sprays his family with his frustrations.

5. When he refuses to lead spiritually: This husband is a believer and a church attendee. But beyond that, he's generally unresponsive to spiritual matters; he therefore never exercises spiritual leadership in his home. And that void blocks the intimacy for which his wife yearns.

We have seen, in conclusion, characteristics of both a no-regrets husband and a husband with regrets. Now, let's make this more personal. If I were to ask your wife how your husbandly love compares to what we've just learned, what would she say? Would she categorize you as a no-regrets husband—or a husband with regrets? How would God evaluate the fruitfulness of your primary ministry to your wife?

Get Started Now

YOU HAVE A SPECIFIC CALLING—love your wife, and sacrificially lead her—just as Jesus loved us and gave Himself for us. This is not a fact to learn; it is a lifestyle to live. And as Jesus said, it is not those who say they love, but those who show it—that really love.[a]   a. Matthew 7:21-23

Just as with every other facet of our spiritual lives, we must repent and go back to where we got off the path. Christ's course for each of us to follow is so clear. If you have lost the joy, lost the vibrancy of your daily walk with your wife, repent and go back to where you veered away. Do as Jesus said in Revelation 2:4-5: Go back to your first love—the love of choice, the love of sacrifice, the love of priority, the love that draws you to sacrifice for her. Start today! Make a list, and follow it back to where God wants you to be:

- From this chapter, note what areas you have neglected, or were even unaware of that needed to be done (1 Peter 3:7).
- Humbly agree with God that you have failed. Ask for the cleansing of forgiveness (1 John 1:9; Matthew 5:23-24; James 5:16). Then sit (or even better—shock your wife and kneel with her) and pray for God to forgive your failures and give you a fresh start together.
- Start over again by remembering that God is the God of New Beginnings (Lamentations 3:23). By God's grace, the whole life of a believer is but "a series of new beginnings."
- Realize that marriage is just like every other dimension of our life in Christ—it only works by the power of the Spirit. Yield to Him, and ask for the fullness of His power to bear the fruit of love in your life, your marriage, and in your family (Galatians 5:16, 22-23).

a. John 14:21
Philippians 2:12-13
James 1:19-24

b. Romans 5:5

c. James 4:2b

God says so often, "If you love Me, you will obey Me."[a] Decide now, in the power of God, to overflow with His love, to begin anew and afresh in this walk with your wife. Ask Him to make His love overflow in your hearts.[b] Don't wait—ask now! There is so much that we *have not* simply because we *ask not.*[c]

What an opportunity to have such a rare and precious ministry. And that is exactly what the Lord offers to each of us. How about it? Are you a no-regrets husband? Is your marriage a no-regrets marriage—or full of grief? Where is your marriage headed? I believe the choice is yours. Why not decide to start in some of these suggested ways—heading toward a marriage that thrills your wife and pleases the Lord?

Why Not Start Two Simple Habits?

LIFE IS SO FULL, DAYS are so short, and time passes so swiftly—so I have chosen two simple habits to freeze time into precious snapshots of my love for my wife and children. Here they are; think about them and try your own version in your family. I'm sure you will be glad you did.

First, I have an ongoing list that I have made for Bonnie. It took about an hour to start, and now I add to it whenever I can. I call it my **"Reasons Why I Love You"** list. I took her out to eat, talked over our wonderful blessings, and then read it to her the first time. Need I say how she received it? She was overwhelmed, overjoyed, and blessed beyond measure. Since then, I add at least one new reason before the special events in the life of our marriage. I give my wife a new and updated list on each of her birthdays and our anniversaries. (I even find the list taped in a place where she can read it over and over each day—to remember just why I love her so much!)

My second simple habit is another important list. Bonnie and I, as a couple, sat together and prayerfully assembled a list we call **"Spiritual Goals for Our Marriage and Family."** It will bless your wife and children if you do the same; begin simply, and watch the list grow. When Bonnie and I started our lives together, for example, we planned to do the following things with each of our children. And as the Lord allows these goals to become reality in our family, they become praise points that encourage us along the road of our marriage and family. Here are just a few examples of simple goals we have made, prayed for, and will rejoice to see God accomplish through us:

- Lead each of our children to Christ.
  Teach them how to have personal devotions with the Lord.
- Train them in simple Bible study methods (marking key topics, study subjects through the entire Bible like "prayer," etc.).
- Begin our children's memorization habits for life.
- Teach them how to mark their Bible with the "Romans Road," and then teach them how to use that to lead a soul to Jesus from the Scriptures. You will find the "Romans Road" at the end of this chapter; these are the four simple truths I mark in every Bible I own, as soon as I obtain it. I hope you will too, and then help your wife and family mark theirs.
- Read God's Word aloud with them at the meal table—aim to read the entire Bible before they grow up and head off to college.
- Look for a time to pray every day with them, either as a couple or alone with them, at the start or end of their day.

Guess what? God has given us every goal we had—every goal we prayed over regularly! He loves to respond to whole-hearted praying: *"But from there you will seek the Lord your God, and you will find Him if you seek [Him] with all your heart and with all your soul"* (DEUTERONOMY 4:29).

Start with a simple habit like one of these, keep going on it, and you will be amazed at how it keeps your marriage and family focused on what will really last!

A Simple Plan for Leading Someone to Salvation In Christ

THE "ROMANS ROAD" IS THE simplest and most direct method I have found to use at a moment's notice in pointing someone to Christ. The best way is to start by writing Romans 3:10 on the first page inside your Bible cover. Then look there as a reminder where to start. Now turn to Romans 3:10—and begin the "Road" of explaining the Gospel.

Here are the "Road Markers" that you need to mark. At the top of the page in your Bible where Romans 3:10 is printed, write clearly:

#1 WE ALL ARE SINNERS
—Romans 3:10-18, 23 (5:8)

Highlight verse 10b: ***"There is none righteous, no not one."*** Then underline and note the following words I have bolded below in Romans 3:10-18 and 23: (Emphasis added to "Romans Road" verses.)

> *10 As it is written: **"There is none righteous, no, not one;** 11 **There is none** who understands; **There is none** who seeks after God. 12 **They have all** turned aside; **They have together** become unprofitable; **There is none** who does good, no, not one." 13 "Their throat is an open tomb; **With their tongues** they have practiced deceit";* [WE SIN BY WORDS] *"The poison of asps is under their lips"; 14 "Whose mouth is full of cursing and bitterness." 15 "**Their feet** are swift to shed blood;* [WE SIN BY DEEDS] *16 Destruction and misery are in **their ways**;* [WE SIN BY HABITS] *17 And **the way of peace they have not known.**"* [WE SIN BY NEGLECT] *18 "**There is no fear of God** before their eyes."* [WE SIN BY IRREVERENCE] *23 **For all have sinned and fall short of the glory of God** ...* [THEREFORE ALL ARE SINNERS]. (5:8)

After Romans 3:23 write in your Bible the next stop on the "Romans Road," which is Romans 5:8. Now turn there with me. Up in the margin somewhere near these verses write the second truth, which you SAY as you guide a seeking soul toward Christ. You say, "Secondly, God's Word says Christ died for sinners. Remember we just saw God's Word say that all of us are sinners, right? Now the good news is that Christ died for sinners!" Next, put in parentheses the third stop on the "Romans Road" (6:23).

#2 CHRIST DIED FOR SINNERS
—Romans 5:8-11 (6:23)

> *8 **But God demonstrates His own love toward us, in that while we were still sinners, Christ died for us.** 9 Much more then, having now been justified by His blood, we shall be saved from wrath through Him. 10 For if when we were enemies we were reconciled to God **through the death of His Son,*** [THIS IS CHRIST'S

SUBSTITUTION "TAKING OUR PLACE ON THE CROSS"] *much more, having been reconciled, we shall be saved by His life. 11 And not only that, but we also rejoice in God through our Lord Jesus Christ, through whom we have now **received the reconciliation.** [THIS IS IMPUTATION—HIS RIGHTEOUS LIFE PLACED UPON US SO WE HAVE HIS PERFECT LIFE].* (6:23)

After explaining the three truths of these verses—Christ died for sinners, took our sins upon Himself, and offers His perfect life to we who are so imperfect—continue to Romans 6:23.

#3 SALVATION IS A GIFT
—Romans 6:23 (10:9-13)

*23 For the wages of sin is death, **but the gift of God is eternal life** in Christ Jesus our Lord. (10:9-13)*

I find it helpful to pull out my pen and ask what a gift really is. I offer my pen and say, "Here you go; this is a gift for you." And then when he or she is holding the pen I stick out my hand and say, "That will be TEN DOLLARS please." And smiling I say, "Was that a gift if I charge for it, or if you try to pay for it?" And then the whole matter of working or earning his or her way to heaven can be explained as impossible. The beauty of God's grace is here explained in simple terms.

Review the three points by asking: "Now we have seen God's Word say that all are sinners, right?" Wait for a response, looking intently at the seeking soul; after this is affirmed, ask, "And what did we see as the ONLY remedy for sins? Christ DIED in the place of sinners like you and me, right?" This is a great time to give a 30-second testimony of how you came to faith in Jesus for your salvation. Then say, "And here in Romans 6:23 we have seen that salvation is a GIFT, right?" Then turn to Romans 10:9-13.

#4 ASK JESUS TO SAVE YOU
— Romans 10:9-13

This is one of the critical moments. Read and show these verses. But don't stop there. So many never lead anyone to the Lord because they never ask the person, "Would you like to ask Jesus right now to forgive and cleanse and save you?" If you don't ask, he or she will have to pray alone, or God will bring someone else along, so please pray for the grace and boldness to ask!

> 9 *That if you* **confess with your mouth** *the Lord Jesus and believe in your heart that God has raised Him from the dead, you will be saved.* 10 *For* **with the heart one believes** *unto righteousness, and* **with the mouth confession is made** *unto salvation.* 11 *For the Scripture says, "Whoever believes on Him will not be put to shame." 12 For there is no distinction between Jew and Greek, for the same Lord over all is rich to all who call upon Him.* 13 *For* "**whoever calls on the name of the Lord** *shall be saved."*

And if God is at work, if the Holy Spirit is drawing, the person will beautifully say, "Yes, that is what I need, that is what I want," and press into the kingdom as you watch him or her cry out to the Lord for salvation.

I hope you pray and sow, and see God give you the harvest; there is really nothing like soul winning in the entire world! Hallelujah, what a Savior!

STUDY GUIDE QUESTIONS

1. **A Word-filled marriage is a no-regrets marriage, which is a small snapshot of the delights of heaven.** Such a marriage is a living portrait of the perfect love of Jesus. How are you striving to be more like Christ in your relationship with and love for your wife?

2. **There is no lack of magnificence to what God calls us to do—and be—as husbands.** There are many scriptural passages that reveal the man's part in marriage. Look up the following key verses and then summarize the man's responsibility in each.

    Genesis 3:16 -

Psalms 127 and 128 -

Proverbs 5:15-19 -

1 Corinthians 7:3-5 -

Ephesians 5:23-33 -

Colossians 3:19 -

1 Timothy 3:4-5 -

1 Peter 3:7 -

3. By God's grace, a husband who believes that his primary ministry is his marriage will faithfully strive to be like Jesus wants him to be. It is as we embrace the humility (the root of all virtue) of Christ that we stop being absorbed by self, and begin thinking of others. Read Philippians 2:1-8. How is God speaking to you personally in this passage?

4. Not only should we love our wives as Christ has loved the church (Ephesians 5:25), **but we should also model Christ's example of gentle, compassionate, servant-leadership.** Read Matthew 20:26b-28. Explain how emulating the spirit of those verses will help you fulfill your two primary responsibilities to your wife—to love and to lead her, as Christ loves and leads you.

9

"Wives, submit to your own husbands, as to the Lord. For the husband is head of the wife, as also Christ is head of the church .... Therefore, just as the church is subject to Christ, so [let] the wives [be] to their own husbands in everything."

— *Ephesians 5:22-24*

Understanding the "S" Word

EVER SINCE THE GARDEN OF Eden, husbands and wives have continually competed for first place. When sin entered the world, the woman desired to rule over the man; the man desired to rule over the woman, and both departed from their God-ordained roles in life. Now, instead of being the Christlike leader of his home, as the biblical head over his wife, the typical man has become dominant and forceful; in reaction, the typical woman has resisted, and sought liberation from such control. And that whole conflict began way back in the Garden!

The idea of wifely submission is therefore not a very popular topic in our day. Some resistance to submission is simply sinful rebellion against the will of God; but sometimes it reflects a wrong understanding of what the biblical wife's submission really involves. Therefore, to clarify a wife's role in biblical submission, we need to correct common misconceptions, and then discuss what Scripture really says about submission.

What Biblical Submission Is *Not*

GOD SAYS, IN THE SECOND chapter of Genesis, *"[It is] not good for man to be alone: I will make a help meet for him"* (GENESIS 2:18, KJV). The key word in that verse is the word "for." God made the woman for Adam—to complete him by adding a quality of life that previously did not exist. Eve was a precious gift to Adam—to fulfill him as a person. And the Lord said that this was "very good."[a] Genesis 1:26-27, 2:23, and Galatians 3:28 all assert the spiritual, mental, and physical equalitarian status and dignity of women and men. However, in spite of this, there are still five common misconceptions about submission:

Misconception #1: Submission is only for women. Actually, we are all commanded to submit to one another in Christ's body. So this is a universal responsibility, not merely for wives.[b]

Misconception #2: Submission is bondage. Wrong. Jesus said that submission to obey what God has commanded is actually a tremendous picture of love.[c]

Misconception #3: Submission means muting. Never. The Scriptures which describe godly wives never state or imply that she may not speak. Rather, she is to become the treasured confidant, advisor, and completer for her man who stands in front protecting her—not silencing her.[d]

Misconception #4: Submission means invisibility. Actually, a submissive wife opens the doors to endless opportunities because by obedience she frees God to give all that He in His plan wants to give to her. It is rebellion which hides anyone's true potential for God.[e]

Misconception #5: Submission means inferiority. God has ordained gender-specific roles for men and women within the church and home. The Scriptures never imply that a woman is

a. Genesis 1:31

b. Ephesians 5:21
Philippians 2:3-4
1 Peter 5:5
Romans 13:1
Hebrews 13:17

c. John 14:21

d. Proverbs 31:26
Acts 18:26
Judges 13:21-23

e. Proverbs 31 depicts the full use that God's ideal wife made of her talents and abilities.

anything less than equal with a man. In history many women have excelled men in many areas. But to excel with God, submission equals obedience to a God-given role. Jesus said, *"I can do nothing on my own initiative, as I hear I judge; ... I do not seek my own will but the will of Him who sent me"* (JOHN 5:30, NASB).

So, if those are the errors, what is the truth?

When Christ's Word Fills Our Hearts—We Obey

A WIFE'S PROPER RELATIONSHIP TO her husband is as a lovely act of worship of Christ in our heavenly Father's eyes. Submission "as to the Lord" provides daily opportunities for the wife to show the Lord's "worthship" through service to her husband. The Lord has prescribed for women, wives, and mothers, a gender-specific role within three realms: the church, the marriage, and the family. This wonderful act of worship is reflected in the following seven truths:

Truth #1: Submission is a choice. Believing wives are asked by God to submit as an obedient response to God. God never *makes* us obey—He *asks* us to obey. Husbands are not commanded to demand submission, but to win it by love.[a] The Holy Spirit applies submission for a godly woman by the structure of Scripture. Submission was inspired as a present tense (that means "ongoing") imperative (that means "non-optional").[b] So submission is a not a choice of whether to obey or disobey a husband, but a choice to obey or disobey the Lord.

a. Cf. Ephesians 5:22 and 1 Peter 3:1.

b. Cf. Ephesians 5:21-22 and 1 Peter 3:1.

Truth #2: Submission is unto the Lord. Submission is really between a woman and her Lord God Almighty. It is a choice to do what He says, whether it is agreeable, understandable, or even possible. It is also only presented in a positive way (what she should do), and never negatively (what she should not do). It is "as to the Lord" (EPHESIANS 5:22). The same One who said, *"If you love me, you will keep my commandments"* (JOHN 14:15, NASB) goes on to say, *"[Be subject] to your own husbands ..."* (EPHESIANS 5:22).

Truth #3: Submission is part of a Word-filled life. The clearest statement of submission for a wife comes in the middle of a much larger teaching. If you trace the word and concept of submission in Ephesians 5:21-6:9, it is actually stated or implied seven times. It is, in other words, a complete (as in the meaning of number 7) guide to the work of God's Spirit empowering us to be like Jesus. Here is the larger context of a wife's submission:

- We all are to submit to each other (5:21).
- Wives are to submit to their husbands (5:22).
- Husbands are to submit to the picture of Christ and the church (5:23-33).
- Children are to submit to (obey) their parents (6:1-4).
- Bondservants are to submit to their masters, as in an employee-to-employer relationship today (6:5-8).
- Masters, business owners and managers of today, are to submit to their heavenly Master (6:9a).
- Everyone is to submit to their Master in heaven (6:9b).

Truth #4: Submission multiplies the blessings of our marriage. When Genesis 2:24 says that two become one, this merging is a public declaration that all the gifts, talents, strengths, goals, dreams, hopes, and desires of two lives are poured into one vessel. That results in a multiplication. Each is doubled. And contra wise, any weaknesses, cares, concerns, and deficits which are lacking are all poured into that larger sphere, and are now reduced greatly.

Truth #5: Submission draws us closer as a couple. A unity candle is often used in weddings to symbolize two becoming one. First, the two outside candles are lit to indicate that the bride and groom were two individual lives, just like the two individual candles. Then they merge their two individual lights into a single center candle, and once it is lit, they extinguish their individual candles. That is the precious truth that unifies a couple as they share all of life.

Truth #6: Submission liberates us to be what God made us to be. When we see submission as God designed it to be, we are amazed. It is not a dungeon, but a delight. It is not bondage, but liberty. It is not a bitter pill to swallow, but a lifelong meal prepared for our enjoyment by our Creator: *"My food is to do the will of Him who sent Me and to accomplish His work"* (JOHN 4:34, NASB). Did Jesus just dutifully obey? No, He delighted in obeying His Father. When we truly submit, we shall also delight.[a]

a. Psalm 40:7-8

Truth #7: Submission opens all of our lives to each other. A godly wife gets to share every part of the life of the one she loves most on earth. That is what Paul said in Ephesians 5:24, NASB: *"Wives ought to be [subject] to their husbands in everything."* Of course, wives are still first of all believers, so God would never ask them to sin or dishonor Him to fulfill their husband's wishes.[b] But any wife who loves God, offers herself in every possible way to willingly be her husband's helper, completer, and companion—one who delights him at all times.[c]

b. Acts 5:28-29

c. Genesis 2:18

What Happens When a Wife Submits to Her Husband?

A WORD-FILLED WIFE WILL LOVINGLY and respectfully submit to her husband's direction. Just like the Proverbs 31 woman, she will evidence a servant's heart toward her life partner. What are some ways that a wife can display a servant's heart? What are the characteristics of such a woman?

1. She draws her husband. A Word-filled woman realizes how hard it is for her husband to live and work in the world. Temptations swirl around him all day long. Weariness and discouragement come at him from all sides. So a wise wife decides that home will be a magnet for him—a shining beacon on a hill that beckons her husband to come. It should be the place he would rather be when he is at work and at play. It should be his place to refocus, be refreshed, and be renewed. She is the guardian of that place. When activities and the urgent overrun this priority, all must be stopped and the home reset to be the place of refuge her husband needs: *"The heart of her husband safely trusts her; So he will have no lack of gain"* (PROVERBS 31:11).

2. She pleases and honors her husband. What man can ever resist this kind of a woman? She has a lifelong desire to do what pleases him: *"She does him good and not evil all the days of her life"* (PROVERBS 31:12). She also honors him in her words, attitudes, and actions: *"Let the wife [see] that she respects [her] husband"* (EPHESIANS 5:33B). Only the Lord has a higher place for this Word-filled wife. No house, no job, no child, no ministry can hold her; she wants to please and honor the man God made for her. That is her calling and role given by the Lord himself.

3. She serves her husband. The Lord designed the men to be out "sweating" to provide, and the women to be inside making his entire world ready for his homecoming. A Word-filled wife directs the house, the children, the schedule, and the meals to all make her husband's life a joy: *"She opens her mouth with wisdom, and on her tongue [is] the law of kindness. She watches over the ways of her household, and does not eat the bread of idleness. Her children rise up and call her blessed; her husband [also], and he praises her: 'Many daughters have done well, But you excel them all' "* (PROVERBS 31:26-29). The reason the Proverbs 31 woman is so amazing is that her marriage was at the center of all she did. It was her primary ministry!

4. She blesses her husband. The Lord said that our words flow from our heart. That means a godly wife, full of the Holy Spirit, would never speak wickedly about her husband or to him. She gives her mouth to God and meditates upon: *"She opens her mouth with wisdom, and on her tongue is the law of kindness"* (PROVERBS 31:26).

"Let no corrupt word proceed out of your mouth, but what is good for necessary edification, that it may impart grace to the hearers. And do not grieve the Holy Spirit of God, by whom you were sealed for the day of redemption. Let all bitterness, wrath, anger, clamor, and evil speaking be put away from you, with all malice.

And be kind to one another, tenderhearted, forgiving one another, even as God in Christ forgave you" (EPHESIANS 4:29-32).

5. She trusts her husband. If you are married, it is God's will. And since it is His will, you need to trust God with the details. The Lord can get your husband to shape up in an infinitely greater way than you ever could. All the Lord asks is this: **"Trust Me with your husband."** So what should you do? Trust your husband as God's man for you—for life!

"Be anxious for nothing, but in everything by prayer and supplication, with thanksgiving, let your requests be made known to God; and the peace of God, which surpasses all understanding, will guard your hearts and minds through Christ Jesus" (PHILIPPIANS 4:6-7).

"Let [your] conduct [be] without covetousness; [be] content with such things as you have. For He Himself has said, 'I will never leave you nor forsake you.' ... But do not forget to do good and to share, for with such sacrifices God is well pleased" (HEBREWS 13:5, 16).

6. She waits for her husband. Many wives are miles ahead of their husbands and can get so frustrated at their plodding. Don't discourage your husband; don't push him—wait for him.

"Walk worthy of the calling with which you have been called, with all lowliness and gentleness, with longsuffering, bearing with one another in love, endeavoring to keep the unity of the Spirit in the bond of peace" (EPHESIANS 4:1B-3).

"Therefore, as [the] elect of God, holy and beloved, put on tender mercies, kindness, humility, meekness, longsuffering; bearing with one another, and forgiving one another, if anyone has a complaint against another; even as Christ forgave you, so you also [must do]. But above all these things put on love, which is the bond of perfection" (COLOSSIANS 3:12-14).

7. She attracts her husband. The God who invented sex, and inspired the Song of Solomon, also designed marriage to complete a man in every way. So, for almost 99 percent of all men—appearance means so much. Be as beautiful as humanly possible for him. Learn what he likes, and then seek as much as possible to look irresistible for him. If you add to it the most beautiful part of your marriage—the spirit that God treasures—you will attract your grateful husband all your days!

> *"Do not let your adornment be [merely] outward—arranging the hair, wearing gold, or putting on [fine] apparel—rather [let it be] the hidden person of the heart, with the incorruptible [beauty] of a gentle and quiet spirit, which is very precious in the sight of God. For in this manner, in former times, the holy women who trusted in God also adorned themselves, being submissive to their own husbands"* (1 PETER 3:3-5).

8. She challenges her husband. Husbands can't resist godly wives. That is what Peter said. So, maintain a spiritual life full of devotion to God. A dynamic ongoing relationship with Christ is the key to being enabled to lovingly and respectfully submit to your husband's leadership.

> *"Wives, likewise, [be] submissive to your own husbands, that even if some do not obey the word, they, without a word, may be won by the conduct of their wives, when they observe your chaste conduct [accompanied] by fear"* (1 PETER 3:1-2).

9. She forgives her husband. Christ's love causes a Word-filled wife to forgive her husband's failures, weaknesses, and struggles. God's grace allows her to look at him with eyes of love and to think the truth. Love him as Christ loves you is her motto.

> *"Love suffers long [and] is kind; love does not envy; love does not parade itself, is not puffed up; does not behave rudely, does not seek its own, is not provoked, thinks no evil; does not rejoice in iniquity, but rejoices in the truth; bears all things, believes all things, hopes all things, endures all things. Love never fails ..."* (1 CORINTHIANS 13:4-8A).

Danger Signs of Wordless Women

WORD-FILLED LIVES SUBMIT TO GOD'S Word—if not, what will happen? Without a commitment to faithfully follow Christ's Word, wives can end up with one or several of the following five common regrets:[a]

a. This section is adapted to wives from the husbands' five common regrets in Robert Lewis and William Hendricks' *Rocking the Roles* (Colorado Springs, CO: NavPress, 1991), p. 156.

1. Without the foundation of God's Word, she will become an irresponsible wife. This wife is nothing but a little girl in search of a daddy, and she seems to have found one in her husband. She is thoroughly self-centered, but manages to appear to others as a loving and devoted wife.

2. Without the power of God's Word, she will become an emotionally-detached wife. This woman may be recognized as one of the most stable and even-tempered women in her community. She is frequently asked to serve on the boards of numerous ministries because of her organized mind and methodical way of making decisions. However, in her home, she is about as detached and emotionally unavailable as a woman can be.

3. Without obedience to God's Word, she will become a dictatorial wife. This woman's idea of wifehood means that nothing happens without her approval. When her husband dares to question her decisions, she resorts to manipulation or intimidating tactics and, if that doesn't work, goes into a blind rage.

4. Without the pattern of God's Word, she will become a workaholic wife. This woman never quits working mentally or emotionally. She lives under pressure, and sprays her family with her frustrations.

5. Without the nurture of God's Word, she will become a spiritually-apathetic wife. This woman is a believer and church attendee. But beyond that, she's generally unresponsive to spiritual matters; she therefore never exercises a sound spiritual testimony in her home. And that void blocks the relationship a godly husband longs to have.

Wives, you are called by God to be in submission to your husband—to be his unique and suitable helper. In this section we have seen what that means. But knowing what it means is of little value unless it is applied to your relationship with your husband. Knowing these facts will not promote oneness in marriage. Performing them will. I therefore ask you to examine your relationship to your husband in the light of these truths. Are you *really* practicing submission with a servant's heart? Are you *really* practicing being your husband's helper?

Marriage is God's training ground to prepare husbands and wives for greater service for Christ. Ever changing, each unique personality is used by the Lord as heavenly sandpaper on the other. It is in the nitty-gritty events of daily living that our true character comes out—not the one we present to others, but the real us. Learning how to biblically handle that day-in-day-out give and take is essential if we are to have a successful marriage. I suggest that where you find yourself to be failing, prayerfully consider this checklist:

- Confess those failures to one another (James 5:16).
- Accept the washing and cleansing that Jesus wants to bring to us through His precious blood, as Revelation 1:5 reminds us.
- Ask the Holy Spirit for power to be different (Galatians 5:16, 22-23).

a. Philippians 2:12-13
James1:19-24

A Word-filled wife genuinely believes that her primary ministry is her marriage. She willingly moves out in obedience to the Word of God, making any necessary changes the Holy Spirit brings to mind.[a] A Word-filled marriage is a small snapshot of the delights of heaven—a living portrait of the perfect love of Jesus!

STUDY GUIDE QUESTIONS

1. Scripture asserts the spiritual, mental, and physical equalitarian status and dignity of women and men. (See Genesis 1:26-27, 2:23, and Galatians 3:28.) God has not only established guidelines for submission to one another in general, but also for gender-specific submission requirements. After you read each of the following verses, briefly state God's view on the matter of submission in general.

Romans 13:1 -

Hebrews 13:17 -

1 Peter 5:5 -

Philippians 2:3-4 -

Ephesians 5:21 -

2. In Ephesians 5:21, God laid the foundation for the principle of submission. Now read Ephesians 5:22-24, which begins a passage addressing gender-specific roles. For wives, proper submission to "your own husband" is meant to be a lovely act of worship "as to the Lord."
    Read John 15:9-11. What implication does this passage have on your response to Ephesians 5:22-24?

3. If you are married, it is God's will. And since it is His will, you need to trust God with the details. Trust that your husband is God's man for you for life. We see this in Ephesians 5:22; the words "your own husband" imply that he is intimately and personally yours—and you are his.
    Read the Song of Solomon 2:16, 6:3, and 7:10. Is this type intimacy representative of your own marriage? If not, list practical ways that you can be used of the Lord to help make this a reality in your own life.

4. A dynamic ongoing relationship with Christ is the key to being enabled to lovingly and respectfully submit to your husband's leadership. Christ's love causes a Word-filled wife to forgive her husband's failures, weaknesses, and struggles. You should read, memorize, and meditate on 1 Corinthians 13:4-7; pray this passage regularly on behalf of yourself—and your family.

10

"I will give you a new heart …."

— *Ezekiel 36:26a*

"So I will restore to you the years that the swarming locust has eaten …."

— *Joel 2:25a*

Triumph Through Failures–
With Our God of New Beginnings

WHY IS PARENTING SO HARD? Because we fail in so many ways! But why do we fail? Because, until heaven, we are all imperfect. So as we look at one of the hardest jobs on earth—raising children—here is my perspective that keeps me going through the hard times and the easy times.

I am an imperfect husband. I married an imperfect wife. We have an imperfect marriage that has produced imperfect children — which we have raised imperfectly. However, we have a Perfect Father in heaven, who has given His flawless Word as a guide to light the pathway for us to follow His plan. That plan is to have a Word-filled way of life. And that is what we have found in God's Word: **Our God is the God of New Beginnings!**

He shows us every way He can that He wants us to know we can start over again with Him. Every day starts new and fresh with a new river of time flowing by at 60 minutes per hour. On Sunday every week we get to start over with a new day that starts a new week. Every month we get to start over with a brand new first day of the month. Every 3 months a new season begins with freshness and variety and newness. Winter melts into spring; spring blossoms into summer; summer sails into fall; and fall fades into winter, and over we go into a new year.

So when we fail, we need to repent and start over again. To help us remember, God's Word records countless failures that the Lord graciously uses. One of my favorites is Peter. I hope this reminder of the new beginning of a Word-filled life stirs your heart as it has mine.

Peter Demonstrates—
The God of the Second Chance

PETER WILL ALWAYS BE AN example in the Bible of one who loved Jesus deeply—but struggled with submitting to His plan. He is a trophy of grace. The Gospel by Mark is the premier Book in God's Word about hope: hope for a new start, hope for complete forgiveness, and hope in the God of the Second Chance. Next to Christ, no one in the New Testament is mentioned by name more than Peter. Peter could never get enough time in Christ's presence because he longed to walk with Jesus. He wanted the Lord with every ounce of his being!

- No one was ever honored like Peter: *"You are Peter, and on this rock I will build My church, and the gates of Hades shall not prevail against it"* (Matthew 16:18).
- No one was ever rebuked as sharply as when Jesus called Peter a tool of Satan: *"Get behind Me, Satan!"* (Matthew 16:23).
- No one ever claimed greater loyalty to Christ: *"If I have to die with You, I will not deny You!"* (Mark 14:31).
- No one ever denied Jesus like Peter—not once, not twice, but three times: *"I do not know the Man!"* (Matthew 26:74).
- No one was ever more totally smitten by their sin in the sight of Jesus: *"And the Lord turned and looked at Peter"* (Luke 22:61).
- No one ever grieved more completely—for no one knew Jesus better, or loved Him more, or wanted His approval more: *"Then Peter remembered the word of the Lord ... [and he] went out and wept bitterly"* (Luke 22:62).
- No one was ever restored more tenderly and completely: *"Feed My lambs"* (John 21:15-17).

The way the story of Peter's darkest hour is written and cast in the Holy Scriptures has the emphasis completely on the forgiving love of Jesus for His failing disciple. God did not want Peter's failure emphasized—He wanted His forgiveness to shine like a ray of light in utter darkness. That is the lesson of Gallicantu, the place where the rooster crowed twice after Peter had denied Christ thrice! Let us now examine the details of Peter's downfall and later triumph.

Jesus and His disciples left the Upper Room, and there they traveled all the way around the wall of Jerusalem to a little garden perched on the slopes of the Mount of Olives. In the Garden of Gethsemane, Jesus, the great High Priest, the One who stands before the throne for us—the Jesus who knew what was going to happen in Peter's future—warned Peter that a spiritual battle was coming his way. Sadly, His warnings went unheeded. But in that garden, Jesus prayed, and prayed, and prayed. Just before Judas arrived with a great multitude armed with swords and clubs, Jesus once more encouraged His disciples to *"rise and pray, lest you enter into temptation"* (LUKE 22:46).

After Judas betrayed Jesus with a kiss, and they laid hands on Him to take Him away, Peter impetuously drew his sword and cut off the ear of the high priest's servant.[a] Jesus had already warned Peter just prior to this that there was a great spiritual conflict coming up. But he armed himself for physical conflict, and totally neglected the real battle. The Lord was not asking for armed guards; He could have called upon six legions of angels to defend Him. Jesus needed Peter and the other disciples to get ready spiritually, but they still had failed to understand the gravity of the situation.

a. Luke 22.50

The disciples at this point all forsook Jesus and fled. Because John Mark was always hanging around, some believe that the Mark 14:51-52 reference to a certain young man following Jesus, wrapped only with a linen cloth around his naked body, was Mark. However, when they grabbed him, he left the cloth and fled away as well.

The mob traveled from Gethsemane across the Kidron Valley and cut through the courtyard of the Temple. The brook in the valley was probably running dark red with the blood of 250,000 sheep that had been slain at the Passover. The blood poured out of the Temple area in special drains to the Brook Kidron all the way to the Dead

Sea. What an amazing time of the year it was! It was over that stream running red with the blood of all those sheep, that Jesus crossed and went up to the home of Caiaphas *"who advised the Jews that it was expedient that one man should die for the people"* (JOHN 18:12-14). This was necessary to fulfill prophecy.

> *"And Simon Peter followed Jesus, and [so did] another disciple. Now that disciple was known to the high priest, and went with Jesus into the courtyard of the high priest. But Peter stood at the door outside. Then the other disciple, who was known to the high priest, went out and spoke to her who kept the door, and brought Peter in"* (JOHN 18:15-16).

Peter's Steps to Defeat

PETER AND JOHN WERE NOT supposed to follow Jesus into the courtyard of the high priest. Peter fell because he was so presumptuous—he had bragged, and flashed his sword, and tried to take on the whole world in his own strength. He was following Jesus because he wanted to present himself as the one who stayed. Thus, he was disobeying the Lord from the start. The Lord had warned that they would enter into temptation, but Peter self-reliantly followed Christ right into the "lion's den." You may say that it was noble for Peter to do that because he loved Jesus so much, but His sheep often do foolish things. So the Lord says to all of us, "Don't put Me to the test like that!"

Peter, by going into that courtyard, was now walking with people who were enemies of the Lord. Immediately my mind goes to Psalm 1. You will see a downward progression in the life of Peter in this horrible time of his life: *"Blessed is the man Who walks not in the counsel of the ungodly,* [Peter was fraternizing with the ungodly in that courtyard to see what would happen to Jesus] *Nor stands in the path of sinners,* [Peter stood with them] *Nor sits in the seat of the scornful;* [Peter sat down by the fire, was tempted, and failed] *But his delight is in the law of the* LORD, *and in His law he meditates day and night* [this pattern of delight characterizes the Word-filled man or woman]."

When they led Jesus away to the high priest, where all the chief priests, elders, and scribes had gathered together, Peter followed at a distance. Old preachers have a lot to say about Peter following at a distance. The danger signs are like the trail of a tornado the day after—the debris could be seen everywhere as he looked back. The Scriptures record five areas that were danger signs:

> *"Then Jesus said to them, 'All of you will be made to stumble because of Me this night, for it is written: "I will strike the Shepherd, and the sheep will be scattered."' But after I have been raised, I will go before you to Galilee.' Peter said to Him, 'Even if all are made to stumble, yet I [will] not [be].' Jesus said to him, 'Assuredly, I say to you that today, even this night, before the rooster crows twice, you will deny Me three times'"* (MARK 14:27-30).

1. PETER BOASTED TOO LOUDLY—A SIGN OF GIVING IN TO PRIDE.

Peter boasted: " *'If I have to die with You, I will not deny You!' And they all said likewise"* (MARK 14:31). Peter had disobeyed the Lord when He said, *"Watch and pray lest you enter into temptation."*[a] Instead, he went to sleep. Jesus woke him up, and asked him to watch and pray again, but Peter went back to sleep once more. When he woke up and saw the crowd, he remembered all of his bragging, so he pulled his sword out and attacked. He missed the servant's head, but cut off his ear.

a. Matthew 26:41b

Probably one of the most touching miracles in the New Testament is Jesus tenderly and completely healing that ear. That was such a statement to Peter: "This is spiritual, not physical. Put away your sword." But Peter had not yet faced his self-absorption, and self-will. He stalked after the crowd which took Christ, planning to prove that he had not failed. This reminds me of Paul's caution: *"Let him who thinks he stands take heed lest he fall"* (1 CORINTHIANS 10:12).

2. PETER PRAYED TOO SPARINGLY—A SIGN OF GIVING IN TO THE FLESH. [b]

b. Matthew 26:38

I always see this in believers' lives who think they have their "act together" spiritually, so they easily lapse into prayerlessness. It is presumptuous to be self-sufficient by attempting to go through a day, an hour, or even a moment without a conscious dependence upon the Lord. When Peter neglected Christ's clear request to watch and pray, he threw away the key that would have enabled him to truly triumph in his darkest hour.

3. PETER SLEPT TOO SOUNDLY— A SIGN OF PRESUMPTION.[a]

a. Matthew 26:41

On that night of nights—the very night Jesus warned Peter about repeatedly—he ignored Christ's admonition to watch and pray, and fell asleep. He was unaware that he was so full of himself. What a sad testimony of being out of step with the Savior, out of touch with what He was doing!

4. PETER ACTED TOO HASTILY— A SIGN OF GIVING IN TO THE WORLD.[b]

b. Matthew 26:51

Peter looked merely at the circumstances in the Garden, and reacted according to his own prideful self-determination by choosing to strike the servant with a sword. He had lost touch with God's pur-

c. James 4:10

pose, and was not humbling[c] himself before the Lord.

5. PETER FOLLOWED TOO DISTANTLY— A SIGN OF SELF-SUFFICIENCY.[d]

d. Mark 14:54

The mark of someone who has allowed the sin of self-sufficiency into their lives is that they start following the Lord at a distance. They go to church, but they are distant from the Lord. They pray and serve, but from a distance. They read their Bible, but feel far away. They always say, "I never get anything out of the Bible." The reason is that they are following too distantly. Then they start getting pressured by people around them, as Peter did in Mark 14:66-71.

He was twice pressured by one of the servant girls. He was pressured by those who stood around him, and reacted by cursing and swearing: *"I do not know this Man of whom you speak!"* In Matthew 26:71-74, he went out to the gateway, and was spotted by another girl. But this time he denied Christ with an oath: *"I do not know the Man!"* (That oath meant calling on the name of God to strike him if he was not telling the truth!) A little later, he was again confronted by those who stood by him. Once more, he cursed and swore, saying, *"I do not know the Man!"* And immediately a rooster crowed.

The timing of that rooster's crow is a miracle. One of God's creatures was waiting for a divine signal to sound the sound that would pierce the heart of one of God's greatest servants. All Peter had to do is hear that sound, and he remembered the words of Jesus, *"Before the rooster crows, you will deny Me three times."* And he went out and wept bitterly.[a]

a. Matthew 26:75

Peter was at the Lord's Supper before all of this happened. He was so confident; he was on top of the world; and he was the closest disciple to Jesus. He was sure that he was going to be either on the right or left hand of Jesus in the kingdom. Peter was characterized by self-determination and self-sufficiency. He was a willful man. (In fact—the only thing he didn't take first place in was the race to the tomb—John beat him there.) Jesus, for that reason, let Satan sift Peter until he realized that he was so full of himself: boasting too loudly, praying too sparingly, sleeping too soundly, acting too hastily, and following too distantly. His life up to this point was a testimony to the truth of Proverbs 16:18: *"Pride [goes] before destruction, and a haughty spirit before a fall."* But our great God of the Second Chance had a wonderful plan; He was not through with Peter!

God Wants to Lift Us Up From Failure

JESUS' PLAN WORKED—AFTER PETER WAS sifted and tried, he painfully came to a humbling end of himself. Listen to the now-aged Peter's testimony as he exhorted a group going through similar suffering:

> *"In this you greatly rejoice, though now for a little while, if need be* [if the Lord knows you need it], *you have been grieved by various trials* [shakings]*"* (1 PETER 1:6).

Peter was thinking of his own sifting; he had been shaken until He did not have anywhere to go but down on his face. He then went on to share, *"You have been grieved by various trials* [just like I was], *that the genuineness of your faith, [being] much more precious than gold that perishes, though it is tested by fire, may be found to praise, honor, and glory at the revelation of Jesus Christ ..."* (1 PETER 1:6B-7). After Peter was purified through the fire, look at all that God did in his life!

God never emphasizes failures; He emphasizes His forgiveness so that He gets the praise, honor, and glory! Any child of God can come back to Him at any moment from any sin and any failure. Anyone born of the Lord Jesus Christ can receive forgiveness: *"If we* [constantly, continually] *confess our sins, He is faithful and just to* [already have forgiven] *us our sins and to cleanse us from all unrighteousness"* (1 JOHN 1:9). There are in that verse, two completely different tenses of the verb. One is "an ongoing present" and the other is "a point of action in the past." Peter confessed his sins, and wept bitterly; he had a contrite heart. He knew he had disobeyed, and he sorrowed unto repentance.[a] There was therefore no condemnation,[b] or separation from the love of God.[c] With true repentance, God promises to forget our sins, and remember them no more: *"As far as the east is from the west, so far has He removed our transgressions from us"* (PSALM 103:12). Hallelujah!

And what was the result of all this refining? Perhaps the greatest life ever lived for the glory of God. Peter stands tallest among all who ever walked this planet.

- Peter, the man Jesus chose, the man Jesus trained, the man Jesus saved from death—
- Became Peter, the man Jesus warned, the man Jesus watched deny Him, the man Jesus protected from the devil—
- Became Peter, the man Jesus restored, the man Jesus used, and the martyr who hung humbly upside down on a cross because he was unworthy to die as Jesus died.

If there is ever a person who shows the love of Jesus, the compassion of Jesus, the patience of Jesus, the forgiveness of Jesus, the restoring power of Jesus, and the empowerment for ministry that Jesus can give—it is Peter! It was in Peter's darkest hour, when he was at his lowest ebb, when he was most overwhelmed with his utter failure in the presence of Christ that Jesus dealt so tenderly with Peter. What I see from Peter's life is that if Jesus ministered to him in that way, and at that time, then Jesus will minister to us when we likewise are at our darkest hour. And at that time, we, too, can remember God's Word—and, like Peter, have hope!

Jesus—in the midst of the darkness that threatened to overwhelm

a. 2 Corinthians 7:10
b. Romans 8:1
c. Romans 8:35

Peter—shed five glorious rays of light upon him. Here are those rays of light to encourage us as well:

Hope for Those Who Have Failed

1. JESUS OFFERS US COMPLETE FORGIVENESS AND NO CONDEMNATION.

Each one of us will at some time fail the Lord, and then hear (in one way or another) "the crowing of the cock." Satan will try to discourage us by whispering something like: *Now you've done it! You are finished! Your future ministry has been destroyed because God can no longer use you—a failure!* But that is not God's message to us. It was certainly not the end for Peter, was it? His restoration was so complete that he was able to later say to the Jews, *"But you denied the Holy One and the Just"* (ACTS 3:14). Although Peter did not have 1 John to read, he experienced the sweetness of 1 John 1:9 in his own heart.

2. JESUS PROMISES US A LIFE OF NEW BEGINNINGS.

The miracle of the cock crowing told Peter that a new day was dawning. After all, that is actually what a rooster's call means each day. It was not a new day for Judas or for the enemies of the Lord, but it was a new day for Peter as he repented and wept bitterly. He experienced: *"A broken and a contrite heart, O God, thou wilt not despise"* (PSALM 51:17, KJV). On resurrection morning, the angel sent a special message to encourage Peter.[a] Then the Lord Himself appeared to Peter that very day to restore him to fellowship,[b] and to offer him a life of new beginnings. What compassion!

a. Mark 16:7

b. Luke 24:34

3. JESUS WANTS US TO REMEMBER HIS WORD IN OUR DARKEST HOURS TO GIVE US HOPE.

The crowing of the cock assured Peter that he could be forgiven. Peter had not been paying close attention to the Word of God. He had argued with it, disobeyed it, and even run ahead of it; but now he *"remembered the word of the Lord"* (LUKE 22:61), which brought him hope. Why? Because with the word of warning was also a promise of restoration!

a. Luke 22:32

Peter was to be converted, and then strengthen his brethren.[a]

Like Peter, we need to remember God's Word at the very moment of our need. Romans 15:4 says, *"For whatever things were written before were written for our learning, that we through the patience and comfort of the Scriptures might have hope."* The whole purpose for God giving us His Word is not to have the best edition, the best cover, the best footnotes, or even the best markings, but to have Word-filled lives. Then, when we are in our darkest hour, and have failed the Lord, in that moment, we are able to remember His precious promises, and thereby obtain hope for that situation.

4. JESUS IS IN CONTROL OF ALL THE EVENTS SURROUNDING OUR LIVES.

For one cock to crow at the right time, while the other birds in the city remained silent, was certainly a miracle. But the crowing of the cock was much more than a miracle that fulfilled our Lord's words; it was also a special message to Peter—a message that helped to restore him to fellowship again. It was an assurance to him that Jesus Christ was still in control of things even though He was a prisoner, bound, and seemingly helpless before His captors. Peter could recall witnessing his Lord's authority over the fish, the winds, the waves, and even over disease and death. No matter how dark the hour was for Peter, Jesus was still in control.

Most of us tend to regard circumstances and happenings as mere coincidences, accidents, or disappointments. However, the Lord wants us to realize that there are no such things—only the appointments of God, which He works for the good of those who love Him.[b]

b. Romans 8:28

5. JESUS WANTS US TO KNOW THAT HE IS WATCHING OVER US IN OUR DARKEST HOURS.

Note who was watching whom. Jesus knew exactly where Peter was, both spiritually and physically—as demonstrated in Luke 22:61: *"And the Lord turned and looked at Peter. Then Peter remembered the word of the Lord, how He had said to him, 'Before the rooster crows, you will deny Me three times.'"* He is in touch with our lives as well. No matter what you and I do, no matter where we are, Jesus has His eyes on us. When the disciples were sinking in the boat during the storm, and Jesus was miles away on top of a lonely mountain, He was watching, and came to them at exactly the right moment. He is always there; He is always watching; He is always rescuing—just when we need Him. God is never too late![a]

Every time we open to the Gospel by Mark, we should remember that in one way or another, all of us, too, have stumbled. And for each of us, Peter's triumph by God's grace should be an incredible source of encouragement!

a. The points on Luke 22 were adapted and drawn from Warren W. Wiersbe's The Bible Exposition Commentary: Luke (Wheaton, IL: Victor Books, 1997).

Prayer Example: *Dear Heavenly Father, how I praise You for Peter's witness that there is nothing that can separate us from the love of Christ! No tribulation, or distress, or persecution, or famine, or nakedness, or peril, or sword—or even failure to live up to Your expectations! I praise You that, like Peter, in all these things I, too, can be more than a conqueror through Him who loved me. For I am persuaded that neither death nor life, nor angels nor principalities nor powers, nor things present nor things to come, nor height nor depth, nor any other created thing, shall be able to separate me from Your love which is in Christ Jesus my Lord. Oh, the depth of the riches of both Your wisdom and knowledge! How unsearchable are Your judgments, and Your ways are past finding out! I humble myself before You, oh High and Lofty One who inhabits eternity! And I praise You for the knowledge that Your plan for me and my family is perfect, whether I understand it fully or not. Help me to honor You by Word-filled living, and by leading my family to do the same! In Christ's name I pray. Amen.*

No Failures Are Permanent

ARE THE EXPERIENCES OF PETER unique? No!

Apart from the brief ministry of His own Son, the history of God's work on earth is the history of His using the unqualified. Even the twelve disciples who became apostles were no exception. They had few characteristics or abilities from the human standpoint that qualified them for leadership and service. Yet God used those men in marvelous ways to do His work, just as He did Noah, Abraham, and the others. God picks normal people and pours His grace on them.

Satan wants our sins and failures to convince us to give up. But one look at the people of the Bible should defeat that temptation. The work of God is performed by weak individuals like us, surrendered to the God whose power is perfected in man's weakness.[a] God has always had only weak and sinful humans with whom to work. Listen to the team God has used to win the championships:

a. 2 Corinthians 12:9

- **Noah** became drunk and acted indecently soon after God had delivered him and his family through the Flood.
- **Abraham**, a sometimes disobedient dad, was chosen to be the father of the faithful. Yet, he doubted God, lied about his wife, and committed adultery with her maid.
- **Isaac**, like his father before him, told a similar lie about his wife when he thought his life was in danger.
- **Jacob** took advantage of his brother Esau's weakness and extorted the birthright from him. He was a cheat and a liar, and yet he became the father of God's people—Israel.
- **Moses** was a murderer as a young man. Later, in pride he struck the rock instead of speaking to it as God had instructed. Though he dragged his feet in obedience, he led and taught the people by knowing God "face to face."
- **Aaron**, Moses' brother, was the first high priest. But he led Israel in erecting and worshiping the golden calf at the very time Moses was on Mount Sinai receiving the law of God.
- **Joshua** was fooled into disobeying the Lord by making a treaty with the Gibeonites instead of destroying them.
- **Gideon** had trouble trusting God at first; he had little confidence in himself, and even less in God's plan and power.
- **Samson** was repeatedly beguiled by Delilah because of his great lust for her.
- **David** was a "ladies man" who committed adultery and murder. He was an almost total failure as a father, and was not allowed to build the Temple because he was a man of blood.
- **Elijah** stood fearlessly before 450 false prophets, but cowered before Jezebel. Having just experienced the exhilaration of Mt. Carmel's victory, he then plunged quickly into deep depression. However, Elijah's life should encourage us all. Why? Because God says he had a nature like ours.[b] Elijah was a man "subject

b. James 5:17

to like passions," meaning literally "of the same experience"!

- **Ezekiel** was brash, crusty, and quick to speak his mind.
- **Jonah** defied God's call to preach to the Ninevites, and then resented His grace when they were converted through his preaching.[a]

a. Adapted from *The Macarthur New Testament Commentary: Matthew 10* (Chicago: Moody Press, 1983), electronic edition.

The list of godly men and women who have experienced failure down through the centuries is endless. Even Mark and Peter were not unique among the disciples; they all fled, and abandoned Jesus in His greatest hour of need! On the eve of Christ's coming death, they all were so self-absorbed that they argued over who would be the greatest in His kingdom! Yet Christ placed the beginnings of our eternal future in the hands of these men. S. D. Gordon, in his book, *Quiet Talks on Service*, gives an imaginary account of Jesus' return to heaven after His ascension. It is as the angel Gabriel greets Jesus, he asks:

"Master, You died for the world, did You not?" to which the Lord replies, "Yes." "You must have suffered much," the angel says; and again Jesus answers, "Yes." "Do they all know that you died for them?" Gabriel continues. "No. Only a few in Palestine know about it so far," Jesus says. "Well, then, what is Your plan for telling the rest of the world that You shed Your blood for them?" Jesus responds, "Well, I asked Peter and James and John and Andrew and a few others if they would make it the business of their lives to tell others. And then the ones that they tell could tell others, and they in turn could tell still others, and finally it would reach the farthest corner of the earth and all would know the thrill and power of the gospel." "But suppose Peter fails? And suppose after a while John just doesn't tell anyone? And what if James and Andrew are ashamed or afraid? Then what?" Gabriel asks. "I have no other plans," Jesus is said to have answered; "I am counting entirely on them."[b]

b. Cited in Herbert Lockyer's *All the Apostles of the Bible* (Grand Rapids: Zondervan, 1972), p. 31.

Jesus planned to do extraordinary things with these ordinary men so that He would be glorified. The disciples' failures were only temporary. Only with the exception of Judas, all of them were beautifully restored to ministry—and by His power they turned the world upside down for Jesus Christ! Jesus was counting on them, just as He is counting on us!

God has given an awesome promise to those who will humble themselves before Him: "*For thus says the High and Lofty One Who inhabits eternity, whose name is Holy: 'I dwell in the high and holy place, With him who has a contrite and humble spirit, To revive the spirit of the humble, And to revive the heart of the contrite ones'*" (ISAIAH 57:15). Wow! What a God of Second Chances and New Beginnings!

And what happens when we allow God to use us as He pleases? Great and marvelous things—exceedingly abundantly above all we can ask or think! And the greatest joy, the greatest power, and the greatest rewards possible are the result of a Word-filled life, a Word-filled marriage, and a Word-filled family!

> **Closing Personal Prayer:** *Dear Father in Heaven, I bow my knees to You, the Father of our Lord Jesus Christ, from whom the whole family in heaven and earth is named. I pray that You will grant the readers of this book, according to Your riches in glory, the great joy of a Word-filled family. Strengthen them with might through Your Spirit in their inner man; may Christ dwell in their hearts through faith; that they may each be rooted and grounded in love, and able to comprehend with all the saints what is the width and length and depth and height of the love of Christ which passes knowledge; that they may be filled with all the fullness of God. Now to You who is able to do exceedingly abundantly above all that we ask or think, according to the power that works in us, be glory forever and ever! Amen.*

STUDY GUIDE QUESTIONS

1. **Peter will always be an example in the Bible of one who loved Jesus deeply—but struggled with submitting to His plan.** There were some very clear steps that led down the path to his biggest defeat. We should learn from his mistakes, so that we can avoid "learning the hard way":

   Peter boasted too loudly. He failed to heed Christ's warnings of dangers ahead. Read Proverbs 16:18 and 1 Peter 5:5b. What does God have to say about the dangers of pride?

   Peter prayed too sparingly. He failed to give prayer the

priority it deserves. Read 1 Thessalonians 5:16-18. What
does God say should be our attitude toward prayer?

Peter was too presumptuous. He failed to heed Christ's repeated
warnings to watch and pray. Read 1 Corinthians 10:12-13. In
contrast to being self-sufficient, what hope does God give
to the person who trusts Him during times of testing?

Peter acted too hastily. He failed to humble himself before
the Lord. The word "humble" means "to make oneself
low." Read James 4:10 and 1 Peter 5:5b-7. What is God's
attitude toward those who are humble in spirit?

Peter followed too distantly. He failed to grasp how crucial
it is to stay near to Christ, because he was characterized
by self-determination and self-sufficiency. Read Hebrews
10:22-23 and James 4:7-8a. What does God promise if we
will draw near (seek after an intimate relationship) to Him?

2. **Each of Peter's downward steps toward failure was rooted in pride,
which is the root of all sin because pride competes with God for
control and glory.** On a scale of 1 to 10—with 10 being the highest—
how would you rate your own present struggle with pride? Make victory
over pride an earnest matter of prayer for yourself as well as your family.

3. **Each one of us will at some time fail the Lord, but, upon
repentance, like Peter, we too can be beautifully restored.** Read
Psalm 51:10, 12, and 17b. If you (or a loved one) are struggling with
failure, make these verses a regular part of your prayer time.

4. **God wants to do extraordinary things with ordinary people so
that He will be glorified.** Read 1 Corinthians 1:26-31. Are you among
the "foolish," "weak," and "base [common]" things of the world? Rejoice!
Immerse yourself in the Word, and Word-filled prayer, and then praise
God as you see Him do the "extraordinary" in your life—for His glory!
Memorize verse 31; ask the Lord to keep you alert to Satan's "pride
darts" so that you will never rob Him of any of the glory He's due.

11

"[The virtuous wife] does [her husband] good and not evil All the days of her life."

— *Proverbs 31:12*

Fulfilling Your Husband's Deepest Needs:
From a Wife's Heart

Note: *My beloved wife, Bonnie, the mother of our precious eight children, is an exemplary model of the Proverbs 31 virtuous woman. I'm asking her to present insights the Lord has given her on how to fulfill a husband's deepest needs. I believe that you will be delighted with what she has to say!*

GOD CLEARLY INSTRUCTS OLDER WOMEN to teach younger women to honor and obey the Bible by loving their husbands and loving their children. The next three chapters (11, 12, 13) focus on these three key areas of instruction from God to women: husbands, children, and older women.[a]

a. Titus 2:3-5

After many years as a pastor's wife, I am convinced that only when we keep God in the formula of marriage (**1 man +1 woman = *not* 2 but 1**) can we continue to grow and improve this sacred relationship between a man and a woman. More than ever, marriages are in a desperate state—and it all started with a lie in the Garden of Eden.

Author Nancy Leigh DeMoss writes:

What took place in the Garden of Eden thousands of years ago was not only an attack on God and on two people, it was an attack on marriage. Marriage was designed by God to reflect His glory and His redemptive purposes. In undermining that sacred institution, Satan struck a forceful blow at God's eternal plan.

It is no coincidence that Satan launched his insidious plan by approaching a married woman. He lied to her about God, about His character and His Word, and about sin and its consequences. She believed and acted on his lie and then turned to her husband and drew him into sin with her. The implications on their marriage were profound.

Shame replaced freedom. Pretense and hiding replaced transparency and fellowship. The oneness Eve and her husband had experienced in their original state now turned to enmity and animosity—not only toward God, but toward each other ... what was intended to be a joyous, fruitful, intimate relationship between a man, a woman, and their God now became a battleground ... and so it has been in every marriage since.[a]

a. Nancy Leigh DeMoss, *Lies Women Believe: And The Truth That Sets Them Free* (Chicago, IL: Moody Press, 2001), pp. 136-137.

Statistics tell us that for every two couples who say "I do" in the United States, one couple is likely to say "I don't any more," and end up in divorce court. Unfortunately, Christians are not exempt from troubled marriages—especially when a couple's basic values conflict.

Everyone has a basic set of values or beliefs. In essence, there are only two belief systems—biblical and non-biblical. Those who hold the non-biblical view have bought into Satan's lie that pleasing *self* rather than *God* will bring them happiness. These people are guided by *feelings*, and they value *getting*. In contrast, the biblically-oriented are guided by the *absolutes* in God's Word, and value *giving*. They believe God's promise that living more abundantly can only come through serving Christ.[b]

b. John 10:9-10

Loving Your Husband: Know His Needs

GOD'S IDEAL FOR MARRIAGE IS that both the husband and wife choose to value what *He* values, and thus be blessed abundantly with an intimate union as was originally intended in Genesis 2:24. John and I have experienced the fruit of this in our own lives, for which we will be forever grateful! Though I believe we have a *wonderful* marriage, and John *is such a blessing*, I know that because there are no perfect people (just forgiven!), there can be no perfect marriages. There is always room for growth and improvement. Since this chapter is addressed to wives, may we each consider its contents as an encouragement to further become all we can be in Christ—and then lovingly, earnestly, and continually seek to fulfill our husbands' deepest needs. What might those needs be? I believe that all husbands have three vital needs in marriage:

1. **All husbands need to be loved spiritually.**[a] This requires following their leadership and submitting to their direction, which will identify with **God's plan** for our lives.

a. 1 Peter 3:1-7

2. **All husbands need to be loved physically.**[b] This requires giving of our love to exhilarate them, which will satisfy **God's man** in our lives.

b. 1 Corinthians 7:1-7
Proverbs 5:15-19

3. **All husbands need to be loved mentally and emotionally.**[c] This requires honoring and encouraging them, which will multiply **God's joy** in our lives.

c. 1 Peter 3:8-9

Fulfilling these needs flows from a Christlike love—a love patterned after the sacrificial love of God as seen in John 3:16. This kind of love is unconditional (without conditions or requirements); it is uninterrupted (without stopping or intervals); it is unselfish (without concern for personal needs or desires *first*); it is unabashedly freely given (without shame or embarrassment).

Let us consider how we can more fully demonstrate such biblical love to our husbands—spiritually, physically, emotionally, and practically.

Word-Filled Wives Love Their Husbands Spiritually

1. By following and submitting to him.

"Wives ... be submissive to your own husbands, that even if some do not obey the word, they, without a word, may be won by the conduct of their wives, when they observe your chaste conduct [accompanied] by fear" (1 PETER 3:1-2).

Wifely submission is not a popular concept today (see also chapter 9). The women's liberation movement considers the idea offensive, old-fashioned, and unjust. But every Christian wife is told in Scripture to submit to her husband just as she submits to Christ. But what does it mean to be submissive? Jesus asks us to yield our bodies and emotions to our husbands as we have given our wills and spirits to Christ. Therefore, loving our husbands is not an option; pursuing them in the way they need and desire is not a take-it-or-leave-it proposition—it is a measure of our true spirituality. We should ask ourselves: *How close am I to Jesus? Do I unreservedly give myself to Him?* If so, we should do the same to our own man. Anything less is a false and self-serving spirituality.

The secret of total submission is an adoring attitude. The servant's attitude is two-fold, and the story of Mary and Martha offers us a choice illustration. In Luke 10:38-42, Martha is concerned about the Lord's comforts; Mary is concerned about adoration and nearness to Him. A wife who desires a proper servant's attitude should notice that both of these types of service are necessary, but Jesus Christ commended Mary for choosing the better role.

Many wives are wonderful servants to their families and husbands. They provide meals, clothes, and a clean environment. But they fail to understand other needs that require the personal attentions of a devoted wife.

2. BY EXPRESSING A SERVANT'S ATTITUDE TOWARD HIM.

"Encourage the young women to love their husbands, to love their children, [to be] sensible, pure, workers at home, kind, being subject to their own husbands, that the word of God may not be dishonored" (TITUS 2:4-5, NASB).

An adoring servant's attitude is a crucial part of real love—submission. A woman trying to *win* a husband shows this attitude continuously before marriage, and the man responds with a tender protective love for her. After marriage, however, the woman often becomes burdened with the cares of the household and neglects the most important responsibility of caring for her husband's need for love and companionship. Therefore, Scripture clearly warns against the destructiveness of Satan's way and reminds wives to follow God's way.

The passage cited above in Titus lists seven elements that God is looking for in your life so the Word of God will be honored. Why not take a moment and underline or circle them in your Bible and write a note there beside those verses to yourself that says something like this: **"God wants ME to cultivate these qualities for HIM."**

3. BY ALLOWING CHRIST TO BE ALL YOU NEED.

"If then you were raised with Christ, seek those things which are above, where Christ is, sitting at the right hand of God. Set your mind on things above, not on things on the earth. For you died, and your life is hidden with Christ in God" (COLOSSIANS 3:1-3)

"The heart of her husband safely trusts her; so he will have no lack of gain. She does him good and not evil all the days of her life" (PROVERBS 31:11-12).

Satan will do all he can to persuade us differently. We must, as women, therefore, be especially alert to his lies, for Eve was easily deceived by that old serpent; Adam was not.[a] Thus we should con-

a. Genesis 3
1 Timothy 2:14

tinually ask the Lord to lead us into truth, which can keep us free of deceptions.[a]

The following comparisons can help you examine your actions in light of scriptural truths. Prayerfully consider which of the two value systems (worldly or biblical) most describes how you relate to your husband:

Satan's Way	God's Way
Are you habitually following Satan's way by harboring a railing and contentious spirit (1 Peter 3:9; Proverbs 19:13b)?	Or following God's way—by displaying a meek and quiet spirit (1 Peter 3:4)?
Are you habitually following Satan's way by withdrawing from your husband's affections and being cold (1 Corinthians 7:3-5)?	Or following God's way—by desiring to please him (Genesis 3:16; 1 Corinthians 7:34)?
Are you habitually following Satan's way by depicting an unresponsive and unsympathetic ear (Proverbs 12:25)?	Or following God's way—by demonstrating consolation and loyal support (Genesis 24:67; Proverbs 31:11)?
Are you habitually following Satan's way by showing resentment of his service for the Lord (2 Samuel 6:20-23)?	Or following God's way—by joyfully helping him, and training your children to understand what Dad is doing (Genesis 2:18)?
Are you habitually following Satan's way by hindering prayers being answered because of wrong attitudes (1 Peter 3:7)?	Or following God's way—by portraying reverence and obedience to your husband (Ephesians 5:33; 1 Peter 3:5-6)?
Are you habitually following Satan's way by presenting an uncaring attitude toward your personal appearance (1 Corinthians 10:31)?	Or following God's way—by exemplifying strength of body, evidencing self-control, exercise, and rest (Proverbs 31:17)?
Are you habitually following Satan's way by allowing jealousy in your heart toward other women's positions or abilities (James 3:14)?	Or following God's way—by relying on His strength to control your mind (Philippians 2:5, 1 Peter 1:13; 2 Timothy. 1:7)?
Are you habitually following Satan's way by exhibiting a destructive attitude (Proverbs 14:1b)?	Or following God's way—by aspiring to keep your home a refuge where he may come for comfort and rest (Titus 2:5; Proverbs 31:27; Proverbs 14:1)?
Are you habitually following Satan's way by feeding a discontented and selfish spirit (1 Timothy. 6:6-8)?	Or following God's way—by evidencing contentment, and a hospitable attitude toward his friends and others in need (Philippians 4:11; Proverbs 31:20; Romans 12:13)?
Are you habitually following Satan's way by being a rottenness to your husband's bones (Proverbs 12:4b)?	Or following God's way—by being a crown to him (Proverbs 12:4a)?

Word-Filled Wives Love Their Husbands Physically

1. By exhilarating him with her love.

God invented sexual intimacy before the Fall and declared it *"very good"* (GENESIS 1:27-28, 31). He designed marital intimacy for pleasure and also for procreation:

> *"May your fountain be blessed, and may you rejoice in the wife of your youth. A loving doe, a graceful deer—may her breasts satisfy you always, may you ever be captivated by her love"*
> (PROVERBS 5:18-19, NIV).

The Scriptures describe the beautiful ecstasy of a couple obeying God's plan,[a] and deeply enjoying one another physically.[b] And this union Christ elevates; He says it portrays His love spiritually for His church.[c] However, God limits this sexual intimacy for marriage only:

a. Song of Solomon 2:3-6
b. Song of Solomon 4:9-11

c. Ephesians 5:31-32

> *"Now for the matters you wrote about: It is good for a man not to marry. But since there is so much immorality, each man should have his own wife, and each woman her own husband"*
> (1 CORINTHIANS 7:1-2, NIV).

That puts a responsibility on us as women to understand a man's need for regular and exhilarating sexual intimacy. Because of differing natures when it comes to sex, the physically intimate side of marriage can really test our character. Women are far more attracted by a man's personality, but men are stimulated by sight. While a man at times may need little or no preparation for the bedroom, a woman needs to be emotionally and mentally prepared by touch and romantic words, often hours in advance. Jack and Carole Mayhall, in their book, *Marriage Takes More than Love*, offer this comparison: "A man is like an electric light bulb—you flip a switch and on he goes. A woman is more like an electric iron—you flip a switch and it takes a little time to warm up. When you turn it off, it takes a bit of time to cool off too."[d]

d. Jack and Carole Mayhall, *Marriage Takes More Than Love* (Colorado Springs, CO: NavPress, 1978), p.22.

Although most women may not possess as strong or as consistent a sex drive as a man, we do have a sex drive. Married love is God's ordained plan for this expression. Did you know that medical professionals attest that the female nervous system is intrinsically tied to the reproductive organs? The act of marriage exists for the propagation of the race and personal enjoyment promoting fidelity and fulfillment, but it also contributes a much needed relaxant to the nervous system.

For most men, the desire for sexual intimacy is almost continual. God designed man to be the aggressor, provider, and leader of his family. Somehow all of that is tied to his sexual desires. A wife may equate her husband's passion with carnality, not realizing that her husband's desires are not unique, but characteristic of most normal men. His sexual desires need a regular release to avoid frustrating his mental and physical well-being. Such intense desires are the gift of God to produce the next generation of humans. That gift not only influences a man's sexual behavior, but also his personality, work, motivation, and almost every other characteristic of his life. Without it, he would not be the man with whom you fell in love. In other words, God has planned that the strong desires of your husband be recognized by you as unselfish affection, and not selfish desire. It is a wise and blessed woman who cooperates with her husband's God-given sexual needs, rather than ignoring, fearing, or fighting against them.

> "The husband should fulfill his marital duty to his wife, and likewise the wife to her husband. The wife's body does not belong to her alone but also to her husband. In the same way, the husband's body does not belong to him alone but also to his wife"
> (1 CORINTHIANS 7:3-4, NIV).

2. BY SATISFYING HIM WITH HER LOVE.

God commands any who wish to be truly spiritual to not interrupt regular sexual intimacy except for a time of devoted prayer.

> "Do not deprive each other except by mutual consent and for a time, so that you may devote yourselves to prayer. Then come together again so that Satan will not tempt you because of your lack of self-control" (1 CORINTHIANS 7:5, NIV).

Frequent, satisfying intimacy shared between a husband and wife is a form of spiritual warfare against one of Satan's favorite targets—a sexually-frustrated husband. Depriving a husband of his legitimate biblical right to intimacy can cause him great hardship and suffering, and thus increase the risk that he may eventually yield to unfaithfulness. If David, a man after God's own heart, succumbed to sexual temptation,[a] so can most men. Listen to the true story of a sexually-frustrated husband and a selfish wife:

a. 2 Samuel 11:1-4

> *Tim confided with his friend, as his eyes followed the feminine form of a stranger crossing in front of his car in the crosswalk, "I love my wife, Pauline, with all of my heart, but I feel like I'm being cheated." Was his wife being unfaithful with another man? No! He further confided, with dejected words, that he and his beautiful wife had shared physical intimacy only four times in their many years of marriage. This man, with all of his being, wanted to be a good and faithful husband; but his wife was so lacking in her love for him that this basic need of her man had been left unmet for years …. She was not only hurting her own self and causing her husband to suffer greatly—living on the edge of temptation at every hand, but she was being disobedient to God who instructs us to live in love caring for the needs of our life partner.*

A sexually-satisfied husband is a man who will rapidly develop self-confidence in other areas of his life. Most men do not realize that some of their irritations can often be traced to their unsatisfied sexual desires, but a wise wife will remain alert to this possibility. When sexual harmony prevails, somehow the world looks better, and difficulties seem less intimidating to a man. It is as though his hard work and the pressures of life are worth it all when he and his wife consummate their love properly. The most beautiful aspect of all this is that God created the experience for man to share only with his wife.

Anything less than a scriptural view of sexual intimacy is a hindrance to our spiritual life, our family life, and is unsubmissive to our Lord. God commands married couples to love one another, and He never demands that we do anything for which He will not provide the strength. *Heeding His instructions will affair-proof our marriages and protect our families from great dangers!*

Word-Filled Wives Love Their Husbands Emotionally

By honoring and encouraging him.

ONE OF THE BEST WAYS to honor and encourage our husbands is to admire them. Note what Peter says:

> *"For in this way in former times the holy women also, who hoped in God, used to adorn themselves, being submissive to their own husbands. Thus Sarah obeyed Abraham, calling him lord ..."* (1 PETER 3:5-6, NASB).

Have you ever marveled at how a loaded jet can rise so seemingly effortlessly? Just as there are physical principles such as the principle of lift, so there are equally vital principles of relationships. One is the principle of admiration. People are attracted to those who admire them and avoid those who look down on them. As a pastor's wife for over 20 years, I have had scores of women come to me for help because their husbands don't spend time with them anymore. It is time for all of us to do a check of our relationships. Admiration, one of man's deepest needs, is the basis of all growing relationships. That is probably why the Scriptures tell wives to respect, or admire their husbands.[a] Peter states that admiration can even motivate a husband spiritually.[b]

The word admire (respect, honor) in the Scriptures basically means "to attach high value to another." When the Word speaks of "fearing God," it simply means that God is to be the most important— number one in our lives—and that is the beginning of wisdom.[c] "Admire, respect, fear, and honor" are similar in meaning, and all tell us to consider one another very worthwhile.[d] Admiring someone is a choice, a decision, a commitment, an act of our will. It is telling ourselves: *God loves and values that person, and so can I.* Your husband might irritate you, offend you, or ignore you; but admiration looks beyond what he does to who he is. Admiration is unconditional.

Men tend to gravitate toward those who admire them. If your husband isn't spending quality time with you, perhaps the following questions might reveal one or more reasons why. Be honest with yourself as you consider these warnings.

a. Ephesians 5:33

b. 1 Peter 3:1-2

c. Proverbs 9:10

d. Romans 12:10

1. Do you express less admiration or thanks to your husband than you do for other men? Your husband may be harboring hurt caused by your esteem for other men. Questions like, "Did you see Jill's ring at the party? Can you believe her husband bought her such an expensive gift?" may be sending a message to your husband that you think he is less successful and less generous than Jill's husband.

Comparing your husband with another man can tell him that you admire someone else more than him. Some men actually find themselves avoiding church because they don't think they could ever measure up to the men their wives brag about every Sunday. Comments such as "The pastor leads *his* family in devotions every morning at 7 A.M." are certainly not words that build up. Be careful not to tear down your mate by unthoughtful words. A man is especially sensitive about his job, his friends, and his abilities. Be careful not to praise other men unless you show even greater appreciation for your husband.

2. Do you make critical remarks about his character or his activities? This is deadly if voiced in front of friends or your children. Professionals recognize that a key principle of leadership is that it is totally unacceptable to belittle a person's character or ability in front of others. I can think of nothing that cuts a husband down more rapidly than criticism in front of his peers or his children.

3. Do you hear yourself nagging your husband? Nagging is another word for pressure from a wife that makes her husband feel incompetent and irresponsible. Proverbs says, "*A continual dripping on a very rainy day* [in a thatched-roof home] *and a contentious woman are alike.*"[a] Rather than motivating him to fulfill his responsibility, it makes him want to ignore it. As you keep nagging, he will seek other people who don't constantly remind him of his inadequacies. Facial expressions and tone of voice have the power to tear down your husband or to build him up.

a. Proverbs 27:15

4. Do you find yourself automatically questioning his choices or decisions? For example, if he decides to go to Home Depot™ on a Saturday morning, do you ask him, "Do you really have to go this morning?" With that single question, you imply you really don't agree with his judgment. All he hears is your challenge of his decision. No one likes to listen to a challenger.

5. Do you interrupt or correct your husband in conversations?
Have you ever listened to a woman who finished every one of her husband's sentences? This is a habit some women don't even realize they have. Decide you will let your husband finish his own sentences and that you won't correct him or argue with him in public. I have actually watched men withdraw from social situations because their wives are so overbearing or rude in their conversational habits. God can give you the wisdom to guard your tongue and fill your mouth with kindness.

6. Can you remember anything that you have complained about this week—his work schedule, leisure time choices, time with the kids, or your "honey do" list? Complaining has the same effect as nagging; it can drive anyone away to other people or other places. Commit these concerns in prayer to the Lord. He cares for your every need. If they need to be discussed with your husband, the Lord will provide the time and place. Complaining is really contagious. Remember the children of Israel in the wilderness?[a] For every time you are tempted to complain, try to think of one thing you can praise the Lord for. Psalm 71:6 encourages us to let our mouths be so filled with praise that there is no room left for complaining.

a. Psalm 106:24

Now that we have pondered the pitfalls to be avoided, what are some positive habits wives can work on to encourage husbands? Let us seek for our husbands to think of home as a refuge—a haven of rest, encouragement, and support.

Word-Filled Wives Love Their Husbands Practically

In Genesis 2:18 the Lord says, *"It is not good that man should be alone; I will make him a helper comparable to him."* Verse 20 continues, *"But for Adam there was not found a helper comparable [suitable] to him."* Do you remember what our All-Wise God did when He saw man's need? Verse 22: *"Then the rib which the Lord God had taken from man He made into a woman and He brought her to the man."* When you were joined in marriage to your husband, you became the one God supplied to be his suitable helper. Don't we have an amazing calling from God as wives? You are the one who has the high calling to know your husband's needs and to help him. By loving and reverencing your helpmate, you are loving and honoring our great God. How can you help your mate and your marriage? Love your husband in practical ways. Many studies have been done on the responses of men. Take a look around you at the ways that peers, secretaries, employers, and friends make a man feel important. Below are the most frequently suggested ways to strengthen your marriage relationship. Remember: knowing all the verses about loving your husband isn't enough. James 1:22 warns us: *"Be doers of the word, and not hearers only, deceiving yourselves."* Put feet to your plans and begin to love your husband in *practical ways* by loving him **"P.R.A.C.T.I.C.A.L.L.Y."**

P: Practice asking your husband what he thinks about every day matters such as daily schedules of family members. Carefully evaluate his input and let him know you value his advice. Maintain a balance by looking for opportunities to seek his opinion. As you receive his ideas, he will see that you consider him to be valuable.

R: Remember your husband's special desires and seek ways to fulfill them. I have learned much from my husband's example. When we were dating, John began writing little notes in the back of his calendar. After 20 years of marriage, he is still taking notes. What does he write down? He *listens* to my words and writes down my favorite things—my favorite foods, colors, places, etc. Just yesterday he took our whole family to a high school football game. This was very unusual for us! During the game he leaned over and whispered in my ear, "Two years ago you told me you loved fall football games and I've wanted to take you to one ever since." Of course, that melted my heart! His sincere desire to know me and to please me has been a constant example. What amazed me was that he remembered my comment and had waited for the opportunity to do something about it.

Ask the Lord to help you remember requests your own husband has made or implied. Maybe it has to do with a romantic date with you—look for the opportunity to please him. It could be a special event he wants to attend, or an activity he has wanted to do; maybe a special meal you haven't made for a long time, or one of his favorite desserts. Work on meeting whichever requests are within your capabilities. The more you do this, the more fulfilling it will become for both you and your husband.

A: Affirm your belief in your husband's godly character qualities. Adore and praise him with words spoken before your children. Confirm your admiration when you are with other people by listening to his ideas and not interrupting or correcting him. Pray for the discipline of your tongue. Pray for God's help to affirm your mate's leadership and your reverence of him.

C: Cultivate an appreciation for your husband's employment. Pray for your husband as he daily completes his work responsibilities. Do not ever belittle his job or the importance of his activities at work. Belittling your husband's efforts to support you will lead to the danger of destroying your husband's self-confidence. Simply being ignorant of your husband's efforts can communicate negatively to your husband. If you cannot accurately explain to someone else your husband's job responsibilities during his normal working day, you don't know enough about his job. When a man feels unimportant because of his job, it tears away at the very heart of his being. Help him discover the value of what he does in your sight and in the Lord's.

T: Teach yourself to withhold immediate negative responses. If you have a tendency to react immediately when you hear an idea, discipline yourself to carefully consider his words. Pray about your thoughts before you react. Practice responding positively and ask the Lord to prompt you in patience and kindness. One of my favorite Bible verses is Proverbs 31:26, *"She opens her mouth with wisdom, and on her tongue is the law of kindness."* You will avoid unnecessary tension in your relationship, and he will enjoy being with you more.

I: Instill a plan to regularly give verbal appreciation to your husband. It has been said that "gratefulness is a sincere appreciation for the benefits you have gained from others." Corporations have found that the highest motivational factor is not income or benefits. The majority of workers report that the one thing that encourages them to work harder is an expression of appreciation for their individual efforts.

If it works in a corporation, it will work at home! Gratefulness expressed through praise is one of the highest motivations for anyone. If you want your relationship with your husband to become more fulfilling, it's essential that you develop a grateful attitude.

Praise expressed from a grateful heart is essential to our walk with God. We actually enter into His presence through praise,[a] and our faith in Him is proven through our willingness to thank Him in all circumstances—no matter how destructive we may think they could be.[b] We have not learned to walk with Christ until we learn to say, "Thank you, Lord, for 'that'! I don't understand it, but I trust that You can work it for my good because I love You."

a. Psalm 100:4

b. 1 Thessalonians 5:18
Romans 8:28

Don't let a day pass without expressing gratitude for at least one thing your husband has said or done during those hours. Remember how much nicer it is to be with people who make you feel special than with those who don't? Why not try a "Purpose to Praise Him." Purpose to offer at least three expressions of appreciation for your husband daily for 31 days, and see what the Lord can do through this loving service to your husband!

C: Consider your understanding of your husband's personal goals. Let him know you pray for and support those goals. His personal goals may involve advancement in his company, higher education, spiritual disciplines, or special ministry pursuits. Sweetly encourage your husband during periods when he may feel like quitting, and praise him each time he attains any of his goals. Help him to keep his eyes on the Lord who enables us day by day and is the same yesterday, today, and forever.

A: Admire your husband in nonverbal ways. Studies of communication between husbands and wives have proven that words alone are responsible for only 7 percent of their total communication. Thirty-eight percent of marital communication is expressed through voice tone, and 55 percent through facial expressions and body language. In other words, when you say something to your husband, the words themselves account for only a small portion of the meaning. Consider the phrase, "I love you." It can be said in a way that communicates, "Of course I love you; I pay the bills don't I?" It could be conveyed as, "I desperately need you to fulfill my needs right now." Or, it could be expressed in a way that says, "I adore you and couldn't live my life without you!"

Here are a few nonverbal ways to show your husband you admire him, and that he is important to you:

1. Be attentive to his concerns when he comes home after work. Don't unload on him about how bad the children have been, or how exhausted you are. Greet him with a kiss and a smile.

2. Look as attractive as possible when he comes home. My college roommate once shared that every afternoon her mom showered and put on a fresh dress, makeup, and perfume to greet her husband after work. If this doesn't seem possible, at least keep a hairbrush, lipstick, and perfume close by so you can do a little "repair work" right before you expect him to arrive.

3. Prepare appetizing meals. Put some extra effort into making meal time a special family time. Fluff some paper napkins, or invest in cloth napkins. Light candles every once in awhile; put on a tablecloth, or make place cards. Play some pleasant worshipful music. Give thanks to God that you are about to entertain dinner guests—your most favorite people in all the world—your family.

4. Show interest in his world outside of your home. Ask questions about his job, activities, problems, and achievements. Avoid giving a quick answer for all of his troubles, or a correction of all his mistakes, or a criticism of his decisions.

5. Listen attentively by focusing your eyes on him. Don't continue writing the grocery list, talking on the phone, or worse yet—watching the TV. Drop everything when he wants to talk. When he doesn't have to compete with the TV, dishes, or even the children, he will know you value his communication with you.

6. Learn to be sensible about your expectations of your husband. This is vitally important. Expectations can be one of the most destructive forces in your marriage. They can bring unnecessary disappointment and discouragement to both you and your husband. Don't expect him to be someone else. Don't expect him to be Superman or the Apostle Paul. Love him for being a provider, being faithful, and being yours.

L: Let no wedges be formed between you—humbly seek your husband's forgiveness whenever you offend him. We all tend to avoid those who offend us. When we were newlyweds, John used this picture. Every hurt or offense that we left unforgiven or undealt with could be a small wedge of difference between us. If left unremoved, many little wedges become a great big wedge causing separation and lack of communication.

When we have been hurt, we usually do not want to hear a simple, "I'm sorry." We want to know that the person realizes he or she was wrong and that he or she hurt us. Perhaps you have offered this kind of apology: *"I'm sorry I did that; I really didn't mean to hurt you."* Or *"I'm sorry I said what I said, but you were wrong too."*

Conditional communications like these leave wedges between us in our marriage. Instead, go to each other; look into each other's eyes and say, "I was wrong. I am sorry. Please forgive me." My husband calls those the nine most necessary words in a marriage! You are then communicating that you care for each other enough not to leave each other with wounded feelings. If your husband does not lead you in prayer, ask him gently if you could pray together—thus uniting your hearts before the Lord. The Scriptures tell us to *"let not the sun go down upon your wrath."*[a] Cultivate a habit of ending your day by holding hands or kneeling beside your mate to close the day in prayer to our Lord.

a. Ephesians 4:26

L: Learn to be his biggest encourager by letting God fill you with praise. God wants your most intimate earthly relationship to be with your husband. Praise God for the mate He provided. Memorize and meditate upon several Bible verses of praise such as those in Psalms 98, 100, and 103. Commit to memory Proverbs 31:12: *"She will do him good and not evil all the days of her life."*

If you want your husband to yearn for quality time with you, you must learn to consistently express a positive attitude. Think back to when you were dating and he came to pick you up for the evening. Did you greet him with complaints and continue the evening with criticisms? Of course not! Honestly ask yourself: *How do I act around company even when I have a headache? How do I act when I'm in a hurry and receive a phone call from a friend who has problems?* We usually find it easy, or at least necessary, to have a positive attitude around our friends. Don't you agree that your husband deserves the same thoughtfulness?

When I turned 40, my husband gave me a cherished gift. He asked me what I wanted for the special occasion and I said, "Please write me a love letter like you did when we were dating and separated by great distances." John did write a letter and in it he listed "40 Reasons Why I Love You." That was a very memorable gift. It has hung on my mirror for years now, and every year my husband updates it with one more reason why he married me and still loves me.

Let God fill your heart and mind with praise to Him. I guarantee it will flow over into your relationship with your husband!

Y: You Decide Which Kind of Love You Will Show. This chapter's focus is upon learning how to biblically love and value our husbands. But what if you don't love your husband? Ask God to fill your heart and mind with His great, unconditional love. To learn more about true love, study 1 Corinthians 13 . One of the most exciting aspects of true love is that God can instill it in our hearts without the presence of affectionate feelings.[a]

a. Galatians 5:22
Romans 5:5

True love is totally different from affection and passion. Affection and passion make us aware of our own needs, and cause us to look to others to meet those needs.[b] Genuine love, as shown by Christ, becomes aware of the needs of others and seeks opportunities to meet those needs. One speaker summarized true love this way: "I see your need; please allow me to meet it." Or, to paraphrase the Apostle Paul, "I submit myself to meeting your needs—your needs are my master" (GALATIANS 5:13-14). The focus of genuine love is not getting (Satan's way); it is giving (God's way).

b. John 15:11-13

True love doesn't always arise from feelings. Although the feelings of affection usually follow, biblical love is primarily a choice to fulfill another person's needs. God loved you so much that He gave His only Son. Jesus Christ gave Himself for you. Developing true love for your husband is to begin seeing him and valuing him as God does.[a] It   a. John 3:16
is choosing to care because he is worthwhile, and because God truly loves him. You decide. Choose your own way or choose God's design. As you obey God's Word in John 15:11-13, you will be rewarded with joy and peace. You will fulfill the deepest needs of your husband and your life will be flooded with God-given peace and joy.

STUDY GUIDE QUESTIONS

1. **The choice to do whatever it takes to fulfill your husband's deepest needs is a choice to value what God values.** The ability to do this must flow from a Christlike love. Read Colossians 3:12-18. How does that passage apply to lovingly fulfilling your husband's needs?

2. **Word-filled wives love their husbands spiritually.** This requires following their leadership and submitting to their direction, which will identify with God's plan for our lives.

   Read 1 Peter 3:1-6. How does your own conduct as a wife measure up to this passage? In areas where you are weak, ask the Lord for the enablement to fulfill the role He's given to you as a wife (1 John 5:14-15).

   Read Titus 2:4-5. List the seven elements that God is looking for in your life so that the Word of God will be honored in your marriage.

3. **Word-filled wives love their husbands physically.** This requires giving of our love to exhilarate him, which will satisfy God's man in our life.

   Read the Song of Solomon 4:9-11. In this passage, can you sense how exhilarated King Solomon was with his beloved wife's physical intimacy? Is this a joy in your

own life? If not, ask the Lord for such a blessing so that
you can better fulfill your husband's deepest needs.

Read 1 Corinthians 7:3-5. What does this passage have to
say about your responsibility as a wife to satisfy your
husband's physical needs on a regular basis?

4. **Word-filled wives love their husbands practically (mentally and emotionally).** This requires honoring and encouraging them, which will multiply God's joy in our lives.

Read Romans 12:9-21. This passage clearly identifies the
characteristics of a Word-filled life. A wife with this spirit
will lovingly and graciously be honoring and encouraging
to her husband. Meditate on this passage, and then make
a list of practical ways that God has revealed for you to
better serve your own husband's deepest needs.

"I have no greater joy than to hear that my children walk in truth."

— 3 John 4

Your family can be the source of your greatest joy in life.
If you want to experience the greatest joy possible on earth—learn what God offers to your family. If you aren't married, or childless—join the club. Paul seems to have been both, yet he may end up with one of the biggest families in heaven (saints he led to Christ, nurtured, and took with him to heaven). For those who are married and have children, here are five chapters that show us that path to the greatest joys on earth!

CHAPTER 12: *A Discipling Mother*

CHAPTER 13: *Learning From Great Women of the Word*

CHAPTER 14: *How to Be a Word filled Dad*

CHAPTER 15: *Moving Families toward Godliness*

CHAPTER 16: *How to Be an Incredible Dad*

PART THREE

A Word Filled Family

There Is *No* Greater Joy

12

"Her children rise up and call her blessed; her husband [also], and he praises her."

— *Proverbs 31:28*

A Discipling Mother

Note: I'm turning this chapter over to Bonnie—my special "portrait of grace"—and the beautiful mother of our eight wonderful children. I am confident that you will be blessed by what she has to share about becoming a discipler of your children!

THERE HAVE PROBABLY BEEN FEW times in history when it has been harder to raise a Word-filled family than in today's culture. More and more, mothers need godly role models to help light the way through these dark and perilous times. Lois and Eunice, Timothy's grandmother and mother, were such "lights" during what many consider to have been the most difficult time to be a follower of Christ. In the first chapter of 2 Timothy, the Apostle Paul acknowledged the wonderful influence these women had upon Timothy's faith. Beginning when he was still young enough to have to be fed, carried, and dressed, they discipled him for Christ through God's Word and His ways.[a] Like the great women of the Word before them, they were

a. 2 Timothy. 3:15

beautiful portraits of God's grace. And today, you, dear mother, can also clearly manifest such grace to your children. God can use *you, by your example and words,* to shape tomorrow!

When I walk around at night and look at those still forms of my children asleep in their beds, my heart leaps within me—for no one on earth holds more sway over their precious little hearts and minds than I do. For many years, I can shape their world by my life, my words, my touch, and my prayers. Even my dear husband who proclaims God's Word so faithfully and fully can't come close to what God has given *me.* I can melt them with love, steel them with truth, shape them with conviction, guide them with insight—and all that is what God called me to do! Fellow women, rejoice! I can't imagine a higher calling in the universe than what God has offered us.

Mothers can tremendously impact the future of the Lord's heritage, as Paul testified about Timothy's start for the Lord: *"... and that from childhood you have known ..."* (2 TIMOTHY 3:15). Young Timothy, in a home with an unbelieving father, was shaped by a Word-filled mother. That is what I prayerfully set out to do every day. During this short life on earth—this prelude to eternity—God has assigned us parents the role of standing in His place to show our children what He is like. My husband says, "God has given us their tiny hands to hold, to walk with in this world, step by step, until we lead them to their heavenly Father, and place their hands in His everlasting hand."

How do we begin holding their hands to disciple them for Christ? How will our children begin to see what God is like through us? Children will better understand what God is like by first learning to honor their father and mother. God says, *"Children, obey your parents in the Lord, for this is right. Honor your father and mother ..."* (EPHESIANS 6:1-2A). The Greek word for "obey," *hupakouo,* means "obedience out of duty." Learning to obey out of duty is essential if children are to understand what God is like. It is improbable that they will learn to obey God, whom they *can't* see physically, until they first learn to obey those they *can* see. Therefore, from the time they are young enough to have to be fed, carried, and dressed, children must be taught "obedience out of duty" because, to God, obedience is better than anything else we could offer Him.[a]

a. 1 Samuel 15:22

Being trained to obey because it is *right* will help create teachable hearts open to learning more and more about our great God and all of His wondrous attributes. As this occurs, rather than obeying the Lord merely out of duty, children should increasingly evidence "submission out of devotion." That spirit was demonstrated by Jesus when, at the age of twelve, He submitted to Mary and Joseph, and Scripture records that He *"increased in wisdom and stature, and in favor with God and men"* (LUKE 2:41-52). Later on in life, Jesus summarized "submission out of devotion" by saying, *"If you love Me, keep My commandments"* (JOHN 14:15).

The question: How can you parent in a way that will not rob your children of the pure joy of honoring and obeying the Lord and you? The answer: By God's grace, increasingly model the characteristics of a genuine disciple of Christ.[a] That is the first key to successful mothering; having a consistent prayer ministry on their behalf is the second key. (Part Four of this book will cover the latter topic in depth.)

a. 1 Corinthians 11:1

Discipling Your Children: Nurture Them in Christ

TODAY, MY NINE-YEAR-OLD SON SAT beaming at our dining room table. He was working on a school project which I had helped him begin. He turned his freckled face toward me just for an instant, long enough to exude his appreciation. "Mom, you're teaching me so much! I am learning so much from you. Thank you for teaching me." Discipling your children by nurturing them in Christ every day brings the reward of great joy. Effective discipleship involves a twofold process:

1. Child training is the process of causing children to come under your authority and respect your word so that they are more likely to be receptive to being discipled.

2. Discipling, then, is a specific type of training that nurtures children in God's Word and His ways. This twofold process applies to all stages of child development.

Nurturing your children begins on day one and continues through their entire development. As you enjoy the seasons of physical growth and changes, so too you should observe the spiritual growth in your children as you nurture and disciple them for Jesus Christ.

INFANT AND TODDLER YEARS

During these years, parents stand as God's visible representative to lovingly, consistently discipline their children with the goal of bringing about outward obedience. Young children obey initially out of duty. However, as a mother of eight, I believe it is never too early to begin teaching a child the Word of God and the love of God. Begin early to reach their hearts. Teach them that love requires obedience.

SCHOOL YEARS

As your children grow in their knowledge and understanding of God, continue to disciple them in the ways of wisdom: "*The fear of the Lord is the beginning of wisdom.*"[a] Pray for salvation and then sanctification. In these formative years, children progress from obedience out of duty to obedience out of devotion.

a. Proverbs 1:7

Pursue knowing each child well enough to measure his or her spiritual pulse. Keep the Word of God always before them and live a life of Christlike self-sacrificing before them. Spend much time together as Deuteronomy 6 instructs so that you can pour into them the truths of God. Be ready for the teachable moments and the open windows of their hearts. Guide them into biblical discipleship as you prayerfully see them become true followers of Jesus Christ.

LAUNCHING INTO LIFE

Our goal in discipling our children is to see them become genuine followers of Christ who are yielded in the Master's hand and useful in His service. After you have faithfully implanted God's Word in their lives, you will have the joy of seeing your children walk in the truth. I was reminded by a Christian camp director recently, "We harvest in a different season than we sow." Sometimes the harvest season seems to come slowly. But I believe God is faithful. What we sow we will reap. Let us not grow weary in well-doing.[b] Being likeminded with Christ, you will find your relationship with your children has grown from one of disciplinarian to nurturer to discipler, and now to friend. As brothers and sisters in God's family, let iron sharpen iron and drink in the sweetness of relationships in Christ.

b. Galatians 6:9

The mother who is a portrait of God's grace fosters an atmosphere in which the type of relationship just described can thrive. You have, as your children's primary discipler, the great privilege of watching God's hand at work in their lives. Can you picture yourself in such a role? What does it take to fulfill such a responsibility?

The Best Ability Is Availability: Be Available to God

GOD WILL HELP YOU, AS you keep a steady focus on the Lord and search for His unchanging truths, to increasingly model the characteristics of a genuine disciple of Christ. Does He expect perfection? No, for that is impossible this side of heaven. **Remember: God isn't after your ability, but your availability.** Simply put, God wants your *heart.* As you surrender yourself unreservedly to Christ, the Holy Spirit will use the Word of God to conform you into the image of God, for His glory.[a]

a. Romans 12:1 2

Amy Carmichael's life is a beautiful portrait of one who unreservedly surrendered all to Christ and bore abundant fruit for His glory. She was born December 16, 1867, in the village of Millisle on the north coast of Ireland, and at the age of eighty-three—after a lifetime of service to the needy outcasts of India—she died. When she died, this beloved "Amma" left behind a spiritual family of thousands! Her bed was covered with flowers, and upon her death, children sang in her honor for an hour and a half! She had suffered, yet faithfully endured to the end.

What kind of home made this remarkable woman? How do you rear children in a way that makes them free from self-indulgence, and ever confident in the goodness of a holy, heavenly Father? Elisabeth Elliot, in her biography of Amy Carmichael, *A Chance to Die*, gives us a glimpse of that remarkable Irish home:

> *There was no question in the minds of the Carmichael children as to what was expected of them. Black was black. White was white. Their parents' word could be trusted absolutely, and when it was not obeyed there were consequences. There is a great biblical principle behind this kind of relationship. Even Ted Koppel of*

[American Broadcasting Company's] Nightline can see it. Speaking to the graduates at Duke University he said that the reason "Honor thy father and thy mother" was included in the first five commandments [which deal with our relationship to God] is that parents stand in the place of God for their children. We are charged by God to show our children what God is like.[a]

a. Elisabeth Elliot, *A Chance to Die: The Life and Legacy of Amy Carmichael* (Grand Rapids, MI: Fleming H. Revell, 1987), p. 77.

What was Amy's own estimation of this awesome, Christlike home? Long afterward, she wrote, "I don't think there could have been a happier child than I was." Her parents stood in the place of God to teach her to say, "Thank you, Father!" for all He brought her way. Her parents' faithfulness reaped Amy's total submission out of devotion. Devotion and faithfulness then became her fruitful pattern for life!

Amy Carmichael's parents seriously followed God's charge to show their children what He is like. Philippians 2:1-8 captures that spirit:

> *"If there is any consolation in Christ, if any comfort of love, if any fellowship of the Spirit, if any affection and mercy, fulfill my joy by being like-minded, having the same love, being of one accord, of one mind. Let nothing be done through selfish ambition or conceit, but in lowliness of mind let each esteem others better than himself. Let each of you look out not only for his own interests, but also for the interests of others. Let this mind be in you which was also in Christ Jesus, who, being in the form of God, did not consider it robbery to be equal with God, but made Himself of no reputation, taking the form of a bondservant, and coming in the likeness of men. And being found in appearance as a man, He humbled Himself and became obedient to the point of death, even the death of the cross"* (PHILIPPIANS 2:1-8).

Note that **love**, **unity**, and **humility** are predominant. With that in mind, let us now consider some ways a discipling mother can manifest this trinity of graces to her children.

WE DISCIPLE BY UNCONDITIONAL LOVE

> *"A new commandment I give to you, that you love one another; as I have loved you, that you also love one another. By this shall all men know that you are My disciples, if you have love for one another"* (JOHN 13:34-35).

The discipling mother understands that children need to be *loved unconditionally*. Her love is not dependent upon whether or not a child performs according to "expectations." Rather, the discipling mother accepts and affirms a child for who he or she is—a child made in the image of God—not for what he or she does. God expresses this kind of love in Romans 8:38-39 when he affirms that nothing can separate us from His love; we thus love Him *because* He first loved us.[a] My pastor-husband says, "There is nothing I can do to make God love me any more or any less."

a. 1 John 4:19

The love chapter, 1 Corinthians 13, beautifully describes Christlike love. Consider how nicely the following paraphrase applies that chapter to a mother's ministry to her children:

If I talk to my children about what is right and what is wrong, but have not love, I am like a ringing doorbell or pots hanging in the kitchen. And though I know what stages they will go through, and understand their growing pains, and can answer all their questions about life, and believe myself to be a devoted mother, but have not love, I am nothing. If I give up the fulfillment of a career to make my children's lives better, and stay up all night sewing costumes or baking cookies on short notice, but grumble about lack of sleep, I have not love and accomplish nothing. A loving mother is patient with her children's immaturity and kind even when they are not; a loving mother is not jealous of their youth nor does she hold it over their heads whenever she has sacrificed for them. A loving mother does not push her children into doing things her way. She is not irritable, when the chicken pox have kept her confined with three whining children for two weeks, and does not resent the child who brought the affliction home in the first place. A loving mother is not relieved when her disagreeable child finally disobeys her directly and she can punish him, but rather rejoices with him when he is being more cooperative. A loving mother bears much of the responsibility for her children; she believes in them; she hopes in each one's individual ability to stand out as a light in a dark world; she endures every backache and heartache to accomplish that. A loving mother never really dies. As for home baked bread, it will be consumed and forgotten; as for spotless floors, they will soon gather dust and heel marks. And as for children, well, right now toys, friends, and food, are all-important to them. But when they grow up it will have been how their mother loved them that will determine how they love others. In that way she will live on. So care, training, and a loving mother reside in a home, these three, but the greatest of these is a loving mother.[a]

a. Dianne Lorang,
Keep the Fire Glowing
(Old Tappan, NJ: Fleming H. Revell Company, 1986),
pp. 152-153.

b. Proverbs 17:17

Love always chooses to act in the best interest of others. In other words, a discipling mother is a friend who loves at all times.[b]

WE DISCIPLE BY GRACE-FILLED LIVES

One of the discipling mother's top priorities is to promote unity among family members—that they may all be of one accord, of one mind. Such peace and harmony can be modeled through the following seven graces:

1. Openness. A discipling mother is graciously open to the close examination of her physical, mental, emotional, and spiritual state by members of her family—even the littlest ones, who seem to notice everything! Of this one thing we can be sure: our lives are like an open letter, *"known and read by all* [children]*"* (2 CORINTHIANS 3:2). Most are very discerning and know when we are doing things God's way, and when we're not. Therefore, God says, *"Confess your trespasses to one another, and pray for one another, that you may be healed. The effective, fervent prayer of a righteous* [woman] *avails much"* (JAMES 5:16).

2. Teachableness. When trying to promote like-mindedness in her family, the discipling mother recognizes that God has created us with differing temperaments. The differences between family members are to be treasured and enjoyed. She never assumes that because she is an adult, she is always right. The discipling mother is therefore willing to listen to what her children have to say, and is often surprised at how much she learns from them. If the Holy Spirit brings about personal conviction, appropriate action is taken to correct deficiencies. God says that *"He who disdains instruction despises his own soul, But he who heeds rebuke gets understanding"* (PROVERBS 15:32).

3. Kindheartedness. Different ways of expressing kindheartedness are tenderness, compassion, sympathy, forbearance, understanding, and thoughtfulness. A mother with such a spirit easily identifies with the pain of others, and desires to be a burden bearer[a]—one who freely extends comfort. When one of her children is hurting, she instinctively senses that there is *a time to keep silence, and a time to speak*" (ECCLESIASTES 3:7B). She withholds unwarranted comments and instead offers compassion, thereby becoming a visible representation of the God of All Comfort.[b] Then, as appropriate, the discipling mother follows, *"Brethren, if a [child] is overtaken in any trespass, you who are spiritual restore such a one in a spirit of gentleness, considering yourself lest you also be tempted"* (GALATIANS 6:1).

a. Galatians 6:2

b. 2 Corinthians 1:4

4. Truthfulness. The discipling mother is discerning enough to know when to confront a problem needing attention, rather than waiting to be asked about it. She knows that *"as iron sharpens iron, so a [woman] sharpens the countenance of [her] friend"* (PROVERBS 27:17).

5. Meekness. The discipling mother has a gentle and quiet spirit, which is very precious in God's sight.[c] She willingly yields her rights and expectations to God. Her heart's cry: *"My soul, wait silently for God alone, for my expectation [is] from Him"* (PSALM 62:1, 5). She is therefore not quickly angered because she has learned to seek God's grace to avoid common pitfalls in parenting that can provoke her children to exasperation.

c. 1 Peter 3:4

6. Trustworthiness. Earning her children's trust is a top priority. The discipling mother knows that if children can't trust their parents, they are not likely to trust God either. Showing confidentiality regarding sensitive matters is very important to this mom, for Proverbs 11:13 tells us that *"a gossip betrays a confidence, but a trustworthy [woman] keeps a secret."*

7. Faithfulness. The discipling mother realizes that all of the above graces are meaningless without a daily testimony of living by faith before her children. She therefore more and more longs to know God personally—what He loves, what He hates, and how to best please Him. Her passion is to be "a woman after God's own heart." Like David, she cries out:

"Give me understanding, and I shall keep Your law; Indeed, I shall observe it with [my] whole heart. … Oh, how I love Your law! It [is] my meditation all the day. … How sweet are Your words to my taste, [Sweeter] than honey to my mouth! Through Your precepts I get understanding; Therefore I hate every false way" (PSALM 119:34, 97, 103-104).

The list of graces that foster love and unity can go on and on. But the point I wish to make is this: **The more you grow in Christlikeness, the more your children can envision what God is like, and thus desire to worship and serve Him with their whole heart, soul, mind, and strength.**

WE DISCIPLE IN THE HUMILITY OF CHRIST

The discipling mother knows that *"a* [woman's] *pride will bring* [her] *low, but the **humble in spirit** will retain honor"* (PROVERBS 29:23, Emphasis added); for *"God resists the proud, but gives grace to the humble"* (JAMES 4:6).

In a storm, a tree is no stronger than its roots—neither are we. A healthy root system leads to life; a defective one leads to death. In the verses above, there are two contrasting root systems. One root system, Satan's way, leads to the death of family harmony; the other, God's way, heals families, promoting like-mindedness for God's glory. Consider the extreme contrasts between the two root systems:

- Satan's way is to be controlled by pride—"self on the throne" competing with God for first place. Pride, which is the root of every sin and evil, is something children will naturally gravitate toward and easily imitate. Every time pridefulness rears its ugly head, it must therefore be firmly resisted.[a]
- God's way is to humbly yield to *Christ's* control, depending upon His power to obey the written, living Word of God. Because humility is the root of all virtue, this is the spirit we want Christ's lambs to imitate.[b]

a. James 4:7

b. 1 Corinthians 11:1
Philippians 2:5-8
Ephesians 5:1

Beloved, be alert to the dangers of a defective root system which can destroy you and your family. Because Satan is fully aware that whoever controls the children controls the future, one of his schemes is to weaken or destroy a mother's godly influence. He would love to ensnare you with the same sin that was his downfall—pride—and thereby conceivably capture the hearts and souls of your children as well.

Every day each of us repeatedly faces this choice: serve self, or God—follow Satan's way, or the Lord's. A friend of mine in school used to always repeat, "Only two choices on the shelf, pleasing God or pleasing self." Being a model of humility will help equip daughters to be virtuous wives and mothers. At the same time, by being a witness to this spirit of humility in the home, sons will be better prepared to assume future leadership, and to make a wise choice when ready to seek a wife.

Love, **unity**, **humility**: This trinity of graces is an essential part of the discipling process to show children what our beloved Savior is like. So is nurturing them in God's Word and His ways—the ultimate key to personally walking hand in hand with God!

My Walk—Hand in Hand With God

THE SECRET TO BEING A successful Word-filled wife and discipling mother is found in Joshua 1:7-9. Basically, God told Joshua, "If you want to prosper everywhere you go, do not turn to the right or to the left; stay on the straight path! If you want to be able to live according to My Word, you must be strong and very courageous. If you want to live prosperously and successfully, you must live according to all that I have written. If you want to live according to all that I have written, you must *meditate day and night in My Word*—and never ever let it be out of your mouth!" The principles of success that God impressed upon Joshua also apply to the leading of our children.

Have you ever had the privilege of knowing a woman who actually lived by Joshua 1:7-9? I have. It was 20 years ago, as a young first grade teacher, that I had the joy of getting a glimpse of a life that continues to touch my life to this day! That beautiful portrait of God's grace was an ultra-busy mother of eleven children. As a professional musician, teacher, wife and mother, she refused to compromise when it came to spending time with her Lord. Her daughter, Sharon, declared to me, "My mother cannot start her day without meeting with God. We are not to disturb her during her devotions. She needs to meet with Jesus for her daily strength."

Sharon was a student of mine, and a wonderful testimony to the reality of Ezekiel 16:44: *"As is the mother, so is her daughter."* Through her, I learned the beauty of a godly mother who is faithful to her Savior, and the simplicity with which a child who could not yet read or write could have devotions. Sharon's mother had taught it all:

- How is my personal time with God?
- Am I heavenly-hearted?
- Am I growing in Christ?
- Am I faithfully hearing, reading, studying, memorizing, and meditating upon the riches of God's Word?
- Is my prayer life abundant and powerful?
- Is prayer as natural as breathing?
- If my children are following me, are they becoming imitators of Christ?

It has been said, "You will never see God until you need Him." Do you need Him every day? Jesus Christ waits for you to meet with Him daily. Is your life so full that time spent with Christ has been crowded out by other activities? Consider one author's picture of Jesus Christ trying to contact you:

Subject: I Love You and Miss You
From: God2@heaven.com (Jesus Christ)
To: Mom@childofGod.com

I never thought I'd have to reach you this way,
but I wanted to make sure you would read this so
you would know how much I love and care for you.
Yesterday I saw you racing through the day. I heard
you laughing and talking with your friend from church
who telephoned you for advice. I had hoped that as
soon as you'd hung up, you'd want to talk with me
too. So as you prayed on the phone with your friend,
I painted a glorious sunset to close your day. I don't
think you even looked. You were already busy with
dishes and laundry. But I just kept on loving you.

As you sat down to work on ... plans for the next
school day, I saw you glancing at your watch and
yawning. I felt your frustration and tiredness. I wanted
to touch you and calm you. I spilled moonlight onto
your window and supplied a refreshing, warm breeze.
I thought maybe you would reach for my Word on
the way to bed, but instead you glanced at the news
and weather while you scanned your schedule for
the next day. You didn't even think of me. I wanted so
much to comfort and cheer you. I wanted you to come
near to me so I could show you I was there to love
you. Did you really think what was happening in your
world was more important than what was happening
in your relationship with me? I loved you anyway.

My love for you is richer than any account you could
land, and your need for me is greater than any entry on
your to do list. But I fear that outside of a direct miracle
there is no way I can get placed on your busy agenda.

Father sends his love; he cares too. Fathers are just
that way. So, please, call on me soon in any way that
suits you. Don't be afraid to call collect; the Holy Spirit
is ready to accept the charges. No matter how long it
takes, I'll keep trying to connect—because I love you.

Your Friend, Savior, and Lord,
Jesus[a]

a. Mark Sanborn, Terry Paulson
   *Meditations for the Road
   Warrior.*
   (Grand Rapids, Michigan:
   Baker Books, 1998) pp. 11–13

Would it take a personal e-mail from Jesus to get your attention?
Do you struggle with ways to find time to strengthen your faith? If
so, you are not alone, but God tells us that *"those who wait on the
LORD shall renew [their] strength; they shall mount up with wings
like eagles, they shall run and not be weary, they shall walk and not
faint"* (ISAIAH 40:31). I therefore exhort you to devote yourself
wholly to God and His Word. Your children *need* to see that your
faith is a personal, disciplined, and exclusive relationship with a
Person—Jesus Christ!

How to Establish a Personal Quiet Time

IT IS THROUGH CONSISTENT QUIET times with the Lord that you, dear sister in Christ, *can* "mount up with wings like eagles" to soar with your God! The following suggestions have worked well in my own life. Prayerfully consider each of these steps to success, and then consistently implement those ideas that will work best in your own situation.

STEP ONE: DEVELOP A PLAN

There is a saying that warns, "If you fail to plan, you plan to fail." (Personally, I even *plan* to exclude many things so that I can more fully focus on Christ.) The highest priority therefore is to create a plan that can establish a regular quiet time with the Lord. Choose a private, comfortable place where you can be alone with Him, without distractions. Plan to give the Lord your "best time"—early in the morning, before your family awakens. If you are not a morning person, ask Him to create this spirit in you: *"O God, You are my God; Early will I seek You; My soul thirsts for You; My flesh longs for You In a dry and thirsty land where there is no water"* (PSALM 63:1).

- Keep all your devotional materials together in one place: Bible, notebook, markers, pen, Bible commentary, Bible dictionary, hymn book, prayer journal or list, and even a favorite treat. This should be the sweetest time of the day with your "Best Friend," so yearn for it, and enjoy it!
- Be flexible and creative, but faithful. By spending 15 minutes a day, the average reader can read the whole Bible through in one year. Reading the Bible through twice a year is even better. Fifteen minutes in the morning and 15 minutes at night is all it takes! (Attorney David Gibbs of the Christian Law Association of Cleveland, Ohio once reported that his teen-aged son challenged him to read the Bible through once a month. Father and son did just that, and David said it revolutionized their lives!) Whatever you decide to do, make this your commitment: "No Bible, no breakfast; no Bible, no bed."

STEP TWO: MEMORIZE GOD'S WORD

Use the "Verses Every Believer Should Know" list in Appendix A, or customize your own list of verses to memorize. You may even wish to choose chapters or Books of the Bible to memorize. Keep verse cards in front of you all day long—in your pocket, on your desk, on the refrigerator, in your purse, in your Bible, on a kitchen counter, etc. If you want to be successful, meditate on the verses all day long.[a]

a. Joshua 1:8

Evangelist Ron Hood suggests this method of memorization: [b]

b. Ron Hood, *HOW TO SUCCESSFULLY MEMORIZE & REVIEW SCRIPTURE: HOLDING THE WORD OF GOD FOREVER*, (Greenville, SC: Spiritual Success Institute, 1974).

- Say the verse(s) 25 times the first day.
- Say the verse(s) 20 times the second day.
- Say the verse(s) 15 times the third day.
- Say the verse(s) 10 times the fourth day.
- Say the verse(s) 5 times the fifth day.
- Say the verse(s) once a day for a month.
- Say the verse(s) once a week for a month.
- Say the verse(s) once a month forever.

STEP THREE: PRAY FROM GOD'S WORD

Pray the Scriptures regularly for your husband and children. Apply Ephesians 3:8, 12, 14; and pray verses 16-21 for them. There are over 200 names of God in the Scriptures.[c] As you come across one of His names in Scripture, mark it in your Bible, and then write it on a list to remember. As you go through the list, pray that God will be known to you and your family. Later we will cover this topic in depth, but for now here are a few simple suggestions:

c. For a free list of these many names and titles of God to get you started on your personal study, e-mail us at namesofgod@dtbm.org and we will send you this exciting study.

- Make prayer lists in a personal prayer journal. A three-ring notebook with dividers for each family member works great!
- Pray for salvation, then sanctification—from infancy through adulthood—that each may become a useful servant of the Lord.
- Make Word-filled prayer a priority, because it is the key that unlocks the doors to your children's hearts!

Remember that the apostles said that before the ministry comes prayer.[d] So ask, seek, and knock at the door of our heavenly Father for the strength to accomplish this goal. It takes *work* to be disciplined in all these areas, but the *rewards* for faithfulness are endless.

d. Acts 6:4; Matthew 7:7

Let us now move on to how to lead our children to walk hand in hand with their everlasting God!

LEADING YOUR CHILDREN TO WALK HAND IN HAND WITH GOD

Our children, in a very real spiritual sense, have the hands of their little hearts reaching out to us as they say, from the depths of their beings, "Hold my hand, Mommy! Lead me so I don't get lost!" Holding your children's hands, lead them step-by-step to faithfully walk by the truths represented in this wonderful old children's hymn:

> *Little children, come to Jesus; Hear Him saying, "Come to Me"—*
> *Blessed Jesus, who to save us shed His blood on Calvary.*
> *Little souls were made to serve Him, All His holy law fulfill;*
> *Little hearts were made to love Him, Little hands to do His will;*
> *Little eyes to read the Bible, Given from the Heavens above,*
> *Little ears to hear the story, Of the Savior's wondrous love,*
> *Little tongues to sing His praises, little feet to walk His ways,*
> *Little bodies to be temples, Where the Holy Spirit stays.*[a]

a. Mrs. C. L. Holmes,
"*Little Children, Come to Jesus,*"
The Children's Hymn Book
(Grand Rapids, MI: The
National Union of Christian
Schools [now Christian
Schools International], 1962),
pp. 162–163.

Practically speaking, this type of discipling occurs through teaching children God's Word "*precept upon precept, line upon line, here a little, there a little*" (ISAIAH 28:10). The importance of this can never be overstated.

How to Establish Quiet Times for Children

YOU WILL NEVER LEAD YOUR children higher than where you already are. Do you want your children to be strong and courageous—to not be afraid because they know God will never forsake them? Do you desire that they have good success in His eyes? If so, be a model mother by consistently trusting and following the Lord. Then lead your children to likewise never let God's Word out of their presence. Teach them diligently to hear, read, study, memorize, and meditate upon the preciousness of God's Word!

Providing the right environment will lay the best foundation for their spiritual growth. When one of our sons was little and he was hungry, he ate all the candy and cookies he could find. So I had to take away the "junk food" and replace it with good, nourishing food. In the same manner, because we want our children to hunger after the Bread of Life, we don't feed them the "junk food" of always watching exhilarating television or movies, or playing with toys that "do everything." When they are young, John and I simplify their lives by consistently choosing what is God's best for them.

As a discipling mother, look for opportunities all day long to talk to your children about God.[a] He wants you to lead them to talk to Him through prayer, and to listen to Him through His Word. They are always watching you, and will want to know, "Who is this God?" Show them that God speaks, hears, listens, cares, answers, teaches, directs, comforts, commands, and promises. The more you yourself are in the Word, the more His Word will naturally minister through you as you tenderly care for your children in their dark nights, splinters, cut knees, bruises, accomplishments, failures, relationships, worries, fears, thanksgivings, burdens for others, and hopes for the future. As a gentle shepherd, lead your lambs to trust the Good Shepherd.

a. Deuteronomy 6:5-7

PRACTICAL SUGGESTIONS FOR CHILDREN: Keeping that home atmosphere in mind, let us now turn to a few practical suggestions for how to further hold your children's hands as you lead them to walk hand in hand with God.

1. Quiet Times for Babies. John and I began to teach our children from the womb that the greatest gift they could ever receive is the gift of eternal life through Jesus Christ, who alone offers forgiveness and payment for our sin. Modern day experts have discovered what the Bible said 2,000 years ago—that babies can hear and react 3 months before birth. The Bible records that 3 months before John the Baptist was born, he recognized the presence of the Lord Jesus Christ in Mary's womb. He was also filled with the Spirit from the womb.[b] So, here are some suggestions according to what has worked well with babies in our own family:

b. Luke 1:15, 39-44

- Give them their own Bible to hold and carry.
- Hold them on your lap during devotions and Bible reading.
- Hold their hands to pray before meals, in
  the car, and throughout the day.
- Before bed, read from the Bible and/or a pictorial Bible story book.
- On their first-words-to-learn list, be sure to include
  "Bible," "Jesus," "Thank you," and "Amen."
- As their vocabulary grows, teach them to talk to God
  in prayer about everything. As soon as they attempt
  to say "Thank you," lead them to respond to God in
  thanksgiving for even the simplest things in life.

2. Quiet Times for Toddlers. It is at this age that John and I begin emphasizing that God is alive. He is a Spirit and does not have a body like man. He is the Creator, Sustainer, and Redeemer of us all. God made us unique and loves us so much that He gave His only Son to die for our sins, and He wants to spend time with us.

Never underestimate how much toddlers can perceive about spiritual matters. God tells adults to become as little children because their faith in Him is so simplistic.[a] You may be surprised at some of the questions they ask. I recall our son asking questions like: "Does God save us *always?*" and "Does God protect us *always?*" His brother wanted to know: "Can God hug me? Can I hug God? Can I hug Jesus?" Here are some suggestions for **toddlers**:

a. Matthew 18:3

- Give them their own Bible and Bible case.
- Establish a daily "quiet time" for them to think about God and pray.
- Read to them from the Bible, a pictorial
  children's Bible, or a Bible story book.
- Lead them to respond to God by listening to His teachings
  in the Word. Ask questions such as: "What do we learn about
  Jesus from these verses (or story)? Will He do that for you?"
- Have your toddlers draw pictures in a blank book or journal about
  what they think about God or a Bible story. Underneath the pictures,
  record what they have to say about their drawings. (You may wish
  to save special ones for a memory scrapbook or spiritual journal.)
- Teach them how to trust and thank God by regularly pointing
  out ways He takes care of them and His creation all around us.

3. Quiet Times for Beginning or Struggling Readers. At this general age, John and I teach our children that they need to realize they have a big problem—sin. But God solved that problem in the Person of Jesus Christ. We use the Bible to explain salvation, and regularly share our own testimonies of what Christ has done for us personally. Here are some suggestions for **young children**:

- Establish a schedule for reading the Bible one Book at a time. Write the dates in the Bible when each Book was started and completed.
- Have them make a Bible notebook to record what they're learning, and a prayer journal to enter prayer requests and answers.
- Encourage them to nightly ask themselves accountability questions like these: "What did we read in the Bible during family devotions today? What did God teach me? What promises did He make? What commands? What lessons can I learn from what we read? How should I respond to God? What is my prayer to God? What answers has He already given?" Make bedtime an unhurried time to talk about the Lord.
- Teach them to apply what they've been learning about God by asking themselves: "What would Jesus do in this situation?"
- Reward Bible reading or memorization. (C. H. Spurgeon's grandfather paid for every Bible verse and hymn young Spurgeon committed to memory.) Use a chart or bulletin board to keep track of their progress. Reward with home-made certificates, coupons, or tickets that can be redeemed for worthwhile "treasures" you and the children decide upon ahead of time. Don't forget the kisses and words of encouragement! A warm look and a "well done" may be the greatest reward you could give your child.
- Pray for missionaries together. Even young children can send cards, pictures, and prayer letters to get to know the many missionaries around the world. Write to missionaries together, invite them into your home, or share a meal when they are in your area.
- Have discipleship tea parties. Ingredients: lemonade, iced tea, juice, or even just water; special treat; lace, china cups, a candle; your Bibles; one child; about 15 minutes of your time—and your hearts ready to be blessed. (To emphasize the purpose of your time together, you may wish to set a third place for the Lord.) Read from your Bibles together, and pray. Talk about the lesson, what has been learned, and listen to what your child has to say. (Even our boys loved these when they were little!)

4. Quiet Times for Independent Readers to Adult. We train our children, by this point, to understand that to grow in Christ, they must continually be seeking to know Him better, and to love and worship Him in spirit and in truth. Here are some suggestions applicable to **older children**:

- Oversee that quiet times with their favorite Bible are consistent.
- Lead them to study particular topics such as: names of God, paths of discipleship, "fear not" passages, prayers in the Bible, evangelism, understanding God's will, and others.
- As a supplement, have them study missionary biographies.
- Have them keep a personal prayer and devotions journal to record their ongoing growth toward spiritual maturity.
- Celebrate their spiritual birthday with a date; share lunch alone and ask them important questions about their walk with Christ.
- Schedule discipleship dates one-on-one at a coffee shop. Be the one to "officially" disciple your child.

Encourage your older children to regularly examine themselves; here is one suggested personal accountability check list:

- How was my time with the Lord? Was I still? (There are eight different Hebrew words for "waiting.") God wants your children to be trained to follow: *"Be still, and know that I [am] God; I will be exalted among the nations, I will be exalted in the earth!"* (Psalm 46:10).
- Did I live in my own strength this week—or in the Lord's?
- How did I do with taking thoughts captive— holding them obedient to Christ?
- How was my submission to the Spirit? Did I keep in step, grieve, or quench Him?
- How was my prayer time? What is God showing me?
- How did I do with my priorities and what are they?
- Did I invest in the eternal this week?
- Did I live in grace—accepting the forgiveness of God and others?
- Was I content and thankful, or did I murmur and grumble in my heart?
- Did I trust God?

BUILD SWEET MEMORIES OF
THEIR SPIRITUAL JOURNEY

The final discipleship idea, for all ages of children, is to keep a "Spiritual Journey Journal" or "Spiritual Journey Scrapbook" for each child. In a journal, record events such as: when they learned to pray, special prayers and how God answered them, when they were saved, date of their baptism, special Bible reading or memorization accomplishments, spiritual challenges, and overall spiritual growth. My friend Beth calls these "deposits in their faith bank."

A "Spiritual Journey Scrapbook" could include both photos and special written memories. The week after our fourth son prayed to be saved, for example, he came to me in a genuinely downcast state and said with concern, "God only saved half of me!" Puzzled, I asked, "Why is that, Jeremiah?" His response? "Because I still get angry at *Joseph!*" (Joseph is one of his brothers.) That is a sweet memory I don't want to forget!

Take photos of special events like these: dedication to the Lord, the day of each child's salvation, baptism, witnessing, family communion, testimonies, and each "spiritual birthday" you celebrate together. The purpose of both the "Spiritual Journey Journal" and "Spiritual Journey Scrapbook" is to build a book of remembrance[a] that will always remind them of God's everlasting hand in their lives.

a. Malachi 3:16

Keeping Your Hand in God's Everlasting Hand

ALWAYS REMEMBER THAT IF YOU keep your hand in God's—by knowing Him personally and having a growing relationship through His Word and prayer—you will stand in God's place to show your children what He is like so that they, too, may ultimately place their hands in the everlasting and wondrous "hand of God"! Never forget that:

- His is the hand that protects (Exodus 33:22).
- His is the hand that disciplines (Hebrews 12:3-11).
- His is the hand that keeps promises (Genesis 24:2).
- His is the hand that saves (Judges 7:2).

- His is the hand that provides for physical needs (Numbers 11:23).
- His is the hand that holds us (Deuteronomy 33:2).
- His is the hand that punishes disobedience (1 Samuel 5:11).
- His is the hand that shows mercy (2 Samuel 24:14).
- His is the hand that gives grace (Ezra 7:9; Nehemiah 2:18).
- His is the hand that holds the life of every creature and the breath of all mankind (Job 12:10).
- His is the hand that holds eternal pleasures (Psalm 16:11).
- His is the hand that gives us satisfaction with our daily work (Ecclesiastes 2:24).
- His is the hand that punishes sin (Isaiah 5:25).
- His is the hand that rules in power (Isaiah 40:10).
- His is the hand that gathers His lambs and holds them close to His heart, gently leading them (Isaiah 40:11).
- His is the hand that has measured the waters and marked off the heavens (Isaiah 40:12).
- His is the hand that holds us securely (John 10:29).
- His is the hand that was pierced for our sin, and beckons us to believe and follow Him (John 20:27).

And for those of you whose family is still growing in numbers, as a mother of eight children I can testify that you are in for the adventure of your life! Having a large family definitely gives you more of *everything!*

More laundry …
More shoes to find for Sunday morning …
More socks to match and holes to mend …
More noses to blow …
More tears to wipe …
More knees to bandage …
More hearts to comfort …
More secrets to share …
More hugs and kisses …
More sins to sorrow over …
More opportunities to teach the Word of God …
More to trust God for—and thus more to pray about …
And, best of all, more hands to place in His!

Amy Carmichael, John Paton, Corrie Ten Boom, Elisabeth Elliot. What do these dear saints all have in common? They all learned to trust and honor God with their whole life at the knee of their mothers, who ultimately placed their hands in God's hands! When your children open the windows of their soft and yielded hearts to your discipling, be prepared to pour in the love of Christ and taste the sweetness of the greatest ministry a mother can ever have!

If we humbly walk with our God as He instructs us, follow His Spirit as He guides us, and obey His Word as He reveals His way, then we can be called blessed by our children and be praised by our husband.[a]

a. Proverbs 31:28

But most of all, if we faithfully obey the Lord by His grace, and finish the course He has mapped out for us—we can live with no regrets. And on that great day when we are ushered into the very presence of the Lamb of God, our "King of kings," we will hold His everlasting hand and hear His words: *"Well done, good and faithful servant; ... Enter into the joy of your Lord"* (MATTHEW 25:21).

STUDY GUIDE QUESTIONS

1. **During this short life on earth—this prelude to eternity—God has assigned parents the role of standing in His place to show our children what He is like.** As a Word-filled mother, God wants to use you to disciple your children for Christ—even if you do not have a believing husband.

   Read 2 Timothy 1:3-5 and 3:14-15. What influence did Lois and Eunice have upon Timothy as he was growing up? Read 2 Timothy 3:16-17. List four ways in which Scripture is "profitable" for bringing children up in the nurture and admonition of the Lord. What does God say should be your ultimate goal?

2. **Where should you begin to "hold your children's hands" to train and disciple them for Christ?** Read Ephesians 6:1-2a and Colossians 3:20. What is the most important character quality to instill into your children from the very beginning of their lives?

How should that training affect their relationship
with Christ as they mature?

**3. Is there a way to train and disciple your children so that they are
not robbed of the pure joy of honoring and obeying the Lord and
you?** Read 1 Corinthians 11:1.
Modeling Christlikeness is an ongoing growth process.
Read 2 Peter 1:3-8. Is the Lord speaking to your heart
concerning graces that He wants you—through His
power— to diligently work on to be more like Him?

**4. As you keep a steady focus on the Lord, and search for His
unchanging truths, God will help you to increasingly model the
characteristics of a genuine disciple of Christ.** What characteristic
should be outstanding in your life? Read John 13:34-35.
Do you love your children unconditionally—regardless
of whether or not they perform according to your
expectations? If this is a struggle for you, make John
13:34-35 a regular prayer for yourself—and your family.

**5. Discipling your children for Christ is a ministry; Scripture clearly
identifies a priority for successful ministry.** What is it? Read Acts 6:4.
If you have not already done so, I urge you to make Word-filled prayer
for your children (and husband) a commitment from now on.
What does Christ say is a prerequisite to fruitful
prayers? Read John 15:5 and 7-8.

13

"And He said to me, 'My grace is sufficient for you, for My strength is made perfect in weakness.'"

— *2 Corinthians 12:9*

Learning From Great Women of the Word

Note: In chapter 2, I discussed five special women—the "Women Energized by Hope." Each of these ladies was a beautiful portrait of God's grace. And now, you are in for a real treat as my dear wife, Bonnie, shares from the riches God has taught her through both biblical and modern-day women whose lives demonstrate His grace so well!

"The older women likewise, that they be reverent in behavior, not slanderers, not given to much wine, teachers of good things—that they admonish the young women to love their husbands, to love their children, to be discreet, chaste, homemakers, good, obedient to their own husbands, that the Word of God may not be blasphemed" (TITUS 2:3-5).

I DIDN'T KNOW, AS AN unsaved child, what my future would hold, or how it would be shaped. I simply accepted that whatever would be, would be. I became a rebellious, independent, strong-willed, daring, sinful young woman. Yet, in God's mercy, Christ drew me up out of the miry pit I was in at age twenty-one, and He set my feet firmly upon the Rock.[a] He graciously forgave my sins and washed me white as snow![b]

My heavenly Potter then gently took the clay of my soft and yielded heart and began molding me into a vessel fit for my Master's use. Based upon God's Word, which I thirsted for continually, I started to make right choices and form lifelong godly habits. I meditated upon His laws, sang His praises, and prayed ceaselessly, often breathing His name in prayer aloud throughout my days. I served the Lord joyfully at every opportunity—witnessing door-to-door, teaching little children, and sharing my testimony of God's grace from New York to California.

When reflecting back upon what I have learned in my journey, my thoughts turn gratefully to the Titus 2 women who have greatly enriched my life. As a young Christian growing in the Lord, I discovered that not only would God mold me through daily personal times with Him and the preaching of His Word, but He would also teach me through the example of others—especially the godly women He placed in my path. Though I knew nothing of Titus 2 at the time, because I yearned to please Christ, I soon found myself carefully studying the lives of women in Scripture, and then observing faithful women living around me. Please join me now as I turn the yellowing pages of my life's photo album to view those "portraits of grace" who have enriched my life so immensely.

1. **Jochebed**: A Mother Who Feared God, Not Man
2. **Elizabeth**: A Righteous Mother Whose Autumn Years God Blessed
3. **Mary**: A Mother Who Praised God in Unexpected Circumstances
4. **Anna**: A Widow Devoted to God
5. **Mary and Martha**: Sisters With Open Hearts and an Open Home
6. **Lydia**: A Business Woman Yielded in Spirit, Serving the Lord
7. **Lois**: A Grandmother With Genuine Faith

In Titus 2:3-5 we see God emphasizing the rare value of older women and the wisdom of learning from them. Imagine a garden full of fragrant flowers. I believe if you pay attention to those God has planted around you, you'll discover that God has placed you in a garden of rich blooms from which you may glean life-changing truths and grow through their godly example.

a. Psalm 40:2
b. Isaiah 1:18

Cultivate the practice of looking around you—as you read about these "everyday" women, seek out the virtuous women God has planted in your life; then begin growing from observing and imitating their righteous example! And then, as the years pass—be a Titus 2 woman to those that God brings into **your life**!

God's "Portraits of Grace"

1. JOCHEBED: A MOTHER WHO FEARED GOD, NOT MAN

"The name of Amram's wife [was] Jochebed the daughter of Levi, who was borne to Levi in Egypt; and to Amram she bore Aaron and Moses and their sister Miriam" (NUMBERS 26:59).

"By faith Moses, when he was born, was hidden three months by his parents, because they saw he was a beautiful child; and they were not afraid of the king's command" (HEBREWS 11:23).

Have you ever played Bible Trivia and missed this one: "Who was the mother of Moses?" Like many mothers, Jochebed's greatness was not found in the public limelight, but through the faith, courage, and devotion she invested in the lives of her children. Jochebed's name, to the average Bible reader, is unnoticed and overlooked. However, in the eyes of the Lord, she was a woman of noble character because she feared God, not man. Jochebed was able to discern the eternal from the temporal—because she believed in God's faithfulness. Her faith affected her life and home. Her blessings were great because she gave so much of herself away. Her name means "the glory of God." This remarkable woman is listed among the heroines of faith in Hebrews 11. Her name is not given; only her title is provided—*"the parent of Moses."* Jochebed's life represents a beautiful portrait of motherhood, one which still speaks to us today through God's record of the fruitful lives of Aaron, Moses, and Miriam.

In 1984, the Lord allowed me to meet and learn from a "modern-day Jochebed." Joy's husband planted churches and smuggled Bibles into communist lands for 43 years. Serving in cold, damp, unfriendly Germany—often without hot water and little heat, no relatives, few friends, and only the Christians they led to the Lord—Joy, like Jochebed, was able to discern between eternal values and merely temporal ones. One afternoon in Germany, I had the privilege of standing in her kitchen as she faced an avalanche of ministry opportunities. Joy cheerfully stretched what food she had to prepare dinner to feed guests, listened to one of her six children's homework recitations, encouraged her husband, and then instructed me as a young wife and mother. She was a wonder to my young eyes watching her serve so graciously!

Two years later, I was with Joy when she visited her sister here in the States. We arrived just as her sister finished a dip in the pool, prepared to grill gourmet salmon steaks, and sipped freshly-brewed iced tea. Though the sisters resembled each other greatly in physical appearance, I was struck with the great contrast in their lifestyles. The sisters were living with totally different values and goals in life. One woman was living for the pleasures and luxuries of this world while the other had chosen to live for the riches of eternity. Joy couldn't wait to return to her mission field of Germany (and her six children). This woman feared God rather than man; she had consistently chosen the eternal over the temporal and became a modern-day portrait of Jochebed.

PRAYER OF YOUR HEART:

Prayerfully look around you to find a woman of example like Jochebed or Joy who has chosen to invest in the eternal rather than the temporal. Take a moment to journal her story and your prayer of commitment to live for the eternal, not the temporal.

I observed the heavenly focus of Joy's life; I treasured the lesson in my heart and silently prayed, *"Lord, help me to throw aside every weight of this world which so easily hinders me. Let me grow into a woman who lives for eternity's riches with my eyes fixed on the Author and Finisher of my Faith—Jesus Christ. Amen."*

2. Elizabeth: A Righteous Mother Whose Autumn Years God Blessed

"Now indeed, Elizabeth your relative has also conceived a son in her old age; and this is now the sixth month for her who was called barren. For with God nothing will be impossible" (LUKE 1:36-37; see also LUKE 1:5-80).

I love the autumn season which marks the end of another year's cycles! Seed time, spring blossoms, and summer's fruits are soon passed. Trees are preparing to shed their leaves, and the earth will soon lie sleeping in winter's cold. But with God, things are not always as they appear. He delights in doing the impossible. His children are often one faith-step away from the miraculous and unexpected. Elizabeth was in the autumn years of her life and she was to savor spring time again. Her name means "God is my oath"; her life is a testimony of God's faithfulness to His Word and His tender mercies toward His children. She is a reminder that God never forgets or abandons His own; His timing is always perfect. Elizabeth was privileged to be the first woman to confess Jesus' coming in the flesh and to experience the glory of His presence as no one ever had before. In a beautiful way, through the birth of her son, John, God made the latter years of this righteous woman the most precious of all.

Autumn came early in the life of my mother, Lavone. Mom was forty-nine when diagnosed with ovarian cancer. I was, at that time, a 9-month-old Christian who had committed my life to serve the Lord in any way He wanted. I had only been at a Bible college for one month when the phone call came conveying my mother's diagnosis. This represented the autumn of Mom's life; yet, in dying she was to taste spring again, as Elizabeth did. Just as Elizabeth was blessed with the birth of her son, Mom was blessed with the spiritual birth of her daughter. We were thus able to share many beautiful moments recalling God's goodness—His blessings, rich mercies, and faithfulness! The perfect timing of my salvation before my mother's "graduation to heaven" is etched in my heart as a portrait of God's perfect timing, and one of His precious gifts of love. In a sense, as with Elizabeth of the Bible, I believe God made the latter years of my mother, a righteous woman, the most precious of all!

My 95-year-old grandmother, Nanny, also experienced God's riches in her autumn years. She was passing through the last season of her earthy life. Sitting by her bed, holding her frail, soft hand, she looked straight into my eyes. Nan pondered her years and sadly shared, "I guess I have a lot to atone for." I was blessed to share with her the Good News: that is exactly what Jesus did for us. He atoned for our sins because we could never pay for our own sins. Jesus Christ died for my sins according to the Scriptures. He gave Himself for me. Nanny placed her faith in Jesus Christ that day—the Son of God who atoned for all her sins (mine and yours also)—and received the gift of eternal life! Two months later she was ushered into the presence of her Savior.

God's tender mercies are new every morning. Perhaps you are in the autumn season of life on earth. If you don't have the peace and joy of eternal life, today is the day to turn to Jesus for forgiveness of your sins and to receive God's wonderful gift of eternal life.

"For God so loved the world that He gave His only begotten Son that whosoever believeth in Him should not perish but have everlasting life. For God sent not His Son into the world to condemn the world but that the world through Him might be saved" (JOHN 3:16, 17, KJV).

PRAYER OF YOUR HEART:

Is there an Elizabeth or Lavone in your pathway of life—one whose latter years God has made her most precious? Share her journey of faith here along with your prayer of commitment to ask God to also use you in every season of life.

"Dear Lord, I know that I belong to You. By grace I have been saved by faith, and that not of myself—I have received Your free gift of everlasting life. When it is my time to walk through my autumn season, help me to trust You and rest securely in your tender mercies."

3. MARY: A MOTHER WHO PRAISED GOD IN UNEXPECTED CIRCUMSTANCES

"Now the birth of Jesus Christ was as follows: After His mother Mary was betrothed to Joseph, before they came together, she was found with child of the Holy Spirit" (MATTHEW 1:18; see also MATTHEW 12:46; LUKE 1-2; JOHN 2:1-11, 19:25; ACTS 1:14).

Mary has been honored more than any other woman in history. God chose her to be the physical vessel to bring forth the Messiah into the world. She was given the honor of nurturing Jesus, helping to raise Him, and being one of His earthly guardians until manhood. Mary knew both great sorrow and great joy. In her poverty, she possessed the truest of riches! Having no earthly title, she was joined to the royal line. Yet as an unwed, teenaged mother, she surely bore the scorn of many in her little village. Her faith, obedience, and quietness of heart are an expression of inward beauty that is well-pleasing to God. Mary is exalted among women because of her profound humility and deep sense of personal unworthiness. She never claimed perfection or boasted of self-righteousness; her response to God's chosen path for her life is a praise song to God Almighty. Mary knew that all she had been given was a result of God's marvelous grace!

Mary was so prepared with her knowledge and understanding of Scripture. She had learned much at her father's knee as he served at the local synagogue in Sepphoris (next door to Nazareth). When what many called disaster came into her life—**Mary trusted God and humbly sang praises to her God** (Luke 1:46-55).

In 1995 God brought Ann into my life. Serving together in church ministries, we became prayer partners and friends. Ann is a joy-filled mother of three children. As in Mary's life, the unexpected entered Ann's life suddenly. Just after celebrating her fortieth birthday, Ann received news that cancer had infected her body.

Ann's story is a story of a woman in the bloom of life stricken down with near death and disease. If disease or disappointment greets you tomorrow, are you prepared to bow before Almighty God and sing His praises that the world may know that there is a God in heaven?

Here is Ann's story in her own words:

"Ann, you have breast cancer," were the words that started a spiritual journey for our family. For someone else, the words may be one of these life-changers: "Honey, I've lost my job"; "Let's test for MS"; "We have to move"; "You have a terminal illness"—or a ringing phone late at night reporting the death of a loved one. Why do seemingly "bad" things have to happen? Why must we go through trials? Scripture gives many reasons that answer the "Why, Lord?" questionings of His hurting children.

One reason is told in Psalm 119:71: "It was good for me to be afflicted so that I might learn your decrees." Another is in Psalm 119:92-93: "If your law had not been my delight, I would have perished in my affliction. I will never forget your precepts, for by them you have preserved my life." That tells us that God wants us to depend on Him completely.

Right after I got home from the diagnosis appointment, my husband, Duke, and I admitted to each other that we were scared and worried. We knew we had to turn to the Lord in prayer and depend on His Word for comfort. We found a promise to us from our Good Shepherd in Isaiah 41:10: "So do not be afraid, for I am with you, do not be dismayed, for I am your God. I will strengthen you and help you. I will uphold you with my righteous right hand." God took away our fear and replaced it with a peace.

Some of you may be facing a serious dilemma right now—perhaps a job loss, financial hardship, relational conflict, or physical problems. In such times, we normally want to pray, "Lord, remove this hardship … ease the pain … take it away." Yet, God often gives a "No" or "Wait" reply. But He has promised to deliver us as we depend on Him. I'm told that the Hebrew word for "deliver" means "to be liberated, equipped to fight, to strengthen." God will deliver those whose hearts are set on Him; however, the deliverance will be in His way, and for His purposes. Instant rescue is rarely the Lord's way. Daniel was delivered, but he still had to spend a night in the lions' den. God spared Abraham from sacrificing Isaac, but Abraham still had to take that long trip up Mt. Moriah. Martha and Mary wanted Jesus to heal Lazarus, but Jesus wanted to do more: He wanted to confirm in their hearts that He was the Messiah; He wanted to deepen their trust; He wanted to make the strongest possible impression on the unbelieving

Jews at the tomb. In other words, Jesus wanted to bring glory to God.

How focused we can become on our own little world, and how easily we grow impatient. We forget that our Father has bigger plans for us—plans to do with His kingdom. Sometimes, this means that He will not answer on the day we cry, but He will always answer.

To have greater intimacy with God is yet another reason for trials. He allows trials for the purpose of revealing Himself more fully to us. Consider His wonderful revelations in just Psalm 145 alone: "The Lord is gracious and compassionate ... good to all ... faithful to all His promises ... loving toward all He has made ... upholds all those who fall and lifts up all who are bowed down ... righteous in all His ways ... near to all who call on Him ... fulfills the desires of those who fear Him ... watches over all who love Him ... My mouth will speak in praise of the Lord."

Our family saw these characteristics of our Lord displayed throughout my year of multiple surgeries and chemotherapy. Over and over He demonstrated His faithfulness, graciousness, righteousness, and love through answered prayer. During all this, Duke and I asked the Lord to use my illness to draw our neighbors closer to Himself. Later we learned that at the same time we were praying a couple in Arizona were also praying for their daughter and son-in-law who had recently moved next door to us. They were specifically praying that neighbors would show them the love of Jesus. You can imagine our delight on the day their daughter came to my home to tell me through tears that she had come back to the Lord after having strayed away for many years! She told me that God had used my response to breast cancer to get her attention. She and I have continued to meet biweekly; and she is reading her Bible regularly, memorizing Scripture, and praying for her husband.

When we find ourselves most helpless, the road most taxing, it is then that the Risen Christ comes and makes Himself known to us. This is the one pure joy for those who sorrow.

We can have true rest as we travel through any trial, for God says, "Come to Me, all you who labor and are heavy laden, and I will give you rest. Take My yoke upon you and learn from Me, for I am gentle and lowly in heart, and you will find rest for your souls. For My yoke is easy and My burden is light" (Matthew 11:28-30). If we want rest, we must first do something: "Come." The search for true rest is ended once and for all in coming to Christ. Does life weigh heavily upon you? Are you hurting? Are you tired of trying to please man? Are you tired of struggling to "fix" a situation? Have you lost hope? You always have a place to go for rest. Better yet, you have a Person to go to. Only Christ can give you complete, satisfying rest. Rest from bitter memories, a broken heart, disappointments, anxiety, or worry. It is inward rest that refreshes and renews for continued service. This rest allows you to trust in the guidance and care of your loving Father.

The goal of trials is not to be comfortable and have everything turn out fine. No, God wants us to dependently, restfully, come to Him so that He can show Himself to us. In His perfect timing, He has a plan to grow us up into the likeness of His Son, Jesus Christ. As we trust and obey, we can make an impact on our dying world: we can demonstrate the genuine faith that overcomes—no matter the circumstances. The world does not want to be told. They must be shown. Wouldn't the world (and our children) learn godliness better if they saw examples of contentment instead of complaints? Obedience instead of rebellion? Peace instead of frustration?

Through this journey of breast cancer, our family has learned to depend upon God first. He gave us rest from anxiety and worry, and revealed Himself to us, His children, in every part of our lives. Learning to wait on the Lord with confident expectation is the best thing we did! We grew closer to the Lord through this trial—more than at any other time in our lives.[a]

a. Quoted from actual e-mails received from Duke and Ann Weir of Owasso, Oklahoma sent out during their fight with cancer.

—Ann and Duke Weir

Whether you are faced with a life-threatening struggle or mundane daily dilemmas (dead car battery, long line at the check out counter, headache, unkind word, forgotten thank you, and so forth), be sure to ask yourself these questions: *Is God trustworthy? Is He sovereign, loving and good? Is He faithful to His promises?* If you find the answer is yes, then you will soar like the eagles above the conflict and people will see your good works and glorify your Father in heaven.

PRAYER OF YOUR HEART:

Look around you to find a woman like Mary or Ann—a woman who has been through unexpected changes and circumstances and praised God through it all. Record her story of faith here and your own prayer of commitment to offer the sacrifice of praise to God when life brings the unexpected.

_____

_____

_____

If disease or disappointment greets you in the morning, are you prepared to bow before God Almighty? *"Lord, help me to be so prepared, so girded by your Word that when troubles come, my life overflows in songs of praise to You—that all the world may know there is a God in heaven!"*

4. ANNA: A WIDOW DEVOTED TO GOD

"Now there was one, Anna, a prophetess, the daughter of Phanuel, of the tribe of Asher. She was of a great age, and had lived with a husband seven years from her virginity; and this woman [was] a widow of about eighty-four years, who did not depart from the temple, but served [God] with fastings and prayers night and day. And coming in that instant she gave thanks to the Lord, and spoke of Him to all those who looked for redemption in Jerusalem" (LUKE 2:36-38).

The name "Anna" means "favor" or "grace." Widowed as a young woman, she spent decades of her life devoted to the Lord, quietly bearing the sweet fragrance of God's presence. Though never in the spotlight, such was the honor of her life that thousands of mothers have named their daughters after her. Her greatest privilege was to be the one who would herald the coming of the Messiah to Jerusalem. For one brief moment, her eyes looked upon the face of Jesus for whom she'd waited her whole life! She was given the privilege of being the first woman missionary to announce the good news of His coming to others. Anna's life is a testament of hope and faithfulness—a message of the beauty of waiting upon God, being loyal to Him in service, and trusting Him to fulfill His promises with perfect timing.

Are there Annas living around you? Has God put someone in your life who has lost her husband, is left alone, and yet is serving God faithfully all her days?

My wonderful friend, Eva, moved to California in the 1930s. She and her new husband lived in the San Fernando Valley, where they became involved in a local church. Eva's husband divorced her, after many years of marriage, and she was left alone. She suffered emotionally from the pain of a broken heart and home for years afterwards—and also from a crippling physical disorder. Many women suffer, but Eva's response to her physical and emotional pain is what made her one of my life long heroines. Eva seldom talked about her own suffering. Instead she quietly and faithfully served the Lord in many capacities. She volunteered weekly at a new ministry center; she served faithfully every week in outreach and children's ministries at her church; she served in the nurseries, Sunday schools, and hospitality ministries every Sunday morning. In Eva's life, as in Anna's, I saw the importance of waiting upon God daily for His sufficiency, through pain being loyal to Him, and through loneliness trusting Him to fulfill His promises perfectly—to my last breath.

PRAYER OF YOUR HEART:

Perhaps God has placed an Anna or Eva in your pathway. Are you encouraging her in her lonely walk through life? Share her story here along with your own personal words of prayer.

_____

_____

_____

"Father, if You choose to allow me to walk alone through life's journey, may I know that You are with me and will never forsake me. May I wait upon You—for You are daily my all-sufficient strength and joy!"

5. MARY AND MARTHA: SISTERS WITH OPEN HEARTS AND AN OPEN HOME

"Now it happened as they went that He entered a certain village; and a certain woman named Martha welcomed Him into her house"
(LUKE 10:38; see also LUKE 10:39-42; JOHN 11, 12:1-3).

If Mary and Martha were living today, they would fit right into most church's women's ministries. Although Martha was corrected by Jesus in Luke 10:41 and Mary was commended for choosing the better part—Martha was a woman of action, with the heart of a servant. Mary stands as our example of a woman who valued being in the presence of Jesus and chose that precious opportunity as her highest priority. Both sisters saw their home as an opportunity to serve family and to extend the blessings of hospitality to friends and strangers. Like the Proverbs 31 woman, Martha worked willingly with her hands, giving attention to details, providing the very best that she could. Martha devoted herself to the needs of her guests. Mary and Martha were used to create warm hospitality, from which guests left feeling both ministered to and refreshed. Even Jesus found Mary and Martha's home to be a welcoming haven of warmth and fellowship! And it was through His visits that Martha learned of the rest and worship that her spirit lacked.

Are you cultivating a ministry of hospitality in your life? Years ago, as a newlywed, I was encouraged to exercise these gifts by a gracious friend named Joannie.

I met Joannie in a Sunday school class and little did I know what big lessons I would learn from her! Both her home and very presence were a welcoming haven: home-cooked meals, curtains she had fashioned, flowers she'd planted, a Bible always open, and words of wisdom and encouragement always upon her tongue. I watched her face trials with growing teenagers and trust God with an aging mother, always growing with continual hope in the Lord.

"She opens her mouth with wisdom, and on her tongue is the law of kindness. She watches over the ways of her household, and does not eat the bread of idleness" (PROVERBS 31:26-27).

Sometimes it is the simplest things in life that are the most profound. Joannie touched my life with her graciousness when our first child was born. She arrived on my doorstep with her home-cooked meal on a lovely tray, adorned with a fresh rose and cloth napkins. Another time, noticing we had no chair for our living room, Joannie found one for us. The list of ways in which Joannie touched my life is long; she invested heavily in this young bride's life by her example and ministry. She was not afraid to reach out and let me into her life. In crowded Los Angeles, Joannie's home and presence were a haven of refreshment. As with Mary and Martha, visiting with Joannie left one feeling both refreshed and ministered to. Joannie's peace-filled life testified to the fact that she had learned both to warmly welcome strangers and to sit daily at Jesus' feet.

PRAYER OF YOUR HEART:

Are there Marys, Marthas, and Joannies in your circle of life from whom you can learn? Do you know enough of Christ's love that you welcome strangers into your life and love them as Christ loves you? Scroll through your memory to see if you have been like Martha and Mary to a younger woman. Take time to thank God here for using you in the lives of younger women.

_____

_____

_____

"Dear Father of Lovingkindness, help me to be so filled with Your Word that Your love overflows from my life into others. Help me to become a woman with an open heart and an open home for Your sake."

6. LYDIA: A BUSINESS WOMAN YIELDED IN SPIRIT, SERVING THE LORD

"And [we went] ... from there to Philippi, which is the foremost city of that part of Macedonia, a colony. And we were staying in that city for some days. And on the Sabbath day we went out of the city to the riverside, where prayer was customarily made; and we sat down and spoke to the women who met [there]. Now a certain woman named Lydia heard [us]. She was a seller of purple from the city of Thyatira, who worshiped God. The Lord opened her heart to heed the things spoken by Paul. And when she and her household were baptized, she begged us, saying, 'If you have judged me to be faithful to the

Lord, come to my house and stay.' So she persuaded us"
(ACTS 16:12-15; see also ACTS 16:40; PHILIPPIANS 1:1-10).

Across the pages of Scripture we see that God calls His children from every walk of life—from palaces to huts, from farms to the blur of big cities. One of God's chosen servants in the early church was from the region of Thyatira, a crossroads of many nations. It was in God's perfect way and timing that He brought the lives of Lydia and the Apostle Paul together by the banks of a river near the city of Philippi. She was a woman wise in the ways of business and diligent in the things of God. Lydia was the first convert added to the church on Paul's initial missionary journey to Europe. She opened her heart to God's Word, and her home to God's people. Lydia skillfully worked with her creative hands, and industriously cared for the needs of others. Amid her highly successful profession, she chose to put God first. Perhaps Paul thought of Lydia when he wrote these words to the Romans: *"Not slothful in business, fervent in spirit, serving the Lord"* (ROMANS 12:11). Last fall, as I stood at the edge of that river in Philippi where Paul met Lydia and read those verses in Acts, my heart began to reflect upon my friend Sally.

Like Lydia, my friend, Sally, rose to the highest levels of business. Although a successful banking executive, she has opened her heart to God's message and her home to God's people. Everything Sally does, she does in an excellent way: teaching her children, encouraging her husband, playing the piano, sewing clothing or draperies, opening her home to friends or strangers, and humbly trusting the Lord through difficult circumstances in life. Sally works skillfully, and willingly cares for the needs of others. Her sensitive yet fervent spirit reminds me of Lydia, and thus Paul's *"not slothful in business, fervent in spirit, serving the Lord."* I count it a privilege to be her friend and to learn from her righteous example!

PRAYER OF YOUR HEART:

Perhaps God has given you talents such as Lydia's or Sally's. Have you yielded those abilities to the Lord? Are you serving Him with a fervent spirit? Do you know a business woman like Lydia who is yielded in spirit and serving the Lord? Tell the Lord how He has used her to encourage you in life.

_____

_____

_____

"Dear Father, thank You for creating each of us with unique abilities. Help me to keep You first in my life and yield those abilities to You so that whatever my hand finds to do, I do all to Your glory. Amen."

7. LOIS: A GRANDMOTHER WITH GENUINE FAITH

"I call to remembrance the genuine faith that is in you [Timothy], *which dwelt first in your grandmother Lois and your mother Eunice, and I am persuaded is in you also"* (2 TIMOTHY 1:5).

Paul, in 2 Timothy, tells us that Timothy had a great spiritual heritage. Like connecting the dots in a picture, Paul points out that the genuine faith was alive in Lois, and then in her daughter, Eunice, and finally in her grandson, Timothy.

Lois knew the privilege and responsibility of passing on to future generations the truths of God. Her most evident possession was an abiding, genuine faith in the living God. Her wealth in Christ became the family heirloom. Lois' name means "desirable," and her life portrays the role of a spiritual "grandmother" graciously. She loved God's Word and His people. Lois was a woman Paul respected and admired, He counted her as a friend, and noted her example of Christian virtue.

Even in her seventies, my friend, Helen, always had room in her home and heart for one more! A visitor to her home would find spotless floors, freshly laundered curtains, walls scrubbed by hand, the Word of God open and worn, and family pictures everywhere. Visits with Helen always included news of the spiritual condition of each of her children, grandchildren, and even great-grandchildren. Though their family grew to fifty or so in number, Helen could tell you exactly where each one appeared to be in his or her spiritual life. She lived before me as a Lois of the Bible who grasped the opportunity to pass on to future generations the claims and privileges of God's kingdom!

PRAYER OF YOUR HEART:

Ask God to give you a Lois or Helen in your life. Pray, and then pursue a Titus 2 relationship. Journal your testimony here to record the blessing of our great God.

_____

_____

_____

"Dear Father, thank You for Helen's example of an older, godly woman—teaching me to be a keeper at home, to honor my husband, and seize the opportunity to pass on to my children and grandchildren a legacy of faith in Jesus Christ. Help me live a life of prayer for the generations who follow me—and to be so filled with Your Word that it overflows into the lives of my children. Amen."

Becoming a "Portrait of Grace"

"He has shown you ... what is good; And what does the LORD require of you, But to do justly, To love mercy, And to walk humbly with your God" (MICAH 6:8).

Through these beautiful "portraits of God's grace"—these devoted wives and mothers—God has shown us a variety of examples of "what is good." Because these women have walked humbly with their God, they have a spot in my personal "Spiritual Hall of Fame"! Although life has been a difficult challenge for many of them, through Christ's strength they have triumphed magnificently. When I think of how much I have learned through their loving witness, I am overwhelmed by God's wonderful grace!

Whether you are a ten-talent woman, a five-talent woman, or a one- or two-talent woman, you, too, can be an inspiration to others. God wants you to "Be all you can be!" Through Christ's strength, you can make the most of who He has fashioned you to be. God wants to use you as a lovely portrait of His grace to point your children to Christ. He wants you to light the paths of women who are younger in the faith than you are right now. And—He wants you to be blessed by the exemplary lives and fellowship of older women who grace your path of life.

STUDY GUIDE QUESTIONS

1. **Jochebed evidenced great faith, courage, and devotion by how she invested in the lives of her children.** She trusted in God's faithfulness, and this affected her life and home. Read Acts 5:29 and 1 John 5:3-4. How did Jochebed's response to a time of severe testing bear witness to the truth of these verses?

2. **Elizabeth is a testimony of God's faithfulness to His Word and His tender mercies toward His children.** Read Genesis 18:14a and Luke 1:37. Like Sarah and Elizabeth, what have you learned from these verses that can give you hope for not only today but also for the future?

3. **Mary is exalted among women because of her profound humility and deep sense of personal unworthiness.** Read Proverbs 15:33. How does this verse reflect the testimony of Mary's life?

4. **Anna is a testament of hope and faithfulness—a message of the beauty of waiting upon God, being loyal to Him in a lifetime of service, and trusting Him to fulfill His promises with perfect timing.** Read Ecclesiastes 3:1, 11a; then read Ephesians 5:15-21. How do these verses parallel Anna's life? How do they parallel yours?

5. **Martha was a woman of action, with the heart of a servant; Mary was a woman who valued being in the presence of Jesus and chose every precious opportunity as her highest priority.** Read 1 Corinthians 10:23-24, 31. How do these verses apply to the differences between Martha and Mary?

6. **Lydia was a woman wise in the ways of business and diligent in the things of God.** She opened her heart to God's Word, and her home to God's people. Read Romans 12:9-13. How does this passage apply to Lydia's life? Is it characteristic of your own?

7. **Lois was a grandmother who knew the privilege and responsibility of passing on to future generations the truths of God.** Her wealth in Christ became the family heirloom. Read 2 Timothy 2:1-2. Lois understood that the process of "passing on the faith" is to be ongoing—until the Lord returns—for both men and women. Are you experiencing this great joy with your own children— and, if applicable, your children's children?

14

"Fathers, do not exasperate your children;
instead, bring them up in the training
and instruction of the Lord."

— *Ephesians 6:4, niv*

How to Be a Word Filled Dad

WHO ARE YOU TAKING WITH you to heaven? Specifically, are you taking your children along with you? I hope so! The most thrilling part of life is to be able to take someone with us to heaven—especially those who are so near and dear to us! Paul was convinced he was taking along saints from his "family," those he ministered to briefly in Thessalonica 20 centuries ago.[a] Are you as convinced about your own family?

a. I Thessalonians 2:19-20

You have about 20 years to raise each child from birth to adulthood. God's greatest reward for Word-filled parenting is to lead your children to Jesus, and then see them faithfully follow Him as they graduate from your home! Therefore, the essence of this book is a challenge to **start now**—no matter where you are, how old your children are, or how strong or weak your marriage is.

Where to begin is always the hardest part of encouraging families to allow the Lord to bless their homes. My counsel from God's Word for over a quarter of a century continues to be: husbands and dads, it really needs to start in you! You can write e-mails all day—but if you are not connected to the internet, they go nowhere. You can type on the keyboard for hours—but if it is not connected to your computer, nothing is recorded. You can obtain countless books, seminars, video series, tapes, and messages on parenting, but if you are not connected to God Himself, you can never fill the role He called you to do. To sum it up, a Word-filled family starts in the heart and life of a husband and dad who becomes full of God and His Word.

What a precious yet awesome responsibility. But the good news is that God has promised that He will never forsake you, nor leave you alone! Along the way, as you travel the parenting path together with God, you can count on Him to provide support through others who have already walked that path. Their seasoned experience can offer biblical wisdom that is usually easy to implement, no matter where you happen to be in the parenting process. Sometimes, this may even take the form of sharing how they would do things differently—if they had the opportunity.

Ever since my first Father's Day, I have benefited from the insights shared by just such a person—a wise dad with grown children. While I was on staff as a new pastor in California, I received a Father's Day tract; and after reading the tract, and thinking about it, I taped it onto the front cover of my Bible. It finally wore out, so I retyped the tract and pasted it once again in my Bible. (The tract specifically addresses fathers; however, its principles apply well to both parents.) And now, as a delighted father of eight wonderful children, here is what I have treasured so much from that dad's wonderful bit of wisdom:

Fathers: Would You Do It Any Differently

"MY FAMILY'S ALL GROWN, AND the kids are all gone. But, if I had to do it all over again, this is what I'd do:

- I would love my wife more in front of my children.
- I would laugh with my children more—at our mistakes and our joys.
- I would listen more, even to the littlest child.
- I would be more honest about my own weaknesses, never pretending perfection.

- I would pray differently for my family—instead of focusing so much on them, I'd focus more on me.
- I would do more things together with my children.
- I would encourage them more and bestow more praise.
- I would pay more attention to little things, like deeds and words of thoughtfulness.
- And then, finally, if I had to do it all over again, I would share God more intimately with my family; every ordinary thing that happened in every ordinary day I would use to direct them to God." [a]

a. John M. Drescher, *If I Were Starting My Family Again*, Rev. (USA: Good Books, 1996), Preface.

As a dad, I have especially loved that last point! The following illustration is an example of how easily we can direct our little ones to God through an "ordinary thing that happens on an ordinary day." In this excerpt, author Charlie Shedd is talking to his tiny son, Peter, telling him about an adventurous trip to the country with Peter's older brother, Philip:

We had been out in the country for a ride. It was evening and we ran out of gas. We were walking along after we had been to the farm house, and I was carrying a can of gas. Philip was only four. He was playing along, throwing rocks at the telephone poles, picking flowers, and then, all of a sudden it got dark. Sometimes night comes all at once in the country. Philip came over, put his little hand in mine and said, "Take my hand, Daddy. I might get lost." Peter, there is a hand reaching to you from the heart of the universe. If you will lay your hand in the hand of God and walk with Him, you will never ever get lost. [b]

b. Charlie W. Shedd, *Letters To Philip On How To Treat A Woman* (USA: Revell, 1970), p. 38.

Today, God's hand is likewise reaching out to you from the heart of the universe. If you will but lay your children's hands in His and help them walk with Him—they will never ever get lost! You can trust Him to lovingly guide you and your family in every stage of life.

It is an awesome task to declare God's requirements for nurturing a Word-filled family. There's no doubt about it: parenting is difficult at times. Just at one bookstore I counted fifty-four titles on marriage and family, with eighteen offering advice on how to train children. Many authors didn't even agree. One well-known authority on life, writer and humorist Mark Twain, had an interesting insight on parenting. Consider this advice if you need a good chuckle during one of those exasperating moments—which all parents at one time or another will experience. Twain's philosophy was this: When a kid turns 13, stick him in a barrel, nail the lid on top, and feed him through the knothole. When he turns 16, plug up the hole.

God does have a better way ...

It is fascinating to read what God recorded about the family in a 3,000-year-old Hebrew manuscript from the Jewish Wisdom Literature called the *Kethubim*, known today as the Proverbs of King Solomon. Throughout Proverbs, God contrasts the wise man with the foolish man. Proverbs says if we have a disobedient son, he:

1. Grieves his mother: *"A wise son makes a glad father, but a foolish son is the grief of his mother"* (PROVERBS 10:1). *"A foolish son is a grief to his father, and bitterness to her who bore him"* (PROVERBS 17:25).

2. Despises his father: *"A fool despises his father's instruction, but he who receives correction is prudent"* (PROVERBS 15:5).

3. Sorrows his father: *"He who begets a scoffer does so to his sorrow, and the father of a fool has no joy"* (PROVERBS 17:21).

4. Ruins his father: *"A foolish son is the ruin of his father ..."* (PROVERBS 19:13A).

5. Shames his parents: *"He who mistreats his father and chases away his mother is a son who causes shame and brings reproach"* (PROVERBS 19:26).

6. Robs his parents: *"Whoever robs his father or his mother, and says, 'It is no transgression,' The same is companion to a destroyer"* (PROVERBS 28:24).

Do we want to feel shame and reproach? If we foolishly neglect our parenting responsibilities, and just don't do anything, that is what we will feel. Dr. Alberta Siegel once wrote in the *Stanford Observer:*

*When it comes to rearing children, every society is only 20 years away from barbarism. Twenty years is all we have to accomplish the task of civilizing the infants who are born into our midst each year. These savages know nothing of our language, our culture, our religion, our values, or our customs of interpersonal relations. The infant is totally ignorant about communism, fascism, democracy, civil liberties ... respect, decency, honesty, customs, conventions, and manners. **The barbarian must be tamed if civilization is to survive.**[a]* (Emphasis added.)

a. *Stanford Observer,* (Stanford, CA: Stanford News Service, October 1973), p. 4.

If we read those words and think our youngsters are excluded, we make a grave error. Every child has the potential of becoming a study in hostility—a heartache—a model of wickedness. There's no denying it: parents must deal with the evil that rests in their children's lives. Those who fail to deal with that evil consistently, and wisely, will face a future of misery.

In a study conducted several years ago, sociologists Sheldon and Eleanor Glueck of Harvard University tried to identify the crucial factors in delinquency. They developed a test that could predict the future delinquency of children 5 or 6 years old. Their follow-up tests, 4 years later, proved to be 90 percent accurate. They identified four necessary factors to prevent delinquency:

1. Discipline must be firm, fair, and consistent.
2. A mother must know where her children are and what they're doing at all times, and be with them as much as possible.
3. Children need to see love demonstrated between the father and mother, and see genuine love lived out before them.
4. A family must be cohesive, regularly spending time together.[b]

b. Sheldon and Eleanor Glueck, *Unraveling Juvenile Delinquency* (Cambridge, MA: Harvard University Press, 1950), pp. 257-271.

Word-filled husbands and fathers recognize that their vocations are important, but their homes are essential. They regularly express deep love for their wives. Such Psalm 15 men are also responsive to their children; they refuse to be counted among the typical dads who give their children only 3 minutes of undivided attention per day. Word-filled dads are keenly aware of their responsibilities listed in Ephesians 6:4.

The Job Description of a Word-Filled Dad

CONSIDER THE CHALLENGES TO US as dads toward godliness in this verse:

> *"Fathers, do not exasperate your children; instead, bring them up in the training and instruction of the Lord"* (EPHESIANS 6:4, NIV).

Note that God specifically expects fathers to be fair, tender, firm, and Christlike. Let us now consider each of these challenges individually.

1. WORD-FILLED DADS ARE FAIR.

> *"Fathers, **do not exasperate your children**; instead, bring them up in the training and instruction of the Lord"* (EPHESIANS 6:4, NIV; Emphasis added).

How do we exasperate our children at times? What are some ways we may be unfair? The great Reformed Bible teacher, William Hendriksen, cautions us to guard the hearts, minds, and spirits of our children.[a] He warns that we must beware of:

a. William Hendriksen, *New Testament Commentary: Galatians and Ephesians* (Grand Rapids, MI: Baker Book House, 1987), p. 261.

Overprotecting them. We should let our boys be boys, and not restrict them so that they end up acting as little girls. Boys need to run, climb, jump, get scraped, and explore—or they will not develop into the leaders and protectors they must become.

Favoring them. Isaac favored Esau, and Rebecca doted on Jacob. Their favoritism eventually split the family. Yet, Jacob didn't learn from his parents' mistakes because he lavished love on Joseph, preferring him above his siblings. This practice embittered others. Having a favorite son or daughter can only lead to jealousy and dissension.

Blurring them. God has made and gifted each of His children uniquely—like beautiful spiritual snowflakes. Therefore, we should never try to make clones of ourselves, but cooperate with God in conforming them to His image, to fulfill His ultimate purpose for creating them.

Neglecting them. As Word-filled dads, we must spend time with our children. Instead of hustling *them* off to bed, we should put our work or TV to bed early—and enjoy special and long times together with our children during those fast-passing childhood days. Neglect is the danger sign of a bad father. Consider the example of Eli, who neglected disciplining himself as well as his children.[a] God said that Eli participated in his sons' sins because he didn't rebuke them.[b] Because he failed to confront sin in his own home, it cost him—and generations to come—dearly![c] Beware of being a modern-day Eli. Like Eli, this involves being preoccupied with a job to the exclusion of family needs. It means refusing to face the severity of our children's actions. A poor father fails to respond quickly and thoroughly to the warnings of others. Often a bad parent rationalizes the wrong he has done, thereby becoming part of the problem rather than part of the solution.

a. 1 Samuel 4:18

b. 1 Samuel 2:29

c. 1 Samuel 3:13

Verbally abusing them. All too often, cutting words[d] spew forth on children instead of blessings, and the end result is their discouragement. We often hear the truth of the warning—tell a child often enough that he's worthless and will never amount to anything and it becomes a self-fulfilling prophecy. Often our children will live up to, or should I say down to those expectations. How many fathers do you know who have blessed their sons? How many sons would give anything for their father's blessing?

d. Ephesians 4:29

Even though they are young, children need to be treated with respect, just as adults need to be. If treated respectfully, they in turn will learn how to respect others. Verbal assaults and physical cruelty ought never to be part of a Christian home, for each form is extremely destructive. This should be the guideline for all discipline: never correct children in anger, *"For the wrath of man does not produce the righteousness of God"* (JAMES 1:20). It is important to note that if we do not consistently follow this principle, our children's tender hearts can become so embittered that they close their hearts and spirits to us, and hence our discipling efforts.

How to Bless Your Family

One of the greatest blessings we have experienced in my own family is practicing the "Jewish Sabbath Dinner" concept of blessing. In some branches of Judaism, there is a custom for the father to stand behind each of his children during Saturday dinner and read a blessing over each one of them—a statement of what he sees in their lives that has blessed and touched him. This is often similar to Jacob's blessing of his sons when he spoke of what their strengths would become.[a]

a. Genesis 49

I have chosen to frame my blessings as, "This is what I see God doing in your life now—" Then I follow with, "—and this is where I see God at work shaping your life."

Amazingly, the smiles, the eyes, and the voices of our children say it all. They are blessed and honored and respond in such a loving way to this special time together, which also sets the entire tone of our preparation for Sunday.

2. Word-filled Dads Are Tender.

*"Fathers, do not exasperate your children; instead, **bring them up** in the training and instruction of the Lord"* (Ephesians 6:4, niv; Emphasis added).

To "bring them up" means "to nourish, to provide for with tender care."[b] Because women are natural nurturers, we would be wise to listen to our wives' concerns, ideas, and constructive criticisms. Most men approach life mechanically. As a result, we tend to make snap decisions and jump in on discipline situations without getting all the facts. For that reason, it is important to first respectfully listen to what a child has to say before deciding upon a consequence. This lets children know their feelings are important to us.

b. Fritz Rienecker, *A Linguistic Key to the Greek New Testament* (Grand Rapids, MI: Zondervan, 1982), p. 540.

Occasionally, we will evidence bad judgment, be harsh, or otherwise be negligent in doing what we know we ought to do. Whenever we fall short in any area, tenderness requires that we quickly ask for forgiveness. If we are tender, we will give plenty of hugs, affectionately hold our children on our laps, and be constant encouragers.

3. WORD-FILLED DADS ARE FIRM.

"Fathers, do not exasperate your children; instead, bring them up in the training and instruction of the Lord" (EPHESIANS 6:4, NIV; Emphasis added).

That word *training* "may be described as training by means of rules and regulations, rewards, and when necessary, punishments. It refers primarily to what is done to the child." By contrast, *instruction* (admonition) means "training by means of the spoken word, whether that be teaching, warning, or encouragement. It refers primarily to what is said to the child."[a] How effectively do most fathers fill this prescription for successful child rearing?

Years back, when members of Britain's royal family toured the United States, they were asked to share the most amazing thing they had observed in America. Without a moment's hesitation, the reporter was told: "The way the parents obey their children."[b] That is quite an indictment against American dads in general, isn't it? But it need not be so for dedicated Christian fathers.

Ken Taylor, whose *Living Bible* paraphrase has touched so many lives, well explains the father's role in discipline:

> *A father's task is many sided, but the most important part of his work is to fit himself and his family into God's plan of family authority. Children are to be encouraged by the father's pat on the back. And, helped to better understand things (when necessary) by the application of the hand or stick to the seat of learning. Of course there are other methods of discipline besides spanking, but whatever is called for must be used. To refuse to discipline a child is to refuse the clear command of God. A child who does not learn to obey both parents will find it much harder to learn to obey God.[c]*

As we set the proper example, it facilitates our children's ability and desire to obey both parents. God even promises to honor such faithfulness. If we have submissive children, and lead our homes well,

a. William Hendriksen, *New Testament Commentary: Philippians* (Phillipsburg, NJ: Presbyterian and Reformed Publishing Co., 1977), p. 62.

b. Steve Farrar, *Point Man: How a Man Can Lead a Family* (Portland, OR: Multnomah Press, 1990), p. 216.

c. *Quotable Quotations* (Wheaton, IL: Victor Books, 1985), p. 1132.

we are eligible to be considered for leadership in His church. However, the opposite is also true: *"If a man does not know how to rule his own house, how will he take care of the church of God?"* (1 Timothy 3:5).

4. Word-filled Dads Are Christlike.

*"Fathers, do not exasperate your children; instead, bring them up in the training **and instruction of the Lord**"* (Ephesians 6:4, niv; Emphasis added).

To be biblical, child training techniques (what is *done* to the child) plus instruction or admonition (what is *said* to the child) must be "of the Lord," based upon God's Word and His principles. The goal should be to disciple our children to be conformed to Christ's image: *"Imitate me, just as I also imitate Christ"* (1 Corinthians 11:1). As dads, we need to demonstrate godly living in the midst of this sinful and fallen race. To do this, we must avoid certain temptations, such as the following dangers. Word-filled dads have the power by God's grace to:

Flee the danger of substituting gifts for time. In 1 Timothy 5:8, God commands that we provide for our own. However, the temptation is to make *presents* substitute for our *presence*. In other words, many men prefer to offer "toys" instead of their time. They would rather stay late at the office, do endless traveling, work weekends, and so forth. But no gift can replace a daddy's presence. When children are grown, and they are asked what they remember most about growing up, chances are that it will not be memories of different "toys." No, it will most likely be the breakfasts with Dad, or trips to the zoo, park, or sports games. It will be the nights waiting up for them, the games cheering for them, and the hours coaching them in the backyard or workshop. Every child desperately wants, and needs, precious time with his or her father! **Pursue time with your family!**

Flee the danger of giving them only leftovers. As men, we constantly are tempted to save our best for the workplace, and give our families the leftovers. That practice can be likened to us being jets at an airport. As jets, we'll exercise, refuel, and taxi out of our hangars to fly to work—full of energy and ideas all day—only to run low on fuel as we land, taxi into our recliners, and shut down for the evening. Does that description fit your life's pattern? Where are you really investing your life? In things that won't matter in 100 years? Be careful! **Pursue investing your best in them!**

Flee the danger of corrupt communications. In Ephesians 4:29, Paul admonishes each of us to never allow "corrupt" (KJV) words out of our mouths. The word used speaks in clear terms. It means "sharp and cutting or sick and rotting." Does that describe talk that comes out inside your home and car?

Just with words alone, some men dice and chop while others put the smell of decay into the hearts and minds of their families. Paul says, "Don't do that. And if you are, *stop!*" As dads, we must avoid making a practice of simply delivering a shotgun of words rather than earning the right to be respected through listening and learning. Remember: *"So then, my beloved brethren, let every man be swift to hear, slow to speak, slow to wrath"* (JAMES 1:19).

Do this test on the words you use at home: Do you simply point out errors, correct problems, and deliver warnings? Are your words primarily negative or positive? Would you keep as a close friend someone who was as negative when they spoke to you as you are to your family? If not, why should they esteem you as their best friend?

The only hope in this area is through the work Jesus does inside of us. He changes our hearts out of which issue our words. If your words have soured at home, ask for the cleansing of forgiveness. Ask God for an infusion of loving words that Christ inspires. *"Let your speech always be with grace ..."* (COLOSSIANS 4:6). Grace-filled words build up, not tear down—encourage, not discourage. Gracious words promote emotional health, and not hurts. Paul ends Colossians 4:6 by saying that our words should be seasoned with salt. That speaks of the power we have even without knowing it. Gracious words have a purifying and preserving influence on all those around us when "salted" with grace by the Holy Spirit. **Pursue grace-filled communication with them!**

Flee the danger of perfectionism. This is such a subtle temptation to some of us dads. We have fallen into the wrong pattern of desiring to be *perfect,* and demanding the same from our families.

Yet, no one can live up to those expectations; nothing is ever good enough. Tom Eisenman describes some of the tendencies of men who are perfectionists:

> *Perfectionists tend to think in dichotomous categories. Everything is either great or bad, perfect or worthless. Perfectionists also engage in minimizing or maximizing. Failures are maximized and successes are minimized. The small thing that went wrong destroys or at least overshadows everything else. Perfectionists set unreasonable goals for themselves and others. Perfectionists judge their personal worth by their **performance**—and others by the same standard.[a]* (Emphasis added.)

a. Tom Eisenman, *Temptations Men Face* (Downers Grove, IL: InterVarsity Press, 1990), pp. 168-170.

We must realize that God is the God of Second Chances. We are sinners. All of us fail Him and others, and we must get right with Him and them, and press on, *"For we do not have a High Priest who cannot sympathize with our weaknesses, but was in all [points] tempted as [we are, yet] without sin"* (HEBREWS 4:15). **Pursue a pattern of forgiveness and recognition of their priceless worth to you and God!**

Flee the danger of undisciplined desires. This primarily reflects the temptation to desire intimate satisfaction outside the bonds of monogamy, such as seeking to find sensual satisfaction in reading, seeking, listening, imagining, or even experiencing any woman other than our own wives. God warns:

> *"Let no one say when he is tempted, 'I am tempted by God'; for God cannot be tempted by evil, nor does He Himself tempt anyone. But each one is tempted when he is drawn away by his own desires and enticed. Then, when desire has conceived, it gives birth to sin; and sin, when it is full-grown, brings forth death"* (JAMES 1:13-15).

Men, we dare not give in to sensual temptations—even for a fleeting peek at online pictures, a lustful glance at immodest women, a quick look in a magazine, a moment on the movie channel, or a secret meeting with a woman! We must say no, flee, and not look back!

If you are struggling with this particular sin, it can help to take reminders of your family to work. Look at their smiling faces in pictures on business trips; place family pictures around your office or work area; talk about your wife as your sweetheart and best friend to your coworkers—especially if they are women. Most of all, remember the lives of your family rest in your care! **Pursue disciplined desires!**

Flee the danger of neglecting spiritual nurturing. If we neglect spiritual nurturing, by default this automatically undermines discipling efforts in every area. We should faithfully cultivate the spiritual appetites of our family members. If we are to nurture Word-filled families, we must lead the way to the Word, church, prayer meeting, verse memorization, and other God-centered activities. Our children should see us praying, reading, studying, witnessing, serving in the Lord's work, helping the helpless, sacrificing resources to invest in eternity, and resisting worldliness and pride. All of these examples are more likely to be "caught" than taught. **Pursue spiritual appetites!**

We must always beware of anything that can spiritually deaden our families. Always keep in mind that if we aren't leading our children in the right way, the world will sweep them away! Dads, I know that none of this is easy, but then nothing worthwhile ever is.

None of us are perfect, especially me. Remember: modeling Christlikeness is costly, and it is not an overnight process. It takes time and dedication, but the eternal rewards are priceless! May I encourage you to keep looking unto Jesus, the author and finisher of your faith, for *"He who has begun a good work in you will complete it until the day of Jesus Christ"* (PHILIPPIANS 1:6B)!

STUDY GUIDE QUESTIONS

1. **Word-filled dads are fair.** By God's grace, Word-filled dads are careful to not exasperate their children.

   Read James 1:19-20. What does God have to say about man's anger?

   Read James 1:26. What does God say about an unbridled tongue?

   Read Ephesians 4:30-32. What is God's antidote for unkindness?

2. **Word-filled dads are tender.** By God's grace, Word-filled dads "bring [their children] up" by nourishing them, tenderly providing for their care.

   Read Psalm 103:13-14. Does this verse represent
      your spirit toward your children?

   Read 1 Corinthians 1:3-4. As a man who desires to be like Christ,
      are you a comforter of your children? Or do they fear you?

   Read 1 Timothy 5:8. Are you a loving provider of your
      household? Are your children well taken care of?

3. **Word-filled dads are firm.** By God's grace, Word-filled dads lovingly train their children "by means of rules and regulations, rewards, and when necessary, punishments."

   Read Proverbs 10:13; 15:20; 17:21; 19:18; 22:6, 15; 29:15. Proverbs
      has a lot to say about child training—and the lack thereof.
      Which verses most characterize your own family's experience?

   Read Proverbs 10:1; 23:15-16, 24-25; 28:7; 29:17. List some
      anticipated results from training children God's way.

   Read Hebrews 12:5-11. What should be the motivation
      and goal of disciplining children?

4. **Word-filled dads are Christlike.** By God's grace, the Word-filled dad's training is "of the Lord," based upon God's Word and its principles. However, such dads understand that modeling Christlikeness is one of the best teachers. We must not just tell our children how to be like Christ, we must show them.

   Read Philippians 4:9. Why could the Apostle Paul make such a
      confident statement to the Philippians? Can you, in all good
      conscience, say the same thing to your children? (To your wife?)
      If not, regularly ask the Lord to make this a reality in your life!

15

"Therefore we also, since we are surrounded by so great a cloud of witnesses, let us lay aside every weight, and the sin which so easily ensnares [us], and let us run with endurance the race that is set before us, looking unto Jesus, the author and finisher of [our] faith …."

— *Hebrews 12:1-2a*

Moving Families Toward Godliness:
The Four Disciplines

THE ULTIMATE GOAL OF WORD-FILLED parenting is to lead our families to love God—nothing spectacular, nothing superhuman, just regular and consistent adoration of the "King of kings and Lord of lords" (1 Timothy 6:12-16). The results can be extraordinary! In a moment we will see snapshots of four dads who lived such a Word-filled life—three from the Old Testament and one from the New Testament. The *encouraging similarity* is that **all of these men were mightily used by God in spite of their imperfections, failures, and struggles!**

Isn't it wonderful that our perfect God does not expect perfection before He can be served in a mighty way? Isn't it amazing that He *wants* to use each of us for His glory? Because of this, with great joy we can press on as husbands and dads to become all God calls us to be! And even when we fail at times, we get to start over again through the cleansing of forgiveness. Each and every day thus becomes His gift of a marvelous new beginning!

Only God Is a Perfect Father

HOW DO WE, WHO ARE so imperfect, even begin to perform one of the most difficult tasks in life—parenting? We begin by seeing our great God as He is, and then, in the power of His Spirit, we emulate Him. Though we will sometimes fail as His students, we can always point our families to their Perfect Father.

The perfect father would be one who knows everything about you, and still loves you. The perfect father would always be on your side. He would be big enough for anything, and never ever let you down. Of course, that description can fit only one Person—God the Father, as declared by Christ, His dear Son.[a] Jesus introduced us to Him as our Perfect Father.

a. John 1:18

1. GOD OUR FATHER IS **ALL-SEEING**: *"Your Father who sees in secret will Himself reward you openly"* (MATTHEW 6:4B; see also MATTHEW 6:6B AND 6:18C).

When you fear that you don't know enough to get the job done—remember who you work with! Nothing escapes our heavenly Father's notice! Jesus calls Him our *"Father who sees all of our secrets."* Whenever we keep our charitable deeds secret, prayers a private act of worship, or fasting strictly between us and the Lord, our Perfect Father sees, and will reward us accordingly. He is always *"keeping watch on the evil and the good"* (PROVERBS 15:3B). Yet, even though we fail Him at times, He still loves us. What a comfort to have God as our Perfect Father, and to know that He is on our side!

2. GOD OUR FATHER IS **ALL-PROVIDING**: *"Every good gift and every perfect gift is from above, and comes down from the Father of lights, with whom there is no variation or shadow of turning"* (JAMES 1:17).

When you feel completely inadequate, remember that we are invited to draw upon our Supplying Father, whose resources are limitless. Have you met and entered into communion with our Father of Mercy? Oh, how much He loves you—and is supremely on your side!

3. God Our Father Is ALL-POWERFUL: *"Furthermore, we have had human fathers who corrected [us], and we paid [them] respect. Shall we not much more readily be in subjection to the Father of spirits and live?"* (HEBREWS 12:9).

This "Father of our spirits" is powerful, and we should therefore trust in His strength to deliver us—even during times of correction. Chastening is always intended for our good; our Perfect Father is able to make us victorious because He is big enough for anything![a]

a. Genesis 18:14a

4. God Our Father Is NEVER-FAILING: *"... the Father of lights, with whom there is no variation or shadow or turning"* (JAMES 1:17B).

When you feel like you have failed again—remember that He never does. His name "Father of lights" reminds us that our God is the Creator of the sun, moon, and stars.[b] However, unlike these "lights" that are subject to movement and change, the incredible truth is that our great God is changeless. He can never be anything less than absolute perfection! In everyday language, that means He is the Father who will never let us down. Therefore, we can constantly be at rest as we place all our hopes in our Secure Father.

b. See Genesis 1:14-19.

5. We Should Imitate God and Those He Uses as Examples: *"Therefore, be imitators of God, as dear children"* (EPHESIANS 5:1).

So we have partnered with our Perfect God and we can accomplish all He calls us to do. To help us know how, He has given us His Word to glean insights from other dads who have done things God's way—especially fathers of the Word. We are therefore going to look at four godly habits to emulate, as demonstrated in the lives of these biblical models: Job, Noah, Abraham, and Joseph.

How does God—through the lens of Scripture—portray these Word-filled men of the past? When He took their "pictures," what images stood out most clearly? I am delighted to say that their wonderful habits are not outdated, but can be followed by us in the twenty-first century as well! Four men, four methods, four examples—God is so good. He tells us what to do, and then shows us how to do it. He then provides His grace and encouragement to go out and *imitate* the same godly characteristics. So as you read about the habits of these Word-filled dads, I exhort you to carefully analyze what they did, and then ask the Lord to guide you in doing the same.

Discipline Number One: Job Models Prayer

THE BOOK OF JOB IS perhaps the oldest book in the world. It is probably the clearest view into the spirit world, the spiritual side of parenting, and the cosmic proportion of conflicts we face as parents. From Job's life example, we can learn how to copy his habit of *prayer*, and by the power of God's Spirit, start making it characteristic of our own lives.

1. JOB PRAYED FOR HIS CHILDREN'S ACTIVITIES

*"**So it was, when the days of feasting had run their course,** that Job would send and sanctify them, and he would rise early in the morning and offer burnt offerings [according to] the number of them all. For Job said, 'It may be that my sons have sinned and cursed God in their hearts.' Thus Job did regularly"* (JOB 1:5, Emphasis added).

Note these words: "when the days of feasting." This indicates that Job prayerfully followed the lives of his children. He knew what was going on in their lives—their cycle of house visits, parties, get-togethers, and so on. He was in touch daily with where they were, and where they were headed. Job followed his children around in his heart, because he had a godly concern and love for them. You and I will never pray effectively for those who are not regularly on our hearts. Do you follow your children's lives in this same manner?

Part of friendship is sharing what's going on in our lives. If our sons and daughters become our brothers and sisters in Christ—the next step is friendship. We stay in touch by love. When apart, we share their days joyfully by praying for them. We ask them to keep us posted so we know what we can be asking the Lord to do. This closeness is only earned by a loving friendship they have experienced with you .

2. JOB PRAYED FOR HIS CHILDREN'S PURITY

"So it was, when the days of feasting had run their course, that **Job would send and sanctify them**, *and he would rise early in the morning and offer burnt offerings [according to] the number of them all. For Job said, 'It may be that my sons have sinned and cursed God in their hearts.' Thus Job did regularly"* (JOB 1:5, Emphasis added).

Job prayerfully sought the personal consecration of his children. This speaks of his high priestly role at the head of his family. He went to God seeking their purity before the Lord. We likewise need to know our children, and seek their sanctification. As fathers, we should tell them when they are out of line, immodest, heading toward sin, and so on. Word-filled men will know the spiritual status of their children, and be prayerfully caring about their growth toward Christlikeness. How can you do this? By asking the Lord to make you sensitive to their struggles, their concerns, their fears, their anticipations. And then, *after* you have both remembered and prayed about these areas, ask your children how you can better encourage and support them. This will open up a new level of your relationship with them.

I write these things down for my family in my prayer journal. *(To help you get started, Appendix B has sample pages.)* Then, as I read the Word, verses actually leap from its pages and into my heart. I pray those verses, asking the Lord to do what He promised in what I found for them. Afterwards, I share a verse or a principle from God's Word that touches their lives. Do you care about the consecration of your children? How about your wife? Then ask the Lord to open His Word to you—**for them**!

3. JOB PRAYED FOR HIS CHILDREN'S RELATIONSHIP WITH GOD

"So it was, when the days of feasting had run their course, that Job would send and sanctify them, **and he would rise early in the morning and offer burnt offerings [according to] the number of them all.** *For Job said, 'It may be that my sons have sinned*

and cursed God in their hearts.' Thus Job did regularly" (JOB 1:5, Emphasis added).

Job prayerfully offered himself to God as an intercessor for his family. Every morning, without fail, he rose early to offer sacrifices on their behalf. This habit wasn't just "talk"; it was work! Prayer is much like holding something for someone we love, and making sure that it is guarded carefully. Have you offered yourself to God as an intercessor for your family?

4. JOB PRAYED FOR HIS CHILDREN'S HEARTS

*"So it was, when the days of feasting had run their course, that Job would send and sanctify them, and he would rise early in the morning and offer burnt offerings [according to] the number of them all. **For Job said, 'It may be that my sons have sinned and cursed God in their hearts.'** Thus Job did regularly"* (JOB 1:5, Emphasis added).

Job prayerfully looked at his family from God's perspective. This godly dad was so vitally concerned about his children's inner spiritual lives that he cried out to God for them! Have you started doing this, Dad?

Job kept himself aware of the constant pressures of the world, the flesh, and the devil. He wanted pure children, a holy family, and strong worshipers of God Almighty. He diligently watched over their lives, trying to see them from the inside out. We likewise ought to sometimes look at our children as they *will* be, instead of as they are right now. After all, God does that for us! In Ephesians 1:3-6, being seated with Christ refers to our future glorified condition, and the Lord relates to us on that basis—never overlooking sin, but always seeing us as we shall be, by His grace. Do you compassionately look at your children as they will become—or only at their present immaturity?

5. JOB NEVER STOPPED PRAYING FOR HIS CHILDREN

"So it was, when the days of feasting had run their course, that Job would send and sanctify them, and he would rise early in the morn-

ing and offer burnt offerings [according to] the number of them all.
For Job said, 'It may be that my sons have sinned and cursed God in
their hearts.' Thus Job did regularly" (JOB 1:5, Emphasis added).

Job prayerfully persisted in his prayer ministry for his family. He
was a great dad because he persevered in prayer—throughout their
entire lives. The way to success in any endeavor is to get started, and
not quit. Job not only started following their lives, offering interces-
sory prayers along the way, but he also wouldn't *stop*. Therefore, he
was ready for the unexpected death of his children, because he had
prepared them for it every day. Have you started? Keep on. Have you
quit? Get started again.

Fathers of the Word will be like Job who interceded prayerfully
for his family. He had five objectives: **1.** Job followed what was
going on in his children's lives; **2.** Job cared about their personal
lives being consecrated; **3.** Job personally stood as priest of his
family by offering atoning sacrifices for their sin in general; **4.** Job
looked not just at appearances but at their hearts; and **5.** Job continually watched over his family with spiritual persistence.

Godly fathers in tune with the Scriptures will know their children
deeply, personally, and directly. They will get involved in making
sure they stay pure, and stand ready to seek their repentance and
restoration as needed. Godly fathers will look at heart attitudes, and
will not ever stop!

Discipline Number Two: Noah Models Obedience

NOAH MODELS ANOTHER FACET OF the Word-filled dad because he
obeyed. Have you ever wondered how Noah ever did it? Every other
family on earth was losing their children, who had all "gone to the
devil"—literally! But Noah's children did not. Why was that? It was
God's grace through a man who had responded and cultivated a
heart for God. There is a pattern to his life we all would do well to
note! Job was a great dad because he prayed! Noah was considered
great because he *obeyed*.

1. NOAH BELIEVED GOD

"By faith Noah, being divinely warned of things not yet seen, moved with godly fear, prepared an ark for the saving of his household, by which he condemned the world and became heir of the righteousness which is according to faith" (HEBREWS 11:7, Emphasis added).

In that one verse, the inspired writer of Hebrews condenses the Genesis 6-9 biography of Noah's life. The character of Noah's whole life is summed up with just one word: *obedience*. Even though the world had never seen anything close to a flood, Noah chose to believe God "by faith," and spent 120 years (Genesis 6:3) obediently carrying out His instructions for building the huge ark. Let me ask you, men: do you believe God enough to follow His instructions for building a godly family?

2. NOAH STAYED IN TOUCH WITH GOD

"By faith Noah, **being divinely warned of things not yet seen,** *moved with godly fear, prepared an ark for the saving of his household, by which he condemned the world and became heir of the righteousness which is according to faith"* (HEBREWS 11:7, Emphasis added).

Fathers of the Word will be like Noah, who believed God and obediently warned his family of things to come. Through both the Word and prayer, Noah kept in spiritual contact with God, and listened to Him. This association led to the spiritual perception of God's will for his family. I hope you likewise will keep in touch with God so you can know with certainty God's will for your family, and obey it.

3. NOAH OBEYED GOD

"By faith Noah, being divinely warned of things not yet seen, **moved with godly fear, prepared an ark** *for the saving of his household, by which he condemned the world and became heir of the righteousness which is according to faith"* (HEBREWS 11:7, Emphasis added).

Have you ever wondered about Noah's initial reaction when God first mentioned the coming judgment, and the need to build an ark? Perhaps he thought: *He wants me to build a what?* When God gave the dimensions, it might have seemed as a "mission impossible." Remember, the ark was a barge-like ship 450 feet long, 75 feet wide, and 45 feet high. The floor space totaled 1 1/2 *million square feet.* This equals *almost 600* railroad stock cars, of which *just one-third* could hold the 21,000 land animals of the *one million plus* total species we know of that lived upon earth. (The average land animal is the size of a sheep.) Noah never let the immensity of the task ahead detract from his commitment to obey Almighty God. If you are facing what seems to be a "mission impossible," like Noah, reach out in faith and trust God to see you safely through.

4. NOAH LED HIS FAMILY

*"By faith Noah, being divinely warned of things not yet seen, moved with godly fear, prepared an ark **for the saving of his household,** by which he condemned the world and became heir of the righteousness which is according to faith"* (HEBREWS 11:7, Emphasis added).

Noah was considered to be a righteous man, who walked with God—just like Enoch.[a] Because of his consistent integrity, both in the world and at home, Noah's family went along with his project, even though it meant standing alone in the whole world! Would your family be willing to pay such a price because of your life's testimony?

Is your testimony one of sitting in front of a TV set? Shopping on eBay? Or serving the Lord by reading the Bible story and praying with your children at night before they go to bed? How about prayer? Do you say "Let's pray" when the family gets in the car? Do you ask what the children learned at school, Sunday school, or youth group? Do you serve the Lord by volunteering to help when needs arise to clean, move, and actually work on your weekend for the Lord? All of these services speak so much louder than words to your family.

a. Genesis 6:9

5. NOAH BRAVELY CONDEMNED SIN

*"By faith Noah, being divinely warned of things not yet seen, moved with godly fear, prepared an ark for the saving of his household, **by which he condemned the world** and became heir of the righteousness which is according to faith"* (HEBREWS 11:7, Emphasis added).

Noah courageously confronted the whole world of sin, and stood against it. This was not easy because of the intense demonic activity prevalent in the days of Noah. Until the end of the world there will never be a time of stronger demonic activity. The entire earth was anti-God, anti-righteousness, and pro-sin. Immorality was at its vilest degrees, murder was rampant, and people were deaf to the Word from God. After 120 faithful years of preaching (Genesis 6:3) there was not one human beyond his family that Noah had convinced that God was right and they were wrong. Only Noah and his family believed in God and entered the ark of safety.

And Scripture tells us that *"as it was in the days of Noah, so it will be also in the days of the Son of Man ..."* (LUKE 17:26). Many Bible scholars believe that we are living in those very days right now. Noah was willing to obey God, regardless of the cost to him and his family. Are you willing to follow Christ with that same depth of devotion?

Today we have no ark to build, but we do have to choose if we will be shaped by the world—or by Christ. For example, measure the influence Jesus has through His Word on the clothes your wife, sons, and daughters wear. **(See chapter 19 for a brief guide to biblical modesty.) Do they reflect Him?** How about the music they listen to? Is it prompting them to seek the Lord or the world? And whatever movies, videos, and amusements they enjoy—do they please God? How about the level of sports involvement in your family's schedule? (A decrease in out-of-the-home events will free up time for the powerful simplicity of reading the Bible at meals and discussing it with your family.) Is the Lord honored by your family's schedule?

6. NOAH LIVED ACCORDING TO FAITH

*"By faith Noah, being divinely warned of things not yet seen, moved with godly fear, prepared an ark for the saving of his household, by which he condemned the world **and became heir of the righteousness which is according to faith"** (HEBREWS 11:7, Emphasis added).*

This is the genealogy of Noah: *"Noah was a just man, perfect in his generations. Noah walked with God"* (GENESIS 6:9). Wow! What a tribute! Wouldn't you love to have God say that about you? Biblical heroes are those men who, like Noah, faithfully saved their families by obediently warning with both word and example.

Word-filled fathers will: **1.** believe God; **2.** stay in contact with Him; **3.** obey the Lord; **4.** live a life of integrity in the world and at home; **5.** confront sin, and stand against it; and **6.** end as heirs of faith.

Discipline Number Three: Abraham Models Leadership

SO FAR WE'VE SEEN THE importance of developing the godly habits of prayer and obedience, as seen through the life examples of Job and Noah. And now we are going to look at a third great father of the Word—Abraham. What habit was it that God admired about this man of faith? *Leadership*: Abraham set the direction of his family.

1. ABRAHAM LED HIS FAMILY BY EXAMPLE

*"For I have known him, in order that **he may command his children and his household after him,** that they keep the way of the LORD, to do righteousness and justice, that the LORD may bring to Abraham what He has spoken to him"* (GENESIS 18:19, Emphasis added).

"After him" in Genesis 18:19 implies that Abraham's family was deeply impacted by his example. So we see that God chose Abraham to "command his family." Did he obey God's rules?[a] Did he have genuine loving concern for each family member?[b] Did he sacrifice

a. See Genesis 21:1-8.

b. See Genesis 21:9-21.

all for God—even the best, closest, and most precious?[a] The answer to every question is yes!

Abraham faithfully directed his family to look beyond the passing fancies of the world system, beyond the materialism of his day in Ur of the Chaldeans. That meant forsaking the gods of this world system, and obeying the true, living, and only God.

Some of the twenty-first century "gods" are comfort, security, and convenience. We lust for material comforts, sacrifice for financial security, and allow life to become a blur in the name of convenience. The notion that "a good paying job is worth the risk of losing our family by neglect" is a false god we serve. The idea that our children should be "successful" financially in a career, instead of useful to their Creator, is a false god we serve. The fear of not having enough money to retire on and lead the "good life" is a false god we serve. It is time to have goals for the future that are not financial but eternal. That is God's call to the Abrahams of today who want to lead Word-filled families.

2. ABRAHAM LED HIS FAMILY FAITHFULLY

*"By faith Abraham, **when called to go to a place he would later receive as his inheritance, obeyed and went, even though he did not know where he was going.** By faith he made his home in the promised land like a stranger in a foreign country; he lived in tents, as did Isaac and Jacob, who were heirs with him of the same promise. For he was looking forward to the city with foundations, whose architect and builder is God"* (HEBREWS 11:8-10, NIV; Emphasis added).

Whenever God said to go, Abraham went. When told to leave it all, he did so by giving up materialism. When God told him, "Give up those gods, and worship only Me," he did, and when God commanded obedience, he obeyed. The greatest leader is one who himself is respectfully submissive to authority. Even Christ was in subjection to His Father, always doing those things which pleased Him.[b]

In the months that followed completion of seminary, I worked for a very large pharmaceutical company, and Bonnie was a stay-at-home mom. I served half-time at my first church staff position while awaiting the next year's budget approval to go full-time. Just before the full-time status arrived at the church, the vice president of the eight-billion-dollar conglomerate I worked for in the mid 1980s flew out and took us to dinner. At dinner that evening, I was offered a national sales position that *tripled* what I was *going* to make full-time at church. In response, Bonnie and I looked that New Yorker in the eye, thanked him, and said no. Why? Money can't buy the satisfaction that only obedience to the Lord brings.

One of our goals in the education of our children has been to allow them to experience and enjoy ministry. They have served at camps, conference centers, and alongside third world missionaries. All that has lessened the other activities of our family, but the trade-off is priceless. They have not been able to be as involved in many of the events that families use to measure and demonstrate their children's successes. Yet we have seen a growing desire in each of our children to consider lifelong ministry for the kingdom of God—as their *first* choice.

One prayer that I trained my children to say from their earliest days was this: "I love the Lord, and I want to serve the Lord, and I want to be a godly woman just like Mom (for our daughters) or a godly man just like Dad (for our sons)." I have had them repeat that hundreds of times over the years, and do you know what? The Lord has caused that simple prayer to become the true desire of their heart! What are your children seeing and hearing modeled by you?

3. ABRAHAM LED HIS FAMILY TO FOCUS ON THE ETERNAL

"By faith Abraham, when called to go to a place he would later receive as his inheritance, obeyed and went, even though he did not know where he was going. By faith he made his home in the promised land like a stranger in a foreign country; **he lived in tents, as did Isaac and Jacob, who were heirs with him of the same promise.** *For he was looking forward to the city with foundations, whose architect and builder is God"* (HEBREWS 11:8-10, NIV; Emphasis added).

Abraham led his family to get out of the world system that is headed away from God, and toward judgment. Rather than putting down physical roots wherever they went, they dwelled in tents.

They kept looking upward, to God, because their focus was upon the real world—the eternal world.

In the world system, many believe in egalitarianism—that all should have equal political, social, and economic rights. But God's view is equal worth, not equal roles. Still others hold to relativism, believing that there are no absolutes. Yet, God is the God of absolutes. There are those who exploit others to get all they can—to "Go for the gusto!" Hedonists live by "Please me, *now!*" And millions upon millions have fallen prey to materialism, believing that life consists in the multitude, quality, and possession of things and privileges.

Beyond those vain and empty philosophies, there are still many gods to give up. Many of Satan's ways permeate this world, such as substance abuse, sexual license for gratification, or the "sounds of sin"—the language and music of rebellion, wickedness, and occultism. Forsake those gods, and bow to the living and true God!

God's design is to leave the quest for things, and start seeking for only that which has eternal value. Lead your family by reading the Word of God to them, directing them in the paths of righteousness, serving together in church, and reaching out to the lost. Dads, there is a world system to renounce. Are you doing so? Is your life's focus, and that of your family's, on things eternal?

Discipline Number Four: Joseph Models Persistence

IN THE NEW TESTAMENT, JOSEPH is another model dad. Everything we see him do is right on target. He is a father who, in the midst of adversity, *persevered* in hope. We can learn much from his godly example.

1. JOSEPH WAS COMPASSIONATE

*"Then Joseph her husband, **being a just [man], and not wanting to make her a public example,** was minded to put her away secretly"* (MATTHEW 1:19, Emphasis added).

According to Jewish law, a betrothed couple was viewed as if already married, even though not yet physically intimate. Therefore, premarital sex with another person was considered adultery, with a penalty of being stoned to death. But Joseph was a good man, a just and merciful man, who did not want to make a public example out of Mary. Therefore, he wanted to quietly get a legal divorce, which is the meaning of "to put her away."

Do you know what the Bible says about an action like his? Love throws a garment over others' mistakes; love does not draw public attention to them. A compassionate person will cover a transgression.[a]

a. 1 Peter 4:8

2. JOSEPH LISTENED TO GOD

"But while he thought about these things, behold, an angel of the Lord appeared to him in a dream, saying, 'Joseph, son of David, do not be afraid to take to you Mary your wife, for that which is conceived in her is of the Holy Spirit.' ... **Then Joseph, being aroused from sleep, did as the angel of the Lord commanded him** *and took to him his wife"* (MATTHEW 1:20, 24; Emphasis added).

Mary's situation was probably on Joseph's mind continually. After all, they lived in a small town; everyone knew Mary was expecting, but unmarried. With a looming death penalty, it was undoubtedly a frightful time. Yet, in the midst of adversity, we see Joseph triumph as a godly role model. He listened to God by immediately obeying His command to marry Mary. Later on in life, James—another one of Mary and Joseph's children—said: *"Be doers of the word, and not hearers only, deceiving yourselves"* (JAMES 1:22). You can almost hear James echoing his father Joseph's righteous example of listening to God.

3. JOSEPH DEMONSTRATED LOVE

"Now when they had departed, behold, an angel of the Lord appeared to Joseph in a dream, saying, 'Arise, take the young Child and His mother, flee to Egypt, and stay there until I bring you word; for Herod will seek the young Child to destroy Him.' When he arose, **he took the young Child and His mother by night and departed for Egypt,** *and was there until the death of Herod ..."* (MATTHEW 2:13-15A, Emphasis added).

In this passage, Joseph demonstrated love for his family. Did you know that moving all the way to Egypt was a Herculean task back then? It was both difficult and dangerous, but Joseph didn't hesitate to obey God and thereby protect his little family. Godly dads like Joseph demonstrate love to their family by not just *feeling* love, but following through with action. They *do* things for their family!

The following is a modern-day application of one way to protect your family. Recently, my children came to me about a write-up on a movie about a curse on some Egyptian tomb and its contents. They thought it was very interesting. But when I told them I wasn't interested in it, they wanted to know why. So they sweetly gathered around Bonnie and me to find out. I explained, "You children don't understand the pervasive influence of the occult in our world. All that stuff about incantations and books of the dead is currently used in the occult. Most people don't know that the witchcraft book of curses is called *The Sixth Book of Moses*. And all of that stems from Egyptian demonology. Why would we ever want to look at something that had to do with Satan?" The youngest ones didn't understand what the occult was, so I continued, "The Bible says that we are to think on things that are true, honest, just, pure, lovely, of good report, and full of virtue and praise.[a] Does that movie fit God's definition of what we're to think about?" They all decided they didn't want to watch that occult stuff!

Like Joseph, we should demonstrate love for our families by keeping them safe from the hazards of this world. When God revealed the danger, Joseph directed: "Family, pack up! We're getting out of here!" In our world, we need to move our families away from being immersed in wickedness. It is coming everywhere; Matthew 24 says the whole world will be deceived, and we should therefore take care!

a. Philippians 4:8

4. JOSEPH KEPT IN TOUCH WITH GOD

"Now when Herod was dead, behold, an angel of the Lord appeared in a dream to Joseph in Egypt, saying, 'Arise, take the young Child and His mother, and go to the land of Israel ...' " (MATTHEW 2:19-20A, Emphasis added).

Many dads pray to God when faced with a family crisis, but Joseph's habit was perseverance in prayer; he never lost touch with God. Thus he was ready to obey just as soon as the Lord gave him his next instruction—to move back to Israel.

Today, we have something better than angel visitations, hearing voices, or having dreams. We have the revealed will of God in print. What a privilege! We don't have to think: *Did I really dream that or not?* No, we can read it in the Scriptures. Are you searching for answers from God's Word! Does your hunger for His truths direct you? Do you stay in touch with God through prayer and His precious Word?

5. JOSEPH WAS A GOOD PROVIDER

*"But when he heard that Archelaus was reigning over Judea instead of his father Herod, he was afraid to go there. And being warned by God in a dream, he turned aside into the region of Galilee. **And he came and dwelt in a city called Nazareth ...**"* (MATTHEW 2:22-23A, Emphasis added).

To get away from Archelaus, and Judea, Joseph went up into the hill country of Israel. Because Nazareth was a small town of probably no more than 400 people, it was a difficult place to find work as a carpenter. Though it was never easy, Joseph persevered in working hard to provide for his family. In fact, Joseph was a leader in God's order for his home. But after Christ was age 12, we never hear about Joseph again. He most likely died in those silent years. Jesus probably took over the carpentry business at that point. Good fathers will leave an inheritance for their children, and even their children's children.[a]

a. Proverbs 13:22; 19:14

6. JOSEPH GAVE LESSONS IN LIVING

"'Is this not the carpenter, the Son of Mary, and brother of James, Joses, Judas, and Simon? And are not His sisters here with us?' so they were offended at Him" (MARK 6:3, Emphasis added).

It is fascinating that Joseph is such a model father. In Mark 6:3, notice that when the riffraff see Jesus, they immediately think of him as the carpenter. Jesus learned that skill by standing alongside His earthly dad. Godly dads like Joseph give their children lessons in living. He was a modeler; he taught Jesus his trade, and that took side-by-side time.

An Assignment for Dads: As a father, it is a joy to teach my children—even in simple things like how to mow a lawn. I remember when my own dad was teaching me about lawn care. At first, I cut designs in the grass—such as my name, tic-tac-toe, and so forth. However, when Dad caught me, he said, "You know what? The purpose in mowing the lawn is to make straight rows so that when you look at it, you see those pretty lines in the grass." I hadn't realized that; all I thought about was that it took up time, so I had fun doing the designs. When my son Johnny was old enough, I then had the joy of telling him, "Okay now, I'm going to tell you what my dad taught me …"

I realize that a mowing lesson is a simple thing, but the idea I want to get across is the need to teach our children practical lessons in how to live. If we can teach them how to mow, and other things about everyday life, then along the way we will also have opportunities to talk with them, like Solomon talked to his sons in Proverbs.

I actually have a list of items I plan to teach each of my children. It is a joy to be the one they will remember—the one who taught them the basics. Here are a few of the goals on my "Teach the Kids" checklist: How to put gas in the car, clean the windows, and check the oil; How to change a tire; How to use the ATM (Automatic Teller Machine), write a check, and deposit money; How to give from the first of my income regularly, proportionately, and sacrificially to the Lord. Why not make your own checklist and start giving lessons in living like Joseph? Men, put some time into your children each week! What a wise investment with eternal dividends such choices can be!

7. Joseph Followed God's Word for Growing Children

*"So he came by the Spirit into the temple. **And when the parents brought in the Child Jesus, to do for Him according to the custom of the law,** he [Simeon] took Him up in his arms and blessed God and said: 'Lord, now You are letting Your servant depart in peace, According to Your word; For my eyes have seen Your salvation Which You have prepared before the face of all peoples, A light*

to [bring] revelation to the Gentiles, And the glory of Your people Israel.' And Joseph and His mother marveled at those things which were spoken of Him" (LUKE 2:27-33, Emphasis added).

According to the custom, Joseph and Mary took Jesus to Jerusalem to be presented before the Lord. Do you know how far it is from Nazareth to Jerusalem? It is about 70 miles! Worshiping families had to make the trip to Jerusalem at least three times a year. They took time off from work to walk, spend the week in Jerusalem for the feast, pay for their housing, pay for the feast, pay for the sacrifices, and then walk back. That was hard on them, and very costly. But godly dads like Joseph followed God's Word for growing children, which said that when sons were born, they were to be presented before the Lord. As they grew, they were then to be brought to each of the great festivals and taught about God. When Simeon took baby Jesus in his arms and blessed God, his parents marveled at the things he said about Jesus. If we follow scriptural principles for training our children, we too will marvel at the blessings God brings along the way—even when it is hard!

To be truly effective, we must reinforce scriptural child training with power—Word-filled prayer! It can be astonishing to see what prayer can do in the hearts of young people. Did you know that prayer is one of the greatest tools we have in parenting? Our prayers can follow our children into their rooms when they are not looking; our prayers can touch them when they are away at school; our prayers can ride in the car with them; by prayer we can ask God to be real to them wherever they are. We can be requesting, entreating, petitioning, and supplicating before God to touch their hearts and lives. Are you availing yourself of this precious and powerful tool for growing godly children? (See the full discussion of this in Part Four.)

A way *we* can present *our* children to the Lord is by solemnly dedicating their lives to Christ, then dedicating ourselves as faithful parents. We see Christ's presentation to the Father by His parents and can draw some lessons for us as parents from God's Word.

"Now when the days of her purification according to the law of Moses were completed, they brought Him to Jerusalem to present Him to the Lord" (LUKE 2:22).

Here is a way we can also present our children in dedication: When parents present their children to the Lord they are saying, "These children belong to you, Lord. We want to publicly acknowledge that." As we closely examine God's Word we see that God never holds us responsible for how our children turn out—only for how we raised them.

Dedication is when parents say:

- **I will raise Your children** as my very own.
- **I will surrender them** back to You.
- **I will have Your peace** when it is hard, and when they are making their own choices that will shape their future lives.
- **I will always pray for them,** always love them, and no matter what happens—
- **I will have Your peace because I gave them to You,** and raised them as best as I knew how for You.

When I call new parents to the front of the church to lead them in this dedication, I ask all the parents in the congregation to reaffirm these five simple truths in their own hearts as well. But what happens when we dedicate them and they don't turn out as we had hoped and planned? For answers to that question, see Appendix C for "How Should a Believing Parent Respond to a Wayward Child?"

8. Joseph Led His Family in Worship

*"His parents **went to Jerusalem every year** at the Feast of the Passover"* (LUKE 2:41, Emphasis added).

Joseph was a worshiper; Joseph was a leader in godliness because he *took* his family to the feast. He didn't send Mary; he didn't send her with the relatives. Nor did he say, "Why don't you guys go?" Scripture says that Joseph took that responsibility upon himself.

Joseph, like all godly dads, led his family in worship. He did not have the New Testament, but he had the Old Testament, and he was probably aware of this great verse: *"Do not remove the ancient landmark which your fathers have set"* (PROVERBS 22:28).

I think this is critical in today's culture, because it seems like everything is eroding so fast. For that reason, I have especially loved reading *The Autobiography of John G. Paton*, a nineteenth-century missionary.

Paton's father, James, had established clear boundaries for his family. Some of his rules were that they would never miss going to the Lord's house and worshiping; they would never miss morning and evening prayers; they would never miss offering their lives as sacrifices to the Lord; they would never let any event make them miss those ancient landmarks. Nothing is more important than God! As a result, all eleven of James's children passionately followed Christ!

John Paton went on to suffer, survive, and rejoice in the glorious work of the Gospel among the cannibalistic tribes of the New Hebrides Islands (now Vanuatu). He testified that for 50 years he maintained the spiritual disciplines his father had developed in his life. A Word-filled home which shared vital worship and prayer on a consistent basis, coupled with integrity and perseverance, was what steeled the heart of this mighty servant of the Lord.

If we remove the ancient landmarks, and keep moving our standards, we should not be surprised at where our children put those landmarks when they grow up. Like the Paton family, children need to see boundary lines that do not move.

We have examined four imperfect dads who made an eternal impact on each of their family members. So what will we do with our lives?

A good way to start moving your family toward godliness is to decide today what you are going to focus upon. May I suggest you pick one element from the disciplines below and get started implementing it. Stay at it and you will see God begin to impact your family.

Here's how to personalize their examples for use in your family:

Discipline Number One: Job Modeled Prayer. **I will, like Job,** pray from now on for my children—their activities, their purity, their relationship with God, and their hearts. **I will seek, like Job,** to never stop praying for my children!

Discipline Number Two: Noah Modeled Obedience. **I will, like Noah,** seek to model obedience—by believing God, obeying Him, leading my family, condemning sin, and living by faith. **I will seek, like Noah,** to never stop trusting God.

Discipline Number Three: Abraham Modeled Leadership. **I will, like Abraham,** seek to lead my family—by example, faithfully, and with a focus upon the eternal. **I will seek, like Abraham,** to be a man you can count on, Lord.

Discipline Number Four: Joseph Modeled Persistence. **I will, like Joseph,** be persistent in my walk with the Lord—being compassionate, listening to the Lord, demonstrating love, staying in touch with God, being a good provider, giving my children lessons in living, following God's Word for growing my family, and leading my family in worship. **I will seek, like Joseph**, to be persistent in my walk with the Lord.

I know we are never perfect this side of heaven, but why not prayerfully begin in these areas and see what God can do through us who are weak, and sometimes failing. Remember: He is the God of New Beginnings and the God of Second Chances!

STUDY GUIDE QUESTIONS

1. **God has given us His Word to glean insights from other dads who have done things God's way—especially fathers of the Word.** From Job's life example, we can learn the importance of developing a lifelong habit of prayer.

   Read 1 Timothy 4:12. Can you envision Job praying in this manner for his sons and daughters? Does this verse represent your own prayers?

   Read 1 Chronicles 28:9. List the ways David's admonition to his son, Solomon, might have paralleled Job's prayers for his children.

2. **Noah's whole life can be summed up with just one word: obedience.** He modeled obedience by believing God, obeying Him, leading his family, condemning sin, and living by faith.

   Read 1 Samuel 15:22-23. What does God say about the importance of obedience? How does He view rebellion?

Read John 14:15. What does Christ say gives
evidence of our love for Him?

3. What habit is it that God admired about Abraham? Leadership:
Abraham set the direction for his family by example. He chose to keep
his primary focus on eternal values rather than temporal ones.
Read Genesis 18.19. Why did God choose Abraham?
What is the meaning of "after him"? What does God
say is the ultimate goal for his parenting?
Read 1 Timothy 6:6-12. In what ways does this passage
reflect the character of Abraham's life? In what
ways does this passage reflect your own life?

4. Joseph is a New Testament example of a model dad. He is a father
who, in the midst of adversity, persevered in hope.
Read Romans 5:3-5. How does this passage reflect the character
of Joseph's life? How does it reflect your own?
Read Hebrews 10:24-25. Joseph was a leader in godliness
because he took his family to worship. How
does your life compare to his example?

16

"Imitate me, just as I also [imitate] Christ."

— *1 Corinthians 11:1*

How to Be an
Incredible Dad

O N FEBRUARY 1, 2003, SEVEN brave souls—the crew of the
United States space shuttle Columbia—were unexpectedly
ushered into eternity. The crew's commander, Rick Husband, was a
quiet man, but not quiet when it came to sharing his faith in Jesus
Christ. At a reception in his honor, at Husband's request, his friend
Steve Green sang this song for him shortly before take-off on what
proved to be his final mission.

"GOD OF WONDERS"
Lord of all creation
Of water, earth and sky
The heavens are Your tabernacle
Glory to the Lord on high

God of wonders beyond our galaxy
You are holy, holy
The universe declares Your majesty
(Precious Lord, reveal your heart to me)
You are holy, holy

Lord of Heaven and earth
Lord of Heaven and earth

Early in the morning
I will celebrate Your light
When I stumble in the darkness
I will call Your name by night

Hallelujah to the Lord of Heaven and earth
Hallelujah to the Lord of Heaven and earth.[a]

a. Note: "God of Wonders"
is included in Steve Green's
CD entitled "Woven in Time,"
produced by Sparrow
Records (c) 2002.
Used by Permission.

Before boarding the space shuttle, Husband stopped all of his crew, and prayed for them. National Aeronautics and Space Administration (NASA) workers later commented that in all their years working there, they had never seen a commander pray for his crew. Just moments before take-off, a NASA control person commented that it was a perfect day for launch, and Husband replied, "The Lord has given us a beautiful day!"

While in space, because he loved the song "God of Wonders" so much, at his wife Evelyn's request, it was played as one of the crew's wake-up songs. In an e-mail to Steve Green, Husband shared just how awesome God's creation was as he viewed it out of the space shuttle window—never realizing just how soon he'd personally be face to face with the Savior he adored!

We can all laud Husband's leadership and courage as an astronaut. And on the home front, we can praise God for his example as a discipling father. Because of not wanting his two children to miss having private devotions with their dad during the 17 days he was to be in space, Husband recorded a daily devotional video for each of them. This meant sacrificing time out of a busy schedule to record those videos. He had no way of knowing what that act of devotion, that desire to disciple, would be leaving as a legacy to his children! Scripture tells each of us: *"Do not boast about tomorrow, for you do not know what a day may bring forth"* (PROVERBS 27:1). Dad, if you yourself were ushered into eternity today—without a moment's notice—what kind of legacy would you be leaving for your children?

Building a Godly Legacy

How CAN WE EVEN BEGIN to build a godly legacy? The Owner of your life, and mine, has written out just what He expects from us. There are an abundance of "how to" parenting instructions in our "Owner's Manual"—the Bible. Nothing will be more vital or practical to our parenting than God's Word, for He has set the standard for the way He designed life to be. God has a lot to say about His expectations for the family— especially to fathers. His parenting mandate is clearly stated in the following verses:

"You shall love the LORD your God with all your heart, with all your soul, and with all your strength. And these words which I command you today shall be in your heart. You shall teach them diligently to your children ..." (DEUTERONOMY 6:5-7A).

That passage reveals our threefold parenting responsibility: **1.** We must love God preeminently, **2.** treasure His Word in our hearts, and **3.** pass on that faith diligently to our children. Nurturing in God's Word and His ways is a specific type of training called discipling. Biblical child training—the process of causing our children to come under our authority and respect our word—leads to teachable hearts that are open to receiving God's Word in the right spirit. **How can we do this in our families?**

1. BY TALKING ABOUT GOD

God commands us to fill our homes with His Word. In contrast to operating in the flesh, God's way is to lead our children—through both word and deed—to love Him with their whole hearts, and to follow Him obediently. Though that is a tall order, His training process is simple:

> *"You shall teach them* [God's Words] *diligently to your children,*
> ***and shall talk of them*** *when you sit in your house, when you*
> *walk by the way, when you lie down, and when you rise up"*
> (DEUTERONOMY 6:7, Emphasis added).

Note that God tells us to talk about all that He has commanded us—not preach, scold, cajole, pound it into them, or dump on them. No, we should make sharing the Lord so natural that we freely talk about Him—anytime, anywhere. Such talk should be unforced, flowing over into every part of life. If we see God in everything, so will they. If God stays strictly at church, they will compartmentalize Him right out of their social lives, private lives, sports lives, dressing lives, recreation lives—and every other part of their lives. As one great old saint said, "There's no difference between the sacred and the secular." That is what Moses is saying: let God flow into all of life. He has given us powerful pointers on ways to do that.

a. v. 7a

Talk about God "when you sit in your house."[a] "Sit in your house" suggests that we are at home, and so are our children. Mealtimes are wonderful opportunities to open up to our families, sharing how we've seen **God's hand** in our lives, **His face** in our devotions, and **His voice** in our hearts as we worship. We ought to tell them how our heavenly Father is so patient with our weaknesses, so loving with our failures, so gentle with our corrections. Then we need to live that out before them.

b. v. 7b

Talk about God "when you walk by the way."[b] One discipling technique is to take "talk walks" with our children. On the way, we ought to *listen* until we hear them through their words, and then talk to the person we see in those words. Another example is to turn off the radio in our cars while on a family outing, and just let our children talk with us. We must seize those opportune moments—while we still have them.

c. v. 7c

Talk about God "when you lie down."[c] One of the most crucial times of ministry for us as dads is at our children's bedtimes. So many little thoughts, little fears, little hurts, can all be worked on. A wise dad takes life and parenting one day at a time. We ought to consistently train our children by leading and guiding them, and then asking God to move in their hearts accordingly. Discipling fathers should treasure those closing moments of the day by making the most of them. I always try to pray with each of my children before they go to sleep, ending with, "I love you and Jesus loves you even more!"

Talk about God "when you rise up."[a] Every morning, we should treat our families in a manner which "makes their day." We can do this by bathing them with the loving presence of Jesus as shown through our kindness, gentleness, and goodness. After we leave for work, our families ought never to have to struggle with remembering our lateness, shortness, and gruffness. Another great time is on the way to school. If you drive your children to school pray with them for strength to take Jesus with them all day long.

a. v. 7d

Talk about God "when away from home."[b] We must make our faith portable, as God directs in this passage: *"Tie them as symbols on your hands* [this speaks of what we do for a living] *and bind them on your foreheads* [this stands for our minds, thoughts and values; God must be a part of all we do and think]. *Write them on the doorframes of your houses and on your gates"* (DEUTERONOMY 6:8-9, NIV). "Doorframes" takes us beyond the literal word and directs us to consider that all that comes and goes (through those doors)—**is to have God's signature upon it**. Is it pleasing to Him? And the "gates" speaks of what those outside our home can see. What impression does our family leave with those who watch us from afar? Is God's Word written upon our behavior in our community? What do our actions declare about the Lord to our neighbors?

b. vv. 8-9

Christ beautifully modeled this art of biblical communication. When He taught, He taught simply. Thus the common people—the unschooled and unpolished—heard Him gladly. Some of the greatest portions of Scripture are the simplest. The Sermon on the Mount, known and loved around the world, is comprised of 60 percent monosyllabic words. First Corinthians 13, the great love chapter, is over 50 percent one-syllable words.

What was Christ's teaching style? Jesus shared from life in general—outdoors, indoors, sitting, walking, standing, any time or place. Because He used the elements of the world, His hearers understood when He spoke of sowers and seeds, reapers and harvests, tombs and bones, plants and animals, coins and jobs, trees and birds, heaven and hell. In other words, Christ etched His mind on hearts through the words and pictures of the common people.

The power of Christ's teaching was His conviction of the truth of what He was saying. Stressing biblical communication, with conviction, is imperative if we are to effectively lead our households. As we nurture in God's Word and His ways, like Jesus, we should keep our "talk" simple, consistent, and focused.

2. By Bringing God Into All of Life

Now let's make all of this more personal. What are some practical ways that you, as a discipling dad, can etch God's Word on every action of your children's lives?

As the leader of your home, you should **initiate the daily reading of God's Word to your family.** Establish a routine, with a definite time and place. For the greatest effectiveness, the level of difficulty and amount of reading ought to be adjusted to the ages and attention spans of your children. As you read, remember that it is exciting to have the privilege of reading God's "Best Seller"—the only one written by God—which will never change nor fade away! It is this spirit that you should pass on to your children.

Varying the methods of Bible times together will enhance their love of God and His Word. In my own family, when our children were all little, we had evening Bible time with them on our laps on the living room floor, or in their bedroom. This was a loving, fun, and favorite part of the whole day! We would pray, read the Word, ask questions, sing, and pray again. We still have this special time with the "little buddies" (the four youngest), but additionally have Bible times around our dinner table at breakfast or lunch, and almost every dinner time.

For variety, we've also read **missionary biographies together;** played Bible charades; watched Bible videos; listened to dramatized versions of Bible audios; and given the children turns at leading devotions, songs, telling stories, or leading in prayer. Telling bedtime stories from our own lives that teach spiritual lessons from our successes and failures has been a favorite. Bonnie and I have shared our personal salvation testimonies regularly, as well as how God's hand has been active in our lives. Our children have learned numerous hymns that teach doctrine. We've memorized verses together, and have had "Sword Drills" in which a Bible reference is called out and the children then find the verse(s) as quickly as possible. The youngest children have also enjoyed having their older siblings read to them.

Since each child's birth, we have **sung the same special hymns** ("My Jesus, I Love Thee," "Be Still My Soul," and "How Great Thou Art") nightly with a child snuggled against our shoulder, or tucked happily in bed. This brings such security and comfort as they close their day singing in their hearts to the Lord. We always close our day in prayer to God, with thanksgiving, and committing to Him any cares that may have come out when "little windows" of their hearts were opened to Dad and Mom.

As your children gain the necessary reading skills, **start a Read-Through-the-Bible Chart for each child**. This will help you better oversee their consistency in daily reading. (Make sure to model this habit as well.) Ask questions about particular passages; explain the meanings as needed.

Select verses or full passages that currently apply to your family's walk with the Lord, then **memorize those together as a family.** (Very young children would do well learning to recite only a phrase or single verse out of a lengthier selection.) Discuss ways to practically apply what you're memorizing.

Establish a monthly breakfast date with each child. This is a key time to grow as friends. We are first of all parents, then friends. Learn to ask questions that they will like to answer. Be sure to listen attentively as each child pours out his or her thoughts, and then address them in an encouraging manner.

- What do you think about our family?
- If you could change anything, what would you change?
- What are your most common thoughts about God?
- What do you like about the way God made you?
- What do you think He wants you to be when you grow up?

Taking "talk walks" is an excellent time to **share stories from when you were a child.** Use them to teach moral, spiritual, and practical lessons on your failures and successes. (Remember: it is important to let children into the interior of your life.)

Take your children on ministry trips. Visit a rest home or a hospital; have your family serve food on Thanksgiving at a mission; go on visitation together, and then model how to evangelize. Be creative! Ask the Lord to provide additional ideas for ways to instill an attitude of outreach and service for Him.

Start a "Spiritual Life Journal" on each child. Keep track of the date of salvation; special prayer requests and answers; desires for service (such as wanting to be a missionary, pastor, church musician, etc.); reading accomplishments in Scripture; and so forth.

As a discipling father, also **initiate meaningful family traditions**—to include fun outings for the family on a regular basis. Why is that important? A family that prays, works, and plays together is likely to stay together.

3. By Not Provoking Our Children to Wrath

"And you fathers, do not provoke your children to wrath, but bring them up in the training and admonition of the Lord"
(EPHESIANS 6:4).

It is not easy to own up to struggling with anger. Yet, survey nearly any group of solid Christians, and a majority of the men will often confess to having a problem with anger. Author H. Norman Wright points out:

> *[Anger] can motivate you to hate, wound, damage, annihilate, despise, scorn, loathe, vilify, curse, ruin, and demolish. When we're angry we might ridicule, get even with, laugh at, humiliate, shame, criticize, bawl out, fight, crush, offend, or bully another person. All of these do very little to build relationships.*[a]

a. H. Norman Wright, *Winning Over Your Emotions* (Eugene, OR: Harvest House Publishers, 1998), p. 49.

Were such actions vented on our children, think of the damaged relationships which can occur! They have no way to defend themselves from our wrath. Instead, they just absorb such meanness right into their little spirits—and then *they* become angry. So the cycle perpetuates itself because anger begets anger.

In the Old Testament Book of Numbers, God reveals the three common causes for anger. These are areas that we all need to remember to avoid. Do you remember what they were so that you can spot situations that often lead to anger? Here they are. Moses was angry because of **FEAR**[a]—the last time the people were without water they tried to stone him in Exodus 17:1-4; he was angry because of **FRUSTRATION**[b]—his sister Miriam had just died and these people thwarted him so often; and Moses was angry because of **HURT**[c]—he had saved their lives in Exodus 32:7-14 when God was ready to destroy them all, and they did not even care about him. Watch out in times of fear, frustration, and hurt—anger lurks nearby.

Because men normally think mechanically rather than relationally, God knows that sinful anger can be a frequent temptation for us as dads. He thus cautions: *"Fathers, do not provoke your children, lest they become discouraged"* (COLOSSIANS 3:21). What are some ways that fathers commonly provoke children to anger?

If you were to do a quick survey of the topic of "anger" in God's Word—this would be a summary of what you would find. Anger is contagious, and we run the risk of raising angry children when we allow our own lives to be out of control.[d] This anger in their lives is fueled when they see that as their parents we are not having marital harmony.[e] This personal and marital struggle leads us to appear to our children that we have a double standard[f]—the high level we try to hold them to, and the reality we at times are sadly living—and this will always fuel their anger and frustration.

Other ways that we actually encourage anger in our children are when we do not take the needed time to talk with them;[g] or we are neglecting their physical needs;[h] or even when we give them too much freedom.[i]

Prayerfully decide that you will not provoke them to anger by never praising them,[j] or having a critical spirit toward them,[k] and even scolding, especially in front of others.[l] Of course we should never evidence a lack of love by making fun of them,[m] or calling them names.[n]

When we are in too much of a hurry to listen to their opinion

a. Numbers 20:2

b. Numbers 20:3

c. Numbers 20:4

d. Proverbs 22:24-25

e. Genesis 2:24
Hebrews 12:15
f. Matthew 23:1-4, 23-24, 28
Philippians 4:9
James 1:17, 22
Matthew 5:37
Colossians 3:9

g. Ephesians 5:15-16
Ecclesiastes 3:1
h. Philippians 2:3-4
Titus 2:4-5
i. Proverbs 29:15
Galatians 4:1-2

j. Proverbs 25:11; 27:2
k. Matthew 7:1-5
2 Corinthians 3:6
l. Matthew 18:15
John 21:15-17
m. Job 17:1-2
n. Ephesians 4:29

a. Proverbs 18:13, 17
b. Matthew 5:23-26
   Job 32:2
   James 5:16
   Proverbs 16:18
   James 4:6
c. Psalm 6:1; 38:1
   James 1:19-20
   Ephesians 4:26-27
d. James 3:17
e. 1 Corinthians 10:13; 13:11
f. 2 Corinthians 10:12
g. Titus 3:2
   Proverbs 22:1
h. Ecclesiastes 8:11
i. Ephesians 4:31-32
   Matthew 18:5-6
   1 Timothy 3:3
   Titus 1:7

or side of the story[a] we plant seeds of anger. Our pride in not admitting when we are wrong[b] also induces anger, just as when we are consistently disciplining in anger.[c]

To protect our children from cultivating anger we must guard against being overly strict,[d] and from having unrealistic expectations for them or by comparing them to others.[e] Another bad habit we slip into that causes resentment and smoldering anger in our children is when we discuss our children's weaknesses and struggles with others, especially in their presence.[f] If we discipline inconsistently,[g] or abuse them emotionally,[h] and especially if one abuses them physically[i]—there is no excuse. We are sinning and they will grow more and more angry. These evils should never be allowed to come into our homes and lives as a family.

In conclusion, Wright made some valid points when he wrote: "Why do you become angry at your family members when they don't respond to you? Why do you get angry at the kids when they don't pick up their room, mow the lawn, or dry the dishes properly? Anger expressed by yelling at a son who does not mow the lawn carefully does not teach him how to do it correctly. Angry words directed to a sloppy daughter do not teach her how to be neat. Step-by-step instruction (even if it has been given before) can help solve the problem."[j]

j. H. Norman Wright,
Winning Over Your Emotions
(Eugene, OR: Harvest House
Publishers, 1998),
p. 68. For an extensive study
in the prevention and cure
of anger in children, read
Lou Priolo's The Heart of
Anger (Amityville, NY: Calvary
Press, 1997).

"So then, my beloved brethren," writes James, *"let every man be swift to hear, slow to speak, slow to wrath; for the wrath of man does not produce the righteousness of God"* (JAMES 1:19-20).

Wrath is a "Goliath" that must be faced and conquered. When David faced his "Goliath," he knew the secret of victory. He refused to trust in his own strength, but claimed in faith: *"The battle is the LORD's, and he will give* [Goliath] *into our hands"* (1 SAMUEL 17:47). *"Is anything too hard for the LORD?"* (GENESIS 18:14A).

4. BY ESTABLISHING BIBLICAL GOALS OF DISCIPLING

There is a common saying that can also be applied to the discipleship of children: If you fail to plan, you plan to fail. In other words, if you fail to establish measurable and intentional goals for the

personal and spiritual growth of your children, you are more likely
to fail in your God-given mandate as a father.

Prayerfully ask yourself this question: *In light of God's Word, what
discipling goals does God want me to accomplish in my children before
they leave home?* As the Holy Spirit leads, make a list of goals to
regularly pray over and implement through a discipling process that
relies on *His strength.*[a] To get you started, consider these unchanging
requirements in light of discipling your children:

a. John 15:5

> *"But also for this very reason, giving all diligence, add to* [their]
> *faith virtue, to virtue knowledge, to knowledge self-control, to self-*
> *control perseverance, to perseverance godliness, to godliness broth-*
> *erly kindness, and to brotherly kindness love. For if these things are*
> [theirs] *and abound,* [they] *will be neither barren nor unfruitful*
> *in the knowledge of our Lord Jesus Christ"* (2 PETER 1:5-8).

What a treasure chest of discipling goals: faith, virtue, knowledge, self-control, perseverance, godliness, brotherly kindness,
and love! As those qualities progressively increase in your
believing children's lives, they will reflect Christ's divine nature
within, and thus their ongoing growth toward the ultimate goal
of discipleship: *"Be imitators of God as dear children. And walk
in love, as Christ has also loved us and given Himself for us ..."*
(EPHESIANS 5:1-2).

Character Training for Our Children

IT IS IMPORTANT TO NOTE that the following character qualities are
not something that we can *make happen* in our children. No, they
are the result of being born again, having the Spirit of God within,
and turning over their lives to God's control. As Jesus said about
radical change in a troubled boy in the Gospels—*"this kind cometh
not but by prayer and fasting"* (MATTHEW 17:21, KJV). We must
faithfully seek God (prayer) and deny ourselves (fasting) on behalf
of our children!

1. Lead them to surrender their lives: *"I beseech you therefore, brethren, by the mercies of God, that you present your bodies a living sacrifice, holy, acceptable to God, which is your reasonable service. And do not be conformed to this world, but be transformed by the renewing of your mind, that you may prove what is that good and acceptable and perfect will of God"* (ROMANS 12:1-2).

In 2 Peter 1:5 we see the need to diligently "add to [their] faith" all the graces necessary for godliness. This will result from presenting themselves unreservedly to Christ, then being renewed in their minds through the written and living Word of God. This should be your highest discipling priority. Here are some suggested discipling goals to affirm prayerfully before the Lord. In a time of prayer before His Word tell Him, "By Your grace, I will lead my children to pursue the following disciplines"—

- To present their eyes, ears, hands, feet, dating lives, and social lives to the Lord (Romans 6:13).
- To present their appetites to the Lord, and to hunger for Him and His righteousness rather than the world (1 John 2:15-17).
- To present their future plans to the Lord to make sure they fit with His (Matthew 6:33).
- To present their friends to the Lord, and only associate closely with those who love and want to serve Him (James 4:4-5).
- To present their past hurts to the Lord as well as all their present troubles (Genesis 41:51-52).

2. Lead them to be an example: *"Let no one despise your youth, but be an example to the believers in word* [what I say], *in conduct* [what I do], *in love* [what I give], *in spirit* [what I feel], *in faith* [what I believe], *in purity* [what I resist]*"* (1 TIMOTHY 4:12).

Virtue is moral excellence that will permeate their lives as they obey the written and living Word of God! Here are some suggested discipling goals to affirm prayerfully before the Lord. In a time of prayer before His Word tell Him, "By Your grace, I will lead my children to pursue the following disciplines"—

- To devour God's Word (1 Timothy 4:13).
- To serve Christ's church (1 Timothy 4:14).
- To excel in spiritual things, not merely in temporal things like sports, the arts, or academics (1 Timothy 4:15).
- To run from sin in any form (2 Timothy 2:22).

3. Lead them to exercise discipline: *"Discipline yourself for the purpose of godliness"* (1 TIMOTHY 4:7B, NASB).

The Greek word for "self-control" has the sense of mastering one's desires and passions. A synonym for self-control is discipline. As a discipling father, developing self-control (self-discipline) in your children ought to be high on your "to do" list. Here are some suggested discipling goals to affirm prayerfully before the Lord. In a time of prayer before His Word tell Him, "By Your grace, I will lead my children to pursue the following disciplines"—

- To be bringing every thought under the control of Jesus Christ (2 Corinthians 10:3-5).
- To diligently seek to walk righteously and speak uprightly, to despise ill-gotten gain, and to stop their ears and eyes from hearing or seeing evil (Isaiah 33:15-17).
- To be self-disciplined in their everyday living (1 Timothy 4:7).
- To show self-control by being orderly in everything they do (1 Corinthians 14:40).
- To show self-control by being hard working rather than lazy (1 Thessalonians 4:11-12).
- To show self-control by being dependable, even when they don't feel like it (Psalm 15:4b).

4. Lead them to deny ungodliness: *"For the grace of God that brings salvation has appeared to all men, teaching us that, denying ungodliness and worldly lusts, we should live soberly, righteously, and godly in the present age, looking for the blessed hope and glorious appearing of our great God and Savior Jesus Christ"* (TITUS 2:11-13).

From these verses, you should easily see the importance of training your children to learn to behave in a godly manner, regardless of the circumstances. Here are some suggested discipling goals to affirm prayerfully before the Lord. In a time of prayer before His Word tell Him, "By Your grace, I will lead my children to pursue the following disciplines—"

- To search God's Word to learn what He hates, and what He loves, and then imitate those areas (Psalm 119:97-104).
- To not look at what God calls evil (Psalm 101:3-4). This includes but is not limited to: going to (or renting) ungodly movies; viewing worldly television shows and commercials; playing questionable computer games; surfing the internet to get a glimpse at lustful or otherwise evil pictures; and participating in violent and occultish video games. All of these enticements have the potential to deaden spiritual lives!
- To not use their mouths to say anything which God considers to be corrupt (Ephesians 4:29).
- To please God in all they do (1 Corinthians 10:31).
- To not cling to old habits, but to look upward— not downward (Colossians 3:1).

The suggested discipling goals we have just covered represent a broad range of godly character-development basics. As you personalize your own goals through prayer, the Holy Spirit will direct you specifically in what He deems to be priorities for your own family. The overall discipling goal should be to strengthen your children's character so that they more and more forsake their own way, and choose to follow Christ instead. This basically is simple, straightforward obedience. It means they will desire to do what God asks them to do; they will want to go where God invites them to go; they will strive to say what God instructs them to say. Those we disciple should learn to act and react in the manner God's Word maintains is in their own best interest, as well as for Christ's glory and honor.

In closing, I exhort you to remember that discipleship is an ongoing, lifelong process by which the Holy Spirit uses the Word of God to conform the child of God into the image of God for the glory of God. As we dads increasingly learn how to be imitators of Christ through the power of the Holy Spirit, He can use us mightily not only in our families' lives, but also in the fulfilling of His great commission to go forth and make disciples of all to whom God sends us. We can then experientially and joyfully teach others to observe all things that He has commanded us![a] It all starts with our obedience, our self-sacrifice and devotion to Christ, so that we may honestly say: *"Imitate me, just as I also imitate Christ"* (1 CORINTHIANS 11:1).

a. Matthew 28:19-20

STUDY GUIDE QUESTIONS

1. **An incredible dad strives to build a godly legacy.** He parents through God's Word, for it is He who has set the standard for the way He designed life to be. Read 2 Timothy 3:16-17. List four ways in which Scripture is "profitable" for bringing children up in the nurture and admonition of the Lord. What does God say should be your ultimate goal?

    Read, memorize, and meditate upon Psalm 119:9-11.
       Why is it so important to establish a Scripture
       memory program for your children?
    Read, memorize, and meditate upon Psalm 119:97, 103-104. As you
       hide these words in your heart, and meditate upon them, pray
       that your love of the Word will be "caught" by your children.

2. **An incredible dad strives to bring God into all of life.** He shares the Lord so naturally that he freely talks about Him—anytime, anywhere.
    Read 1 Peter 3:15. As your children ask questions, are you able
       to clearly articulate why you biblically believe the way you
       do? Can you give a "Thus says the Lord …" response?
    Read 2 Timothy 2:15. What does God say is
       necessary to bring Him into all of life?

3. **An incredible dad strives to not provoke his children to wrath.**
    Read Colossians 3:21. What does God say can happen to children
    if they are continually provoked? What are some ways that fathers
    commonly provoke their children to anger?
       Proverbs 22:24-25. What can happen in a family who
          is regularly exposed to an angry person?

Read James 3:17-18. In these verses, God contrasts mean-
spiritedness with "the wisdom that is from above." List the
characteristics that will help avoid provoking children to wrath.

4. An incredible dad provides consistent biblical child training. He
recognizes the need to help his children, by God's grace, to diligently
"add to [their] faith" all the graces necessary for godliness. Read 2 Peter
1:5-7. List these graces.

Read Isaiah 28:10. What child training principle
do we see in this verse?

**5. Becoming an incredible dad starts with our obedience, our self-
sacrifice, and our devotion to Christ.** Ask the Lord to make
1 Corinthians 11:1 a reality in your life—as well as your family's.

"Again, I tell you that ***if two of you on earth agree*** about anything you ask for, it will be done for you by my Father in heaven."

— ***Matthew 18:19, niv,*** *emphasis added*

"If you believe, you will receive ***whatever you ask*** for in prayer."

— ***Matthew 21:22, niv,*** *emphasis added*

"Husbands, in the same way be considerate as you live with your wives, and treat them with respect as the weaker partner and as heirs with you of the gracious gift of life, so that ***nothing will hinder*** your prayers."

— ***1 Peter 3:7, niv,*** *emphasis added*

"Ye have not, ***because ye ask not.***"

— ***James 4:2b, kjv,*** *emphasis added*

Jesus never taught His disciples how to preach, *He only taught them how to pray. The one lesson that His disciples made their priority after the Ascension was recorded in Acts 6:4, and that is our priority also if we want to get His work done, His way, with His power. Learn to pray without ceasing for the Lord to be at work in your life, in your marriage, and in your home. One of the most powerful elements of marriage is the ability to have complete spiritual unity and agreement in our prayers. God's Word says in Matthew 18:19 that the unhindered agreement (of a mother and father) in prayer is one of the greatest powers possible! And to unleash those Word-filled prayers we will learn the following lessons:*

PART FOUR

A Word Filled Prayer Life

There Is *No* Greater Power

17

"If you abide in Me, and My words abide in you, you will ask what you desire, and it shall be done for you. By this My Father is glorified, that you bear much fruit, so you will be My disciples."

— *John 15:7-8*

Prayer: Our Most Powerful Tool

AFTER OVER TWO DECADES AS parents, our philosophy of great parenting can be summed up in just one sentence: you raise a godly family "one prayer at a time." Faithful prayer, in step with God's plan in His Word, is God's most powerful key to unlock children's hearts as we disciple them for Christ.

What did those who spent the most time with Jesus on earth remember about Him? When He had returned to heaven, and His disciples were left to get the message out, they all confessed to the method they had learned, and had made the focus of their lives: *"We will give ourselves continually to prayer and the ministry of the Word."*[a]

a. Acts 6:4

Don't miss the point Christ's disciples were making. There is a simple starting point when you face the greatest task imaginable. (For the disciples, it was evangelizing the whole world; for us it is raising a godly family.) That starting point is to let the Word fill your heart, mind—**and prayers!** There it is: the simplest and most powerful truth of parenting—Word-filled men and women of prayer.

The **Word-filled family** is built upon the foundation of a **Word-**

filled life, or personal spiritual life in daily touch with the Lord. Then we can have a **Word-filled marriage** where we share the ultimate partnership possible in this world with the one He chose to complete our life. From those two streams flow the **Word-filled prayers** of godly husbands and wives, moms and dads. There is no greater power on earth that can ever be unleashed than the prayers of two hearts united with a holy passion for God, and the family that He has given to them.

What we pray about reflects what fills our hearts. When God fills us, His Word spills out in our prayers. The more we reflect on what His Word says we are to believe and do, the more we meditate upon it, and the more it becomes our constant prayerful ministry. Then parenting isn't a struggle to force God into their lives—it is a joyous relationship with the Lord in our lives that overflows onto them.

As you read this chapter, I hope you will pause and affirm to the Lord that you will also be starting anew today by giving yourself continually to prayer. The Greek word used for "give ourselves continually" literally means "to adhere, persevere, and be in constant readiness" and actually is a form of the Greek word *kratos*, which is a New Testament word for "power." It is a verb in the future indicative tense, so it means "*from now on we will constantly be going to the real source of power which is prayer and the serving of God's Word*" (author's translation).

That is what the Fathers of the church, the apostles, concluded was the only way to "raise" the family of God. As the fathers and mothers God has raised up for our families, we need to commit to that also.

I keep a prayer card—with key verses from the next four chapters— in my car over the visor, in my Bible, in my DayTimer, and in my wallet. No matter where I find myself with a few moments—as I drive, wait for an appointment, sit on an airplane, or just wait in the car for my wife or family—I pull this card out and make a progression in prayer through each point and the verses. My goal in Word-filled praying is to pray through this card once a day for my family.

I would commend this simple habit to any and all of you who desire to see Christ reflected in your family, your marriage, and through your children. These areas are what we will learn to pray about in the next four chapters.

1. PRAYING THEY EXPERIENCE REALITY IN THEIR SPIRITUAL LIVES:

By Saving Faith—*"Open their eyes, in order to turn them from darkness to light, and from the power of Satan to God, that they may receive forgiveness of sins and an inheritance among those who are sanctified by faith in Me"* (ACTS 26:18).

By Loving God's Word—*"I have not departed from the commandment of His lips; I have treasured the words of His mouth More than my necessary food"* (JOB 23:12).

By Living Victoriously—*"You shall KNOW the truth, and the truth shall make you free. ... Therefore, if the Son makes you free, you shall be free indeed"* (JOHN 8:32, 36).

By Thinking of Heaven—*"If then you were raised with Christ, seek those things which are above, where Christ is, sitting at the right hand of God. Set your mind on things above, not on things on earth"* (COLOSSIANS 3:1-2).

By Hating Sin—*"I will declare my iniquity; I will be in anguish over my sin"* (PSALM 38:18).

By Staying Tender Toward God—*"The sacrifices of God [are] a broken spirit, A broken and contrite heart—These, O God, You will not despise"* (PSALM 51:17).

2. PRAYING FOR INTEGRITY IN THEIR PERSONAL LIVES:

By Maintaining a Clear Conscience—*"The purpose of the commandment is love from a pure heart, [from] a good conscience, and [from] sincere faith"* (1 TIMOTHY 1:5).

By Learning to Stand Alone—*"His divine power has given to us all things that pertain to life and godliness, through the knowledge of Him who called us by glory and virtue"* (2 PETER 1:3).

By Seeking to Stay Pure in Mind and Body—*"Beloved, I beg [you] as sojourners and pilgrims, abstain from fleshly lusts which war against the soul ..."* (1 PETER 2:11).

By Evidencing a Servant's Heart—*"Whoever of you desires to be first shall be slave of all. For even the Son of Man did not come to be served, but to serve, and to give His life a ransom for many"* (MARK 10:44-45).

By Not Being Bitter in Trials—*"Let all bitterness, wrath, anger, clamor, and evil speaking be put away from you, with all malice. And be kind to one another, tenderhearted, forgiving one another, even as God in Christ forgave you"* (EPHESIANS 4:30-32).

3. PRAYING THEY REFLECT CHRIST'S LOVE IN THEIR RELATIONSHIPS:

By Cultivating Love for Others—*"BELOVED, let us love one another, for love is of God; and everyone who loves is born of God and knows God. He who does not love does not know God, for God is love"* (1 JOHN 4:7-8).

By Trusting God When Troubles Come—*"Rebellion is as the sin of witchcraft, and stubbornness is as iniquity and idolatry"* (1 SAMUEL 15:23A).

By Loving God's Plan for Their Lives—*"I will praise You, for I am fearfully [and] wonderfully made; Marvelous are Your works, And [that] my soul knows very well"* (PSALM 139:14).

By Waiting for God's Chosen Partner—*"Do not be unequally yoked together with unbelievers. For what fellowship has righteousness with lawlessness? And what communion has light with darkness?"* (2 CORINTHIANS 6:14).

4. PRAYING THEY ARE LIVING FOR HEAVEN:

By Choosing a Life of Contentment—*"I have learned in whatever state I am, to be content: I know how to be abased, and I know how to abound"* (PHILIPPIANS 4:11-13).

By Choosing a Life of Consecration—*"If anyone desires to come after Me, let him deny himself, and take up his cross, and follow Me"* (MATTHEW 16:24).

By Choosing a Life of Commitment—*"No one, having put his hand to the plow, and looking back is fit for the kingdom of God"* (LUKE 9:62).

By Giving Their Life Back to God—*"Know the God of your father, and serve Him with a loyal heart and with a willing mind; for the LORD searches all hearts and understands all the intent of the thoughts. If you seek Him, He will be found by you; but if you forsake Him, He will cast you off forever"* (1 CHRONICLES 28:9).

What Can Prayers Accomplish?

AN AMAZING TESTIMONY TO THE power of prayer may be seen in the life of a quiet man from Bristol, England. This man read the Bible through 200 times during his lifetime! Born in the early nineteenth century, George Mueller lived an exemplary life of powerful praying for "his children." In his lifetime, Mueller personally fed, clothed, educated, and discipled 120,000 orphans and poor children in the five orphan homes he built plus the seventy-two day schools he maintained in England and three other countries. And he did so *solely* by *secret prayer*!

Through extensive diaries that he kept during his remarkable life of 93 years, a picture of powerful praying can be pieced together. In summary, by prayer alone, this man raised 7.2 million nineteenth-century dollars, or $111.6 million dollars in today's currency—all without mass mailings, television ads, internet blitzes, or a huge financial machine behind him.

Without ever asking a soul for even one penny, Mueller's prayers touched the finances of countless individuals who were led by God to give him staggering sums of money freely. For over 60 years, day after day, the exact amount of money to supply thousands of orphans a home, food, clothing, and an education flowed into

George Mueller's office. He diligently studied God's Word and then prayed, telling only the Lord his requests. As a result of his simple faith, people all over the world were drawn to send or bring him gifts at an incredible, miraculous rate.

Mueller's testimony bears repeating because it so clearly reveals the secret of his success:

> To one who asked him the secret of his service, Mr. George Mueller replied: "There was a day when I died, utterly died to George Mueller ... to his opinions, preferences, tastes, and will; died to the world, its approval or censure; died to the approval or blame of even my brethren and friends. Since then I have studied to show myself approved only unto God."[a]

a. Mrs. Charles E. Cowman, *Streams in the Desert* (Grand Rapids, MI: Zondervan, 1977), p. 13.

Mueller's fruitful life is living proof of the truth of John 15:7-8: "*But if you make yourselves at home with me and* **my words are at home in you**, *you can be sure that whatever you ask will be listened to and acted upon. This is how my Father shows who he is—when you produce grapes, when you mature as my disciples*" (*The Message*, Emphasis added).

The key to unleashing prayers that God always answers is to have them flowing from a Word-filled life! Jesus spoke His Word so that it would stay with us, live with us, walk with us, talk to us, meet with us, travel with us. He intends His Word to fill our hearts, fill our minds, fill our days, and all our ways. Prayers that flow from a Word-filled life are simple, direct, and biblical. If we seek to pray simply, directly, and biblically, it will harmonize our prayers to the Lord, His will, His Spirit, and we will experience the power of a Word-filled life.

The Praying Life of Christ

OUR HEAVENLY FATHER'S DESIRE IS that we learn to pray as Jesus demonstrated through His life and words. Prayer is to be a total way of life—an open communication with God which goes on all the time. And if prayer is to be a way of life, then we need to understand how to pray.

1. **HOW did Jesus pray?** Jesus never taught about the circumstances of prayer because any circumstance will do. The Bible records prayers that were offered to God in all types of situations. Consider how Jesus Himself prayed:

Jesus prayed standing: *"Then He commanded the multitudes to sit down on the grass. And He took the five loaves and the two fish, and looking up to heaven, He blessed and broke and gave the loaves to the disciples; and the disciples gave to the multitudes ..."* (MATTHEW 14:19). *"Then they took away the stone from the place where the dead man was lying. And Jesus lifted up His eyes and said, 'Father, I thank You that You have heard Me' "* (JOHN 11:41).

Jesus prayed on His face: *"He went a little farther and fell on His face, and prayed, saying, 'O My Father, if it is possible, let this cup pass from Me; nevertheless, not as I will, but as You will' "* (MATTHEW 26:39).

Jesus prayed on His knees: *"And He was withdrawn from them about a stone's throw, and He knelt down and prayed ..."* (LUKE 22:41).

Jesus prayed walking and looking up: *"Jesus spoke these words, lifted up His eyes to heaven, and said: 'Father, the hour has come. Glorify Your Son, that Your Son also may glorify You ...'"* (JOHN 17:1).

Jesus prayed with loud crying: *"Who, in the days of His flesh, when He had offered up prayers and supplications, with vehement cries and tears to Him who was able to save Him from death, and was heard because of His godly fear ...' "* (HEBREWS 5:7).

Jesus prayed from the Scriptures: *"Then I said, 'Behold, I have come—In the volume of the book it is written of Me—To do Your will, O God' "* (HEBREWS 10:7).

2. **WHERE did Jesus pray?** Everywhere! Jesus never taught about praying in a specific place because we are to pray everywhere. In the Bible, prayer was offered in many different locations:

In a closet: *"But you, when you pray, go into your room, and when you have shut your door, pray to your Father who is in the secret place; and your Father who sees in secret will reward you openly"* (MATTHEW 6:6).

In a garden: *"Then Jesus came with them to a place called Gethsemane, and said to the disciples, 'Sit here while I go and pray over there' "* (MATTHEW 26:36).

On a mountain: *"Now it came to pass in those days that He went out to the mountain to pray, and continued all night in prayer to God"* (LUKE 6:12).

In solitude: *"Now in the morning, having risen a long while before daylight, He went out and departed to a solitary place; and there He prayed"* (MARK 1:35).

In the wilderness: *"So He Himself often withdrew into the wilderness and prayed"* (LUKE 5:16).

On a cross: *"And when they had come to the place called Calvary, there they crucified Him, and the criminals, one on the right hand and the other on the left. Then Jesus said, 'Father, forgive them, for they do not know what they do.' And when Jesus had cried out with a loud voice, He said, 'Father, into Your hands I commit My spirit.' Having said this, He breathed His last"* (LUKE 23:33-34, 46).

3. WHEN did Jesus pray? Jesus never taught about specific times to pray because we are to pray at all times. God welcomes prayers any time of the day or night. Consider these examples:

Early morning: *"Now in the morning, having risen a long while before daylight, He went out and departed to a solitary place; and there He prayed"* (MARK 1:35).

Day and night: *"And this woman was a widow of about eighty-four years, who did not depart from the temple, but served God with fastings and prayers night and day"* (LUKE 2:37).

Before meals: *"Then He commanded the multitudes to sit down on the grass. And He took the five loaves and the two fish, and looking up to heaven, He blessed and broke and gave the loaves to the disciples; and the disciples gave to the multitudes"* (MATTHEW 14:19).

Always: *"Then He spoke a parable to them, that men always ought to pray and not lose heart ..."* (LUKE 18:1).

As He died: *"And when Jesus had cried out with a loud voice, He said, 'Father, into Your hands I commit My spirit.' Having said this, He breathed His last"* (LUKE 23:46).

4. **WHAT did Jesus pray for?** The following section describes the most evident areas of Christ's specific prayers. We should learn from His example how to face similar needs in our lives. Jesus prayed for **consecration for ministry:** *"When all the people were baptized, it came to pass that Jesus also was baptized; and while He prayed, the heaven was opened"* (LUKE 3:21). He also prayed for **daily strength:** *"However, the report went around concerning Him all the more; and great multitudes came together to hear, and to be healed by Him of their infirmities. So He Himself often withdrew into the wilderness and prayed"* (LUKE 5:15-16).

We can often see how Jesus prayed for **clear guidance** when choosing His disciples: *"Now it came to pass in those days that He went out to the mountain to pray, and continued all night in prayer to God"* (LUKE 6:12). He also prayed for **God's direction** as He faced the stresses of life when facing the multitudes: *"However, the report went around concerning Him all the more; and great multitudes came together to hear, and to be healed by Him of their infirmities. So He Himself often withdrew into the wilderness and prayed"* (LUKE 5:15-16). Another drain on His strength is seen by how **Jesus prayed when healing the sick:** *"And the whole city was gathered together at the door. Then He healed many who were sick with various diseases, and cast out many demons; and He did not allow the demons to speak, because they knew Him. Now in the morning, having risen a long while before daylight, He went out and departed to a solitary place; and there He prayed"* (MARK 1:33-35).

As a prime example to us—**Jesus prayed before starting His days:** *"Now when it was day, He departed and went into a deserted place. And the crowd sought Him and came to Him, and tried to keep Him from leaving them ..."* (LUKE 4:42). He also prayed for **personal encouragement** before the first prediction of His death: *"And it happened, as He was alone praying, that His disciples joined Him, and He asked them, saying, 'Who do the crowds say that I am?' "* (LUKE 9:18).

In difficult times Jesus prayed for **God's comfort.** His emotions were sheltered by prayer even in the presence of uncaring friends. *"Then Jesus came with them to a place called Gethsemane, and said to the disciples, 'Sit here while I go and pray over there.' And He took with Him Peter and the two sons of Zebedee, and He began to be sorrowful and deeply distressed. Then He said to them, 'My soul is exceedingly sorrowful, even to death. Stay here and watch with Me.' He went a little farther and fell on His face, and prayed, saying, 'O My Father, if it is possible, let this cup pass from Me; nevertheless, not as I will, but as You will' "* (MATTHEW 26:36-39). This is also seen as Jesus prayed to **prevent discouragement** over misguided disciples: *"Therefore when Jesus perceived that they were about to come and take Him by force to make Him king, He departed again to the mountain by Himself alone"* (JOHN 6:15).

In every area we see Jesus at prayer. He prayed for **wisdom** before teaching the disciples to pray: *"Now it came to pass, as He was praying in a certain place, when He ceased, that one of His disciples said to Him, 'Lord, teach us to pray, as John also taught his disciples' "* (LUKE 11:1). He also prayed for **insight for ministry** when the seventy returned with their report: *"In that hour Jesus rejoiced in the Spirit and said, 'I thank You, Father, Lord of heaven and earth, that You have hidden these things from the wise and prudent and revealed them to babes. Even so, Father, for so it seemed good in Your sight' "* (LUKE 10:21).

Amazingly, Jesus even had to pray for **personal victory** in the Garden of Gethsemane:

" 'Father, if it is Your will, take this cup away from Me; nevertheless not My will, but Yours, be done.' Then an angel appeared to Him from heaven, strengthening Him. And being in agony, He prayed more earnestly. Then His sweat became like great drops of blood falling

down to the ground. When He rose up from prayer, and had come to His disciples, He found them sleeping from sorrow. Then He said to them, 'Why do you sleep? Rise and pray, lest you enter into temptation'" (LUKE 22:42-46).

He also had to ask for **God's protection** while facing the great events of His life—His baptism;[a] choosing the twelve;[b] preparing for the cross;[c] and His transfiguration.[d] This is followed by His prayers for **God's preparation** for the great events and challenges of His ministry—feeding the 4,000;[e] feeding of the 5,000;[f] walking on water;[g] and healing the insane boy.[h]

In everything Jesus prayed for **God's will** in the consummation of His life. It was met in prayer as His last breath on the cross.[i] We can affirm that He prayed for **God's goals**. His earthly prayer life may be seen as:

a. Luke 3:21-22
b. Luke 6:12-13
c. Luke 9:18, 21-22
d. Luke 9:28-36
e. Matthew 15.36
f. John 6:11
g. Matthew 14:23-33
h. Mark 9:14-29

i. Luke 23:46

• **Harmony with God's plan, which was His passion:** *"I have glorified You on the earth. I have finished the work which You have given Me to do"* (JOHN 17:4).

• **Thankfulness in all His life:** *"In that hour Jesus rejoiced in the Spirit and said, 'I thank You, Father, Lord of heaven and earth, that You have hidden these things from the wise and prudent and revealed them to babes. Even so, Father, for so it seemed good in Your sight'"* (LUKE 10:21). God's glory, not His personal needs, was primary to Jesus!

• **Confidence to the end:** Jesus always had confidence in God's hearing and answering. *"And I know that You always hear Me, but because of the people who are standing by I said this, that they may believe that You sent Me"* (JOHN 11:42). Every part of Christ's life demonstrated submission.

Why Must We Pray?

As JESUS TOLD HIS DISCIPLES in Mark 9:29, there is a territory we will never enter with Him without learning the secret of supplication, which is **fasting** (denying ourselves) and **prayer** (seeking God's intervention and help for specific events and people). To be a genuine disciple of Christ, all of us need to exercise ourselves in ceaseless prayer, for prayer is the *only key* to unlock God's provisions for us:

> *"Ask, and it will be given to you; seek, and you will find; knock, and it will be opened to you. For everyone who asks receives, and he who seeks finds, and to him who knocks it will be opened. Or what man is there among you who, if his son asks for bread, will give him a stone? Or if he asks for a fish, will he give him a serpent? If you then, being evil, know how to give good gifts to your children, how much more will your Father who is in heaven give good things to those who ask Him!"* (MATTHEW 7:7-11).

1. We must pray—or we become disobedient. We can only avoid sin, disobedience, and temptation by prayer: *"Watch and pray, lest you enter into temptation. The spirit indeed is willing, but the flesh is weak"* (MATTHEW 26:41).

2. We must pray—or we become weak. We can only experience the power God has for us as we wait upon Him, seek the fullness of His Spirit, and yield to His work through us moment by moment: *"So He said to them, 'This kind can come out by nothing but prayer and fasting' "* (MARK 9:29).

3. We must pray—or we become blind. We can only understand and comprehend the ways of the Lord in His Word through prayer for illumination, guidance, and obedience: *"And He opened their understanding, that they might comprehend the Scriptures"* (LUKE 24:45).

4. We must pray—or we become foolish. We can only have wisdom when we ask of God, who loves to give His wisdom and direction: *"If any of you lacks wisdom, let him ask of God, who gives to all liberally and without reproach, and it will be given to him"* (JAMES 1:5).

5. We must pray—or we become spiritually poor.

- We can only lay up treasures in heaven by a prayerful life on earth (Matthew 6:19-21).
- We can only fill our bowls of worship around God's throne by prayerful living (Revelation 8:3).
- We can only stay in touch with God by prayer (Matthew 26:41).
- We can only stay in love with Jesus by prayer (John 14:21).
- We can only stay in step with the Spirit by prayer (Galatians 5:16).

We have no idea how much the Lord wants to do in and through us until we *ask!* What are you and I wasting by not asking? God wants to do something we can't plan, that we can't program, that we can't calculate, so that when He *does* it—*He* gets all the glory! Consider this exciting treasure chest of prayer promises: (Emphasis added.)

*"And **whatever things you ask in prayer,** believing, you will receive"* (MATTHEW 21:22).

*"And **whatever you ask in My name,** that I will do, that the Father may be glorified in the Son"* (JOHN 14:13).

*"And in that day you will ask Me nothing. Most assuredly, I say to you, **whatever you ask the Father in My name** He will give you"* (JOHN 16:23).

*"And **whatever we ask we receive from Him,** because we keep His commandments and do those things that are pleasing in His sight"* (1 JOHN 3:22).

*"The Spirit also helps in our weaknesses. For **we do not know what we should pray for as we ought,** but the Spirit Himself makes intercession for us with groanings which cannot be uttered. Now He who searches the hearts knows what the mind of the Spirit [is], because He makes intercession for the saints according to [the will] of God .... And if we know that He hears us, whatever we ask, we know that we have the petitions that we have asked of Him"* (ROMANS 8:26-27; 1 JOHN 5:15).

How Can We Pray Like Jesus?

WE CAN DRAW SOME SIMPLE truths from Christ's life that we should all be trying to imitate. We can exercise the discipline of prayer daily by following these six simple habits:

1. When like Jesus—we make the time to pray. Take time! You cannot "find time." Prioritize the time God gives you, and you will be more effective for the things eternally important: *"But seek first the kingdom of God and His righteousness, and all these things shall be added to you"* (MATTHEW 6:33).

a. Mark 1:35

b. Matthew 6:6

2. When like Jesus—we choose a place to pray. Set a specific place to pray, as Jesus had a "solitary place"[a] and spoke of entering into an inner room or closet.[b] Remember: Jesus had no home of His own; He was always staying with others. Ninety-five percent of all homes ever found dating from Christ's time had four rooms—eating, working, storing, and sleeping rooms. Don't think for a moment that Jesus had His own room, and a quiet office in which to study. He was in the midst of trailing disciples, curious onlookers, and determined roof-crashing health seekers. When you add demons and enemies to that scenario, His life was difficult, to say the least!

> *"But you, when you pray, go into your room, and when you have shut your door, pray to your Father who is in the secret place; and your Father who sees in secret will reward you openly"* (MATTHEW 6:6).

Have you ever done much traveling? Or lived in a college dormitory, military barracks, on the road, or with relatives? It is precisely those times that we often slip in our devotional lives. We like to say that we can't find any privacy or even the time to do so. But that describes every single day of Christ's three and one-half years of ministry! What was His secret? First, He chose a place, and then He made time: *"Now in the morning, having risen a long while before daylight, He went out and departed to a solitary place; and there He prayed"* (MARK 1:35).

3. When like Jesus—we pray as often as possible. Pray many times during the day, and at night: *"Evening and morning and at noon I will pray, and cry aloud, And He shall hear my voice"* (PSALM 55:17). And *"we will give ourselves continually to prayer and to the ministry of the word"* (ACTS 6:4).

I once read an article in a missions newsletter called *Non Stop Prayer.* That article motivated me to start cultivating some fresh habits of prayer. In 1 Thessalonians 5:17, Paul tells us that we are to pray without ceasing. If the Word of God says "Pray without ceasing," that must mean that we are able to do so. Right? If you will just start practicing this concept, you will be taking vital steps toward obeying this teaching.

Learn a New Way to Pray All Through Each Day

DO YOU FEEL BURIED BY the pace and volume of life? I receive over 100 e-mails a day plus calls, letters, and visits. How can we ever even hope to *keep up* with all that comes through life each day? I discovered a new way to pray once that has really stuck with me as a life-shaping plan. Here are just a few simple habits that many have learned to practice. If you find extended prayer difficult, these methods can revolutionize your prayer life:

- **Reading Prayer:** Don't simply read through letters, but read and pray. After each paragraph, quickly pray about what you just read.
- **Watching Prayer:** When you watch something take place live, or on television, immediately pray about what you are seeing. (Especially do this after news programs.)
- **Talking Prayer:** When you're on the phone, pray for the person you are talking with. If it is a believer, you can pray together on the phone. This will likely lead you to a double ministry of prayer and encouragement!
- **Listening Prayer:** As you hear things in a meeting, on the radio, or almost anywhere, quickly lift to God in prayer what you are hearing.
- **Writing Prayer:** As you send e-mails, do so with a touch of God requested by prayer. When you write a letter or card (which is a great ministry in itself), pray about what you are writing and, of course, for the person to whom you are writing.

4. When like Jesus—we pray for specific individuals. When we meet people, we should consider them as a "prayer opportunity." This type of thinking will truly expand our prayer life. Consider these examples of prayer:

> "And the Lord said, 'Simon, Simon! Indeed, Satan has asked for you, that he may sift you as wheat. But **I have prayed for you**, that your faith should not fail; and when you have returned to Me, strengthen your brethren' " (LUKE 22:31-32, Emphasis added).

> "O Lord, I pray, please let Your ear **be attentive to the prayer** of Your servant, and to the prayer of Your servants who desire to fear Your name; and let Your servant prosper this day, I pray, and grant him mercy in the sight of this man. For I was the king's cupbearer" (NEHEMIAH 1:11, Emphasis added).

> "Then the king said to me, 'What do you request?' **So I prayed** to the God of heaven" (NEHEMIAH 2:4, Emphasis added).

5. When like Jesus—we pray with people throughout the day. Seek out some meaningful opportunity to pray with others. Note that most of the passages on prayer in Acts are group prayer situations, as in Acts 13:1-2: "Now in the church that was at Antioch there were certain prophets and teachers: Barnabas, Simeon who was called Niger, Lucius of Cyrene, Manaen who had been brought up with Herod the tetrarch, and Saul. As they ministered to the Lord and fasted, the Holy Spirit said, 'Now separate to Me Barnabas and Saul for the work to which I have called them.' "

- **Pray with your marriage partner** to start the day. God has given a powerful promise in Matthew 18:19: *"Again I say to you that if two of you agree on earth concerning anything that they ask, it will be done for them by My Father in heaven."*
- **Pray with your children** to begin their day with a positive note.
- If you have someone in the car with you, **pray together** before you drive away.
- When traveling with a companion or your family, **pray together** at the airport when departing and arriving.

- When you're shopping, or waiting in line at the checkout counter, **look for an opportunity to pray with (or for) someone** whom you sense has a need.
- Pray with thanksgiving **when you hear** good news and with intercession when you hear bad news.
- **Pray on the phone** when people call and ask for help, or when they share their burden.
- **Close phone calls** to loved ones with a prayer.
- **Pray at meals** to show thanksgiving.

6. When like Jesus—we pray systematically. Jesus was surrounding the lives of His disciples He loved and trained with His systematic prayers. Listen to His words to Peter in Luke 22:32: *"But I have prayed for you, that your faith should not fail; and when you have returned to Me, strengthen your brethren."*

Be organized. Use any means to help you do this, but depend on the Lord, not on the means. A prayer list or prayer book can help. Learn to make it a habit to take advantage of time to pray during showers, shaving or putting on cosmetics, mowing the lawn, driving, walks, waiting in a dentist's or doctor's office, changing oil in a car, doing calisthenics, and other things that allow the mind freedom to do this.

Learn a New Way to Guide Your Family Prayers

START A DAILY FAMILY SYSTEM of prayer, emphasizing a different element of prayer each day of the week. It is good to introduce a note of variety into family prayer.[a] For instance, each day of the week you can concentrate on a different prayer project. At one time our prayer-week ran something like this:

a. For a powerful presentation of family prayers see Larry Christenson's, *The Christian Family* (Minneapolis, MN: Bethany Fellowship, Inc., 1974), pp. 174-176. This prayer week is adapted from this book.

1. Monday—The Prayer of Faith. Each member of the family picks out a prayer project with the objective of obtaining an answer before the week is out. It is important to distinguish between the different kinds of prayer, because each prayer has a different objective and approach. If we come to prayer in a vague way, we may pray well enough, but we may pray the wrong kind of prayer for that particular situation. A prayer of faith has as its objective getting a job done. Pray that a child who is afraid of the nursery would be comforted this Sunday, or that a newcomer to Sunday school would feel welcome, or that a witnessing opportunity would be opened and courage to speak would come—all of these are prayers of "faith."

2. Tuesday—Prayer for Family (Far or Near). Each one picks a relative or a member of the immediate family and prays for some specific need which that person may have.

3. Wednesday—The Lord's Prayer. To provide variety, one method I use is to pray the Lord's Prayer (Matthew 6:9-13) a sentence at a time. After each sentence prayer, family members then offer specific petitions related to that prayer. For example, under "*Your kingdom come*" may come a prayer for the peace of His kingdom to come in our own home (or in our nation). Or, the prayer sentence "*Forgive us our debts, as we forgive our debtors*" may prompt confession of a resentful and unforgiving attitude toward a playmate.

4. Thursday—Prayer for Missionaries. Each person picks a missionary to pray for. This helps project the family's concern for Christ's kingdom "*to the ends of the earth.*" Sometimes it is fun to vary this by first praying silently for one's particular prayer project. Afterwards, each has an opportunity to act out his or her missionary as a charade while the others try to guess who or what was prayed for.

5. Friday—Prayers of Confession. Each family member openly confesses one sin that has disturbed peace and harmony within our home. To begin with, this may well be more difficult for parents than for children. Children are used to being corrected and chastened within the family, but not the parents. Yet parents, too, stand in need of forgiveness. Here is a setting in which irritations and resentments can be dealt with—not in the context of anger and recrimination, but in the healing light of forgiveness. For instance, if on Friday, one of the children seems at a loss to recall anything to confess, brothers and sisters make fine auxiliary consciences! Parents can also both give and receive suggestions in order that genuine sins and hurts are brought out. Of course, we watch closely the way in which this kind of thing is done so that no spirit of impudence or bitter accusation develops. When it is done in love, it can produce genuine and even deep repentance.

6. Saturday—Prayers for Our Church. Each one of us picks out some aspect of the Sunday services to pray about: choir, Sunday school, sermon, Communion, particular individuals in the congregation, or any other need that has to do with our common life and worship in the body of Christ.

7. Sunday—Prayers for Our Worship. On the way to church we ask for God's blessing and power to flow in and through us as we gather with our brothers and sisters to worship. Then at lunch we try to capture some of what we just experienced around the table; we ask for the worship we have enjoyed and offered to continue to flow through our lives in the week ahead.

As we close this introductory chapter on prayer, it is *my* prayer that God will give you a personal vision for how to pray more effectively:

For yourself and your marriage partner—that you may both be Christlike examples to your children first, and then to others God places in your path.

For the discipling of your children—that this would be your unwavering commitment to them: *"As for me, far be it from me that I should sin against the LORD in ceasing to pray for you; but I will teach you the good and the right way. Only fear the LORD, and serve Him in truth with all your heart ..."* (1 SAMUEL 12:23-24A).

In the remaining chapters of this book, you will learn how to pray powerfully for your children's spiritual lives, personal lives, and relational lives, so that they may firmly lay hold of eternal life. May this be your continual song of prayer, as it is mine and Bonnie's:

"A Christian Home"

O give us homes built firm upon the Savior,
Where Christ is Head and Counsellor and Guide;
Where every child is taught His love and favor
And gives his heart to Christ, the crucified:
How sweet to know that though his footsteps waver
His faithful Lord is walking by his side!

O give us homes with godly fathers, mothers,
Who always place their hope and trust in Him;
Whose tender patience turmoil never bothers,
Whose calm and courage trouble cannot dim;
A home where each finds joy in serving others,
And love still shines, tho days be dark and grim.

O Lord, our God, our homes are Thine forever!
We trust to Thee their problems, toil, and care;
Their bonds of love no enemy can sever
If Thou art always Lord and Master there:
Be Thou the center of our least endeavor—
Be Thou our Guest, our hearts and homes to share.
Amen.[a]

a. Jean Sibelius, "A Christian Home," (USA: Singspiration, Inc., 1965), as cited in *Hymns for the Family of God* (Nashville, TN: Paragon Associates, Inc., 1976), p. 538.

STUDY GUIDE QUESTIONS

1. Our heavenly Father's desire is that we learn to pray as Jesus demonstrated through His life and words. We can exercise the discipline of prayer daily by following these basic habits:

Like Jesus—we should make the time to pray. Read, memorize, and meditate upon Matthew 6:33. Is this verse representative of your prayer life?

Like Jesus—we should choose a place to pray. Read Matthew 6:6. Do you have a "solitary place" to get alone with God?

Like Jesus—we should pray as often as possible. Read Psalm 55:17 and Acts 6:4. Does praying in this manner

characterize your life? If not, I exhort you to pray these
verses earnestly for yourself as well as your family.

2. **To be a genuine disciple of Christ, we need to exercise
ourselves in ceaseless prayer, for prayer is the only key
to unlock God's provisions for us.** However, to unlock His
provisions successfully, He has given us certain requirements:
> Read Mark 11:22-26. What two things does Jesus say are
> necessary for successful prayer? How can Psalm 66:18
> be applied to verse 26 and the matter of prayer?
> Read 1 Peter 3:7. What does God say will hinder a husband's
> prayers? Read 1 John 3:21-22 and 5:14-15. In what ways can we
> have confidence that God hears our prayers and will answer us?
> Read Psalm 37:4. What does God say is a key to
> having the prayers of our heart answered?
> Read Matthew 7:7-11. What is our heavenly Father's attitude
> toward the specific prayers of His children? How is
> God speaking to your heart through these verses?
> Read Philippians 4:6-7. What is to be our attitude in
> prayer? What does God promise as a result?

3. **Above all, we should delight in God Himself through
prayers of worship.** Read Psalm 18:46; 27:4-5; 29:1-2;
Psalm 33:8,18,20-22; 34:1-3; 89:1-2,6-8; 90:1-2; and 150:1-21.
Worshipfully pray these—and other like verses—to the Lord!

18

"We will give ourselves continually to prayer and to the ministry of the word."

— *Acts 6:4*

Experiencing Spiritual Reality

Prayers for Experiencing Spiritual Reality:

Saving Faith (2 Timothy 3:15)
Loving God's Word (Job 23:12)
Living Victoriously (John 8:32, 36)
Thinking of Heaven (Colossians 3:1-2)
Hating Sin (Psalm 38:18)
Staying Tender Toward God (Psalm 51:17)

W E NEED TO PRAY FOR reality in the spiritual lives of those in our family. So often we don't know where to start, and even more—how to pray for them. This chapter examines elements that measure the depth of spiritual life and make Christ's life real in them.

As we saw in the last chapter, the people who were closest to Jesus Christ—those who knew His heart and priorities from watching Him minister as they ate, slept, walked, and talked with Him for 3-plus years—adopted as their first and chief method of ministry the giving of themselves continually to prayer.[a] They understood that God wants to do something great in and through each of us. He wants to do something *we* can't plan, program, or calculate so that *He* gets all the honor and the glory. Those closest to Jesus understood that prayer catapults us to the frontiers of whatever God is doing around the world.

a. Acts 6:4

Front Line Praying

HERE IS A MODERN DAY testimony of a real-life drama and subsequent incredible answer to prayer. It came to me from one of our deacons at Tulsa Bible Church in an e-mail from 2002.[a]

Do you remember the news in late May of 2001? Reports that two American missionaries in the Philippines were abducted and being held for ransom sent shock waves around the world. Countless numbers of God's people prayed faithfully for Martin and Gracia Burnham during their tortuous 377-day ordeal in the jungle. As it turned out, Martin was brutally murdered shortly before his wife was freed. At Martin's memorial service in Rose Hill, Kansas, a dear saint from Tulsa Bible Church, Marilyn Sargent, discovered how our Savior had ministered to Gracia in a very special way throughout her captivity—a direct result of one person's specific prayer on her behalf.

After the memorial service, Marilyn spotted Gracia sitting in the receiving line. Gracia wept as she grasped Marilyn's hand and expressed how much of a blessing she, and especially her brother, Ron, had been in her life. All three knew each other in their college years, but Gracia and Ron had ministered together as members of a touring singing ensemble from Calvary Bible College. While on tour, Ron frequently sang a special solo based upon Psalm 18—"Tower of Strength." Its message that God is the tower we can flee to for strength during times of great need would later impact Gracia's life when she was out in the jungle. This became evident when she tearfully expressed to Marilyn, "During a very hard time in the jungle, there were many nights that I needed special encouragement, and it was just like I could hear Ron's voice in my heart clearly singing 'Tower of Strength' to me!"

Marilyn couldn't stop thinking about what Gracia had said. When she arrived home, she hurriedly called Ron and started to say, "I was just at Martin's memorial service and you wouldn't believe what Gracia ..."

Ron excitedly interrupted her: "You know what? When I first heard about their abduction, and began to pray for them, I was reminded of Gracia's love of hymns."

"Yes," Marilyn said, "You always knew where she was in the college dorm because she was always singing to the Lord!"

"So," Ron continued, "I went into a room and closed the door, then loudly sang all the hymns and songs I could think of that Gracia knew and loved, and I prayed, 'Lord please use that to encourage Gracia!' And I sang and prayed for Gracia many times."

Then Marilyn exclaimed, "Ron do you know what Gracia tearfully told me? She said that she could clearly hear your voice in her heart singing 'Tower of Strength' and many other songs, and every night God used music to minister to her, as Martin would sing to her."

Ron himself then started crying with joy over the power of even one person's faithful praying!

Surely, "the effective fervent prayer of a righteous man avails much" (James 5:16b)! Beloved, God-answering prayers are not only for the Rons of this world but also for those who will diligently pray for their loved ones. It is true! As a result of such faithful prayers, God does indeed want to do something great in and through each of us—something so grand that we cannot even imagine the marvelous things He has in store for our children who are discipled to follow Christ with their whole heart, soul, mind, and strength! With that thought in mind, we are now going to look at some specific areas to pray over in our children's lives.

How to Pray for Reality in Your Children's Spiritual Lives

To BEGIN WITH, HOW CAN we pray most effectively for our children? The Apostle Paul—who labored in prayer for his children of faith night and day—reveals the answer in Galatians 4:19: "My little children, for whom I labor in birth again until Christ is formed in you." What an amazing verse! Paul is likening the intensity of his praying to the physical act of giving birth. For most women, giving birth requires intense focus and exertion of every part of their will power and strength. In other words, effective praying means laboring in prayer for our children with the same type of strength and focus that it took to bring them into this world. The starting place is to specifically pray that in their spiritual lives Christ will be formed in them.

And what is the content of the prayers to be? How do we know what God will respond to or even want us to pray? The answer is obvious—God's Word! Word-filled praying is a call for God to sanctify those we are praying for. Jesus told us the means of sanctification in John 17:17: *"Sanctify them by Your truth. Your word is truth."*

1. PRAY THEY WILL BE GENUINELY SAVED

"From childhood you have known the Holy Scriptures, which are able to make you wise for salvation through faith which is in Christ Jesus" (2 TIMOTHY 3:15).

We should pray to see our children genuinely saved. What is genuine salvation? In the verse above, Paul is talking to Timothy, his son in the faith. He is saying, *"Timothy, from the time you were still young enough to have to be fed, dressed, and carried, you have had a knowledge of and been acquainted with the sacred Writings, which are able to instruct you and give you the understanding for salvation which comes through faith in Christ"* (AV). Exposure to the Word of God opens the heart to make a person wise, which in turn leads to salvation by placing faith in Christ Jesus.[a] We believe in Him, and He transforms us. That is genuine salvation.

a. See also Romans 10:17.

We ought to regularly pray that our children will know the Holy Scriptures so that they will become wise unto their need of God's supernatural work inside of them. It is so easy for our children to just know the facts and not experience the reality of seeing their lostness. Only God at work drawing, convicting, and converting can save them.

Do you know what biblical wisdom is? It is Truth in action—Truth that is acted upon, Truth that is lived out. We should pray that they will live out this Truth, this wisdom, leading them through the Scriptures to salvation. Below is a simple but powerful prayer—evangelistic praying—and something we should each be involved in for those we love.

Prayer Example: Lord, help my children to know the Scriptures! Give them the wisdom to see that they are lost without Christ, and then help them to have faith in Him.

2. PRAY THEY WILL LOVE GOD'S WORD

"I have not departed from the commandment of His lips; I have treasured the words of His mouth More than my necessary food" (JOB 23:12).

We should pray to see our children loving God's Word. Any spiritual life must be built upon the Scriptures, which are our only real source of nourishment. In the verse above, Job is confessing that he has not departed from the commandments of God's lips. Isn't that interesting? When we read the Bible, we are getting instructions from God's very lips. Isn't that simply amazing? Through the Scriptures, He is actually talking to *us!*

Job went on to say, "*I have treasured the words of His mouth more than my necessary food.*" Have you ever paid attention to how hungry kids eat? Wow! They can eat *volumes* of food! In fact, I've told Bonnie that I don't know if I can *afford* raising five sons. It's unbelievable how much they can eat! But, do you know what? Job 23:12b is saying that we should hunger for God's Word with that same voracious appetite.

How are you doing in this area? Do you love God's Word more than food itself? Remember that common saying often heard at Christian camps? **"No Bible, no breakfast; no Bible, no bunk."** That adage simply means that we should make it a priority to spend time with the Lord before ever starting or ending our day. God wants us to enjoy being with Him even more than whatever we love to eat. Just as we have to eat to live physically, so we have to eat the Word of God—the Bread of Life—to live spiritually.

We should model Psalm 119:97 to our children: *"Oh, how I love Your law! It is my meditation all the day."* Meditation is likened to cows that eat grass, chew on it, and then ruminate[a] because they want to get everything possible out of their food, and so should we with our spiritual food—the Bible. We should love it so much that we think about it (keep chewing) all the time. The effect of loving and meditating upon God's Word is seen in Psalm 119:165: *"Great peace have those who love Your law, And nothing causes them to stumble."* If our children see that spirit in us, and they learn to love the Scriptures in the same manner, they will not stumble or fall when faced with new situations. The more they learn to love and meditate upon God's

a. Ruminate means "to chew again what has already been chewed slightly and swallowed."

Word, the more they'll develop the ability to make wise decisions and have proper responses in all circumstances.

While reading through the Bible, a good prayer habit is to write your loved one's name beside a verse that you want to pray for them. For example, consider Jeremiah 15:16a: *"Your words were found, and I ate them."* You might say, "Lord, I pray that [name] would find Your Word and eat it." What you are asking is that they would get the Bible out and devour it as they would a fine meal. And, just as a prayer of thanksgiving ought to be offered before eating physical food, so we should pray before eating spiritual food: *"Open my eyes, that I may see wondrous things from Your law"* (PSALM 119:18). Sometimes readers don't get anything out of the Bible because they have failed to ask God to prepare them so that they could get something out of it. As parents, we should ask the Lord to help us fully delight in God's Word and then to see our children do likewise.

> **Prayer Example:** *Lord, help me be a godly example to my children. May they not want to depart from the commandments of Your lips, and may they treasure the words of Your mouth more than their necessary food! I pray that they will think about Your words all day long and desire to live by them—because they love You so much!*

3. PRAY THEY WILL LIVE VICTORIOUSLY

> *"And you shall know the truth, and the truth shall make you free. ... Therefore, if the Son makes you free, you shall be free indeed"* (JOHN 8:32, 36).

We should pray to see our children living victoriously. In John 8:32 and 36, Jesus gives us the key to victory. The context of those verses is seen in verse 31: *"If you abide in My word, you are My disciples indeed."* Christ's disciples were liberated because they knew "the Truth"—a Person—who had set them free.

I recently read an interesting article that illustrates this topic well. A man went to a counselor and confessed that he was a 29-year-old pornography addict. He wanted to know what counsel he would offer. Do you know what that counselor said? He told the man that he did not need counsel or therapy. He didn't need someone to pray for him.

He just needed to repent. That is exactly what the Bible says. In verse 36 Jesus said, *"If the Son makes you free, you shall be free indeed."*

A lot of people want others to pray for them or give them counsel or therapy. However, they do not really want to change—to repent. Do you know what we should pray? We should pray that those we love will live in victory. Living in victory means that they won't want to be in bondage to any sin—to be ensnared, to live in the gutter, in the darkness, in the ways of this world. It means that they would rather be led by Christ, to live according to Truth.

How do we pray for that? We pray John 8:32 and 36 for them. Verse 32 is another good place to write a loved one's name as a prayer. Say, "Lord, help [name] to know the Truth." What does "know" mean? That word means "to intimately experience." Now let's apply that to verse 32. Who is "the Truth"? It is a *Person.* Jesus said, *"I am the way, the truth, and the life"* (JOHN 14:6). If you come to know Jesus intimately and personally, He can make you free!

We are also asking for God to do what He promised He can do—grant them repentance: *"In humility correcting those who are in opposition, if God perhaps will grant them repentance, so that they may know the truth, and that they may come to their senses and escape the snare of the devil, having been taken captive by him to do his will"* (2 TIMOTHY 2:25-26).

"Set the people free" has been the marching order of missionaries for the past 2,000 years. Missionaries have gone to the heart of Africa, to the opium-ravaged lives of China during the 1800s, to India where the people were enmeshed in darkness and demons, and to cannibal-infested islands. The only thing they took with them was the Bible, which they preached faithfully. Through the Word, pagans were immediately delivered from cannibalism, demonism, sensuality, Hinduistic and Polytheistic beliefs. Why is that? Because that is how God works; He sets men and women free who come to know the Truth, Jesus Christ, and if the Son makes you free, you will be free indeed.[a]

a. John 8: 36

If you are not personally set free, you haven't intimately experienced the Truth. For Jesus says, *"Most assuredly, I say to you, whoever commits sin [practices sin habitually] is a slave of sin"* (JOHN 8:34). The ultimate bondage is not political or economic enslavement but spiritual bondage to sin and rebellion against God.[b] We need to hate sin and rebellion: *"Behold, to obey is better than sacrifice, ... For rebellion*

b. *The MacArthur Study Bible,* (Nashville, TN: Thomas Nelson, 1997), p. 1599.

is as the sin of witchcraft, And stubbornness is as iniquity and idolatry" (1 SAMUEL 15:22-23). We therefore ought to faithfully pray for victory in our own lives as well as those we love!

The world is a dangerous place, full of temptations aimed at leading our youngsters astray. To protect our families, should we drop out of society—like a child born with no immune system who is forced to continually live within a plastic bubble to avoid exposure to dangerous germs? No, withdrawal is not God's way. In fact, look at how Jesus actually prayed for us: *"I do not pray that You should take them out of the world, but that You should keep them from the evil one"* (JOHN 17:15). We should not try to put our children in a bubble, or make them wear earplugs, or put blinders on them. Instead, we must pray for their immune system so that they will *want* to live in victory—want to know the Truth. God's way to keep children from evil is this: *"Sanctify them by Your truth. Your Word is truth"* (JOHN 17:17). And so we must pray that through intimacy with the Word of God they will learn to live victoriously!

> **Prayer Example:** *Lord, I pray that I will be a godly example to my children. May they learn to love abiding in Your Word so they will intimately know the Truth who can set them free. Keep them from the evil one. Cause them to hate sin and not want to be in bondage in any way. Wholly sanctify them through Your Truth.*

4. PRAY THEY WILL LOVE THINKING ABOUT HEAVEN

"If then you were raised with Christ, seek those things which are above, where Christ is, sitting at the right hand of God. Set your mind on things above, not on things on the earth" (COLOSSIANS 3:1-2).

We should pray to see our children loving to think about heaven. That will not come naturally to them because everyone is born with a desire to seek things here on earth. Proverbs 23:7a says, *"For as he thinks in his heart, so is he."* In other words, whatever or whomever we think about most is what we will eventually become. That is how I can always tell where people's affections are. For instance, avid fans of rock or popular music begin to act in the same fleshly manner as the stars they want to imitate. Others opt to wear a favorite entertainer's brand of sunglasses, or adopt one of his or her hair styles. Why? They want to be like their heroes and heroines. But God's way is that His children are to be imitators of *Him*.[a]

a. Ephesians 5:1

To help you prepare your own heart to pray for a heavenly-mindedness in your family, may I suggest a great overview of heaven? Note the footnoted site.[b]

b. One of the most moving studies of my life was a ten-year, intensive time in the final book of the Bible, The Revelation of Jesus Christ. My verse-by-verse devotional commentary entitled *"365 Days of Worship in Revelation"* is available free of charge online at **www.dtbm.org.**

According to the Greek, Colossians 3:1a should more literally read: *"Since then you were raised with Christ* [it's a fact], *seek those things which are above ...."* What the Apostle Paul is addressing here is this: Since you have been raised with Christ, change what you are focusing on and start laying up treasures in heaven instead.[c] This involves a willful, conscious choice. Verse 2 tells us how to do that: *"Set your mind* [affections] *on things above, not on things on the earth."* Whatever we love, we will talk about. Whatever we love, we want. Whatever we love, we usually get. Most of us will strive to get anything we really, really want—even at the cost of great sacrifice. Well, God says, "Really, really want *Me!"*

c. See Matthew 6:19-21.

Set your affections on things above, not on things on the earth. Wow! That is not easy; it is supernatural. So you should pray about it. Colossians 3:1 is another good verse to write a name beside as a prayer. Say, "Lord, I pray that [name] will seek those things which are above, where You are. I pray that they will be drawn to You today." Beside verse 2, write the name again and say, "God in Heaven, I pray earnestly that they will today set their affection on things above and that their affection for things on earth will be loosened."

Do you know what? You can almost measure your earth-mindedness by how much you love to be in touch with what is going on down here. And what is the primary medium for staying in tune with everything that's going on? The electronic media of television, internet, and radio? If you are constantly struggling between being heavenly-minded and the lure of the enticing media, then what you are saying is this: "I know this is true, but I really have set my sights down here, and I just want to be totally in touch. I want to know about every flood, every car or plane crash, every murder, every war. That is really where my true affections are—not on things above." Think about it. What are you drawn to most?

While we are on the subject of thinking about heaven, here is another great verse: *"Fight the good fight of faith, lay hold on eternal life, to which you were also called ..."* (1 TIMOTHY 6:12). Knowing that John 11:26 says that whoever lives and believes in Christ will never die ought to motivate us to make each day count for eternity! We should then pray to see this spirit in our children as well.

> **Prayer Example:** *Dear Lord, I pray that You will help me to make each day count for eternity! Help my children to also be heavenly-minded by setting their affections on things above, and not on this earth. May our whole family fight the good fight of faith, and lay hold on eternal life as we should be, for that is what You have called each of us to do.*

5. Pray They Will Find Sin Repulsive

> *"By faith Moses, when he became of age, refused to be called the son of Pharaoh's daughter, choosing rather to suffer affliction with the people of God than to enjoy the passing pleasures of sin"*
> (HEBREWS 11:24-25).

As I was writing these words, I was sitting on an airplane ready to take off from Burbank, California. My cell phone rang, and Bonnie told me she was having trouble with one of our children at home. My instantaneous, Spirit-prompted response (after I listened to exactly what happened) was to say, "Honey, I will pray right now for God to get a hold of their heart!" More powerful than a stern word from Dad over the phone is the humble cry to the throne of God from a Word-filled dad on behalf of his child!

When Bonnie picked me up at the airport, my first question was about that child. She smiled and said, "I know you prayed. They were remarkably quiet and changed from anger to quietness." I was then able to much more effectively deal with their heart when I returned home. Dads, be men of *prayer!*

Jesus told two prayer stories in Luke 11 and 18. The theme of each was humble persistence. **A single earnest prayer will do more for your children than a thousand anxious thoughts or angry words!**

We should pray to see our children grow by the power of the Spirit of God to find sin repulsive. Some things we all find disgusting—like finding a hair in your salad. Yuk! For me, my most repulsive lesson was learned as a little boy.

Our church was built in a courtyard around beautiful apple trees. As soon as church was over, I loved to scurry outside to climb one particular tree. One Sunday, before I even got out the door, my mom warned, "Johnny, don't eat any of those apples! They haven't been sprayed, and have worms in them!" Naturally, because I was five, I knew more than she did.

I picked an apple, checked for any telltale holes, and it seemed perfectly fine to me. (I thought worms came from the outside-in, eating toward the middle.) I remember the joy of polishing that delectable-looking apple, and then taking a big bite. Chomp, chomp, chomp. Yum! No worm …

When Mom caught me eating the apple, I proudly said, "It's great!" She then asked, "Did it have a worm in it?" Suddenly I looked down and saw twitching—half of a worm remaining … Yuk! Worms taste just awful! I will never forget the sight of seeing what was left of that twitching body. Oh, it was so disgusting! To this day, every time I take a big bite out of an apple I remember that lesson, and I look to make sure there's no twitching before I chew and swallow. From that point on, eating worms has been repulsive to me!

In Hebrews 11:25, we see that Moses chose to suffer affliction with the people of God rather than to enjoy the passing pleasures of sin. Somebody had taught Moses that sin has pleasure—like my first bite of that delectable apple. However, he also knew that pleasure is pass-ing—like the shock of quickly finding half of a twitching worm. We need to pray that in our ministry to those we love, God will enable us to build up a wall of Truth in their lives. Truth mixed with the mortar of prayer is what will hold that Truth together in their lives until they themselves come to the place of finding sin truly repulsive.

Another great verse on this subject is Proverbs 20:17: *"Bread gained by deceit is sweet to a man, But afterward his mouth will be filled with gravel."* What this means is that at first a secret sin may seem to be sweet because nobody knows about it. But those moments can quickly turn sour because of this scriptural principle: *"You have sinned against the LORD; and be sure your sin will find you out"* (NUMBERS 32:23). As a parent, be thankful when God reveals hidden sins in your children's lives. This gives you both prayer and training opportunities.

On more than one occasion over the past 20 years of shepherding our children, we have stepped into their lives *at the exact moment* that exposed some form of willful disobedience. Each time it was a divine appointment to shepherd their hearts. What an answer to prayer! Are you praying that God will expose hidden sin in your children's lives?

> **Prayer Example:** *Lord, once again, I ask You to help me be a godly example to my children. We can't keep our kids in a bubble, totally isolated from the world. We can't keep blinders and earplugs on them, or keep them on a leash. But if they ever do stray into sin, I pray that it will be found out and taste like gravel in their mouths. Let them see the ugliness of that twitching worm so that it will become so distasteful, so repulsive, that they'll never want to taste it again.*

6. PRAY THEY WILL STAY TENDER TOWARD GOD

"The sacrifices of God [are] a broken spirit, A broken and a contrite heart—These, O God, You will not despise" (PSALM 51:17).

We should pray to see our children stay tender toward God. Have you ever broken a bone and, even after it is healed, you are still protective of it? Perhaps it was a wrist, an arm, or an ankle that crumpled under you. It is tender. You have an operation, or a cast put on, and it is still tender. In Psalm 51:17, David is likening that scenario to his heart. He is saying, "Lord, I want to keep my heart tender toward You. I want such a broken spirit that You don't have to knock the door down to get my attention. I want both a broken and contrite heart so that I will humbly come before You and say, 'Yes, Lord, I fail You often. Yes, I'm sinful and weak. And Lord, I'm not going to think that apart from You I can do anything.' "

James 4:6b and 10 says: *"God resists the proud, But gives grace to the humble. … Humble yourselves in the sight of the Lord, and He will lift you up."* That word "humble" comes from a word meaning "to make oneself low." Because pride is the root of all sin, and humility is the root of all virtue, we ought to pray that our children will have broken and contrite hearts before the Lord.

> **Prayer Example:** *Lord, I pray that You will start with me by giving me both a broken and a contrite heart. May pride never rule in my life! Help my children to likewise humble themselves by hating sin and depending upon You alone for victory in every circumstance! Make our family truly honoring to Your name!*

By the way, did you know that you can't pray any of these things for someone else if in that area you are regarding iniquity in your heart? For God says: *"If I regard iniquity in my heart, The Lord will not hear me"* (PSALM 66:18). In other words:

- If you are not genuinely saved, your prayers cannot be answered.
- If you are not loving God's Word personally, how can you ask God to prompt your *children* to love God's Word?
- If you are not living in victory, you have no grounds to say, "God, help them to live in victory."
- If you yourself are earthly-minded, how can you possibly, in the name of Jesus and His character and His Person, by faith ask Him to help someone else live in a heavenly-minded way?

You see, to have an effective prayer life, it calls for our own lives to be checked out first by our Master "mechanic." Therefore, we must continually watch out for the need of a tune-up so that we can more effectively pray for our loved ones.

Building a Strong Foundation

PARENTING IS MUCH LIKE BUILDING a wall, a foundation for our children. I liken this to my watching contractors build a 150,000 square foot Super Target™ store near my home. As I observed their progress, I was bothered by the fact that they put this big wall up, then put a large prop on each side of it. I thought to myself: *Do they think that wall is going to fall down? You know, I'm not sure I'm going to go in there and shop.* But then they finished the roof, pulled away the props, and the building stood firm.

To me, that construction process was a beautiful picture of parenting. In 1 Corinthians 3:11 we read: *"For no other foundation can anyone lay than that is laid, which is Jesus Christ."* We lay the foundation of Christ in our children's lives through various building blocks mortared together with prayer. We prop up the walls in their lives with our standards, our parenting rules and expectations, plus punishments and rewards. Then we pray for God to install the ceiling—His "above work," or spiritual dimension of their lives—tying it all together by His Spirit working in their hearts. All the while, we keep praying. We keep on praying that Truth will become cemented and hardened in their lives, to become a part of them. And then, when it is the appropriate time, we pull away those props, and find them standing firm in His Truth.

So, what are we seeking to launch from our homes? Word-filled children who look like this:

- They are genuinely saved.
- They love God's Word and meditate on it all day long.
- They are thinking about heaven, measuring what they're going to do with their lives and how it can count for eternity.
- They find sin all along the way repulsive.
- They have hearts tender toward God.
- They live in victory because they want Christ to set them free. They don't want to be in bondage to sin.

How does all that happen? It happens by mirroring what Jesus taught His disciples—He gave Himself continually to prayer. Jesus prayed in the morning, all day long, at night, a great while before day, a great while into the night, all night long sometimes, all day long other times. The disciples saw Him always praying. And if Jesus Himself needed to pray, how much more should we! Let us therefore devote ourselves to prayer.

Prayer Example: *Father in Heaven, I thank You that the "Tower of Strength" and other songs prayed in Your name were a ministry night after night after night, as Ron sang in the day, and on the*

other side of the world Gracia was ministered to through the night
watches. Oh Lord, what an encouragement to see how You hear
and answer prayers so incredibly! I pray that I won't consider this
chapter as simply another message on prayer, with some more
truth, but that I will be both a hearer and a doer of the Word. Help
me to learn how to pray effectively and earnestly desire to see You,
oh Christ, formed in my life and in the lives of those I love. In the
name of Jesus, I ask all these things. Amen.

I wonder, have your children ever "caught" you praying for them?
I hope they will—very soon!

STUDY GUIDE QUESTIONS

1. We should pray to see our children genuinely saved.
>   Read 2 Timothy 3:15 and Romans 10:17. What is it that God says
>   will open a child's heart to salvation through Christ Jesus?
>   Read 1 John 5:11-13. Can a person—even a young
>   child—truly know that he or she has eternal life?

2. We should pray to see our children loving God's Word. Any
spiritual life must be built upon the Scriptures, which are our only real
source of nourishment. Read Joshua 1:8. What does God say is the key
to our being prosperous and having good success?
>   Read Psalm 119:97, 103. To capture that spirit personally, I encourage
>   you to read and meditate upon Psalm 119 every day for a
>   month. For 22 of those days, read a section to your children for
>   devotions, and then pray those verses together as a family.

3. We should pray to see our children living victoriously. In John 8:32
and 36, Jesus gives us the key to victory. What is that key?
>   Read 2 Timothy 2:25-26. How should we correct our
>   children when they are in rebellion? What should be
>   our prayer at such times? Read John 17:15-17.

What is God's way to keep children from evil? Make this a
daily prayer for yourself as well as your family.

4. We should pray to see our children loving to think about heaven.
That will not come naturally to them because everyone is born with a
desire to seek things here on earth.
Read Colossians 3:1-2. What does God say is to be our mindset?
In what ways can you model this to your children?
Read 1 Timothy 6:12. How is this verse a good
motivator for making every day count?

5. We should pray to see our children finding sin repulsive. Read
Proverbs 8:13. What is it that will cause a child to hate evil? Why does
God hate pride so much?

6. We should pray to see our children staying tender toward God. Read
Psalm 51:17. How does this verse reflect a tender heart toward God?
Read James 4:6b-8a and 10. What is the root of all virtues
that will help our children stay tender toward God?
How does God say that victory can be achieved?

**Note: At the end of Appendix B's "Monday" prayer section is a list
of verses that correspond to this chapter's prayer suggestions. That
list provides a handy reminder of what to pray for your children on
a regular basis.**

19

"Moreover, as for me, far be it from me that I should sin against the LORD in ceasing to pray for you; but I will teach you the good and the right way."

— *1 Samuel 12:23*

Lives of Integrity

Prayers for
Lives of Integrity:

Maintaining a Clear Conscience (1 Timothy 1:5)

Learning to Stand Alone (2 Peter 1:3)

Seeking to Stay Pure in Mind and Body
(1 Peter 2:11)

Evidencing a Servant's Heart (Mark 10:44-45)

Not Being Bitter in Trials (Ephesians 4:31-32)

IN MY HALF-CENTURY OF LIFE on earth, the strongest temptation to compromise my personal integrity came in the summer of 1979. I'm going to share that account because I want to spur each of you parents to *pray* for the purity and integrity of your children!

Right before my parents sent me off to work in Eastern Europe as a Bible courier, my mom pressed into my hands a special pocket Bible she had written in. Along with that Bible she added this admonition: "Remember what I have always told you since you were a little boy. I am praying for you, and God is always watching—flee sin." With those words, I set off again to work for 10 weeks hauling thousands of Bibles through a maze of communist border guards, searches, dark and winding back roads, and immense spiritual warfare.

It was an incredible summer! We managed to deliver over 25,000 Bibles into the trembling hands of countless house-church leaders, pastors, students, and evangelists all across Eastern Europe—which was at that time under the Soviet Union's "iron fist" made of concrete walls, barbed wire, and iron gates.

When the summer was almost over, we were all exhausted from driving continuously through Romania delivering to villages that had nothing but dirt paths and fields. Before our final week-long push into Poland, we took a short break. Some generous believers in Vienna had invited us to visit them and get renewed. As we pulled up to the address, we were quite impressed. It was a 40-room villa on a beautiful garden-lined, winding road. They were so kind to invite all of the team, which numbered almost twenty.

After dinner and all the fellowship ended, I returned to my room and spotted one of the team's young ladies sitting on my bed. She looked up, and simply said, "This is where I'm spending the night—with you ..." Immediately, I felt both an incredibly strong temptation as well as an overpowering revulsion to such sin.

I reached into the room, grabbed my backpack, and literally fled. I slept in a room with two other fellows from my team, and never saw that girl again. When I arrived home 2 weeks later, my mom asked what had happened on the trip. I discovered that she had been up in the middle of the night and was praying until dawn for me—at *almost precisely the same time* I was being confronted with that temptation.

To this day, I am convinced that night of prayer for my mom, and the choice I made, has shaped every bit of blessing in my marriage, home, and ministry. As a result, it gave me a lifelong awareness of the fearsome power of temptation—and a desire to flee lust in any form. Beloved, *our prayers do impact*—more than we may ever realize!

God wants to do something great in and through each of us through prayer! For when parents pray, God hears and responds. Can we see results like this from our own prayers? Can we see our children doing anything of eternal magnitude? Can we penetrate the lives of those we love with these truths? Can we see God unleashed in their lives? Yes! If we will go forward by prayer and acknowledge that apart from Christ we can do nothing.[a] Jesus gave us a wonderful challenge to pray when He said:

> "So I say to you, ask, and it will be given to you; seek, and you will find; knock, and it will be opened to you. For everyone who asks

a. John 15:5

*receives, and he who seeks finds, and to him who knocks it will be
opened. If a son asks for bread from any father among you, will
he give him a stone? Or if [he asks] for a fish, will he give him a
serpent instead of a fish? Or if he asks for an egg, will he offer him
a scorpion? If you then, being evil, know how to give good gifts to
your children, how much more will [your] heavenly Father give the
Holy Spirit to those who ask Him!"* (LUKE 11:9-13).

From this passage we learn how important it is to keep on asking, keep on seeking, and keep on knocking. We must keep going in
prayer, and never give up. God wants us to be *"praying always with
all prayer and supplication in the Spirit"* (EPHESIANS 6:18). But what
are we supposed to pray specifically for our children? We should pray
that they will lay hold of eternal life, and that they see reality in their
spiritual lives, integrity in their personal lives, and stability in their
relational lives. In the last chapter, we learned how to pray for reality
in our children's spiritual lives. Now let us consider what to pray for
regarding integrity in their personal lives.

Pray for Integrity

Integrity is a life without hypocrisy. It is walking in the fear of God
while seen by others, and when seen only by God. The Bible speaks
often of the system placed by our Creator within each of us that
monitors our integrity. That monitor is called our conscience.

Our conscience is an innate warning system—much like an
altitude sensor unit on an airplane. For example, about 10 years
ago, a plane crashed full speed into the Andes Mountains in South
America. The reason it crashed was failure to remove the duct tape off
the sensor after de-icing the plane's wings. (The duct tape protects the
sensing unit from being damaged by the de-icing spray.) When the
pilots forgot to take the duct tape off the sensor, it was immobilized
and could not alert them to danger ahead. Many people, like those
pilots, go through life with duct tape over their sensors and their
automatic warning systems become immobilized. And that is why
so many crash into devastating mountains of sin—they never saw it

coming! But that is not according to God's perfect design for us.

Our conscience is a gift of God—a spiritual part of our humanity to warn us to "pull up" before we blindly crash into sin. It is part of our personhood, a part of being made in God's image, an innate ability to sense right and wrong. (Even the most uncivilized pagans have a conscience.) We need to understand that the conscience is not a revelation; God does not reveal Himself through it. It is not God actually speaking—it is a part of us as humans and therefore is both fallible and prone to injury. A conscience can become diminished, calloused, and even seared so that it is incapable of operation. A fully operative and sensitive conscience is essential if we and our children are going to be characterized as having integrity. Therefore, that is the first thing we should pray for.

1. Pray They Will Maintain a Clear Conscience

"Now the purpose of the commandment is love from a pure heart,
[from] a good conscience, and [from] sincere faith" (1 TIMOTHY 1:5).

Maintaining a clear conscience is an integral part of integrity. These Scriptures, in particular, can aid our understanding of this relationship:

God works through our conscience: *"Because your heart was tender, and you humbled yourself before God"* (2 CHRONICLES 34:27).

In the Old Testament, the conscience is called the heart. The verse above shows the conscience—the heart—at work; the conscience was tender and responsive. You know, the conscience is much like a glass window. A clean window lets light in so that we can better see what we are doing in our daily activities. However, if dirt and grime is allowed to build up over the years, its light will become dimmer and dimmer until we can no longer see clearly, and will likely stumble or fall.

Second Chronicles 34:27 is a good place to write your loved ones' names and pray, "Lord, keep their hearts tender. Keep them humble before You. Help them to always let Your light clearly shine through their lives so that their consciences don't become clouded with the debris and junk of sin."

Beloved, we need to faithfully pray a hedge of protection around our children, that they will never become calloused—having a hardened heart toward God and others—but that they will stay sensitive and tender toward God.

We must keep our conscience clean and clear: *"Create in me a clean heart, O God, And renew a steadfast spirit within me"* (PSALM 51:10).

As soon as Nathan the prophet confronted David about his sin, he repented and asked God to give him a pure conscience so that he could get back on track with the Lord. If not carefully maintained and scrutinized, a conscience can easily become defiled.

We ought to pray regularly for ourselves and our children: *"Search me, O God, and know my heart; Try me, and know my anxieties; And see if [there is any] wicked way in me, And lead me in the way everlasting"* (PSALM 139:23-24).

We live out in the country on the edge of a creek, but I call it a "river." To me, it is a river because it has beavers in it, all kinds of flora and fauna, vermin, plus everything else common to rivers. Creatures from that "river" regularly crawl into our yard. One day, we spotted a sickly-looking possum slinking in. Well, that monster had the nerve to die underneath our deck. What happens after something dies? It starts to *stink*. And so I had to search to find out where that awful smell was coming from so that I could promptly remove it. That is what sin is like.

In Psalm 139:23-24, David is asking God to search out anything in his life that is defiling his relationships. He wants to know what God would not want in his life. You see, our conscience begs us to do what is right, and hinders us from doing what we believe is wrong. That is why God gave us such a sensing device. If we follow our conscience by obeying what God says, it praises us and brings tranquility and self-confidence. But if we go against it, our conscience will condemn us. It will trigger feelings of apprehension, dismay, disgrace, torment, and penitence. In verse 23 David is basically telling the Lord, "My conscience is troubling me and I don't know why. What possum has snuck in under the deck of my life and is stinking up this relationship? I want to get rid of it!" Just as I put a shovel under the deck, pulled out that dead possum, then hauled the corpse off to where it came from, so David is saying, "Go back where you came from, you monstrous sin!" And then He asked God to give him a clean heart—a fresh-smelling start—and to lead him in the way everlasting.

Conscience care is life long: *"This being so, I myself always strive to have a conscience without offense toward God and men"* (ACTS 24:16).

That was Paul's constant prayer. In fact, Paul talks about the conscience twenty-three of the thirty times it is mentioned in the New Testament. In Acts 24 he gave his testimony of how he was able to serve the Lord so greatly. He basically said, "I myself always strive to keep the 'sensors' un-taped, so that I don't damage my sensitivity. I want a conscience void of offense toward God and others because I want to be a man of integrity—one who is responsive to God's Word."

Only God's Word can protect our conscience: *"Stand therefore, having girded your waist with truth ..."* (EPHESIANS 6:14).

The way Paul says to be a person of integrity—one whose conscience is clean and void of offense toward God and others—is to cinch yourself tightly with the truth of Scripture. When a New Testament era Roman soldier was tightening his belt just before combat, it was because he had to draw up his tunic and cinch it so that he didn't become entangled in it. The belt also kept the sword, which is a symbol for the Sword of the Spirit.[a] Paul is saying that a conscience must be trained, bound, and guided by God's Word. A conscience must be cleaned regularly with the Word of God: it must be filled, calibrated, and constantly reoriented to His Word.

a. Ephesians 6:17

We can have a clear conscience if we want one. God's offer is for all of us. It starts by coming to Christ. Jesus said that if we come to Him, He will give us a new heart, a new conscience. If you don't have a clear conscience, the first thing you might ask yourself is: *Am I even saved? Am I truly born again?* If you live by faith, whenever you have grieved and quenched the Spirit of God by defiling yourself, He will forgive and cleanse you. There will no longer be a guilty conscience, and you will have the joy of cleansing and forgiveness.

Prayer Example: *Father in Heaven, I thank You for John's testimony of how faithfully his parents prayed for him, and that You*

*heard and answered those prayers. That is such an encouragement
to persistently pray for my own children, and to never give up. I
pray that You will help me keep my own conscience pure so that
I will be full of integrity, and can lead my children to do the same.
Give them sensitive hearts, Lord. May we as a family always strive
to keep our consciences void of offense toward You and others.*

2. PRAY THEY WILL LEARN TO STAND ALONE

"But Daniel purposed in his heart that he would not defile himself"
(DANIEL 1:8).

We should pray to see our children learning to stand alone by having
the conviction that their character is more important than popularity or pleasure. One of the most profound examples in Scripture of
a youth daring to stand alone like that is recorded in the Book of
Daniel. Daniel was in the royal family, of the line of David, and living in Jerusalem with the royal family when Nebuchadnezzar broke
down the wall and stormed in to capture the royal family. He took
the best of them as his servants, sold others as slaves, and killed the
rest. Daniel's parents were probably either in slavery or dead when
he found himself all alone in a far away, glitzy, glamorous, Las Vegas-
type place. But Daniel did not want to violate his God whom he
loved, so he purposed in his heart that he would not defile himself
with the king's meat, wine, or any other enticements. Therefore, he
asked to be excused from such indulgences.

Daniel was basically saying, "The temple that I lived by in
Jerusalem, the worship that I participated in, the Word of God that
I heard—I am not going to be just a spectator of it; I choose to personally embrace it." And so he proved that he had personal integrity
by standing alone. Personal integrity tends to also rub off on friends.
Shadrach, Meshach, and Abed-Nego had been watching Daniel, and
they agreed with him about God. When they were told to bow down
to another god or face the fiery furnace, they bravely said to the king,
*"O Nebuchadnezzar, we have no need to answer you in this matter. If
that [is the case], our God whom we serve is able to deliver us from
the burning fiery furnace, and He will deliver [us] from your hand, O
king. But if not, let it be known to you, O king, that we do not serve*

your gods, nor will we worship the gold image which you have set up" (DANIEL 3:16-18).

Standing alone means this: "We will not serve other gods, no matter what." When our children go off to school, camp, class trips, overnights at friends, the work place, or to life on their own, we must pray that they will stand alone by saying, "I will not serve the gods of pleasure, convenience, promiscuity, popularity, or unethical business practices. I'm going to call sin, sin, just as God does. As His representative, I choose to be honest in all that I do, wherever I am."

How do we get that to happen? The most powerful thing we can do for our children is to pray verses on their behalf. Remember: write your loved ones' names by the verses you want to pray for them, such as 2 Peter 1:3: *"His divine power has given to us all things that pertain to life and godliness, through the knowledge of Him who called us by glory and virtue."* What a precious promise! Have you ever meditated upon the fact that God has already given us every spiritual resource necessary to have and to maintain a clear conscience—a sensitive heart toward Him? By His power, He has given us the ability to stand alone, in spite of temptations around us. This is what personal integrity is all about.

> **Prayer Example:** *Lord, I pray that You will give my children all the things that pertain to life and godliness. I pray that they would choose to purpose in their heart to not defile themselves, to not bow to other gods. I pray that they will not worship at the idols of pleasure, convenience, promiscuity, popularity, or unethical business practices. Help them to love having a clear conscience, void of offense toward You and others!*

3. PRAY THEY WILL SEEK TO STAY PURE IN MIND AND BODY

> *"As obedient children, not conforming yourselves to the former lusts, [as] in your ignorance; but as He who called you [is] holy, you also be holy in all [your] conduct, because it is written, 'Be holy, for I am holy.' ... Beloved, I beg [you] as sojourners and pilgrims, abstain from fleshly lusts which war against the soul ..."*
> (1 PETER 1:14-15; 2:11).

We should pray to see our children seeking to stay pure in both mind and body. That is quite a challenge! Today's children are regularly bombarded with an electronic world full of evil images, music, and games. Even books and toys are not exempt. Someone once commented about the dangers from just our media alone; they said something like this: "Our American society is such a constant, mindless engagement with the media; trash is heaped on trash and the bizarre becomes commonplace. It has left us morally exhausted and without discernment."

Thus, we must be on constant alert to safeguard our children's minds. Remember: what they think upon most, they will become.[a]

a. Proverbs 23:7a

- We must help them spot the deceptions of philosophies and traditions of men that are according to worldly principles and not according to Christ.[b] When clear examples arise, point to and explain the errors being taught.

b. Colossians 2:8

- We must teach them how to bring their "every thought into captivity to the obedience of Christ" (see 2 Corinthians 10:3-5). We show them when they are afraid they must clearly choose to say no to fear and say aloud to the Lord, "I will trust in You over my fears." The same is true with anger, "I will give my hurt to You and not hold it." The same is true for lust, "Lord deliver me, and I turn from that desire." And so on—this is vital to train and give them practice. Along that line, Romans 12:2 is a good prayer verse: *"Do not be conformed to this world, but be transformed by the renewing of your mind, that you may prove what [is] that good and acceptable and perfect will of God."*

How Can We Encourage Biblical Modesty?

We have a big day coming. Note these words in 2 Corinthians 5:10. *"For we must all appear before the judgment seat of Christ, that each one may receive the things done in the body, according to what he has done, whether good or bad."* If you think about it, what will be the major chosen activity of your body in your lifetime?

- Eating? At an hour each day it is only 4 percent of your life.
- Sleeping? Even at 8 hours a day we only get 33 percent of life.

- Working or schooling? At 40 hours a week it only makes up 24 percent of life.
- No, there is something that you will choose to do for all your waking hours of almost all your life—wearing. Yes, each day you will choose what your body will be wearing.

In the most literal sense we will each be examined by God for what we do with our body. Wearing clothes—what kind, how modest, and so on—will be a major part of what we will answer for, to God. You and I will answer to God about the choices we made in obeying His command that we cover our bodies in such a way that it pleases Him.

As I have stood before young people in some of the finest Christian schools and colleges across America, I have loved to challenge them about the goal of our lives—standing before Christ's throne and hearing His "Well done."

As I draw the picture for them of that awesome moment, standing with the redeemed of all the ages around the throne, I pause … and briefly remind them of what we will look like at that moment.

When God gets us ready for such a wondrous event as standing in front of Him, the holy angels, and all the saints—what does He have us wear? That is a very sobering thought.

You see, God invented clothing. It was all His idea. He has much to say about what we will wear then—and about what we should wear *now!*

With that in mind, will you join me for a study of clothing, biblical modesty, and how to influence the generation living in one of the greatest seasons of evil since the days of Noah? Let's start our study in *heaven!*

Our Clothing Should Reflect What Is Worn in Heaven. Whenever we see someone in heaven or coming from the presence of God what do they look like? What characterizes them?

- **Look at What Jesus Wears.** "And in the midst of the seven lamp stands, One like the Son of Man, clothed with a garment down to the feet and girded about the chest with a golden band" (Revelation 1:13).
- **Look at What We Are Going to Wear.** "After these things I looked, and behold, a great multitude which no one could number, of all nations, tribes, peoples, and tongues, standing before the throne and before the Lamb, clothed with white

robes, with palm branches in their hands" (Revelation 7:9).

- **Look at What God's Special Representatives Wear.** "And entering the tomb, they saw a young man clothed in a long white robe sitting on the right side; and they were alarmed" (Mark 16:5).
- **Look at What God Expects Us to Wear—Righteousness.** "I will greatly rejoice in the Lord, My soul shall be joyful in my God; For He has clothed me with the garments of salvation, He has covered me with the robe of righteousness, As a bridegroom decks himself with ornaments, And as a bride adorns herself with her jewels" (Isaiah 61:10).
- **Look at What God Offers Us to Wear—Christ.** "The night is far spent, the day is at hand. Therefore let us cast off the works of darkness, and let us put on the armor of light. Let us walk properly, as in the day, not in revelry and drunkenness, not in lewdness and lust, not in strife and envy. But put on the Lord Jesus Christ, and make no provision for the flesh, to fulfill its lusts" (Romans 13:12-14).

What are the robes of Christ and the angels pointing toward? Holiness. Christ's robes were those of a priest; He is our Great High Priest—and we are to be holy in all we do. The emphasis upon robes in these verses doesn't mean we need to go get robes—it means we need to think of ourselves as God sees us now, and as we shall be: priests of our Holy God. Listen to how Peter and Paul applied these truths:

- "But you are a chosen generation, a royal priesthood, a holy nation, His own special people, that you may proclaim the praises of Him who called you out of darkness into His marvelous light " (1 Peter 2:9).
- "Therefore 'Come out from among them And be separate, says the Lord. Do not touch what is unclean, And I will receive you. I will be a Father to you, And you shall be My sons and daughters, Says the Lord Almighty.' Therefore, having these promises, beloved, let us cleanse ourselves from all filthiness of the flesh and spirit, perfecting holiness in the fear of God" (2 Corinthians 6:17-7:1).

Are you acting, thinking, and dressing like you are part of the holy priesthood of God? We see from these verses that God has a strong desire that we walk before Him each day in holiness—both on the inside and on the outside. That desire God has for us extends all the way to what we look like this very moment.

So biblical modesty starts when we as parents and children want to present every part of our bodies as a living sacrifice—holy and acceptable to God (Romans 12:1). Purity of heart is usually reflected by modesty of life.

Since modesty of life is most often reflected in our clothing, what do the Scriptures present as the wardrobe we should wear? In the Bible, we see clothes that reflect these timeless principles from God for His children:

Our Clothing Was Invented by God to Cover Our Bodies. *"Also for Adam and his wife the LORD God made tunics of skin, and clothed them"* (GENESIS 3:21). We should remember that in the Garden of Eden God introduced clothing as a covering for His creatures. Before the Fall, Adam and Eve felt no shame in their nakedness (GENESIS 2:25). However, after the Fall, they were embarrassed and desired that their bodies be covered, so they sewed fig leaves together to clothe themselves (GENESIS 3:7). Because of the fallen, lustful human heart, God says, "Don't allow yourself by a lack of modesty to become a wicked picture in an evil person's heart." Peter explains why we should be so careful about our dress. Our lack of modest dress can allow our body to become an evil picture in an evil person's mind. *"With eyes full of adultery* [literally, this is the plural form of adulter-esses—a mind full of women that are lusted after who become the man's adulteresses], *they never stop sinning; they seduce the unstable; they are experts in greed—an accursed brood!"* (2 PETER 2:14, NIV).

Our Clothing Is to Prevent Confusion. *"A woman must not wear men's clothing, nor a man wear women's clothing, for the LORD your God detests anyone who does this"* (DEUTERONOMY 22:5, NIV). We live in an androgynous (blurred male/female roles) world—we must clearly be masculine as men and feminine as women. That is God's will.

Our Clothing Can Be Either Beautiful or Lustful. *"She makes coverings for her bed; she is clothed in fine linen and purple"* (PROVERBS 31:22, NIV). *"Then out came a woman to meet him, dressed like a pros-titute and with crafty intent"* (PROVERBS 7:10, NIV). Every choice we make in clothing either reflects our God of order and beauty or the god of this world (Satan) and his trademark, which is lust. Remember the words of Paul in the New Testament gallery of beautiful women? God emphasizes a beauty of the unseen character. The flesh flaunts the body, and God beautifies the spirit: *"I also want women to dress modestly, with decency and propriety, not with braided hair or gold or pearls or expensive clothes"* (1 TIMOTHY 2:9, NIV).

Our Clothing Should Help Us Avoid Sin So We Never Play With God's Mercy. *"She took hold of him and kissed him and with a brazen face she said: 'I have fellowship offerings at home; today I fulfilled my vows' "* (PROVERBS 7:13-14, NIV). There is no fear of God, the future consequence, or the present destructiveness of her actions. Galatians warns us: *"Do not be deceived, God is not mocked; for whatever a man sows, that he will also reap. For he who sows to his flesh will of the flesh reap corruption, but he who sows to the Spirit will of the Spirit reap everlasting life"* (GALATIANS 6:7-8).

Our Clothing Should Help Us Avoid Being Manipulative in Our Goals. *"With her enticing speech she caused him to yield, With her flattering lips she seduced him. Immediately he went after her, as an ox goes to the slaughter, Or as a fool to the correction of the stocks, Till an arrow struck his liver. As a bird hastens to the snare, He did not know it [would cost] his life"* (PROVERBS 7:21-23). An ungodly woman is self-driven and wants her way. A beautiful woman wears the heavenly beauty of God's authority over her life: *"And let the beauty of the LORD our God be upon us, and establish the work of our hands for us; Yes, establish the work of our hands"* (PSALM 90:17). *"Instead, it should be that of your inner self, the unfading beauty of a gentle and quiet spirit, which is of great worth in God's sight"* (1 PETER 3:4, NIV).

Our Clothing Must Not Be Ostentatious. *"Beware of the teachers of the law. They like to walk around in flowing robes and love to be greeted in the marketplaces and have the most important seats in the synagogues and the places of honor at banquets"* (LUKE 20:46, NIV). Beware of clothes that are designed to show you off. Pride is hard to resist, and God *hates* it.

Our Clothing Is to Show Separation From the World. *"And do not be conformed to this world, but be transformed by the renewing of* *your mind, that you may prove what is that good and acceptable and perfect will of God"* (ROMANS 12:2).

What are the characteristics of the "hooter girls" or female fashion models of this world? Tight, body-accentuating, form-fitting, and body-revealing clothes—open buttons, plunging necklines, well-placed slits, short shorts and short skirts that draw the eyes to follow the lines and curves in a sensual way. That is the model that the world has placed before us. God says, "Do not allow that model to become the pattern you follow."

- *"When you come into the land which the Lord your God is giving you, you shall not learn to follow the abominations of those nations"* (Deuteronomy 18:9).
- *"Thus says the Lord: 'Do not learn the way of the Gentiles; Do not be dismayed at the signs of heaven, For the Gentiles are dismayed at them'"* (Jeremiah 10:2).
- *"Therefore 'Come out from among them And be separate, says the Lord. Do not touch what is unclean, And I will receive you. I will be a Father to you, And you shall be My sons and daughters, Says the Lord Almighty.' Therefore, having these promises, beloved, let us cleanse ourselves from all filthiness of the flesh and spirit, perfecting holiness in the fear of God"* (2 Corinthians 6:17, 18-7:1).

Our Clothing Reflects Christ. *"Let us walk properly, as in the day, not in revelry and drunkenness, not in lewdness and lust, not in strife and envy. But put on the Lord Jesus Christ, and make no provision for the flesh, to fulfill its lusts"* (ROMANS 13:13-14). Each day as you dress, make a conscious choice to think about whose body it is you are clothing. Remember: we belong to Him!

Our Clothing Is to Cover God's Temple. *"Do you not know that your body is the temple of the Holy Spirit [who] is in you, whom you have from God, and you are not your own?"* (1 CORINTHIANS 6:19). We should pray to see our children understand that in the New Testament God expects clothing to be a reflection of His righteousness and our modesty as His temple! Because of the Fall, we must be on guard at all times. The flesh wants to rise up!

Our Clothing Is to Declare God's Ownership of Our Bodies. *"For you were bought at a price; therefore glorify God in your body and in your spirit, which are God's"* (1 CORINTHIANS 6:20).We should use God's Word to explain to our children so they understand that in the Old Testament God regulated clothing to be a testimony of His ownership. His ownership included the prohibition of tattoos and other body modifications: *"Do not cut your bodies for the dead or put tattoo marks on yourselves. I am the LORD"* (LEVITICUS 19:28, NIV).

Our Clothing Must Not Feed the Lust of the Flesh. God never wants our clothing to be sensuous: *"I also want women to dress modestly, with decency and propriety, not with braided hair or gold or pearls or expensive clothes"* (1 TIMOTHY 2:9, NIV).

Our Clothing Is Not to Detract From Our Holiness. *"Your beauty should not come from outward adornment, such as braided hair and the wearing of gold jewelry and fine clothes. Instead, it should be that of your inner self, the unfading beauty of a gentle and quiet spirit, which is of great worth in God's sight. For this is the way the holy women of the past who put their hope in God used to make themselves beautiful. They were submissive to their own husbands"* (1 PETER 3:3-5, NIV). James equally warns us: *"My brothers, as believers in our glorious Lord Jesus Christ, don't show favoritism. Suppose a man comes into your meeting wearing a gold ring and fine clothes, and a poor man in shabby clothes also comes in ..."* (JAMES 2:1-2, NIV). True beauty flows from within. Your character should be reflected by what you wear—and *is* whether you realize it or not!

Our Clothing Is to Demonstrate Humility. *"Likewise you younger people, submit yourselves to your elders. Yes, all of you be submissive to one another, and be clothed with humility, for 'God resists the proud, But gives grace to the humble' "* (1 PETER 5:5).

- Most of God's people in ancient Jerusalem didn't even know (or maybe care) that God watched what they wore. Tragically, it appears that believers of today have also forgotten "the God who sees." *"The LORD says, 'The women of Zion are haughty, walking along with outstretched necks, flirting with their eyes, tripping along with mincing steps, with ornaments jingling on their ankles. Therefore the LORD will bring sores on the heads of the women of Zion; the LORD will make their scalps bald.' In that day the Lord will snatch away their finery: the bangles and headbands and crescent necklaces, the earrings and bracelets and veils, the headdresses and ankle chains and sashes, the perfume bottles and charms, the signet rings and nose rings, the fine robes and the capes and cloaks, the purses and mirrors, and the linen garments and tiaras and shawls. Instead of fragrance there will be a stench; instead of a sash, a rope; instead of well-dressed hair, baldness; instead of fine clothing, sackcloth; instead of beauty, branding"* (ISAIAH 3:16-24, NIV).

Our Clothing Is to Prevent Causing Mental Pictures That Feed Lust. Because of the fallen, lustful human heart God said don't allow yourself, by a lack of modesty, to become a wicked picture in an evil person's heart: *"With eyes full of adultery* [literally, this is the plural form of 'adulteresses'— a mind full of women that are lusted after who become the man's adulteresses] *they never stop sinning; they seduce the unstable; they are experts in greed—an accursed brood!"* (2 Peter 2:14, NIV).

Our Clothing So Often Reflects Where We Are in Our Discipline of Our Flesh. What are you today? A wise child or a foolish one? Bring your life up to the X-rays of God's Word and see what He finds.

- Are you loud, assertive, boisterous, whiney, and the center of attention? Or are you quiet, submissive, gentle and humble?
- Do you dress in a way that draws others to think about your body and its enticements or your spirit and its beauty?
- Do you have a holy hatred of sin or do you have a desire to watch sinners [TV and movies] as they live out their fleshly fantasies?
- Do you use all in your power to get your own way? Do you manipulate by tears, looks, and whatever it takes to accomplish your ends?
- Are you argumentative, easily quarreling, and fighting with your parents or your brothers and sisters? Or are you peaceable, gentle, and easily entreated?

If these symptoms are present to any degree or amount, and you do not deal with them now in your youth, the prognosis for the future is bleak. One gifted expositor in writing about these verses said, "We may say with a surgeon's frankness, your life will be like Scarlett's—troubled, torn down, and literally *Gone with the Wind*."

We should pray that we will want to wear our true clothing, which is to reflect Jesus Christ. For God says, *"Let us walk properly, as in the day, not in revelry and drunkenness, not in lewdness and lust, not in strife and envy. But put on the Lord Jesus Christ, and make no provision for the flesh to [fulfill its] lusts"* (ROMANS 13:13-14).

Prayer Example: Lord, I pray that I will be obedient and not desire to conform to the world—to its pride of life, lust of the flesh, and lust of the eyes. May I always dress modestly, and reflect You in my appearance and demeanor. Oh, God of heaven, I pray that You will help me keep my mind and body pure for Your sake—as well as for the one I will someday marry.

4. PRAY THEY WILL EVIDENCE A SERVANT'S HEART

"Let a man so consider us, as servants of Christ and stewards of the mysteries of God" (1 CORINTHIANS 4:1).

We should pray to see our children evidencing a servant's heart. As parents, the greatest goal we have spiritually is to raise children who are useful to God. Usefulness in Christ's kingdom is defined by one very precious quality—servanthood. The words "servants," "service," and "bondservants" are used over 1,000 times in the New Testament, which amounts to about once every seven verses. That is very frequent! It is clear that God expects us to be Christ's servants, always following His example.

It has been estimated by historians that at the time of Paul there were as many as 60 million slaves owned by masters in the Roman Empire. Therefore, slaves and slavery were well-known themes to the New Testament world. That is why Paul's testimony to the church at Corinth was so powerful. In 1 Corinthians 4:1 they knew what he meant when he declared that he and his companions wanted to be regarded as "servants." The word "servants" in the original language was *huperetes*, which literally meant "under rowers." That term communicated a vision of humility and absolute servility.

"Under rowers" hardly means anything to us, but it was a loath-some term to the Corinthians of the first century. Corinth sat astride the isthmus that joined the southern peninsula to mainland Greece. In Paul's time it was the wealthiest and most prominent of all Greek cities. One of the most common sights to the people of Corinth was the ship tramway that moved vessels overland to the opposite shore. Like the Panama Canal today, that overland transport system was in constant use and saved days of travel time for all who used it. The most numerous boats were the galley slave ships, each with three banks of oars in three levels, one above another. The slaves who sat chained to the bottom oars were called the "under rowers."[a]

a. This is an adaptation of an article published in *Discipleship Journal* (Colorado Springs, CO: NavPress), *"Are You an Under Rower for Christ?"* (Issue 30, November 1985).

Life at the bottom of the ship: The under rowers' life at the bottom of the ship was tough, always busy, and permanent. Most died in service; the chains about their ankles were grim reminders of their bondage. And there were five aspects of their work that Paul and his companions could identify with in calling themselves "servants of Christ":

1. **Galley slaves had to row to the captain's beat.** To keep as many as 150 oars together, the captain beat a rhythmic tempo on a drum and each slave had to row with that beat.

2. **Galley slaves had to row together.** Often two or three rowers moved 30-foot oars. They quickly learned that one could not lean on the oar, another push, and another pull; they had to work as a team.

3. **Galley slaves had to trust the captain.** In the gloomy depths of the boat, slaves had no idea where they were, where they were going, or when they would arrive. Their labors were of total faith and obedience. As the captain's beat grew more and more rapid, it could signal an enemy attack, a storm to be avoided, or a hurried schedule. Slaves could not question the captain; they could only obey.

4. **Galley slaves were committed for life.** Their trip was always a one-way trip. The damp, hard benches were no relief to weary bones after a day's labor. The lack of sunshine and fresh air, combined with the leg chains, meant repeated illness during service; every slave was bound to the ship with deadly certainty. And if the ship went down in a storm or in conflict, slaves had no way of escape.

5. **Galley slaves received no honor; only the captain was visible to the outer world.** Although there were dozens of men who gave

their lives and very breath to keep the ship going, they were never seen. They rowed on and on, day in and day out, invisible to and unrewarded by the world. If an under rower was ever seen, it was because he was not doing his job.

So what was Paul's goal in his life? To be Christ's servant. What should be our personal goal? The same. We must become, by habit, "under rowers" for our Captain—Jesus Christ! As we set the example of humility and absolute servility, we should be praying that our children will do likewise. I encourage you to read 1 Corinthians 4:1 again, and then enter the names of your loved ones in your Bible, and pray that verse for them.

> *Prayer Example: Lord, I humbly acknowledge You as the Captain of my life. Help me to row to Your beat, to work together as a team, to trust You when the storm clouds gather, to be committed to Your leadership in all circumstances, and to give You the honor and glory You so rightly deserve. Make me a true and loving servant, dear Jesus. And I pray this for my children as well. May our family please You in all our ways!*

5. PRAY THEY WILL NOT RESIST GOD OR BECOME BITTER WHEN TRIALS COME

> *"Do not grieve the Holy Spirit of God, by whom you were sealed for the day of redemption. Let all bitterness, wrath, anger, clamor, and evil speaking be put away from you, with all malice. And be kind to one another, tenderhearted, forgiving one another, even as God in Christ forgave you"* (EPHESIANS 4:30-32).

We should pray that our children will not resist or become bitter in trials. God uses trials as one of His three very special tools to shape our lives into Christlikeness. The other two tools are God's Word and prayer. It is easy to love God's Word and prayer; yet, rarely will someone love trials. But if we resist the troubles and trials of life, and become angry at our circumstances and those who hurt us, we will miss one of the greatest tools God uses in our lives.

Staying angry about life and refusing to forgive those who hurt us causes a dangerous weed called bitterness to grow, take root, and gradually choke out our life. A heart filled with anger and hatefulness grieves the Holy Spirit. When grieved, God's Spirit won't bear fruit in our lives. Though His Spirit cannot leave us (because we are sealed until that day when Christ returns to take us home), we are emptied of joy and blessing.

Bitterness hurts the bitter person the most. Bitter people act like their father, the devil, treating others as he treats them. A soul consumed with bitterness denies our Father in heaven who loved us even when we were His enemies. The way out of bitterness is to remember the cross of Christ. There the power of sin was broken. Because of this, the once bitter person can confidently say: *I no longer have to allow myself to be hurt. I no longer need to get even. I am empowered by God's grace to see His hand even in people and events that hurt me.* Here are simple ways to teach our children to not become embittered. We must teach them these three timeless truths:

1. Adversaries are placed in life by God. David and his son, Solomon, recognized this scriptural principle: *"Let him alone, and let him curse; for so the Lord has ordered him"* (2 SAMUEL 16:11). Later on in the life of David's son we see the divine record of where adversaries really come from: *"Now the Lord raised up an adversary against Solomon, Hadad the Edomite; he was a descendant of the king in Edom"* (1 KINGS 11:14).

2. Bitterness is deadly. For that reason, God commands us to: *"Pursue peace with all people, and holiness, without which no one will see the Lord: looking carefully lest anyone fall short of the grace of God; lest any root of bitterness springing up cause trouble, and by this many become defiled"* (HEBREWS 12:14-15).

3. Trials are vital. Those who respond in humility to being corrected and refined by God are being further conformed to Christ's image: *"My brethren, count it all joy when you fall into various trials, knowing that the testing of your faith produces patience. But let patience have [its] perfect work, that you may be perfect and complete, lacking nothing"* (JAMES 1:2-4).

That is the end result of trials: maturity, completeness, not lacking in anything of spiritual importance and value. *"After you have suffered for a little while,"* Peter assures us, *"the God of all grace, who called you to His eternal glory in Christ, will Himself perfect, confirm, strengthen and establish you"* (1 PETER 5:10, NASB).[a]

We must all learn Joseph's secret. He understood that God is in control, working all things for the good of those who love Him:

a. John MacArthur Jr., *James: The MacArthur New Testament Commentary* (Chicago: Moody Press, 1998), electronic edition.

> *"Joseph said to them, 'Do not be afraid, for [am] I in the place of God? But as for you, you meant evil against me; [but] God meant it for good, in order to bring it about as [it is] this day, to save many people alive' "* (GENESIS 50:19-21).

In that passage, Joseph shows God's cure for self-pity and bitterness. From a human standpoint, he had plenty of reasons for becoming angry, resentful, and unforgiving:

- He was rejected by his brothers.
- He was abused by them and exiled from his own country.
- He was accused falsely of moral laxity.
- He was unjustly imprisoned to get revenge.
- He was injured and forgotten by co-workers and employers and friends.

In other words, from all outward appearances, Joseph's life had all the makings of a disaster. Yet, Joseph knew the Lord was ordering his life's events.[b] He understood the Lord was working all things together for his good.[c] Therefore, he could resist self-pity. How did he do that?

b. Psalm 105:16-20

c. Romans 8:28

- Joseph chose to forget. He intentionally forgot past hurts; he never nursed them (Genesis 41:51).
- Joseph chose to be fruitful. He purposefully looked for God's hand guiding and blessing him (Genesis 41:52).

Joseph's testimony reminds us all that the Lord wants us to use the "weed killer" of bitterness that God has provided: *"Let us draw near with a true heart in full assurance of faith, having our hearts sprinkled from an evil conscience and our bodies washed with pure water"* (HEBREWS 10:22).

Prayer Example: Lord, I pray that I will never forget the lesson from Joseph's life of how to forgive and to forget offenses against me. Search my heart, oh God, and reveal if there is anything that needs to be made right. Help my children to not give in to anger and bitterness toward others, but rather let love be a covering when offenses occur. Help us as a family to have peace and harmony in our home—ever rejoicing that You are in control of the events of our lives, working them for good because we love You!

God's Training Plan for Life

GOD HAS THREE POWER TOOLS He uses to shape our lives—His Word, prayer, and suffering. Electricity only flows through a conductor, so the Holy Spirit can only work through the means God has provided. As we read the Word and pray, we become more like Christ; and the more we become like Christ, the more the unsaved world opposes us. This daily "fellowship of His sufferings"[a] drives us as believers back to the Word and prayer, so that all three "tools" work together to provide the spiritual power we need to glorify Christ.[b]

a. Philippians 3:10

b. Wiersbe, *The Bible Exposition Commentary: Philippians* (Wheaton, IL: Victor Books, 1985), electronic edition.

God wants troubles to push us toward Him—to refine us, to purge us, to build us up, and to overflow our lives with blessings. But that only comes when we respond correctly to those adversaries (people) and those adverse circumstances that we didn't expect. Through it all, no matter what, He wants us, and our children, to exercise integrity in our personal lives by:

- Maintaining a clear conscience.
- Standing alone for Christ's sake.
- Staying pure in mind and body.
- Evidencing a servant's heart.
- Not resisting or becoming bitter in trials.

Our overall goal as parents is to raise, nurture, and launch our children to be pleasing to the Lord. Acts 6:4 gives us the key to success. As the apostle said, "*We will give ourselves continually to prayer and the ministry of the Word."* How do we minister the Word to our children? We pray the Scriptures for them—unceasingly—for when parents pray, God hears and responds.

> **Prayer Example:** *Dear Father, open my heart to the truth that troubles are coming; they can't be avoided. Help me not to run from them, but rather embrace them by Your grace as a shaping tool. You are the one who raises up adversaries to know my heart. You are the one who rocks my boat and gives me unexpected losses so I can make a choice. Either I can try valiantly to go on alone or I can be pushed into Your arms, into Your care, under Your wings, feeling Your strength. I recognize that the way of bitterness is the way of smoldering, angry resentment for the troubles of life. The way of Christlikeness is to yield to You, to allow Your shaping, Your refining, Your purging, Your cleansing. I thank You that You only make me weak so that in Christ I can be gloriously strong. Help me to embrace this truth, to live by it, and to share this with those I love. Help us each to stay tender toward You and others, to be characterized as a family that is full of integrity in our personal lives! In the name of Jesus I pray. Amen.*

STUDY GUIDE QUESTIONS

1. We should pray to see our children maintaining a clear conscience. Integrity is a life without hypocrisy. It is walking in the fear of God while seen by others, and when seen only by God. Read Psalm 139:23-24. How is praying these verses a safeguard against allowing what God would not want in your life—and in your family's lives?

Read Psalm 51:10. If your conscience has become defiled, how can you get back on track? How can you lead your family to do the same?

2. We should pray to see our children learning to stand alone by having the conviction that their character is more important than popularity or pleasure.

Read Daniel 1:8a. Through Daniel's example, can
you see how important it is to pray for this
strength of conviction for your children?

Read 2 Peter 1:3. As your children are learning to stand
alone, what promise has God given which gives hope
for victory through the power of persistent prayer?

3. **We should pray to see our children seeking to stay pure in both mind and body.** Read Colossians 2:8. What warning has God given concerning our society—which is morally exhausted and lacks discernment?

Read 2 Corinthians 10:3-5. How does this
passage give hope for victory?

Read Ephesians 6:17b-18. Name the two mighty weapons
God has provided to tear down Satan's strongholds.

Read Romans 13:12-14. Use these verses to pray that each of
your children will want both their inner being and outer
appearance to reflect Jesus Christ, who is their "true clothing."

4. **We should pray to see our children evidencing a servant's heart.** Read Mark 10:44-45. How are these verses reflected in your life? What fruit are you seeing in your children's lives as a result of your example?

5. **We should pray to see our children not resisting God or becoming bitter in trials.** Read Ephesians 4:31-32. Which of these verses most reflect how your children respond to daily trials? If verse 31 is mostly true of their lives, faithfully pray verse 32 on their behalf.

Note: At the end of Appendix B's "Thursday" prayer section is a list of verses that correspond to this chapter's prayer suggestions. That list provides a handy reminder of what to pray for your children on a regular basis.

20

"But the end of all things is at hand; therefore be serious and watchful in your prayers. And above all things have fervent love for one another, for 'love will cover a multitude of sins.' "

— *1 Peter 4:7-8*

Reflecting Christ's Love

Prayers for Reflecting Christ's Love:

Cultivating Love for Others (1 John 4:7-8)

Trusting God When Troubles Come
(1 Samuel 15:23a)

Loving God's Plan for Their Lives
(Psalm 139:14)

Waiting for God's Chosen Partner
(2 Corinthians 6:14)

JESUS HAS ISSUED EACH OF us an identification tag to wear throughout our
lives. In John 13:35, Jesus said that His
children are to wear the identification
badge of His ownership: *"By this all will
know that you are My disciples, if you have
love for one another."* The characteristic mark of a genuine disciple—
Christ's identification badge—is love. Are you wearing His badge in
your marriage? As a parent? At church? In all other relationships? It
is crucial that you do, because Christlike love is the foundation that
a Christian family and all other relationships must be built upon.
Without the security of such love, it is doubtful that your children
will develop stability in their relational lives.

Consider this far-reaching impact from just one Christian family's
failure to visibly wear Christ's I.D. tag. While attending a university
in London, Mahatma Gandhi, the future leader who would sway the

hearts of hundreds of millions of his own people in India, became almost convinced that the Christian religion was the one true, supernatural religion in the world. Upon graduation, and still seeking evidence that would make him a committed Christian, young Gandhi accepted employment in East Africa and for 7 months lived in the home of a family who were members of an evangelical Christian church. As soon as he discovered that fact he decided that here would be the place to find the evidence he sought.

But as the months passed and he saw the casualness of their attitude toward the cause of God, heard them complain when they were called upon to make sacrifices for the kingdom of God, and sensed their general religious apathy, Gandhi's interest turned to disappointment. He said in his heart: *No, it is not the one true, supernatural religion I had hoped to find. A good religion, but just one more of the many religions in the world.*[a]

a. Evangelical illustrations as quoted by Paul Lee Tan, *Encyclopedia of 7,700 Illustrations* (Garland, TX: Bible Communications, Inc., 1996), electronic edition.

b. 1 John 4:21

Gandhi's conclusion is a sad but shockingly true reminder of the neglected power of a Christian family. Loving one another is not optional;[b] it is the way the entire world will know we are Christ's disciples. As His disciples, we are all part of God's family, brothers and sisters in Christ—like an individual Christian family should be. In a very real sense the way we live, the way we talk, and the way we respond to our brothers and sisters in the Lord reflects who we really are as believers. As we reflect the stability of Christ's love in those areas, we should pray that He will help us lead our children to do likewise.

How to Pray for Christ's Love in Your Children's Lives

THE MOST PROMINENT CHARACTERISTIC OBSERVED by outsiders in the early church was their genuine love. Relational stability is just another way of saying "getting along" with those we live with, go to school with, and work around. This relational stability develops as we practice loving our brothers and sisters in Christ. Doing so demonstrates that we are in God's family: *"He who loves his brother abides in the light, and there is no cause for stumbling in him"* (1 JOHN 2:10). Let's look at what God says in 1 John about what it means for brothers and sisters in Christ to love each other:

1. Love Is Prompted by the Holy Spirit Within Us

God commands that we love one another: *"Beloved, let us love one another, for love is of God; and everyone who loves is born of God and knows God"* (1 JOHN 4:7).

See also 1 JOHN 3:11, 23; 4:11-12; 2 JOHN 5.

Loving our brothers and sisters is obedience to God: *"By this we know that we love the children of God, when we love God and keep His commandments"* (1 JOHN 5:2).

Love means we are willing to die to our plans, our desires, our agenda—and serve our brother or sister: *"By this we know love, because He laid down His life for us. And we also ought to lay down our lives for the brethren"* (1 JOHN 3:16).

A loving family member responds to the needs of his brother or sister: *"But whoever has this world's goods, and sees his brother in need, and shuts up his heart from him, how does the love of God abide in him?"* (1 JOHN 3:17).

Loving our brothers and sisters is an action, a way of life: *"My little children, let us not love in word or in tongue, but in deed and in truth"* (1 JOHN 3:18).

Empty lives lack love. God has given this test for whether or not we are a genuine Christian: *"If someone says, 'I love God,' and hates his brother, he is a liar; for he who does not love his brother whom he has seen, how can he love God whom he has not seen?"* (1 JOHN 4:20).

Not loving our brothers and sisters is ungodly: *"In this the children of God and the children of the devil are manifest: Whoever does not practice righteousness is not of God, nor is he who does not love his brother"* (1 JOHN 3:10).

Not loving our brothers AND sisters is like being attached to a corpse: *"We know that we have passed from death to life, because* *we love the brethren. He who does not love his brother abides in death*" (1 JOHN 3:14). The penal system of the Roman Empire had a gruesome way to deal with murderers. They often punished murderers by tying them face-to-face, body-to-body, with the corpse of the person they murdered until the death of the corpse permeated their living body and killed them also. Therefore, using that piece of history—an unloving member of the family is a living, walking, poisonous corpse that deadens those around them.

An unloving person who hates his brother or sister is like a murderer in God's sight: "*Whoever hates his brother is a murderer, and you know that no murderer has eternal life abiding in him*" (1 JOHN 3:15).

God certainly has a lot to say about how serious hatred is, doesn't He? Perhaps you've struggled in this area yourself and may be thinking: *How is it even possible to demonstrate the stability of Christ's love in our relational lives?* Sometimes, reading the amazing things New Testament saints lived and did for God seems overwhelming. Words like this may come to mind: *Unbelievable! Incredible! Unattainable!* Isn't that where most of us get to after awhile? Unbelievable, incredible, but alas, unattainable for me—and even less so for my children!

Well, I have good news! God never asks anything of us that can't be achieved through His power for "[We] *can do all things through Christ who strengthens* [us]" (PHILIPPIANS 4:13). Through prayer and letting the Holy Spirit continuously fill us, both we and our children can have the stability of a loving, abundant, joyful life!

2. PRAY THEY WILL LOVE THEIR BROTHERS AND SISTERS

"BELOVED, LET US LOVE ONE another, for love is of God; and everyone who loves is born of God and knows God. He who does not love does not know God, for God is love" (1 JOHN 4:7-8).

We should earnestly pray that our children will cultivate a love for their brothers and sisters. Loving in this manner is a result of Spirit-filled living. This means living in the conscious presence of the Lord

Jesus Christ, letting His mind, through the Word, dominate every-thing that is thought and done. Being filled with the Spirit is the same as walking like Jesus did on earth, which is the key to developing stability in our relational lives.

The Spirit of God wants to be taking the Word of God to shape us to look like the Son of God in our daily lives. We are to be living portraits of Christ. Word-filled lives welcome God to make lifelong changes in them. Our Father wants to prune and shape us into the image of Jesus more each day. The status of that process of change is measured by the attitude and action fruits of our lives. This "fruit of the Spirit" monitors the areas that are given over to the Spirit's culti-vation. Any unsurrendered ground bears weeds and no fruit.

Our Imperative: Cultivating the Fruit of the Spirit

AT ANY POINT IN TIME, we are either walking in the flesh or in the Spirit. There are fifteen manifestations of the flesh in Galatians 5:19-21. Of these, eight deal with interpersonal problems. It is not enough to say that we have always struggled in these areas, or to say "I sinned" and go on. Instead, the Scriptures show us that a truly spiritual person will be growing in a visible way in each of the nine areas described as "the fruit of the Spirit" in Galatians 5:22-23—all of which will greatly impact our relational lives:

1. **Love** is the absence of selfishness. It is the product of the Holy Spirit present in our lives,[a] so it remains even in the harshest and most difficult times because we don't produce the love—the Holy Spirit does! The word *agape* is the love of *choice*, referring not to an emo-tional affection, physical attraction, or a familial bond, but to respect, devotion, and affection that leads to willing, self-sacrificial service.[b]

a. Romans 5:5

b. John 15:13
Romans 5:8
1 John 3:16-17

Ask yourself: Can others trace my progress in expressing God's love? Am I less selfish and self-seeking than I was last month?

2. **Joy** is the spiritual quality that releases us from circumstances because our happiness is based on unchanging divine promises and

eternal spiritual realities. Christian joy is not a shallow emotion that, like a thermometer, rises and falls with the changing atmosphere of the home. Rather, Christian joy is a deep experience of adequacy and confidence in spite of the circumstances around us. The Christian can be joyful even in the midst of pain and suffering. This kind of joy is not a thermometer but a thermostat. Instead of rising and falling with the circumstances, it determines the spiritual temperature of the circumstances. Paul put it beautifully when he wrote, *"I have learned in whatsoever state I am, therewith to be content"* (PHILIPPIANS 4:11). Joy is a gift from God; as such, believers are not to manufacture it but to delight in the blessing they already possess.[a]

a. Romans 14:17
Philippians 4:4

> *Ask yourself: Do those who know me and watch my life see me as a joyful person?*

3. Peace is the internal serenity that only God can give. Jesus said not to live tomorrow's challenges today, but to trust what lies ahead to Him. Troubles are not absent; rather, God is present! When the Holy Spirit is not grieved, the Dove of Peace is able to alight on the heart. Peace is an inner calm that results from confidence in one's saving relationship with Christ. The verb form denotes binding together and is reflected in the expression "having it altogether." Like joy, peace is not related to one's circumstances.[b]

b. John 14:27
Romans 8:28
Philippians 4:6-7, 9

> *Ask yourself: Has peace become more and more a way of life for me this year?*

4. Patience ("longsuffering" in KJV) is the absence of personal irritation at the actions of others. It is that gentle patience with people that Paul spoke of in 1 Corinthians 13:4-7. Patience is also one of the supreme attributes of God. It is His character that is revealed as being gracious and longsuffering.[c] This is patience—the ability to endure injuries inflicted by others and the willingness to accept irritating or painful situations.[d]

c. Exodus 34:6
Numbers 14:18
2 Peter 3:9

d. Ephesians 4:2
Colossians 3:12
1 Timothy 1:15-16

> *Ask yourself: Am I more patient than I was three months ago? Or less? If I am not increasing in patience, is it because I am not yielding and submitting to the Holy Spirit?*

5. Kindness is a beautiful reflection of God in our lives. It is when we choose to avoid an abrasive manner in our dealings with people. It is when we choose to live out Ephesians 2:8 and 4:32. Kindness is seen as sensitivity toward others that produces deeds of self-sacrifice and love—even toward the unlovely and undeserving. Kindness will soften any word or act that might hurt another.

Ask yourself: Is my character showing an increasing tendency toward personal kindness in the way I treat others?

6. Goodness is being Godlike, which is the opposite of fallen humanity. Look at Jesus in Acts 10:38: *"God anointed Jesus of Nazareth with the Holy Spirit and with power, who went about doing good …."* When the Holy Spirit anointed Christ's life, what came out? He simply went about doing "good." The example of Jesus should be our guide for life—everywhere we are we should touch those around us with His goodness. Believers are commanded to exemplify goodness.[a]

a. Galatians 6:10
2 Thessalonians 1:11

Ask yourself: Am I a visibly better person than last year? Do the Lord and the godly mentors He has put in my life see me doing good to all those around me?

7. Faithfulness refers to a trustworthy and dependable life. A faithful person keeps his own life in order so you can count on him. Like Psalm 15 describes, this type of person always keeps his word. Faithfulness is the same as loyalty and trustworthiness.[b]

b. Lamentations 3:22
Philippians 2:7-9
1 Thessalonians 5:24
Revelation 2:10

Ask yourself: Am I making strides in reliability and dependability?

8. Gentleness is better translated "meekness," which is the opposite of asserting ourselves. The Lord said the meek are the ultimate winners.[c] Those who are servants of the Lord must not strive.[d] They must resist selfish ambition because that is a reflection of Satan, not God.[e]

c. Matthes 5:5

d. 2 Timothy 2:24

e. James 3:14-16

Ask yourself: What shape is my personal agenda in? Is it intact and my rights being defended? Or, is it as Christ desires—crucified with Him and fading?

a. 1 Corinthians 9:25
   2 Peter 1:5-6

9. Discipline ("self-control" in KJV) refers to restraining passions and appetites[a] and is defined by the Greek dictionary as "a virtue, which consists in mastery of the appetites and passions, especially the sensual ones." The only force that can control our flesh is the Holy Spirit. When yielded to the Spirit, we become vessels that are worshipful sacrifices to Him, and no longer to self. Self cannot control self; flesh is not able to harness flesh.[b] Only the Spirit can discipline us.

b .J. Oswald Sanders, *Spiritual Discipleship*, (Chicago: Moody Press, 1994), p. 118.

Ask yourself: Do others see me as graciously under the control of God's Spirit of Discipline? Am I beating under and giving knockout blows to my flesh—like Paul in 1 Corinthians 9:27?

When God's Spirit is at the helm, there is a remarkable change in our homes, churches, and lives. We see that as believers we are in the same family—God is our Father. We are headed toward a common goal—heaven. We serve a common Master—Jesus. We follow the same Guide—His Word. And share the same passion—Christ, who gets all the glory.

Prayer Example: Dear Lord, I pray that You will make Colossians 3:12-17 a reality in my family's lives! Help us to put on tender mercies, kindness, humility, meekness, and longsuffering. Enable us to be bearing with one another, and forgiving one another. If anyone has a complaint against another, even as You have forgiven us, so help us to forgive others. And above all these things, help us to put on love, which is the bond of perfection. May Your peace rule in our hearts and home. May we always be thankful in all circumstances because Your Word dwells in us richly in all wisdom! Enable us to be teaching and admonishing one another in psalms and hymns and spiritual songs, singing with grace in our hearts to You, oh Lord. And whatever we do in word or deed, may it be done all in Your name, giving thanks to God the Father through You!

PRAY THEY WILL TRUST GOD
WHEN TROUBLES COME

"So Samuel said: 'Has the LORD [as great] delight in burnt offerings and sacrifices, As in obeying the voice of the LORD? Behold, to obey is better than sacrifice, [And] to heed than the fat of rams. For rebellion [is as] the sin of witchcraft, And stubbornness [is as] iniquity and idolatry. Because you have rejected the word of the LORD, He also has rejected you from being king' " (1 SAMUEL 5:22-23).

The Lord says we are to yield ourselves to all levels of authority over us (unless they ask us to disobey a clear command of God's Word). No matter what the conditions, the command was the same: submit, trust, wait, and hope. The Lord expects the same from us today, and that is why we have come to our next area of prayer for our children's relational stability—seeing them learning to trust God with hard situations, and not rebelling.

Is that really possible? It is not only possible, it is imperative. Anything less becomes the breeding ground for one of the deadliest of all spiritual conditions—rebellion. Rebellion is an inward choice to resist and go against the will of an authority over us. Though often unseen at first, rebellion grows. The results of rebellion are infinitely more dreadful than any mistreatment or hard situation. Therefore, as our children face challenges, hardship, and unfair situations we must pray that they never harden their hearts and rebel against God's ordained authorities in their lives.

I love biographies. Since childhood I have marveled at the lives of Edison, Lincoln, Einstein, Churchill, and the likes. Each life story had my rapt attention because they each touched the world in a special way. We can learn great lessons from biographies. Even more, Bible biographies can be a tool to shape the heart of your family. I have spent years finding the key lessons from the biographies God included in His Book. Some were winners and pleased Him; others were losers and turned away from Him.

One of the most sobering lessons on the destructive power of stubbornness, disobedience, and the deadliness of rebellion is seen in God's account of the personal shipwreck of the life of King Saul. "The Fruit of the Flesh" below is just one example of lessons I have shared with my children from the life of King Saul, a colossal failure. Fifteen glaring warning lights "blinked" impending disaster in his life.

Saul's Biography: Cultivating the Fruit of the Flesh

JUST AS THE SPIRIT OF God bears fruit, so does the flesh. When we don't obey God we are in rebellion against Him. There is no middle ground. The fruit of the flesh is also quite easily spotted in ungodly attitudes and actions. King Saul would not walk in step with God, so his flesh reigned in his life. Saul lived a life of ignoring the warnings of departure from God's way! What were those signs? His pathway of rebellion involved the following elements. These are still danger signs to caution anyone who loves and seeks to follow the Lord to this day: (Emphasis added to the verses below.)

1. Impatience: *"Then he waited seven days, according to the time set by Samuel.* **But Samuel did not come** *to Gilgal; and the people were scattered from him"* (1 SAMUEL 13:8). Saul was impatient with God's plan. He sought the approval of man before he sought the approval of God.

2. Neglect: *"So it came about, on the day of battle, that* **there was neither sword nor spear found in the hand of any of the people** *who were with Saul and Jonathan. But they were found with Saul and Jonathan his son"* (1 SAMUEL 13:22). Saul neglected to provide for those entrusted to his care. He made sure he had what he needed to defend himself, but not that those he cared for were armed for the battle. In the New Testament, God says such a person is worse than an infidel: *"If anyone does not provide for his own, and especially for those of his household, he has denied the faith and is worse than an unbeliever"* (1 TIMOTHY 5:8).

3. LAZY INDIFFERENCE: *"AND SAUL **was sitting** in the outskirts of Gibeah under a pomegranate tree which is in Migron. The people who were with him were about six hundred men. Ahijah the son of Ahitub, Ichabod's brother, the son of Phinehas, the son of Eli, the Lord's priest* *in Shiloh, was wearing an ephod. But the people did not know that Jonathan had gone"* (1 SAMUEL 14:2-3). Saul became lazy and indifferent; he was unaware of his son, the battle, and even the victory. He missed it all!

4. Rash words: *"And the men of Israel were distressed that day, for Saul had **placed the people under oath**, saying, 'Cursed is the man who eats any food until evening, before I have taken vengeance on my enemies.' So none of the people tasted food"* (1 SAMUEL 14:24). Saul spoke with no thought of what the implications were to his family or nation.

5. Incomplete obedience: *"**But Saul and the people spared Agag** and the best of the sheep, the oxen, the fatlings, the lambs, and all that was good, and were unwilling to utterly destroy them. But everything despised and worthless, that they utterly destroyed"* (1 SAMUEL 15:9). Saul used selective, self-serving obedience in place of total and God-honoring obedience.

6. Not cultivating personal worship: *"Then he said, 'I have sinned; yet honor me now, please, before the elders of my people and before Israel, and return with me, that I may worship the Lord **your God**' "* (1 SAMUEL 15:30). Saul did not seek God on a personal level; nor did he worship the Lord from his heart.

7. Doubting the power of God: *"When Saul and all Israel heard these words of the Philistine, they were **dismayed and greatly afraid**"* (1 SAMUEL 17:11). Saul had no concept of the awesome God who had revealed Himself to him. He and his followers thought that mere mortals (the Philistines) were greater than the Ancient of Days!

8. Self-focus: *"Then Saul was very angry, and the saying displeased him; and he said, 'They have ascribed to David ten thousands, **and to me** they have ascribed only thousands' "* (1 SAMUEL 18:8). Saul measured the worth of his life by what others said, rather than by the Lord.

9. Insecurity: *"Now what more can he have **but the kingdom?**"* (1 SAMUEL 18:8B). Saul surrendered the care of his future security to himself and took it away from the Lord. Fear is always the realm of Satan.

10. Jealousy: *"So **Saul eyed David** from that day forward"* (1 SAMUEL 18:9). Saul was driven by the lust for self—desiring to keep others from having something he wanted for himself! This is the worst form of jealousy. Jealousy darkens our eyes to anything good about another; in Saul's mind, David was unable to ever measure up to Saul's expectations.

11. Wrong value system: *"Now Saul was afraid of David, **because the Lord was with him,** but had departed from Saul"* (1 SAMUEL 18:12). Saul neither treasured nor sought God's blessing, favor, presence, or even involvement in his life. He valued himself, neglected God, and feared David because the Lord was with him. What a tragic, misdirected life!

12. Neglecting his marriage: *"Then Saul's anger was aroused against Jonathan, and he said to him, '**You son of a perverse, rebellious woman!** Do I not know that you have chosen the son of Jesse to your own shame and to the shame of your mother's nakedness?' "* (1 SAMUEL 20:30). Saul confessed his failure to nurture and care for his wife. An undiscipled wife breeds many painful days.

13. Seeing things entirely from an earthly perspective: *"For as long as the son of Jesse lives on the earth, you shall not be established, **nor your kingdom.** Now therefore, send and bring him to me, for he shall surely die"* (1 SAMUEL 20:31). Saul wasn't able to see the eternal, the divine, and the spiritual parts of life. He looked on his family, his future, and their success as only a physical pursuit, not a spiritual heritage. God was always left out of the equation for security, prosperity, and happiness.

14. Having no fear of God: *"Then **the king said** to the guards who stood about him, 'Turn and **kill the priests of the Lord**, because their hand also is with David, and because they knew when he fled and did not tell it to me.' But the servants of the king would not lift their hands to strike the priests of the Lord"* (1 SAMUEL 22:17). Saul did not see

God, so he did not fear God. Thus there was no limit to his actions because he saw no consequence in offending the Lord by his life.

15. Not hating the enemies of the Lord: "***And the king said to Doeg,*** *'You turn and kill the priests!' So Doeg the Edomite turned and struck the priests, and killed on that day eighty-five men who wore a linen ephod*" (1 SAMUEL 22:18). If we love someone, we hurt when they do. We are loyal and reverent of the name of those we cherish. Saul had none of these qualities because he failed to cherish God enough to carry out His fierce wrath against the Amalekites, He uses one of God's enemies (an Edomite) to kill God's choice servants (the Levites).

The end of Saul was a catastrophe. He crashed against the rocks of his own disobedient life and sank into the dark waters of sin. He was a disgrace to himself by his ignominious death; to his family he failed to protect; to his country he betrayed and brought to defeat; and to his God he ignored and dishonored. What a colossal failure and a grim testimony of neglected warning signs that led to a shipwreck of a very promising life!

Saul's failures can serve to drive us to pray to live in such a way that these areas don't get solidified in the lives of those we love!

Prayer Example: Dear Father in Heaven, thank You for the important lessons learned from Saul's shipwrecked life! I pray when I or members of my family face challenges, hardships, and unfair situations, we will live by 1 Peter 3:8-14. Make us all of one mind, having compassion for one another; let us love as brothers and sisters in Christ. Keep us tenderhearted and courteous, not returning evil for evil or reviling for reviling, but on the contrary blessing, knowing that this is what You have called us to do. Teach us to love life and see good days, to refrain our tongues from evil, and our lips from speaking deceit. We know Your eyes are on the righteous, and Your ears are open to our prayers! Thank You that no one can harm us if we are followers of what is good, and even if we should suffer for righteousness sake, we will be blessed through it all. And Lord, help us to not be afraid of threats, nor to be troubled by them. Give us each obedient hearts—sensitive hearts—to do Your precious will!

PRAY THEY WILL LOVE GOD'S
PLAN FOR THEIR LIVES

*"For You formed my inward parts; You covered me in my mother's
womb. I will praise You, for I am fearfully [and] wonderfully made;
Marvelous are Your works, And [that] my soul knows very well. My
frame was not hidden from You, When I was made in secret, [And]
skillfully wrought in the lowest parts of the earth. Your eyes saw
my substance, being yet unformed. And in Your book they were all
written, The days fashioned for me, When [as yet there were] none
of them. How precious also are Your thoughts to me, O God! How
great is the sum of them! [If] I should count them, they would be
more in number than the sand; When I awake, I am still with You"*
(PSALM 139:14-18).

We were created for God's glory! Each of us was built to a perfect and
intricate set of plans, engineered by God Himself. Within every cell
of our body is a set of those "divine fingerprints" called our DNA. The
human genome is a wonder of precise engineering that laid down
everything about our physical body. Who we are, where we were
born, how we look, all of our imperfections and weaknesses, and
countless other details are all part of God's marvelous design. We are
the handiwork of God—like spiritual snowflakes—no two are exactly
alike! Like rare and precious jewels, no one is worthless or unimportant in God's plan. Each person was especially designed by God for
divine purposes, which brings me to my main point.

Do you know what God's perfect plan is for your sons as men,
and your daughters as women? In some areas the Lord wants similar
character for boys and girls, but in most areas, His plan for a young
man *greatly differs* from His plan for a young woman.

The Lord Almighty, God of the Universe, has made men and
women with different qualities, roles, and purposes within His great
plan. As we look at some scriptural passages, we will see a portion of
that wondrous plan of how young men and women are to please Him
by their lives, choices, and conduct. The key to successful training is
in our understanding that more is caught (discipleship) than taught
(lecture). Fathers and mothers, what *you* are is very much what *they
will become!*

God's Plan for Our Sons

*"Likewise, urge the young men to be sensible; in all things show your-
self to be an example of good deeds, with purity in doctrine, dignified,
sound in speech which is beyond reproach, so that the opponent will be
put to shame, having nothing bad to say about us"* (TITUS 2:6-8, NASB).

GOD WANTS YOUNGER MEN (12 and older) to stand out in our culture
because they represent future leaders in the cause of Christ! He wants
the older men to teach them to exercise sound judgment in all things
by showing reality in their spiritual lives, integrity in their personal
lives, and stability in their relational lives. From Titus 2:6-8, we see
that sons need to see their fathers being role models characterized by:

1. Sensibility. We've seen Paul use this characteristic of elders,
older men, and younger women. Young men need to develop self-
control and balance, discernment and judgment.[a] The phrase "in all   a. Cf. 2 Timothy 2:22; 1 Peter 5:5.
things" stretches this matter of mental balance and self-mastery in
the Christian life to an almost infinite level. Young men—so potentially volatile, impulsive, passionate, arrogant, and ambitious—need
to become masters over every area in their lives. Dad, do your boys
see this type of Spirit-controlled living in you?

2. Good deeds. Paul turns from the young men in general to
encourage Titus to "show [himself] to be an example of good deeds."
One of the most important qualities of a leader is the example he sets.
Paul wanted Titus to be a model first of "good deeds." That refers to
his inherent righteousness, nobility, and moral excellence. A godly
young man is to model righteousness in everything he does. Dad, do
your boys see this type of Spirit-controlled living in you?

3. Purity in doctrine. "With purity in doctrine" is how God wants
good deeds to be accomplished. A better way to translate the Greek
word is "uncorruptness." Titus and young men were to live in perfect
accord with sound doctrine, and without defect. Young men must

know the Word of God and live according to it. Psalm 119:9 says: *"How can a young man keep his way pure? By keeping it according to Thy Word."* Living in obedience to God's Word is what keeps us in line. Dad, do your boys see this type of Spirit-controlled living in you?

4. Dignity. At the end of Titus 2:7, Paul adds that Titus and young men were to be "dignified"—a characteristic that should also be true of men and women, deacons and older men. That means young men are to be serious. Youth tends to be somewhat frivolous, particularly in our culture where entertainment has become an all-consuming passion. While that doesn't mean young men can't enjoy life, they should have a mature understanding of life, death, time, and eternity. Dad, do your boys see this type of Spirit-controlled living in you?

5. Soundness in speech. Finally, Paul encourages Titus to *"[Be] sound in speech which is beyond reproach."* "Sound" means "healthy" or "wholesome." In reference to one's words, Paul wrote: *"Let your speech always be with grace, seasoned, as it were, with salt, so that you may know how you should respond to each person"* (COLOSSIANS 4:6). Young men need to learn that what they say should be worth saying—that it edifies hearers to the point that it is "beyond reproach." [a] Dad, do your boys see this type of Spirit-controlled living in you?

a. John MacArthur, *Different by Design* (Wheaton, IL: Victor Books, 1996), p.29.

So, how are we as fathers doing in these areas? David Wilkerson, author of *The Cross and The Switch Blade*, and now pastor of Times Square Church, gave an amazing testimony to his congregation based upon Jesus calling us *"kings and priests to His God and Father"* (REVELATION 1:6) and *"a chosen generation, a royal priesthood ... being built up [as] a spiritual house, a holy priesthood ..."* (1 PETER 2:5, 9). Wilkerson asked parents to evaluate which priesthood described their lives most:

A Half-hearted Manifestation of Jesus in the Home Produces a Passive Heart in the Children

It's sad but true: many Christian parents are sending their kids straight to hell. Dad is to be the priest in the home. Mother is a member of God's royal priesthood too.

For years I was a youth evangelist, traveling the nation and

*ministering to thousands of young people. During that time, I had
conversations with many troubled teenagers from Christian homes.
These kids were completely turned off to church. They wanted
nothing to do with their parents' religion. They spoke of their dad
and mom's angry fights, blatant hypocrisy, awful gossip, secret sins.
They heard constant grumbling and complaints about their minister, church members, family, and friends.*

*Usually in such cases, the dad was active in church. People saw
him as dedicated and full of Jesus. But his kids knew how to read
his life, and they saw him as he really was: a phony. He mistreated
their mother with abusive language. Or he had a secret stash of
pornographic magazines. Or he was caught watching filthy videos.*

*Such a dad serves in the Eli priesthood. He has no spiritual
authority. And in turn, he has no respect. He might lecture his kids,
or threaten them, or try to demand obedience. But he's wasting his
breath. It's all to no avail.*

*We see this illustrated in Eli's life. Eli had two sons named
Hophni and Phinehas, who also served as priests. God called these
men "sons of Belial," or children of the devil. Yet Eli never dealt
with his sons about their sin. He never spoke to them more than an
empty word of caution. After all, he knew anything he might say to
them was in vain, because of his own spiritual sloth.*[a]

a. David Wilkerson,
"A Manifestation of Jesus"
(New York, NY: Times Square
Church E-mail, 7-12-02).

Be what God desires men to be. Oh, how our young men need
to be discipled by fathers who can honestly say, *"Imitate me, just as
I also imitate Christ"* (1 CORINTHIANS 11:1)! That is a verse every
dad should memorize, and then meditate upon until it is a habit. In
1 Timothy 2:8, Paul points out four ways that a Word-filled dad can
express his walk with the Lord: *"I desire therefore that the men pray
everywhere, lifting up holy hands, without wrath and doubting."*

- Word-filled fathers **"pray everywhere"**—at the table, at bedtime,
  before school, before travel, on the road, alone, in public, and so forth.
- Word-filled fathers are men of purity who are **"lifting up holy
  hands."** When their hands, lives, and secrets are exposed all that
  shows are holy hands, cleansed and kept pure by a Spirit-filled walk!
- Word-filled fathers are men of patience," **without wrath"**—
  longsuffering, with a patience that grows and takes over their responses!

- Word-filled fathers are men of faith who are **"without doubting"**—they believe God's Word enough to actually live it!

God's Plan for Our Daughters

The older women are to encourage the younger *"to love their husbands, to love their children, to be sensible, pure, workers at home, kind, being subject to their own husbands, so that the Word of God will not be dishonored"* (TITUS 2:4-5, NASB).

GOD WANTS YOUNGER WOMEN TO also stand out in our culture. However, that is the exact opposite of what they are being taught. Women today are encouraged to love whomever they want, to farm out their children to someone else's care and influence, not to worry about being sensible or pure, and to do whatever pleases them in fulfilling their desires.[a] But that is not God's way!

a. John MacArthur, *Different by Design* (Wheaton, IL: Victor Books, 1996), p.29.

Our young women need to be discipled by mothers who can honestly say, *"Imitate me, just as I also imitate Christ!"* (1 CORINTHIANS 11:1). From Titus 2:4-5, we can see that daughters need to see their mother being a role model characterized by seven elements:

Note: *If you don't have Titus 2:4-5 marked in your Bible, I encourage you to stop, get a pen, and mark these seven characteristics you are to model.*

1. Love for her husband. This means being a one-man woman, totally devoted to him—in tune with his needs, plans, and desires. Mom, do your girls see this type of Spirit-filled love in you?

2. Love for her children. Being a lover of children is a woman's high calling.[b] Obviously, God doesn't want all women to be mothers or they would be. Those women who have no children mean a great deal to God's kingdom because He has given them freedom to serve in unique ways. But God wants women who are mothers to love their children, which involves making personal sacrifices for their benefit. Loving your children is not based on emotion. Rather, it is

b. 1 Timothy 2:15

your responsibility to pour yourself into their lives so that they grow up to love Christ. Mom, do your girls see this type of Spirit-filled love in you?

3. Sensibility. This refers to using common sense and making sound judgments. Those things are learned best by example, and that's where the older women can have such an influence. Mom, do your girls see this type of Spirit-controlled living in you?

4. Purity. A godly wife and mother is morally pure, virtuous, and sexually faithful to her husband. A pure wife is devoted to her man in body and spirit. What she reads, listens to, and watches on television or movies, should declare loyalty and devotion to the real man she lives with—not a dream or fantasy man who only exists in her mind. Mom, do your girls see this type of Spirit-controlled purity in you?

5. Working at home. A woman's responsibility is in the home because it is the place where she can have the greatest impact on the world by raising godly men and women. God has designed the family to be her sphere of responsibility. This doesn't mean she should spend 24 hours a day there, however. The woman in Proverbs 31 left her home when she needed to buy a field or when she needed supplies, yet even those trips benefited her family. She poured her life into her family—she woke up early and went to bed late for the sake of those in it. Mom, do your girls see this type of Spirit-filled focus upon God's will in you?

6. Kindness. This means being kind, gentle, tenderhearted, and merciful toward others. Mom, do your girls see this type of Spirit-filled kindness in you?

7. Subjection to her husband. This requires being willingly and lovingly subject to your husband. This echoes Paul's instruction in Ephesians 5:22. A godly young woman understands God's created order and submits to it.[a] Mom, do your girls see this type of Spirit- a. Cf. 1 Corinthians 11:5.
controlled godliness in you?

As the world crumbles, as society disintegrates, and roles and genders are obliterated—God's Word still stands. As even the

Christian community erases masculinity from the Bible versions, and families abdicate God's standards for the family, the Word-filled home is getting harder and harder to build. But one truth remains: God has promised His blessing on those who will believe Him enough to obey Him!

Through this brief study of God's design for the differing roles of men and women, I hope you have seen anew and afresh that praying, teaching, and modeling the Word of God is the key to raising, nurturing, and launching children who please the Lord. I pray that you are gaining a greater understanding of the vital need to be learning how to pray for your children from the Scriptures!

> *Prayer Example: Dear Lord, I pray, with all my heart, that You will help me to be able to honestly say to my children, "Imitate me, just as I also imitate Christ!" May my testimony be such that they will heed my admonitions when I remind them of the truth of Ecclesiastes 12:1a and 12:13-14. May they never forget You in the days of their youth! I pray they will fear You always, and lovingly keep Your commandments. May they meditate on the fact that You will bring their every work into judgment, including every secret thing, whether good or evil, and then live their lives accordingly. Oh Father, grant my children listening ears and seeing eyes! Have mercy upon us all, and cause us to be a family who has Spirit-filled stability in our relational lives! In Jesus' name I ask. Amen.*

Pray They Will Wait for God's Chosen Partner

> *"Do not be unequally yoked together with unbelievers. For what fellowship has righteousness with lawlessness? And what communion has light with darkness?"* (2 CORINTHIANS 6:14).

THE SECOND GREATEST DAY OF OUR LIVES

As I have stood in front of crowded churches for decades at weddings, I almost always say the same thing: "You are witnessing the second greatest day of this couple's life." There is often a gasp or two from the audience who is obviously thinking this wedding is their greatest day.

I then continue, "The greatest day was the day these two individuals repented of their sins, believing in Jesus for their salvation."

Are we as parents spending regular time prayerfully preparing our children for the "second greatest day of their lives" after salvation? If not, maybe these paragraphs will challenge you.

God has a simple rule about marriage: a believer may only marry another believer. If we believe what God's Word says, then our sons and daughters should never even date someone who is not a genuine Christian. Evangelistic dating for the purpose of getting someone saved, so that they become a good prospect for a marriage partner, is never wise. According to God's Word, if that rule is violated, another of God's rules will hold true: *"Do not be deceived, God is not mocked; for whatever a man sows, that he will also reap"* (GALATIANS 6:7). Teach in your Bible times around your table that it is not God's will for a Christian to marry or date an unbeliever. The Greek word for "communion" is also used for "marriage." What marriage can light have with darkness? It simply doesn't work! It is not God's will, and is therefore sin.

Remember: our sons and daughters will only get one chance in life to start with a wonderful biblical marriage. Teach them it is worth the wait! Pray they will not squander one of the greatest blessings of life by doing their own thing instead of God's! If you haven't already been doing so, start praying now for their future mates—even if no one is yet on the horizon. At this very moment, those future sons- and daughters-in-law are in the process of developing their intellect, giftedness, abilities, and most of all who they will become as men and women. Why not have a precious ministry to them—and your sons and daughters—by being prayer warriors on their behalf!

A DESCRIPTION OF A WONDERFUL HUSBAND FOR YOUR DAUGHTER

James reminds us that "we have not because we ask not." What are you asking God for in your future sons-in-law? Look at what God says a young man can be by His grace. This is what he should want to be, what he should want to be around, and what he should be drawn toward. Pray that your future sons-in-law will be young men who are seeking to become:

1. A Man of Wisdom. *"A wise man will hear and increase learning, And a man of understanding will attain wise counsel"* (PROVERBS 1:5). The Lord has already told us in James 3:17 the wise man has wisdom from above. He is characterized as pure, peaceable, gentle, and easy to talk things over with, full of mercy, and wanting to do good. Pray your future sons-in-law will be wise men of great understanding!

2. A Man of Happiness. *"Happy is the man who finds wisdom, And the man who gains understanding"* (PROVERBS 3:13). The Sermon on the Mount says it all. Happy are the pure in heart, the meek, the humble, the peacemakers, the righteousness seekers, and those who are hungry for God! Pray your future sons-in-law will be happy in the sense Jesus described in Matthew 5:3-10.

3. A Blessed Man. *"Blessed is the man who listens to me, Watching daily at my gates, Waiting at the posts of my doors"* (PROVERBS 8:34). As Psalm 1 says, the blessed man is rooted deep in God's Word, is full of God's fruit, and won't walk, stand, or sit with those who mock God. Pray your future sons-in-law will be blessed because their heart belongs wholly to God.

4. A Seeker of Justice. *"Give instruction to a wise man, and he will be still wiser; Teach a just man, and he will increase in learning"* (PROVERBS 9:9). This quality of being "just" is like the English word "straight." A just man is straight—in his talk, walk, habits, and convictions. There is no doubt as to who he is, and where he is going. Pray your future sons-in-law will be just in their talk, walk, habits, and convictions!

5. Merciful in Attitude. *"The merciful man does good for his own soul, But he who is cruel troubles his own flesh"* (PROVERBS 11:17). Hitler surrounded himself with men who were evil and cruel. Together they made the darkest blot yet seen in history. Pray your future sons-in-law will stay away from those who delight in cruel words, attitudes, and actions!

6. A Seeker of Good. *"A good man obtains favor from the Lord, But a man of wicked intentions He will condemn"* (PROVERBS 12:2). True goodness is a fruit of the Spirit within a person's life. There is no clearer indicator of what a man will be like than his goodness level. Pray your future sons-in-law will be drawn toward what is good, and not evil. Few people turn out very far from where they are headed right now! A word of caution: *"The backslider in heart will be filled with his own ways, But a good man will be satisfied from above"* (PROVERBS 14:14). The surest sign of danger in a man is when you detect that he is full of himself. He talks about himself, shows himself off, promotes himself, and on and on he goes. This is a life that is sliding backward toward an abyss; don't allow a daughter to attach herself to such a person or she will be pulled down into the pit with him!

7. A Lover of Righteousness. *"A man is not established by wickedness, But the root of the righteous cannot be moved"* (PROVERBS 12:3). As Psalm 1 and Jeremiah 17:8 both say, righteousness holds us firmly in the place where God can make us flourish fruitfully and securely. Such a young man will seek to be righteous in every day life: *"A righteous man regards the life of his animal, But the tender mercies of the wicked are cruel"* (PROVERBS 12:10). Perhaps an animal might have been his transportation, so this could be applied to having the Lord be evident in a future son-in-law's car. How he drives, keeps up, and decorates his car declares a lot about him. Or, an animal might have been his work; God says righteousness invades all of life—even the barnyard (or work). A righteous man exhibits the Lord in how he treats the indefensible, the weak, and the common. Pray your future sons-in-law will be gentle and kind to all around them!

8. Prudent in Responses. *"A fool's wrath is known at once, But a prudent man covers shame"* (PROVERBS 12:16). A fool lets it all out, vents, rages, and carries on, but a godly young man will be Spirit-controlled. Pray your future sons-in-law will be prudent, that they will know how to respond in hard, difficult, or shameful times.

9. Diligent at Work. *"The hand of the diligent will rule, But the lazy man will be put to forced labor"* (PROVERBS 12:24). Proverbs describes the lazy (a sluggard) 14 times. How much heartache would be avoided if a lazy man was not an option to a daughter, because laziness normally only gets worse. Pray your future sons-in-law will be diligent, hard workers, with godly initiative and ambition to provide properly for your daughters and future grandchildren.

10. Wisely Cautious. *"A wise man fears and departs from evil, But a fool rages and is self-confident"* (PROVERBS 14:16; also 12:8). Brashness, overconfidence, and foolhardiness are not noble virtues. Pray your future sons-in-law will be Spirit-controlled, and thus wisely cautious.

11. Upright in Walk. *"The way of the lazy man is like a hedge of thorns, But the way of the upright is a highway"* (PROVERBS 15:19). Here is another one of the fourteen verses containing "lazy man" warnings. The way of the righteous is a God-designed path that the wise follow. It is an exhilarating life of adventure, excitement, and wonders—walking on the high places of the earth as Isaiah describes it. But the wicked, in all their seeming gaiety, are actually walking through a hedge of thorns and getting cuts, scrapes, and scratches every step they take. Pray your future sons-in-law will habitually choose the way of the upright, and that they will always evidence integrity in their personal lives.

12. A Wonderful Son. *"A wise son makes a father glad, But a foolish man despises his mother"* (PROVERBS 15:20). Watch carefully how a son relates to his parents. What he is at home will touch his life with blessing or be lacking all the days of his life. Pray your future sons-in-law will be respectful of their parents, and will continue to love and honor them for a lifetime.

13. Humble in Attitude. *"Before destruction the heart of a man is haughty, And before honor is humility"* (PROVERBS 18:12). Pride is the root of all sin, and humility is the root of all virtue. Therefore, the key to God's blessing is a humble life because haughtiness will only invite disaster. Pray your future sons-in-law will manifest humility in spirit before God and others!

14. A Man of Excellence. *"Do you see a man who excels in his work? He will stand before kings; He will not stand before unknown men"* (PROVERBS 22:29). The mark of an excellent man, who will excel in whatever he does, is that he practices and perfects a skill in his life. There is no limit, God says, to what He can do with one who works hard at what he does! Pray your future sons-in-law will be men of excellence who desire to do all things for the glory of God!

Obviously, all these areas of prayer for your future sons-in-law should also be discipling goals for your sons. Make your discipling of them a top priority; pray they will become honorable husbands for your future daughters-in-law. And, above all, pray your sons will patiently wait for God's chosen marriage partner for them!

A Description of a Wonderful Wife for Your Son

Have you ever checked the recipe in God's Word for a marvelous daughter-in-law? The verses below I have highlighted in my Bible. When I go out for a father/daughter time, these are the themes I bring up, discuss, share, and train my three daughters to hold on to as God's desires for them. I call this "The Habits of a Woman Who Honors the Lord."

If you have sons, why not make this a part of regular prayers for the Lord to provide women who honor the Lord to become your future daughters-in-law! Now look at what God says a young woman can be by His grace. This is what she should want to be, what she should want to be around, and what she should be drawn toward. Pray your future daughters-in-law will be young women who are seeking to become:

1. Modest in Dress: *"I also want women to dress modestly, with decency and propriety, not with braided hair or gold or pearls or expensive clothes"* (1 TIMOTHY 2:9, NIV). A godly young lady's clothing will point to her Father in heaven and His holiness, and not to her. Remember the words of Paul in the New Testament's gallery of beautiful women? God's emphasis is always on beauty of character, as should your sons' be. Pray your future daughters-in-law will dress modestly, for the Lord's sake, as is fitting for His children.

2. Holy in Conduct: *"Do you not know that your body is a temple of the Holy Spirit, who is in you, whom you have received from God? You are not your own; you were bought at a price. Therefore honor God with your body"* (1 CORINTHIANS 6:19-20, NIV). A godly woman fears the Lord. She seeks His "well done" over the approval of anyone else on earth. Her fear of God makes her aware of the future consequence of her choices. Such a godly woman avoids any present situation that would be destructive for her future usefulness to God. Pray your future daughters-in-law will desire to be holy in conduct, and thus useful to God.

3. Gentle in Spirit: *"And the Lord's servant must not quarrel; instead, [she] must be kind to everyone, able to teach, not resentful"* (2 TIMOTHY 2:24, NIV). A foolish woman is loud and defiant; she is disrespectful, hostile, aggressive, and cunning. But a godly woman is pure, peace-loving, considerate, submissive, full of mercy and good fruit, impartial and sincere.[a] Most of all remember what God delights in: *"Let it be the hidden person of the heart, with the incorruptible beauty of a gentle and quiet spirit, which is very precious in the sight of God"* (1 PETER 3:4). Pray your future daughters-in-law will be full of wisdom from above!

a. James 3:17

4. A Dedicated Homemaker: *"She seeks wool and flax, And willingly works with her hands"* (PROVERBS 31:13). As Paul said, a godly woman is a worker at home.[b] She loves to tangibly serve others with food and skills; she has an open and hospitable home; and she is given to ministry to the sick and needy and less fortunate. Pray your future daughters-in-law will desire to make their homes a "castle" for your sons, honoring the Lord in all that they do.

b. Titus 2:5

5. A Servant at Heart: *"She also rises while it is yet night, and provides food for her household, and a portion for her maidservants. She extends her hand to the poor, yes, she reaches out her hands to the needy"* (PROVERBS 31:15, 20). This dear lady has learned the love of Christ for others. Pray your future daughters-in-law will have learned that servanthood is the secret to God's greatest blessings in life!

6. Worthy of Trust: *"The heart of her husband doth safely trust in her, so that he shall have no need of spoil. She will do him good and not evil all the days of her life"* (PROVERBS 31:11-12, KJV). Pray your future daughters-in-law will be trustworthy so your sons can rejoice in their goodness within their marital relationship.

7. Prudent in Finances: *"She considers a field and buys it; from* her profits she plants a vineyard. She makes linen garments and sells [them,] and supplies sashes for the merchants" (PROVERBS 31:16, 24). Such a woman is a saver, not a spender, because she can see beyond today alone. Pray your future daughters-in-law will be wise in the matters of finance because this area in particular can create many marital difficulties if not brought into line with God's standards.

8. A Hard Worker: *"She girds herself with strength, and strengthens her arms. She stretches out her hands to the distaff, and her hand holds the spindle"* (PROVERBS 31:17,19). God puts a premium on hard work and so this godly young lady moves toward it, not away. There is no slothfulness, indolence, or lack of motivation in her behavior. Pray your future daughters-in-law will be hard workers, and not lazy in any area.

9. Of Good Reputation: *"Her husband is known in the gates, When he sits among the elders of the land"* (PROVERBS 31:23). Consider also: *"Moreover he must have a good testimony among those who are outside, lest he fall into reproach and the snare of the devil"* (1 TIMOTHY 3:7). A son who desires to be a future elder in the Lord's church must consider carefully the quality of woman he marries. Her role in the home will play a large part in his eligibility for leadership. So pray your future daughters-in-law will be true helpmeets to your sons so they can be even more useful in the body of Christ, as God so leads.

10. Wise in Biblical Truths: *"She opens her mouth with wisdom, And on her tongue [is] the law of kindness"* (PROVERBS 31:26). The Word is in this godly young woman's heart and life, and so it comes out of her mouth. And when it does, it is dressed in the clothes of the Spirit, gentle and kind. Pray your future daughters-in-law will be continually growing in biblical wisdom, gentleness, and kindness!

A godly young woman will seek to live these secrets of true womanhood. As Solomon said, *"Strength and honor [are] her clothing; She shall rejoice in time to come"* (PROVERBS 31:25). Your sons will praise such wives for doing right, and your grandchildren will rise up to bless them![a] This kind of woman is a blessing to all because she is a builder of the home and family.

a. Proverbs 31:28

Obviously, each of these areas of prayer for future daughters-in-law should also be discipling goals for your daughters. Make your discipling of them a top priority; pray they will become worthy wives for your future sons-in-law! And, above all, pray your daughters will patiently wait for God's chosen marriage partner for them!

> **Prayer Example:** *Dear Lord, I pray our family will fervently cultivate a First Corinthians 13 love for one another, for I know love covers a multitude of sins! Help me to prepare my children well for Your chosen marriage partners for them, and that they will patiently wait for Your direction in this area. May they evidence love in action through their patience and kindnesses toward others. May they never become envious, braggarts, or arrogant. Keep them from being rude or overbearing—easily irritated and angered by others. May they never insist on their own way, but, in humility, love serving others. Keep my children from ever finding pleasure in someone else's sin; instead, help them to rejoice in Your truth. Give them a love that protects, believes, hopes, and endures all things. And help me to lead the way by setting the example in all these areas!*

No Family Is Perfect

Do you have a marriage after God's own heart—or after your own? Where are you headed in your marriage? As a family? You will never get anywhere you are not headed right now. Beloved, if you are not careful, you can be headed for unhappiness, unfaithfulness, hardness, and divorce. God warns: *"Let him who thinks he stands take heed lest he fall"* (1 Corinthians 10:12). Many a marriage has ended up "on the rocks" when one of the spouses never even saw it coming. Most of us only faintly realize the dangerous climate we live in—a culture soaked with the stain of divorce that has penetrated to the depths of all our institutions. Related to that, I'd like to share my personal testimony:

> *Growing up in Michigan as a child was delightful. We lived by a lake and fished all summer, had fish frys with most of our neighbors, and enjoyed many fun moments as a family at church.*

That was life at 5 years old.

As the years passed and my perception of the world around me grew, I noticed the family next door was different. They could be heard at all hours screaming, banging, throwing things, and fighting. I was told that all the fighting meant they were separating as a couple, and would soon divorce. Then, while making a family tree for a school project, I noticed that my dad's mother, Grandma Barnett, had changed her name to Grandma Miller. My mom's mother also stopped living with Grandpa, her husband, and moved in with my uncle. But most devastating of all was when I began to notice as a young boy tension growing inside our own home. That was what it was like growing up at the onset of the cultural war against the godly family of the 1960s.

That sadness, tension, and conflict drove me to the Psalms for comfort. At a young age, I began to pray: "Lord, please let me have a home, a wife, and a family like Psalms 127 and 128 seem to promise." That prayer never stopped.

I most distinctly remember a repeated prayer I made while daily walking through the backwoods at Bob Jones University in Greenville, South Carolina: "Lord, don't let me go my own way. I only want to marry the one You have prepared for me. I want Your will—not mine!" And our faithful God heard those prayers! He has given me a wonderful wife, a wonderful family, and a wonderful home life—a true biblical marriage!

From my testimony, I hope you can see that having a background of sadness, tension, and conflict need not be a deterrent to having a truly biblical marriage. God wants to do something great in and through each of us through prayer! If you are already enjoying a biblical marriage, praise God, and safeguard that precious relationship with your spouse! If your marriage is going through troubled waters right now, as are so many these days, ask the Lord to give you a truly biblical marriage. Begin by working on your own God-given responsibilities within your family, as defined in the Bible and elaborated in this book. Never take your spouse for granted. Refuse to squander one of the greatest areas of your life by doing your own thing instead of God's.

As you pray for your children, pray also for yourself. Ask the Lord to grant reality in your spiritual life, integrity in your personal life, and stability in your relational life by enabling you to: **1.** cultivate Christlike love for your spouse—and other brothers and sisters in Christ, **2.** trust God when troubles come, **3.** love God's plan for His differing roles of men and women, and **4.** teach your children the importance of patiently waiting for God's timing and choice of a marriage partner.

In closing, in light of all we've learned from God's Word in this chapter, I pray that your I.D. tag—Christlike love—is clearly visible as a spouse, as a parent, as a brother or sister in Christ at church, and in all other relationships. This is crucial because His love is the foundation upon which a Christian family and all other relationships must be built:[a] *"And now abide faith, hope, love, these three; but the greatest of these [is] love"* (1 CORINTHIANS 13:13)!

a. Psalm 127:1-5

STUDY GUIDE QUESTIONS

1. **We should earnestly pray that our children will cultivate a love for their brothers and sisters.** The characteristic mark of a genuine disciple—Christ's identification badge—is love. Christlike love is the foundation that a Christian family and all other relationships must be built upon. Loving in this manner is a result of Spirit-filled living.

    Read Galatians 5:22-23. What are the nine characteristics of "the fruit of the Spirit"? How would the development of these fruits—through the Holy Spirit's power—impact your children's relational lives? Pray these verses regularly for yourself and your family.

    Read 1 John 4:7-11. What does God identify as the true source of love? How is the presence of biblical love—or the lack thereof—an indicator of the general health of your children's spiritual lives?

2. **We should pray that our children will trust God when troubles come.**
    Read 1 Samuel 15:22-23. When King Saul faced his troubles, he chose

to not trust the Lord—and his rebellion cost him his kingdom!
Why then is it so important to faithfully train your children
to trust God in trials by choosing to do things God's way?

Read 1 Peter 3:8-15. How will living by this passage help
to prevent the pitfalls King Saul experienced?

3. We should pray that our children will love God's plan for their lives.

Read Psalm 139:14-18. Each of us was built to a perfect
and intricate set of plans, engineered by God Himself.
Do you believe your Master Designer has a perfect
plan for your life—for your children's lives? How is
that manifested in your walk with the Lord?

Read Titus 2:6-8. What things are older men to teach the
younger as God's perfect plan for their lives? As a father,
are you being faithful to instill these character qualities
in your sons—by word, example, and prayer?

Read Titus 2:4-5. What things are older women to teach
the younger as God's perfect plan for their lives? As a
mother, are you being faithful to instill these desires in
your daughters—by word, example, and prayer?

4. We should pray that our children will wait for God's chosen partner.

Read 2 Corinthians 6:14. How does this verse apply to your
children's dating practices? To their future lifelong partners?

Read Titus 2:6-8 and 4-5 again. Meditate upon these
passages; include future sons- and daughters-in-law
when praying these verses for your own children.

**Note: At the end of Appendix B's "Wednesday" prayer section is a
list of verses that correspond to this chapter's prayer suggestions.
That list provides a handy reminder of what to pray for your
children on a regular basis.**

21

"For our citizenship is in heaven, from which we also eagerly wait for the Savior, the Lord Jesus Christ."
— *Philippians 3:20*

"Command those who are rich in this present age not to be haughty, nor to trust in uncertain riches but in the living God, who gives us richly all things to enjoy. [Let them] do good, that they be rich in good works, ready to give, willing to share, storing up for themselves a good foundation for the time to come, that they may lay hold on eternal life."
— *1 Timothy 6:17-19*

Living for Heaven

Prayers for Living for Heaven:

Choosing a Life of Contentment
(Philippians 4:11-13)

Choosing a Life of Consecration
(Matthew 16:24)

Choosing a Life of Commitment (Luke 9:62)

Giving Their Life Back to God (1 Chronicles 28:9)

D ID YOU KNOW THAT WE have dual citizenship? On earth we are citizens of the land of our birth. We become citizens of heaven by the new birth. Paul encourages saints in Philippi by reminding them of this truth and thus getting them focused upon what life on earth is to be all about. One of the greatest attributes we could pray for those we love is that they be heavenly-minded. What exactly is that? It means that the Lord, and the fact that we will be forever with Him, factors into every choice we make through life. So we as husbands, wives, moms, and dads need to add to our prayers these elements that mark someone who thinks about what matters to the Lord, and decides to honor Him by their choices. What do we prayerfully ask the Lord to do in us and them? We pray that they will be living for heaven.

One of my hobbies is to follow global trends. As Americans, we are often so fixated on our own country that we are out of touch with issues upon which the rest of the world is focusing. For example, many major world newspapers have reported that another world-wide influenza pandemic is long overdue. In the twentieth century, the 1918, 1957, and 1968 "Super-Flu" outbreaks caused forty million deaths between them—one percent of the world's population. If one percent of Americans were to die of flu this year, that would mean an extra three million deaths![a]

a. British Broadcasting Company World News, "Health," 11-02-02. http://news.bbc.co.uk/2/hi/health/default.stm

As serious as that would be, an even worse pandemic is running rampant throughout America right now, and it is so dangerous that it has gained worldwide attention. What is it? It is the disease of a sick and dying soul—*affluenza*—an obsession with acquiring more and more money and other possessions.

In September of 1997, the American Public Broadcasting Station (PBS) aired a special television program entitled "Affluenza." The topic was a warning against what the public sector has identified as the "modern-day plague of materialism." Below is their self-diagnosis questionnaire. I encourage you to carefully examine the list to determine whether or not you have any of the symptoms of this dreadful disease. (Please evaluate each item as honestly as possible.)

SYMPTOMS OF BEING INFECTED WITH AFFLUENZA

- My life would be happier if I had more money.
- I often feel overwhelmed by the amount of stuff I have and the amount of time it takes to pay for, maintain, and store it all.
- My partner and I have different views on spending and saving; it's hard to talk about these subjects without arguing.
- My children seem more materialistic than I was at their age.
- I never seem to have enough "quality time" with my family and other loved ones.
- Our family loves clothing with the fashionable logos on it, and we're usually among the first on the block to see the latest hit movie.
- I hardly know my neighbors, I feel disconnected from my local community.
- I very often feel rushed, with too much to do and not enough time to do it all.
- I don't enjoy my job, I would quit if I didn't have to work for money.

- I don't feel that I live my life in total alignment
  with my values and beliefs.
- I don't know what the interest rates are on my credit
  cards or exactly how much debt I have.
- I pay only the monthly minimum payment on my credit cards.
- I do not put money into savings regularly.
- I spend much more time shopping each month
  than I do being involved in my community.
- I sometimes buy something because it's cool or
  fashionable, not because I love it or need it.
- I know I have more "extras" in my life than my parents
  and grandparents did, but I don't feel as satisfied about
  my standard of living as I think they were.[a]

a. pbs.org/kcts/affluenza
escape/

The amazing conclusion of this PBS series was exactly what Paul said 20 centuries ago: Material wealth can't make people happy. History records the testimony of some of the wealthiest people of their day:

- "The care of $200 million is enough to kill anyone.
  There is no pleasure in it." —W. H. Vanderbilt
- "I am the most miserable man on earth." —John Jacob Astor
- "I have made many millions, but they have brought
  me no happiness." —John D. Rockefeller
- "Millionaires seldom smile." —Andrew Carnegie
- "I was happier when doing a mechanic's job." —Henry Ford

Affluenza is most evident as the modern-day plague of materialism. Believers will show the symptoms of this virus when they lose their grip on eternal life; it is a deadly poison. Is there an antidote—a cure for this disease? Yes, there is! The cure: *"Fight the good fight of the faith. Take hold of the eternal life to which you were called ..."* (1 TIMOTHY 6:12, NIV). Paul goes on to say:

"Command those who are rich in this present world not to be arrogant nor to put their hope in wealth, which is so uncertain, but to put their hope in God, who richly provides us with everything for our enjoyment. Command them to do good, to be rich in good deeds, and to be generous and willing to share. In this way they

will lay up treasure for themselves as a firm foundation for the
coming age, so that they may take hold of the life that is truly life"
(1 TIMOTHY 6:17-19, NIV).

Eternity *Is* Reality

WE ARE NOW GOING TO do something very hard for us as people living on the planet earth—we are going to try to think about our eternal life instead of merely our temporal life. Temporal life is everyday life: aches and pains, deadlines and pressures, hopes and fears, ups and downs. It is a life of getting up, going to school or work, and waiting for special things like dinners, dates, vacations, and events. It is a life that is framed by our body, our car, our job, and the world we have experienced. In other words, it is daily life as we all know it.

A Word-filled life is like a compass—everything is oriented toward heaven. What we do, what we say, where we go—all is scrutinized by what it means to our Master in heaven. Does it please Him or not? Any situation, any relationship, any possession should be tested by this question: "What will this mean to God a hundred years from today?"

When we were saved, and the Lord regenerated us by the new birth, we were born a second time. Our first birth put us in the temporal life; our second birth puts us in the eternal life.[a] Both run parallel for 30, 40, 50, 60, or even 80-plus years. Unfortunately, most of us barely experience the eternal part of life. We know it is there; we hope in it for the future; but we don't exactly know what to do with eternal life today because we are so completely overwhelmed by our temporal or physical world. For that reason, Jesus warned:

a. See John 3:3-8, 16.

- *"It is written, 'Man shall not live by bread alone, but by every word that proceeds from the mouth of God'"* (Matthew 4:4).
- *"Do not lay up for yourselves treasures on earth, ... but lay up for yourselves treasures in heaven, ... For where your treasure is, there your heart will be also. ... No one can serve two masters; for either he will hate the one and love the other, or else he will be*

loyal to the one and despise the other. You cannot serve God and
mammon [material possessions] *"* (Matthew 6:19-21; 24).

- *"And He said to them, 'Take heed and beware of*
  covetousness, for one's life does not consist in the
  abundance of the things he possesses' " (Luke 12:15).

The antidote for the poison of materialism is contentment— "being satisfied with one's possessions, status, or situation."[a] Contentment leads to renewed vitality in our eternal life. Contentment means we are alive and thinking and motivated by the fact that we are already immortal. We are thinking eternally when we start seeing what our moments look like as observed from God's throne. All of a sudden, we see that our life span and resources were all given us by Another, who owns us and wants a return on His investment.

a. *Merriam Webster's Collegiate Dictionary, Tenth Edition* (Springfield, MA: Merriam-Webster, Inc., 2002), p. 249.

In light of that, we must earnestly pray that vitality in our children's eternal lives will show up in their choosing to be content. Parenting is an ongoing ministry; Word-filled praying keeps us on the front lines of our children's lives. Word-filled praying is the power key that unlocks God's blessings so they can take hold of the eternal life to which they were called. We therefore need to be deeply and continually engaged in prayer that our children get and maintain vitality in their eternal lives—beginning with contentment.

1. CHOOSING A LIFE OF CONTENTMENT

"Not that I speak in regard to need, for I have learned in whatever
state I am, to be content: I know how to be abased, and I know
how to abound. Everywhere and in all things I have learned
both to be full and to be hungry, both to abound and to suf-
fer need. I can do all things through Christ who strengthens me"
(PHILIPPIANS 4:11-13).

Contentment is liberating! Choosing contentment over an obsession with money or possessions is a major reflection of living for heaven. The New Testament mentions contentment five times, using one of two Greek words which mean either "to be satisfied" or "independent of external circumstances." Let's look at them and learn a lesson on being content.

In the New Testament world there were many reasons to be discontent, but the consistent message was to resist that temptation. *"And the soldiers likewise demanded of him, saying, 'And what shall we do?' And he said unto them, 'Do violence to no man, neither accuse any falsely; and be content* [satisfied] *with your wages' "* (Luke 3:14, KJV).

The Apostle Paul traveled widely and had to be able to minister in an amazing variety of circumstances. How did he do it? *"Not that I speak in respect of want: for I have learned, in whatsoever state I am, therewith to be content* [independent of external circumstances]*"* (Philippians 4:11, KJV). To be content is to accept where God has placed us in life. A content person is willing to devote all energies to the advancement of God's kingdom rather than their own.

To young Timothy starting out in ministry Paul admonished: *"But godliness with contentment* [satisfaction] *is great gain"* (1 TIMOTHY 6:6, KJV). He was teaching Timothy what one author has well said, "Contentment lies not in what is yours, but in whose you are."[a] Paul continues in 1 Timothy 6:8: *"And having food and raiment let us be therewith content* [independent of external circumstances]*"* (KJV). In this verse, "content" means not wanting to be like, have, or do what others are doing!

Finally we find in Hebrews 13:5 what is probably the strongest call to this godly lifestyle: *"Keep your lives free from the love of money and be content* [satisfied] *with what you have, because God has said, 'Never will I leave you; never will I forsake you' "* (NIV).

God is telling us contentment frees us from the turmoil and anxiety our possessions can produce. We can then enjoy the peace of God no matter what our financial circumstances may be. The Spirit of God frees us from the constant bondage of our circumstances. We begin to surrender them to the Lord, and we are flooded with His security and satisfaction.

2. ESCAPING MATERIALISM

How do we learn so that we can teach contentment to our families? The best way is to enroll in "Contentment 101," and diligently study the course manual found in 1 Timothy 6:7-12 and 15-19. From those passages, we can derive important keys to contentment. Here they

a. Richard A. Swenson, M.D. *The Overload Syndrome* (Colorado Springs, CO: NAVPRESS, 1998), p. 198.

are: (Why don't you jot them down in your Bible?)

Always remember things are only temporary: *"For we brought nothing into [this world, and it is certain] we can carry nothing out"* (v. 7).

Only seek necessities, wait for the rest. *"And having food and clothing, with these we shall be content"* (v. 8).

Avoid a consuming desire for prosperity: *"But those who desire to be rich fall into temptation and a snare, and into many foolish and harmful lusts which drown men in destruction and perdition. For the love of money is a root of all kinds of evil, for which some have strayed from the faith in their greediness, and pierced themselves through with many sorrows"* (vv. 9-10).

Flee materialism: *"But you, O man of God, flee these things and pursue righteousness, godliness, faith, love, patience, gentleness"* (v. 11).

Cling to eternal life: *"Fight the good fight of faith, lay hold on eternal life, to which you were also called and have confessed the good confession in the presence of many witnesses ... which He will manifest in His own time, He who is the blessed and only Potentate, the King of kings and Lord of lords, who alone has immortality, dwelling in unapproachable light, whom no man has seen or can see, to whom be honor and everlasting power. Amen"* (vv. 12, 15-16).

Pin your hopes on God: *"Command those who are rich in this present age not to be haughty, nor to trust in uncertain riches but in the living God, who gives us richly all things to enjoy"* (v. 17). When our trust and hopes are not focused on God, we can fall prey to this type of thinking: *I hope we have enough to ... I hope that this investment will ... I hope this job will last ...*

Give until it hurts: *"Let them do good, that they be rich in good works, ready to give, willing to share, storing up for themselves a good foundation for the time to come, that they may lay hold on eternal life"* (vv. 18-19).

Finally, what will be the result of living by the Bible's definition of contentment? If we are content we will enjoy the present rather than being anxious about the future: *"Do not worry about your life, what you will eat or what you will drink; nor about your body, what you will put on. Is not life more than food and the body more than clothing?"* (MATTHEW 6:25). We will also be liberated to truly enjoy the successes of others around us without envy. We learn: *"Rest in the LORD, and wait patiently for Him; Do not fret because of him who prospers in his way, Because of the man who brings wicked schemes to pass. Do not fret—[it] only [causes] harm. For evildoers shall be cut off; But those who wait on the LORD, They shall inherit the earth"* (PSALM 37:7-9). Finally, we will be able to let the Lord build a true sense of thankfulness about everything: *"Rejoice always, pray without ceasing, in everything give thanks; for this is the will of God in Christ Jesus for you"* (1 THESSALONIANS 5:16-18).

Contentment is a habit of life that helps us avoid anything that deeply offends and grieves our heavenly Father. By God's grace, a person who has escaped from the deadly "affluenza" disease will no longer manifest the symptoms of a sick and dying soul which are on the following checklist:

- The desire for things **more** than God.
- The desire for pleasure **more** than godliness.
- The desire for satisfaction through things **more** than to be satisfied by God.
- The desire for better things and additional things that others have **more** than thanking God for what we have.
- The desire for the rewards of the physical world **more** than a desire for eternal rewards.

In Luke 14:26-33, Jesus called out to all who would listen: "Come follow Me and be My disciple! Don't waste your life; don't end life horribly unprepared for the true afterlife." Making a clear choice to unreservedly give themselves to Christ marked His true followers. This call expresses the two opposing approaches to life:[a]

a. Warren W. Wiersbe, *The Bible Exposition Commentary: Luke* (Wheaton, IL: Victory Books, 1997), electronic edition.

Either:	Or:
We belong to Jesus.	We belong to our self.
We deny our self.	We live for our self.
We give everything back to God.	We keep our stuff.
We take up our cross.	We ignore the cross.
We follow Christ.	We follow the world.
We lose our life for His sake.	We save our life for our own sake.
We forsake the world.	We try to gain the world.
We keep our soul.	We lose our soul.
We share His reward and glory.	We lose His reward and glory!

Obviously, the first step toward sharing in Christ's reward and glory is to take hold of eternal life through faith. Once we belong to Jesus, our love for Him should then motivate us to deny self, choosing to be content in whatever circumstances God has placed us. Thus we will be better able to devote our energies to the advancement of Christ's kingdom, rather than our own.

Denying self by rejecting the enticements of materialism is a habit we want our children to "catch" from us. The more we learn to be content, the more they will likely do the same. To that end, we must continually pray that our families learn to be content so that they aren't destroyed by the deadly "affluenza."

> **Prayer Example:** *Dear Lord, help us as a family to be content regardless of our external circumstances. Help us to place our focus on who we are, and not on what we have! May we never place our trust and hopes in temporal things, but only in You. I pray we will not catch "affluenza," but choose to lay up treasures in heaven instead. Enable us to fight the good fight of faith, to lay hold on eternal life! For You are the King of kings and Lord of lords—to whom be honor and everlasting power. Amen.*

3. Choosing a Life of Consecration

"If anyone comes to Me and does not hate his father and mother, wife and children, brothers and sisters, yes, and his own life also,

> *he cannot be My disciple. And whoever does not bear his cross*
> *and come after Me cannot be My disciple. ... [And] whoever*
> *of you does not forsake all that he has cannot be My disciple"*
> (LUKE 14:26-27, 33).

The essence of the passage above is this: "Lord, I give myself to You!" Living a life of consecration is the second mark of living for heaven. This requires total consecration to the Lord of our body, our future, our time, and all our resources. We need to pray for, model, and teach consecration to Christ in every part of our homes, marriages, and jobs. All of us are consecrated to something, and, as we've just seen in the "Either—Or" chart, that something will either fit into the category of godliness or worldliness. To contrast those two conditions, travel back in your mind for a moment to Cairo, Egypt. Picture yourself as having just walked into the King Tut exhibit. Now consider these impressions a pastor shared after viewing that exhibit:

> *The King Tut exhibit at the Egyptian national Museum was mind-*
> *boggling. Tutankhamun, the boy king, was only seventeen when*
> *he died. He was buried with solid gold chariots and thousands of*
> *golden artifacts. His gold coffin was found in a burial site filled*
> *with tons of gold. The Egyptians believed they could take earthly*
> *treasures into the afterlife. But all the treasures intended for King*
> *Tut's eternal enjoyment stayed right where they were until Howard*
> *Carter discovered the burial chamber in 1922. Tutankhamun's*
> *tomb glittered with unimaginable wealth.*[a]

a. Randy Alcorn,
The Treasure Principle
(Sisters, OR: Multnomah
Publishers, 2001), pp. 34-36.

Next, travel with me to view a second, lesser-known grave in Cairo. We will choke through the gray dust of the city of twelve million Egyptians to go down a long dirty alley (only findable by a guide) and into a fenced cemetery—the Protestant Cemetery of Cairo. In a plot of overgrown grass are rows of sun-scorched tombstones. If you dust off the right one, these words faintly appear: William Borden, 1887-1913. Below those words is etched an epitaph that testifies of Borden's love and sacrifices for the kingdom of God and the Muslim people. The words end with a penetrating phrase: "Apart from faith in Christ, there is no explanation for such a life."

In 1904, William Borden, a member of the Borden Dairy family, finished high school in Chicago and was given a world cruise as a graduation present. While traveling through the Near East and Far East, he became heavily burdened for the lost. After returning home, he spent 7 years at Yale and Princeton University, the first four in undergraduate work and the last three in seminary. To reach Muslims, he chose to reject a life of ease by giving away his fortune. After he did so, he penned these words in the back of his Bible: **"No reserves."**

On his way to China to witness to Muslims, he stopped in Egypt to learn Arabic. As he studied there, in the back of his Bible underneath his former entry of "No reserves," he penned **"No retreats."**

After 4 months of intense studying and regular evangelism among the poor of Cairo, Borden contracted cerebral meningitis. He died within a month at age twenty-five. Just an hour after his death, his mother arrived at his bedside. As she was looking through his Bible, she discovered the third and final set of words: **"No regrets."**

William Borden's life was a life consecrated to Christ's call, and he summed it up in only six words: **No reserves; No retreats; No regrets!** Are you as struck as I am by the contrast between these two graves?

- Today Borden's grave is obscure, dusty, and hidden off the back alley of a street littered with garbage. Tutankhamun's tomb and treasures travel the world, glittering with unimaginable wealth. Yet where are these two young men now?
- One, who lived in opulence and called himself king, is most likely in the misery of a Christless eternity. The other, who lived a modest life on earth in service of the one true King, is enjoying his everlasting reward in the presence of his Lord.
- Tut's life was tragic because of an awful truth discovered too late—*he couldn't take his treasures with him.* William Borden's life was triumphant. Why? Because instead of leaving behind his treasures, *he sent them on ahead.*

We will each part with our money. The only question is when. Jesus warns us not to store up treasures on earth. Not just because wealth might be lost, but because wealth will *always* be lost. Either it leaves us while we live, or we leave it when we die. No exceptions.

Christ does want us to store up treasures; He just tells us to be sure to store them in the right place. Anything we put into the Father's hands will be ours for eternity. If we give instead of keep, if we invest in the eternal instead of the temporal—we will store up treasures in heaven that will never stop paying dividends. You can't take it with you, but you can send it on ahead.[a]

Because we know clearly what Jesus wants in this area, we should be compelled to pray for our children to consecrate their lives to Christ. Here are some passages particularly applicable for such prayers:

Consecration means believing that in God's system—losers are keepers: *"Then Jesus said to His disciples, 'If anyone desires to come after Me, let him deny himself, and take up his cross, and follow Me. For whoever desires to save his life will lose it, but whoever loses his life for My sake will find it. For what profit is it to a man if he gains the whole world, and loses his own soul? Or what will a man give in exchange for his soul? For the Son of Man will come in the glory of His Father with His angels, and then He will reward each according to his works'"* (MATTHEW 16:24-27).

Consecration means returning to the Lord the title deed to all we own. Jesus has this to say about the qualifications of such a disciple: *"If anyone comes to Me and does not hate his father and mother, wife and children, brothers and sisters, yes, and his own life also, he cannot be My disciple. And whoever does not bear his cross and come after Me cannot be My disciple. For which of you, intending to build a tower, does not sit down first and count the cost, whether he has enough to finish it—lest, after he has laid the foundation, and is not able to finish, all who see it begin to mock him, saying, 'This man began to build and was not able to finish.' Or what king, going to make war against another king, does not sit down first and consider whether he is able with ten thousand to meet him who comes against him with twenty thousand? Or else, while the other is still a great way off, he sends a delegation and asks conditions of peace. So likewise, whoever of you does not forsake* [literally: "turn over the control of"] *all that he has cannot be My disciple"* (LUKE 14:26-33).

Consecration means giving our bodies, minds, and everything else to the Lord: *"I beseech you therefore, brethren, by the mercies of God, that you present your bodies a living sacrifice, holy, acceptable to God, which is your reasonable service. And do not be conformed to* *this world, but be transformed by the renewing of your mind, that you may prove what is that good and acceptable and perfect will of God"* (ROMANS 12:1-2).

Consecration means believing we were bought and paid for by the Lord: *"Or do you not know that your body is the temple of the Holy Spirit who is in you, whom you have from God, and you are not your own? For you were bought at a price; therefore glorify God in your body and in your spirit, which are God's"* (1 CORINTHIANS 6:19-20).

Consecration means giving our self back to God: *"And not only as we had hoped, but they first gave themselves to the Lord, and then to us by the will of God"* (2 CORINTHIANS 8:5).

So then, consecration means believing that losers are actually keepers. It means returning to the Lord the title deed to all we own—our bodies, minds, and everything else. We must do this because the Lord bought and paid for us; consecrating ourselves to God is simply our reasonable service! A spirit of devoted consecration is what we should faithfully pray for so our children have vitality in their eternal lives.

Prayer Example: Heavenly Father, by Your mercies, please enable my whole family to present our bodies as living sacrifices, holy and acceptable to You. Begin with me first, Lord! Keep me from any desire to be conformed to this world, but transform me by the renewing of my mind through Your Word so I may prove what is Your good and acceptable and perfect will—and then help me to lead my family to do the same!

4. LIVING A LIFE OF COMMITMENT

"Now it happened as they journeyed on the road, [that] someone said to Him, 'Lord, I will follow You wherever You go.' And Jesus said to him, 'Foxes have holes and birds of the air [have] nests, but the Son of Man has nowhere to lay [His] head.' Then He said to another, 'Follow Me.' But he said, 'Lord, let me first go and bury my father.' Jesus said to him, 'Let the dead bury their own dead, but you go and preach the kingdom of God.' And another also said, 'Lord, I will follow You,

but let me first go [and] bid them farewell who are at my house.' But Jesus said to him, 'No one, having put his hand to the plow, and looking back, is fit for the kingdom of God' " (LUKE 9:57-62).

God's desire for each of us is that we finish the course with joy! Living a life of commitment is the third mark of living for heaven. In the above passage, when Christ gave the instruction "Follow Me," He was met with excuses for their general *lack* of commitment. In contrast, David Livingstone, a nineteenth-century missionary to Africa, never made excuses; his life was wholeheartedly committed to Christ's calling on his life.

Late in the summer of 1873, the shadow of a 60-year-old man was silhouetted against the canvas of a small tent deep within the rain forests of Africa. The flickering candle cast a golden aura inside as he knelt beside a small wood and canvas cot. Rhythmic tropical rain lightly pelted the tent as he prayed beside his bed.

Outside, the native porters, guides, and cooks who had followed this man for nearly 20 years through the jungle heard the low sound of his voice communing with God as he always had done before bed. Then the candle flickered out and they also retired to sleep through the rainy night.

The next morning the cold and stiff body of David Livingstone was still kneeling beside the cot when his beloved native brothers found him. He was so thin from the countless bouts with malaria; his skin darkened by the years of Equatorial African sun was loosely draped over the bones of his earthly tent now vacant. His spirit had soared immortal, making its flight from the darkness of a disease-ridden, weak and failing body, to the realm of light and life in the presence of Jesus his King to whom he had consecrated his life.

On Livingstone's last night on this planet earth, he would have prayed a prayer that he had written out many years before. If you were able to hear what God heard that last night, it would have sounded much like this:

O Lord since Thou hast died, To give Thyself for me,
No sacrifice would seem to great, For me to make for Thee.
I only have one life, and that will soon be past;
I want my life to count for Christ, What's done for Him will last.

I follow Thee my Lord, And glory in Thy Cross;
I gladly leave the world behind, And count all gain as loss.
Lord send me anywhere, Only go with me;
Lay any burden on me, Only sustain me.
Sever any tie, Save the tie that binds me to Thy heart.
Lord Jesus my King, I consecrate my life Lord to Thee!

At his death that night in 1873, such was their love for him that his native companions bore his body fifteen hundred miles to the coast. One of them was among the huge crowd at the funeral in Westminster Abbey. Some words on Livingstone's tombstone there summarize his achievements: "For thirty years his life was spent in an unwearied effort to evangelize the native races, to explore the undiscovered secrets, to abolish the desolating slave trade of Central Africa."

Of his life, David Livingstone wrote in his journal, "People talk of the sacrifice I have made in spending so much of my life in Africa. Can that be called sacrifice, which is simply paid back as a small part of the great debt owing to our God, which we can never repay? … Away with such a word, such a view, and such a thought! It is emphatically no sacrifice. Say rather it is a privilege. Anxiety, sickness, suffering or danger now and then, with a foregoing of the common conveniences and charities of this life, may make us pause and cause the spirit to waver and sink; but let this only be for a moment. All these are nothing when compared with the glory, which shall hereafter be revealed in and for us. I never made a sacrifice. Of this we ought not talk when we remember the great sacrifice, which He made who left His Father's throne on high to give Himself for us."[a]

a. *Livingstone's Private Journal: 1851-53, ed. 1. Schapera* (London: Chatto & Windus, 1960), pp. 108, 132.

5. BUILDING A FIREPROOF LIFE

Consecration of the depth we've just seen reflects a life of commitment. Livingstone was committed in that manner because he had vitality in his eternal life—he personally knew, served, loved, and obeyed the Lord! In 2 Peter 3:10-14 and 17-18, Peter lists the following areas of commitment he was charging early believers to grasp:

A lack of commitment clouds our minds. Therefore, we must expectantly put our hand to the plow and **commit to keep alert:** *"But the day of the Lord will come as a thief in the night, in which the* *heavens will pass away with a great noise, and the elements will melt with fervent heat; both the earth and the works that are in it will be burned up. Therefore, since all these things will be dissolved, what manner [of persons] ought you to be in holy conduct and godliness ..."* (vv. 10-11).

A lack of commitment clutters our lives. If we are to have vitality in our eternal lives, we must extinguish materialism. Therefore, we must expectantly put our hand to the plow and commit to build a fireproof life: *"... looking for and hastening the coming of the day of God, because of which the heavens will be dissolved, being on fire, and the elements will melt with fervent heat. Nevertheless we, according to His promise, look for new heavens and a new earth in which righteousness dwells"* (vv. 12-13).

A lack of commitment closes our eyes. We need to live a pure life! Therefore, we must expectantly put our hand to the plow and commit to look up: *"Therefore, beloved, looking forward to these things, be diligent to be found by Him in peace, without spot and blameless"* (v. 14).

A lack of commitment crowds out our Bibles. We need to guard our heart so that we can live maturely. Therefore, we must expectantly put our hand to the plow and commit to study the Book: *"You therefore, beloved, since you know [this] beforehand, beware lest you also fall from your own steadfastness, being led away with the error of the wicked"* (v. 17).

A lack of commitment corrodes our wills. We need to grow spiritually—and expectantly put our hand to the plow and commit to obey Jesus. *"Grow in the grace and knowledge of our Lord and Savior Jesus Christ. To Him [be] the glory both now and forever. Amen"* (v. 18).

What drives God's servants like the William Bordens and David Livingstones of this world to make such great sacrifices? Devotion to Christ—and devotion sacrifices! Oh, how we need to pray that our children will learn divine priorities, and desire to live such a devoted and committed life! Why? Because—

God wants His children to be fruitful: *"Now he who received seed among the thorns is he who hears the word, and the cares of this world and the deceitfulness of riches choke the word, and he becomes unfruitful"* (MATTHEW 13:22).

God wants His children to give no excuses: *"Then He said to him, 'A certain man gave a great supper and invited many, and sent his servant at supper time to say to those who were invited, "Come, for all things are now ready." But they all with one [accord] began to make excuses. The first said to him, "I have bought a piece of ground, and I must go and see it. I ask you to have me excused." And another said, "I have bought five yoke of oxen, and I am going to test them. I ask you to have me excused." Still another said, "I have married a wife, and therefore I cannot come." So that servant came and reported these things to his master. Then the master of the house, being angry, said to his servant, "Go out quickly into the streets and lanes of the city, and bring in here [the] poor and [the] maimed and [the] lame and [the] blind." And the servant said, "Master, it is done as you commanded, and still there is room." Then the master said to the servant, "Go out into the highways and hedges, and compel [them] to come in, that my house may be filled. For I say to you that none of those men who were invited shall taste my supper'"* (LUKE 14:16-24).

God wants His children to be unentangled: *"No one engaged in warfare entangles himself with the affairs of [this] life, that he may please him who enlisted him as a soldier"* (2 TIMOTHY 2:4).

A committed servant is a fruitful servant—one who never makes up excuses for not "taking hold of the life that is truly life." Christ's genuine disciples will avoid entanglement with the cares and enticements of this world. Instead, they will choose to pursue vitality in their eternal lives through a commitment to know, serve, love, and obey the Lord. This should be our prayer goal for ourselves first, and then for our children as well.

Prayer Example: Dear Heavenly Father, I pray that you will enable me and my family to be committed to studying Your Word! Enable us through obedience to Your Word to be growing in the grace and knowledge of Jesus Christ, our Savior. Keep us alert to anything that might entangle us in the cares or enticements of this life. In all our ways, may we be pleasing to You! Help me, dear Lord, to model such a committed and devoted walk—and then lead my children to do the same.

6. GIVING THEIR LIFE BACK TO GOD

"I [Paul] am already being poured out as a drink offering, and the time of my departure is at hand. I have fought the good fight, I have finished the race, I have kept the faith. Finally, there is laid up for me the crown of righteousness, which the Lord, the righteous Judge, will give to me on that Day, and not to me only but also to all who have loved His appearing" (2 TIMOTHY 4:6-8).

"I love the Lord, and I want to serve the Lord" echoes as a prayer in each of my precious children's hearts! I have prayed that little prayer with my children hundreds of times, and it sounds so simple, but it sure is powerful! One hymn writer expressed it like this: "Such love constrains me to answer His call, follow His leading, and give Him my all. Oh Jesus Lord and Savior, I give myself to you!" That is what we should supremely want for ourselves and our families!

Giving our lives back to the Lord is the final mark of living for heaven. As Paul neared the end of his life, he was able to look back without regret or remorse. In 2 Timothy 4:6-8, he examines his life from three perspectives: **1. the present** reality of the end of his life, for which he was ready; **2. the past**, when he had been faithful; and **3. the future**, as he anticipated his heavenly reward. ... Paul saw his coming death as his final offering to God in a life that had already been full of sacrifices to Him.[a]

David, a man after God's own heart,[b] likewise had a life full of sacrifices to the Lord. King Saul offered great rewards for anyone who would face Goliath, but, even as a boy, David was willing to do so "in the Name of the LORD" (1 Samuel 17:45). As a young man, he had trophies of his great triumphs, but he also gave those back to the Lord at the Tabernacle.[c]

At the end of David's life, he confessed that while he was winning every battle, conquering and plundering every kingdom around

a. *The MacArthur Study Bible* (Nashville, TN: Thomas Nelson Publishers, 1997), pp. 1880-1881.

b. Acts 13:22

c. 1 Samuel 21:9

Israel, he had been following a plan: he was storing up all the treasures he could for the Lord.[a] In today's currency, David amassed over 60 billion dollars in gold and silver! That is an amazing sum for any era of the world, but especially for a shepherd boy! It is almost as if he knew already what Jesus would later promise—that those who sacrifice on earth would receive "a hundred times as much" in heaven.[b] That is an impressive 10,000 percent return!

Someone once said, "We're most like God when we're giving."[c]

Gaze upon Christ long enough, and you'll become more of a giver. Give long enough, and you'll become more like Christ. Giving jump-starts our relationship with God; it opens our fists so that we can receive what God has for us. Then, as we see what it does not only for others but also for us, we will open our fists sooner—and wider—when the next opportunity to give comes along.

Did you know the Lord's willingness to answer our prayers is directly affected by whether we are caring for the hungry, needy, and oppressed?[d] God says, *"If a man shuts his ears to the cry of the poor, he too will cry out and not be answered"* (PROVERBS 21:13, NIV). Do you want to empower your prayer life? Give! Then learn all you can about what it means to give your life back to God. The starting place? Be a wise steward of all that He has entrusted to your care.

God is the owner of all our resources; we are only employees. Christ asks that He be above all our treasures on earth—both money and possessions.

> *"Jesus said to him, 'If you want to be perfect, go, sell what you have and give to the poor, and you will have treasure in heaven; and come, follow Me' "* (MATTHEW 19:21).

The believers in Corinth were doing what they pleased with their bodies and their lives. After all, they reasoned, "Why not? It's *my* life." But Paul replied, "No, it's *not* your life. You own nothing—not even yourself. When you came to Christ you surrendered the title to your life. You belong to God, not yourself. He is the only one who has the right to do what He wants with your life: your body, your sexual behavior, money, possessions, and everything else. You therefore owe Him your full obedience." A true steward recognizes that all we have has come from the Lord.

a. 1 Chronicles 22:14

b. Matthew 19:29

c. Randy Alcorn, *The Treasure Principle* (Sisters, OR: Multnomah Publishers, 2001), pp. 30-32.

d. See Isaiah 58.6-10.

"For who makes you differ [from another]? And what do you have
that you did not receive? Now if you did indeed receive [it], why do
you boast as if you had not received [it]?" (1 CORINTHIANS 4:7).

The world has two parts: "God's" and "not God's." Whatever is not
God's is of the world. So, anything not given to God becomes worthless. Wow! That is a deep thought to ponder: what we have sought to
retain the ownership of is a way that we despise the Lord.

If we were to interview the rich businessman of Luke 12, we would
find that God called him a fool because he thought all his possessions were actually his. He would have this to say about his life now:
"What I had in life was mine temporarily. What I kept to the end I
lost forever!"

LOSERS ARE REALLY KEEPERS

Jesus said that what you lose for His sake lasts forever, right? So how
do we learn to give our lives back to God on a daily basis, instead of
spending our lives accumulating more and more so it is harder and
harder to leave it all behind?

Beloved, stewardship is actually resisting Satan's strategy. Since
money is one of the essentials of the work of the kingdom, it is not
surprising that God's great adversary does all in his power to prevent
it from finding its way into God's treasury—and for that he has many
tricks in his bag:

1. **Spending:** Satan encourages overcommitment in buying.
Purchasing more than one can afford on time payments leaves little
left over to give to God.

2. **Upgrading:** Satan plays on our competitive instincts and incites
us to constantly upgrade our standard of living; any increases in
income are already committed. When John Wesley was earning 30
British pounds a year, he lived on 26 British pounds, and gave the rest
to God. When his salary was raised to 60 British pounds, he lived on
26 British pounds, and gave the rest to God.

3. **Waiting:** Satan dries up the fountains of generosity in the heart
by suggesting postponement of giving to some future date. The

stifling of a generous act today makes it easier for us to do the same tomorrow.

4. Leveraging: Satan so arranges things that the assets of the generous man become frozen or overcommitted so that he cannot give what he genuinely wishes to give. Expanding business too rapidly often demands reinvestment on a scale that leaves little for giving.

5. Keeping It to the End: We live in such an age of uncertainty. Many elderly fear that their savings will be exhausted before they expire. Many others want to pass the wealth on to their children. This causes us to be guilty of undue stacking. We all need to be sure we give all we can in our lifetime, and have the joy of seeing our money work for God. God promises a reward for "deeds done in the body," not out of it. Being generous with God—using right motives—brings its reward here as well as hereafter.

To be giving and sacrificing is to be Christlike and blessed. It is as wise to prayerfully plan to sacrifice as it is to think Henry Flagler was wise when he trusted John D. Rockefeller for those few shares at the infancy of his new company, Standard Oil. Flagler's shares went on to be worth hundreds of millions of dollars in the 1920s! What a wonderful investment he made. Would you like to be just as fortunate? Then get Christ's heart for this world! Be moved with compassion, and ask for the grace of giving! And the Lord will work wonders through the treasures you give Him—of any size! True treasures are what we keep beyond this life; false treasures are what we have only for the moment.

How then should we pray for our families? God's Word has a powerful illustration in one of the truly great prayers of a father for his son:

> "As for you, my son Solomon, **know the God of your father, and serve Him with a loyal heart and with a willing mind;** for the LORD searches all hearts and understands all the intent of the thoughts. **If you seek Him, He will be found by you;** but if you forsake Him, He will cast you off forever" (1 CHRONICLES 28:9, Emphasis added).

Notice that when we seek to raise our children for the Lord we don't wait until we are perfect. We never are perfected until heaven, so start now. Be encouraged by David's example. David wasn't perfect, but he prayed. David made many mistakes, but he always loved the Lord. David's children may not have all turned out to be saints, but he was God's man. David might have failed here and there as a father—but in God's sight he was "a man after God's own heart."

I pray that you, too, will desire to be a parent after God's own heart! As you seek to be living for heaven—by contentment, consecration, commitment, and giving your life back to God—through Word-filled praying, your children can "catch" that same joyful walk in Truth!

> *Prayer Example: Dear Jesus, I don't want to be the type of person who holds onto things with grasping, clenched fists—and loses them. For I recognize that You are the Giver of all that I have. You alone are the Owner of all things. I want to be Your servant forever. I give myself, and all my possessions, back to You! When You want anything back just tell me, and they are Yours to do with as You see fit! No longer do I want to think about how much of MY money I should give, but how much of YOUR money should I keep! Help me to show vitality in my eternal life through this commitment of all I am, and have, to You. Then enable me to lead the family YOU have given me to do the same!*

Word Filled Praying Is a Lifelong Commitment

PARENTING IS LIFE LONG. BEFORE we are parents **we are praying;** while we are up to our ears in those child-filled years **we are praying;** and after they launch out into their own lives **we are still praying.** Why? Praying keeps us on the front lines of our children's lives. Successful parenting of a godly family only has two requirements: **1.** get started in Word-filled praying, and **2.** never quit![a]

a. For additional suggestions on how to systematically pray the Scriptures for your loved ones, see Appendix C.

My philosophy for great parenting will always be that you raise a godly family "one prayer at a time." Word-filled praying is the key to raising, nurturing, and launching children who please the Lord:

- Living like Christ's child leads to fruitful praying for reality in our children's spiritual lives. This means seeing them become genuinely saved, loving God's Word, living in victory, thinking of heaven, finding sin repulsive, and staying tender toward God.
- Looking Christlike in all we do leads to fruitful praying for integrity in our children's personal lives. This means seeing them maintaining a clear conscience, learning to stand alone, seeking to stay pure, having a servant's heart, and never becoming bitter in trials.
- Loving one another leads to fruitful praying for the stability of Christ's love in our children's relational lives. This means seeing them cultivating a love for their brothers and sisters, learning to trust God when troubles come, loving God's plan for them as young men or women, and waiting to meet God's chosen life partner for them.
- Laying hold on eternal life leads to fruitful praying for vitality in our children's eternal lives. This means seeing them choose a life of contentment, consecration, commitment, and giving their lives back to God.

In summary, the goal of Word-filled praying is to see our children desire God more than things; godliness more than pleasure; *gratitude* to God for what they have, rather than being discontent over what they don't have; and, finally, to desire eternal rewards more than the temporary rewards of this physical world! The means: *"Fight the good fight of the faith. Take hold of the eternal life to which you were called ..."* (1 TIMOTHY 6:12, NIV).

Prayer: Oh, Heavenly Father! What a challenge to learn how to fight the good fight of the faith—to learn how to take hold of the eternal life to which You have called us! Lead each member of my family to personally trust in Christ, who richly provides us with everything for our enjoyment. May we be rich in good deeds— generous and willing to share. Above all, may we lay up treasure for ourselves as a firm foundation for the coming age, so that we may indeed take hold of the life that is truly life! Amen.

STUDY GUIDE QUESTIONS

1. We should pray to see our children choosing a life of contentment.
To be content is to accept where God has placed us in life.
Read Philippians 4:11-13. How did Paul choose to respond to his
numerous troubling circumstances? In verse 13, to what did
Paul attribute his ongoing victory over negative circumstances?
How can you pass this strength of faith on to your children?
Read 1 Timothy 6:6-10 and Hebrews 13:5. What does God say
should be our view of material possessions and money?
How can you best instill these values in your children?

**2. We should pray to see our children living a life of consecration to
the Lord.** Read Matthew 16:24-26. What is the essence of living "a life
of consecration"?
Read Romans 12:1-2. Have you given your body, mind, and
everything else to the Lord? Memorize this passage as a
family; pray that God will make it a reality in your lives.

**3. We should pray to see our children living a life of commitment to
the Lord.** Read 1 Corinthians 6:19-20. What great debt do we owe to
our God? How should that affect the way we live?
Read Psalm 127:3. Who really owns our children? How
should that affect the way we train and pray for
the children He has entrusted to our care?
Read 2 Peter 3:10-14 and 17-18. List five areas of commitment
that Peter was charging early believers to grasp:

4. We should pray to see our children giving their lives back to God.
Read 1 Corinthians 4:7. Is there anything in our lives which is truly
ours? The world thinks there are two parts: "God's" and "not God's."
What portion of your life is God's? How is your life's testimony in this
area being reflected in your children?

Read, memorize, and meditate upon 1 Chronicles 28:9. This is one of the truly great prayers of a father for his son. As you seek to be living for heaven—by contentment, consecration, commitment, and giving your life back to God—through Word-filled praying, your children can "catch" that same joyful walk in Truth!

5. **Word-filled praying is a lifelong commitment.** Praying keeps us on the frontlines of our children's lives. Read 1 Samuel 12:23. How does this sum up our responsibility as parents?

Read 3 John 4. Can there be any greater joy than this?

Note: At the end of Appendix B's "Friday" prayer section is a list of verses that correspond to this chapter's prayer suggestions. That list provides a handy reminder of what to pray for your children on a regular basis.

APPENDIX A:

Some Verses of a Word-Filled Life: Verses Every Believer Should Know

"This Book of the Law shall not depart from your mouth, but you shall meditate in it day and night, that you may observe to do according to all that is written in it. For then you will make your way prosperous, and then you will have good success" (JOSHUA 1:8).

Note: We can never meditate on what we have not read; nor can we meditate on what we have not downloaded by memorization. I therefore suggest you and your family systematically memorize this list of important verses every believer should know. These are also excellent verses to use when practicing Word-filled praying! [1]

WORD OF GOD

Hear the Word. "So then faith comes by hearing, and hearing by the word of God" (Romans 10:17).

Read the Word. "Blessed is he who reads and those who hear the words of this prophecy, and keep those things which are written in it; for the time is near" (Revelation 1:3).

1. All verses are in the New King James Version.

Study the Word. "Be diligent to present yourself approved to God, a worker who does not need to be ashamed, rightly dividing the word of truth" (2 Timothy 2:15).

Memorize the Word. "How can a young man cleanse his way? By taking heed according to Your word. With my whole heart I have sought You; Oh, let me not wander from Your commandments! Your word I have hidden in my heart, That I might not sin against You" (Psalm 119:9-11).

Meditate on the Word. "Meditate on these things; give yourself entirely to them, that your progress may be evident to all" (1 Timothy 4:15).

"This Book of the Law shall not depart from your mouth, but you shall meditate in it day and night, that you may observe to do according to all that is written in it. For then you will make your way prosperous, and then you will have good success" (Joshua 1:8).

Obey the Word. "Be doers of the word, and not hearers only, deceiving yourselves" (James 1:22).

"To him who knows to do good and does not do it, to him it is sin" (James 4:17).

BASIC DOCTRINE

Christ Is the Center of the Believer's Life.
"I am the vine, you are the branches. He who abides in Me, and I in him, bears much fruit; for without Me you can do nothing" (John 15:5).

"I have been crucified with Christ; it is no longer I who live, but Christ lives in me; and the life which I now live in the flesh I live by faith in the Son of God, who loved me and gave Himself for me" (Galatians 2:20).

"For the love of Christ compels us, because we judge thus: that if One died for all, then all died; and He died for all, that those who live should live no longer for themselves, but for Him who died for them and rose again" (2 Corinthians 5:14-15).

"And whatever you do, do it heartily, as to the Lord and not to men, knowing that from the Lord you will receive the reward of the inheritance; for you serve the Lord Christ" (Colossians 3:23-24).

Death and Hell.
"For the wages of sin is death, but the gift of God is eternal life in Christ Jesus our Lord" (Romans 6:23).

"And as it is appointed for men to die once, but after this the judgment …" (Hebrews 9:27).

"But the cowardly, unbelieving, abominable, murderers, sexually immoral, sorcerers, idolaters, and all liars shall have their part in the lake which burns with fire and brimstone, which is the second death" (Revelation 21:8).

Holy Spirit.
"Do you not know that your body is the temple of the Holy Spirit who is in you, whom you have from God, and you are not your own? For you were bought at a price; therefore glorify God in your body and in your spirit, which are God's" (1 Corinthians 6:19-20).

"For by one Spirit we were all baptized into one body—whether Jews or Greeks, whether slaves or free—and have all been made to drink into one Spirit" (1 Corinthians 12:13).

"I say then: Walk in the Spirit, and you shall not fulfill the lust of the flesh. For the flesh lusts against the Spirit, and the Spirit against the flesh; and these are contrary to one another, so that you do not do the things that you wish" (Galatians 5:16-17).

Inspiration.
"For this reason we also thank God without ceasing, because when you received the word of God which you heard from us, you welcomed it not as the word of men, but as it is in truth, the word of God, which also effectively works in you who believe" (1 Thessalonians 2:13).

"It is the Spirit who gives life; the flesh profits nothing. The words that I speak to you are spirit, and they are life" (John 6:63).

"All Scripture is given by inspiration of God, and is profitable for doctrine, for reproof, for correction, for instruction in righteousness, that the man of God may be complete, thoroughly equipped for every good work" (2 Timothy 3:16-17).

Salvation.
"Sanctify them by Your truth. Your word is truth" (John 17:17).

"Born again, not of corruptible seed but incorruptible, through the word of God which lives and abides forever" (1 Peter 1:23).

"Open their eyes, in order to turn them from darkness to light, and from the power of Satan to God, that they may receive forgiveness of sins and an inheritance among those who are sanctified by faith in Me" (Acts 26:18).

Second Coming of Christ.
"The grace of God that brings salvation has appeared to all men, teaching us that, denying ungodliness and worldly lusts, we should live soberly, righteously, and godly in the present age, looking for the blessed hope and glorious appearing of our great God and Savior Jesus Christ …" (Titus 2:11-13).

"We must all appear before the judgment seat of Christ, that each one may receive the things done in the body, according to what he has done, whether good or bad" (2 Corinthians 5:10).

"And anyone not found written in the Book of Life was cast into the lake of fire" (Revelation 20:15).

"Each of us shall give account of himself to God" (Romans 14:12).

FELLOWSHIP WITH GOD

Surrender to God.
"Do not let sin reign in your mortal body, that you should obey it in its lusts. And do

not present your members as instruments of unrighteousness to sin, but present yourselves to God as being alive from the dead, and your members as instruments of righteousness to God" (Romans 6:12-13).

"I beseech you therefore, brethren, by the mercies of God, that you present your bodies a living sacrifice, holy, acceptable to God, which is your reasonable service. And do not be conformed to this world, but be transformed by the renewing of your mind, that you may prove what is that good and acceptable and perfect will of God" (Romans 12:1-2).

"Whether you eat or drink, or whatever you do, do all to the glory of God" (1 Corinthians 10:31).

Confess Sins Daily.

"He who covers his sins will not prosper, But whoever confesses and forsakes them will have mercy" (Proverbs 28:13).

"If we confess our sins, He is faithful and just to forgive us our sins and to cleanse us from all unrighteousness" (1 John 1:9).

Maintain Fellowship With Others.

"They continued steadfastly in the apostles' doctrine and fellowship, in the breaking of bread, and in prayers" (Acts 2:42).

"[Be] not forsaking the assembling of [y]ourselves together, as is the manner of some,

but exhorting one another, and so much the more as you see the Day approaching" (Hebrews 10:25).

"That which we have seen and heard we declare to you, that you also may have fellowship with us; and truly our fellowship is with the Father and with His Son Jesus Christ" (1 John 1:3).

"Behold, how good and how pleasant it is For brethren to dwell together in unity!" (Psalm 133:1).

PROMISES OF GOD

His Forgiveness.

"You, Lord, are good, and ready to forgive, And abundant in mercy to all those who call upon You" (Psalm 86:5).

"He has not dealt with us according to our sins, Nor punished us according to our iniquities. For as the heavens are high above the earth, So great is His mercy toward those who fear Him; As far as the east is from the west, So far has He removed our transgressions from us" (Psalm 103:10-12).

"Do not grieve the Holy Spirit of God, by whom you were sealed for the day of redemption. Let all bitterness, wrath, anger, clamor, and evil speaking be put away from you, with all malice. And be kind to one another, tenderhearted, forgiving one another, even as God in Christ forgave you" (Ephesians 4:30-32).

His Guidance.

"Trust in the Lord with all your heart, And lean not on your own understanding; In all your ways acknowledge Him, And He shall direct your paths" (Proverbs 3:5-6).

"Now they have known that all things which You have given Me are from You" (John 17:7).

"Your word is a lamp to my feet And a light to my path" (Psalm 119:105).

His Peace.

"Great peace have those who love Your law, And nothing causes them to stumble" (Psalm 119:165).

"You will keep him in perfect peace, Whose mind is stayed on You, Because he trusts in You" (Isaiah 26:3).

"Peace I leave with you, My peace I give to you; not as the world gives do I give to you. Let not your heart be troubled, neither let it be afraid" (John 14:27).

His Presence and Protection.

"Have I not commanded you? Be strong and of good courage; do not be afraid, nor be dismayed, for the Lord your God is with you wherever you go" (Joshua 1:9).

"Fear not, for I am with you; Be not dismayed, for I am your God. I will strengthen you, Yes, I will help you, I will uphold you with My righteous right hand" (Isaiah 41:10).

"Let your conduct be without covetousness; be content with such things as you have. For He Himself has said, 'I will never leave you nor forsake you.' So we may boldly say: 'The Lord is my helper; I will not fear. What can man do to me?'" (Hebrews 13:5-6).

"No evil shall befall you, Nor shall any plague come near your dwelling; For He shall give His angels charge over you, To keep you in all your ways" (Psalm 91:10-11).

"But whoever listens to me will dwell safely, And will be secure, without fear of evil" (Proverbs 1:33).

"For thus says the High and Lofty One Who inhabits eternity: 'I dwell in the high and holy [place], With him [who] has a contrite and humble spirit, To revive the spirit of the humble, And to revive the heart of the contrite ones' " (Isaiah 57:15).

"The angel of the Lord encamps all around those who fear Him, And delivers them" (Psalm 34:7).

His Provision.

"Seek first the kingdom of God and His righteousness, and all these things shall be added to you" (Matthew 6:33).

"Delight yourself also in the LORD, And He shall give you the desires of your heart" (Psalm 37:4).

"He who did not spare His own Son, but delivered Him up for us all, how shall He not

with Him also freely give us all things?" (Romans 8:32).

"My God shall supply all your need according to His riches in glory by Christ Jesus" (Philippians 4:19).

His Strength.

"Wait on the Lord; Be of good courage, And He shall strengthen your heart; Wait, I say, on the Lord!" (Psalm 27:14).

"Those who wait on the Lord Shall renew their strength; They shall mount up with wings like eagles, They shall run and not be weary, They shall walk and not faint" (Isaiah 40:31).

"Let us therefore come boldly to the throne of grace, that we may obtain mercy and find grace to help in time of need" (Hebrews 4:16).

His Victory.

"No temptation has overtaken you except such as is common to man; but God is faithful, who will not allow you to be tempted beyond what you are able, but with the temptation will also make the way of escape, that you may be able to bear it" (1 Corinthians 10:13).

"Thanks be to God, who gives us the victory through our Lord Jesus Christ. Therefore, my beloved brethren, be steadfast, immovable, always abounding in the work of the Lord, knowing that your labor is not in vain in the Lord" (1 Corinthians 15:57-58).

"I can do all things through Christ who strengthens me" (Philippians 4:13).

PRAYER

Note: The key to unleashing prayers that God always answers is to have them flowing from a Word-filled life! God intends His Word to fill our hearts, fill our minds, fill our days, and all our ways. Prayers that flow from a Word-filled life are simple, direct, and biblical. If we seek to pray simply, directly, and biblically, it will harmonize our prayers to the Lord, His will, His Spirit, and we will experience the power of a Word-filled life.

Prayer in General.

"We will give ourselves continually to prayer and to the ministry of the word" (Acts 6:4).

"Evening and morning and at noon I will pray, and cry aloud, And He shall hear my voice" (Psalm 55:17).

"If you abide in Me, and My words abide in you, you will ask what you desire, and it shall be done for you. By this My Father is glorified, that you bear much fruit, so you will be My disciples" (John 15:7-8).

"And whatever things you ask in prayer, believing, you will receive" (Matthew 21:22).

"Be anxious for nothing, but in everything by prayer and supplication, with thanksgiving, let your requests be made known to God; and the peace of God, which surpasses all understanding, will guard your hearts and minds through Christ Jesus" (Philippians 4:6-7).

"And whatever we ask we receive from Him, because we keep His commandments and do those things that are pleasing in His sight" (1 John 3:22).

Note: Memorize and meditate upon the following verses as preparation for praying them for your children. To pray them for someone else, they already need to be part of you!

1. Prayer for Reality in Spiritual Lives:

Saving Faith. "And that from childhood you have known the Holy Scriptures, which are able to make you wise for salvation through faith which is in Christ Jesus" (2 Timothy 3:15).

Loving God's Word. "I have not departed from the commandment of His lips; I have treasured the words of His mouth More than my necessary food" (Job 23:12).

Living Victoriously. "And you shall know the truth, and the truth shall make you free. …Therefore, if the Son makes you free, you shall be free indeed" (John 8:32, 36).

Thinking of Heaven. "If then you were raised with Christ, seek those things which are above, where Christ is, sitting at the right hand of God. Set your mind on things above, not on things on earth" (Colossians 3:1-2).

Finding Sin Repulsive. "For I will declare my iniquity; I will be in anguish over my sin" (Psalm 38:18).

Staying Tender Toward God. "The sacrifices of God [are] a broken spirit, A broken and contrite heart—These, O God, You will not despise" (Psalm 51:17).

2. Prayer for Integrity in Personal Lives:

Maintaining a Clear Conscience. "Now the purpose of the commandment is love from a pure heart, [from] a good conscience, and [from] sincere faith" (1 Timothy 1:5).

Learning to Stand Alone. "As His divine power has given to us all things that pertain to life and godliness, through the knowledge of Him who called us by glory and virtue" (2 Peter 1:3).

Seeking to Stay Pure in Mind and Body. "Beloved, I beg [you] as sojourners and pilgrims, abstain from fleshly lusts which war against the soul …" (1 Peter 2:11).

Evidencing a Servant's Heart. "And whoever of you desires to be first shall be slave of all. For even the Son of Man did not come to be served, but to serve, and to give His life a ransom for many" (Mark 10:44-45).

Not Being Bitter in Trials. "Let all bitterness, wrath, anger, clamor, and evil speaking be put away from you, with all malice. And be kind to one another, tenderhearted, forgiving one another, even as God in Christ forgave you" (Ephesians 4:31-32).

3. Prayer for Stability in Relational Lives:

Cultivating Love for Brothers and Sisters. "Beloved, let us love one another, for love is of God; and everyone who loves is born of God and knows God. He who does not love does not know God, for God is love" (1 John 4:7-8).

Trusting God When Troubles Come. "For rebellion is as the sin of witchcraft, And stubbornness is as iniquity and idolatry" (1 Samuel 15:23a).

Loving God's Plan for Their Lives. "I will praise You, for I am fearfully [and] wonderfully made; Marvelous are Your works, And [that] my soul knows very well" (Psalm 139:14).

Waiting for God's Chosen Partner. "Do not be unequally yoked together with unbelievers. For what fellowship has righteousness with lawlessness? And what communion has light with darkness?" (2 Corinthians 6:14).

4. Prayer for Vitality in Eternal Lives:

Choosing a Life of Contentment. "For I have learned in whatever state I am, to be content: I know how to be abased, and

I know how to abound" (Philippians 4:11b-12a).

Choosing a Life of Consecration.
"If anyone desires to come after Me, let him deny himself, and take up his cross, and follow Me" (Matthew 16:24).

Choosing a Life of Commitment.
"No one, having put his hand to the plow, and looking back, is fit for the kingdom of God" (Luke 9:62).

Giving a Life Back to the Lord.
"Know the God of your father, and serve Him with a loyal heart and with a willing mind; for the LORD searches all hearts and understands all the intent of the thoughts. If you seek Him, He will be found by you; but if you forsake Him, He will cast you off forever" (1 Chronicles 28:9).

SALVATION

Sin.
"As it is written: 'There is none righteous, no, not one …'" (Romans 3:10). "All have sinned and fall short of the glory of God" (Romans 3:23).

"Through one man sin entered the world, and death through sin, and thus death spread to all men, because all sinned …" (Romans 5:12).

"Do you not know that the unrighteous will not inherit the kingdom of God? Do not be deceived. Neither fornicators, nor idolaters, nor adulterers, nor homosexuals, nor sodomites, nor thieves, nor covetous, nor drunkards, nor revilers, nor extortioners will inherit the kingdom of God" (1 Corinthians 6:9-10).

Christ Died for Us.
"Christ also suffered once for sins, the just for the unjust, that He might bring us to God, being put to death in the flesh but made alive by the Spirit …" (1 Peter 3:18).

"God so loved the world that He gave His only begotten Son, that whoever believes in Him should not perish but have everlasting life" (John 3:16).

"God demonstrates His own love toward us, in that while we were still sinners, Christ died for us" (Romans 5:8).

Salvation Is Not by Works.
"To him who works, the wages are not counted as grace but as debt. But to him who does not work but believes on Him who justifies the ungodly, his faith is accounted for righteousness …" (Romans 4:4-5).

"By grace you have been saved through faith, and that not of yourselves; it is the gift of God, not of works, lest anyone should boast" (Ephesians 2:8-9).

"Not by works of righteousness which we have done, but according to His mercy He saved us, through the washing of regeneration and renewing of the Holy Spirit …" (Titus 3:5).

Salvation Is Only in Christ.
"Jesus said to him, 'I am the way, the truth, and the life. No one comes to the Father except through Me' " (John 14:6). "Nor is there salvation in any other, for there is no other name under heaven given among men by which we must be saved" (Acts 4:12).

"There is one God and one Mediator between God and men, the Man Christ Jesus, who gave Himself a ransom for all, to be testified in due time …" (1 Timothy 2:5-6).

Repent of Sins.
"Unless you repent you will all likewise perish …" (Luke 13:3).

"Repent therefore and be converted, that your sins may be blotted out, so that times of refreshing may come from the presence of the Lord …" (Acts 3:19).

"Repent therefore of this your wickedness, and pray God if perhaps the thought of your heart may be forgiven you" (Acts 8:22).

"They should repent, turn to God, and do works befitting repentance" (Acts 26:20).

Receive Christ.
"But as many as received Him, to them He gave the right to become children of God, to those who believe in His name …" (John 1:12).

"He who believes in the Son has everlasting life; and he who does not believe the Son shall not see life, but the wrath of God abides on him" (John 3:36).

"Behold, I stand at the door and knock. If anyone hears My voice and opens the door, I will come in to him and dine with him, and he with Me" (Revelation 3:20).

Assurance of Salvation.
"My sheep hear My voice, and I know them, and they follow Me. And I give them eternal life, and they shall never perish; neither shall anyone snatch them out of My hand" (John 10:27-28).

"Being confident of this very thing, that He who has begun a good work in you will complete it until the day of Jesus Christ ..." (Philippians 1:6).

"And this is the testimony: that God has given us eternal life, and this life is in His Son. He who has the Son has life; he who does not have the Son of God does not have life. These things I have written to you who believe in the name of the Son of God, that you may know that you have eternal life, and that you may continue to believe in the name of the Son of God" (1 John 5:11-13).

Witness.
" 'Go therefore and make disciples of all the nations, baptizing them in the name of the Father and of the Son and of the Holy Spirit, teaching them to observe all things that I have commanded you; and lo, I am with you always, even to the end of the age.' Amen" (Matthew 28:19-20).

"God was in Christ reconciling the world to Himself, not imputing their trespasses to them, and has committed to us the word of reconciliation. Now then, we are ambassadors for Christ, as though God were pleading through us: we implore you on Christ's behalf, be reconciled to God" (2 Corinthians 5:19-20).

"For whoever is ashamed of Me and My words in this adulterous and sinful generation, of him the Son of Man also will be ashamed when He comes in the glory of His Father with the holy angels" (Mark 8:38).

"But you shall receive power when the Holy Spirit has come upon you; and you shall be witnesses to Me in Jerusalem, and in all Judea and Samaria, and to the end of the earth" (Acts 1:8).

APPENDIX B:
Prayers of a Word-Filled Life:
How to Develop a Prayer Journal

"We will give ourselves continually to prayer and
to the ministry of the word" (Acts 6:4).

Personal Prayer Times.
Developing a Daily Prayer Journal can help you establish systematic Word-filled praying—the power for godly parenting (and a joyful marriage). Faithfulness in this can produce the sweetest relationship possible between you and your God, and seeing His sovereign hand move in response to righteous prayers is exciting beyond words!

In Matthew 6:9-14, Christ gives us a simple model for prayer. Using "The Lord's Prayer" as my model, I have divided its verses into a seven-day prayer theme. Of course, this does not mean to imply that your prayer should be limited to these times, and this content. Rather, since we are to pray without ceasing, throughout the day offer up prayers of worship, prayers for

ministry, prayers for family needs, prayers for forgiveness and reconciliation, prayers for victory, prayers of reflection, and prayers of praise and thanksgiving. As you become familiar with this style prayer journal, personalize it by adding special prayer verses God has given you. (For this purpose, space under "Additional Prayer Verses" is provided at the end of each day's theme.)

A good format to use is a 3-ring notebook with seven dividers labeled Sunday-Saturday. (Feel free to duplicate this seven-day plan as a foundation for how to practice praying Word-filled prayers systematically.) Use additional sheets of notebook paper to record dates specific prayers were made, and God's answers. You may wish to also keep a record of such prayers, and on each

child's wedding day, present him or her with "A Book of Remembrances." God keeps such a book that chronicles when we think upon Him (as Malachi 3:16 teaches). So we should also record when we have held the needs of our precious children before the throne of God. Such a book prayed over for our children's growing up years would be a priceless treasure to present to them. This can be a real faith builder for both parent and child!

Each daily prayer theme contains a list of verses, to be prayed back to the Lord (like the "Prayer Examples" in Chapters 16-21). The language of some verses will be easy to pray; for others, you will need to adapt it to a prayer. For example, Psalm 27:1 could be made a prayer simply by changing the wording as follows:

"You, oh Lord, are my light and my salvation; Whom shall I fear? You are the strength of my life; Of whom shall I be afraid?" (Psalm 27:1 Emphasis added).

Note: The whole Book of Psalms is a marvelous resource for practicing Word-filled praying! Like David, and the other psalmists, you, too, can pour your heart out to the Lord through volumes of glorifying worshipful prayers and petitions.

Another aspect of fruitful praying is through scriptural songs. A great saint, Martin Luther, once stated: "I am strongly persuaded that after theology there is no art that can be placed on a level with music; for besides theology, music is the only art capable of affording peace and joy of the heart. ...The devil flees before the sound of music almost as much as before the Word of God." So, beloved, sing thematic Psalms, and hymns, and spiritual songs to the Lord as deep prayers of your heart!

Family Prayer Times:
Many of the suggestions for "Personal Prayer Times" may be adapted, according to the ages of your children, to daily "Family Prayer Times." In addition, once a week, I recommend having a special "Family Night." An excellent resource for this is Jim Weidmann's and Kurt Bruner's series called *Family Nights Tool Chest.*

The concept behind family nights is rooted in the biblical mandate summarized in Deuteronomy 6:5-9. As one dad put it, "Our investment of time and energy into family nights has more eternal value than we may ever know." Why? Because family nights are intentionally teaching children at the wisdom level—the level at which children understand and can apply. Family nights should be exciting, as well as instructive.[3] The family night series contains these excellent biblical teaching aids (12 lessons each): Introduction to Family Nights, Christian Character Qualities, Holidays, Money Matters, Wisdom Life Skills, and Bible Stories for Preschoolers.

The Bible as a Prayer Book for Your Children: In addition to developing a personalized Prayer Journal, you may also wish to make your Bible a prayer book for your children. For the past decade or more, as I have read through the Word and spotted an applicable verse for one of my children, I have noted at the top of the page in my Bible what I am praying about (the character trait, etc.). By the verse(s), I entered the child's name and the date I started praying that for them. In the back of my Bible, I have a compiled list of all the elements. I know where to turn when I open the Word, and I pray that passage every way I can think of for them. So, in effect, the Bible has also become a special prayer book.

In closing, I pray the Lord will draw you ever so close to Him through continual prayer and ministry of His Word!

SUNDAY: PRAYERS OF WORSHIP

"Our Father in heaven, Hallowed be Your Name ..." (Matthew 6:9b).

"God is everywhere, watching, superintending, overseeing, governing everything in the highest interest of man, and carrying forward His plans and executing His purposes in creation and redemption. He is not an absentee God. ...The wonders of God's power are to be kept alive, made real and present, and repeated only by prayer."[4]

Note: What better way to prepare yourself for the Lord's Day services than to fill your heart and mind beforehand with prayers of worship!

Prayers of Worship:

"Oh, worship the Lord in the beauty of holiness! Tremble before Him, all the earth" (Psalm 96:9).

"Make a joyful shout to the LORD, all you lands! Serve the LORD with gladness; Come before His presence with singing. Know that the LORD, He [is] God; [It is] He [who] has made us, and not we ourselves; [We are] His people and the sheep of His pasture. Enter into His gates with thanksgiving, [And] into His courts with praise. Be thankful to Him, [and] bless His name. For the Lord [is] good; His mercy is everlasting, And His truth [endures] to all generations" (Psalm 100).

2. Cited in *Hymns for the Family of God* (Nashville, TN: Paragon Associates, Inc., 1976), Preface.

3. This helpful series can be ordered through Family Life at **www.familylife.com**; click on "Online Store," and enter "Jim Weidmann" or "Family Night Tool Chest" under "Search." (Or call 1-800-FL TODAY to order.)

"The LORD lives! Blessed [be] my Rock! Let the God of my salvation be exalted" (Psalm 18:46).

_____

_____

"Give unto the LORD the glory due His name: Worship the LORD in the beauty of holiness" (Psalm 29:2).

_____

_____

_____

_____

"O LORD, how manifold are Your works! In wisdom You have made them all. The earth is full of Your possessions— … May the glory of the LORD endure forever; May the LORD rejoice in His works" (Psalm 104:24, 31).

"Let all the earth fear the LORD; Let all the inhabitants of the world stand in awe of Him" (Psalm 33:9).

"LORD, You have been our dwelling place in generations. Before the mountains were brought forth, Or ever You had formed the earth and the world, Even from everlasting to everlasting, You [are] God" (Psalm 90:1-2).

"One [thing] I have desired of the LORD, That will I seek: That I may dwell in the house of the LORD All the days of my life, To behold the beauty of the LORD, And to inquire in His temple" (Psalm 27:4).

"Holy, holy, holy, Lord God Almighty, Who was and is and is to come! You are worthy, O Lord, To receive glory and honor and power; For You created all things, And by Your will they exist and were created" (Revelation 4:8b, 11).

Additional Prayer Verses:

MONDAY: PRAYERS FOR MINISTRY

"Your kingdom come. Your will be done" (Matthew 6:10).

"God requires to be represented by a fiery Church, or He is not in any proper sense, represented at all. …The great and eternal interests of heaven-born, God-given religion are the only things about which His Church can afford to be on fire." 5

Note: The servants of God are on the front line of a spiritual battle for the souls of men, women, and children! They need our faithful prayer support! And don't forget prayers for your own ministry to others—and especially to your wife and children!

Prayers for Ministries in General:

Church Leadership (and All Authorities). "I exhort first of all that supplications, prayers, intercessions, [and] giving of thanks be made for all men, for kings and all who are in authority, that we may lead a quiet and peaceable life in

all godliness and reverence. For this [is] good and acceptable in the sight of God our Savior …" (1 Timothy 2:1-3).

Pastors. "For I determined not to know anything among you except Jesus Christ and Him crucified. … And my speech and my preaching [were] not with persuasive words of human wisdom, but in demonstration of the Spirit and of power, that your faith should not be in the wisdom of men but in the power of God" (1 Corinthians 2:2, 4-5).

Missionaries. "According to my earnest expectation and hope that in nothing I shall be ashamed, but with all boldness, as always, so now also Christ will be magnified in my body, whether by life or by death. For to me, to live [is] Christ, and to die is gain" (Philippians 1:20-21).

Personal Ministry to Others. "As for me, far be it from me that I should sin against the LORD in ceasing to pray for you; but I will teach you the good and the right way. Only fear the LORD, and serve Him in truth with all your heart …" (1 Samuel 12:23-24a).

Ministry to Family. Pray for Reality in Your Children's Spiritual Lives:

Saving Faith. "Open their eyes, in order to turn them from darkness to light, and from the power of Satan to God, that they may receive forgiveness of sins and an inheritance

4. Appendix C's prayer comments (at the beginning of each day's suggestions) were taken from this wonderful classic—E. M. Bounds, *A Treasury of Prayer: The Best of E. M. Bounds on Prayer in a Single Volume* (Minneapolis, MN: Bethany House Publishers, 1961). This particular quote is from pp. 190-191.5. Ibid., p. 133.

among those who are sanctified by faith in Me" (Acts 26:18).

Loving God's Word. "I have not departed from the commandment of His lips; I have treasured the words of His mouth More than my necessary food" (Job 23:12).

Living in Victory. "You shall know the truth, and the truth shall make you free. …Therefore, if the Son makes you free, you shall be free indeed" (John 8:32, 36).

Thinking of Heaven. "If then you were raised with Christ, seek those things which are above, where Christ is, sitting at the right hand of God. Set your mind on things above, not on things on earth" (Colossians 3:1-2).

Finding Sin Repulsive. "I will declare my iniquity; I will be in anguish over my sin" (Psalm 38:18).

Staying Tender Toward God. "The sacrifices of God [are] a broken spirit, A broken and contrite heart—These, O God, You will not despise" (Psalm 51:17).

Additional Prayer Verses:

_____

_____

_____

_____

TUESDAY: PRAYERS FOR FAMILY NEEDS

"Give us this day our daily bread" (Matthew 6:11).

"Prayer goes by faith into the great fruit orchard of God's exceeding great and precious promises, and with hand and heart picks the ripest and richest fruit. The promises, like electricity, may sparkle and dazzle, yet be impotent for good till these dynamic life-giving currents are chained by prayer, and are made the mighty forces which move and bless." [6]

Note: We should regularly pray for family needs—whether its members are near or far. This may include physical needs, financial needs, spiritual needs, or specific personal needs. But when we approach God's throne of grace, we need to do so in faith. For "without faith, it is impossible to please Him" (Hebrews 11:6).

Prayers for Family Needs:
"I have been young, and now am old; Yet I have not seen the righteous forsaken, Nor his descendants begging bread" (Psalm 37:25).

"Therefore I say to you, do not worry about your life, what you will eat or what you will drink; nor about your body, what you will put on. Is not life more than food and the body more than clothing? Look at the birds of the air, for they neither sow nor reap nor gather into barns; yet your heavenly Father feeds them. Are you not of more

6. Ibid., pp. 178-179.

value than they? Which of you by worrying can add one cubit to his stature? So why do you worry about clothing? Consider the lilies of the field, how they grow: they neither toil nor spin; and yet I say to you that even Solomon in all his glory was not arrayed like one of these. Now if God so clothes the grass of the field, which today is, and tomorrow is thrown into the oven, will He not much more clothe you, O you of little faith? Therefore do not worry, saying, 'What shall we eat?' or 'What shall we drink?' or 'What shall we wear?' … For your heavenly Father knows that you need all these things. But seek first the kingdom of God and His righteousness, and all these things shall be added to you" (Matthew 6:25-33).

"Delight yourself also in the LORD, And He shall give you the desires of your heart" (Psalm 37:4).

"He who did not spare His own Son, but delivered Him up for us all, how shall He not with Him also freely give us all things?" (Romans 8:32).

"My God shall supply all your need according to His riches in glory by Christ Jesus" (Philippians 4:19).

"Be anxious for nothing, but in everything by prayer and supplication, with thanksgiving, let your requests be made known to God; and the peace of God, which surpasses all understanding, will guard your hearts and minds through Christ Jesus" (Philippians 4:6-7).

"Whatever we ask we receive from Him, because we keep His commandments and do those things that are pleasing in His sight" (1 John 3;22).

Additional Prayer Verses:

_____

_____

_____

_____

_____

WEDNESDAY: PRAYERS FOR FORGIVENESS AND RECONCILIATION

———————

"And forgive us our debts, As we forgive our debtors" (Matthew 6:12).

"Men must walk in upright fashion in order to be able to pray well. ... Praying takes its tone and vigor from the life of the man or the woman exercising it. When character and conduct are at a low ebb, praying can but barely live, much less thrive."[7]

Note: Immediately following the Lord's Prayer, Jesus said that if we don't forgive the trespasses of others, then our heavenly Father will not forgive us (Matthew 6:14). Furthermore, God tells us that if we regard iniquity in our heart, He will not

hear our prayers (Psalm 66:18). While it's true that sins should be confessed daily (1 John 1:9), we also need a regular quiet time of concentrated examination to insure that our walk is not slowly being tarnished by undetected "black spots" like the sterling silver in the Silver Room (Chapter 3). Keeping "clean accounts" with God and others is imperative if we are to live the Word-filled life.

Prayers for Forgiveness and/or Reconciliation:

"He who covers his sins will not prosper, But whoever confesses and forsakes them will have mercy" (Proverbs 28:13).

"You, Lord, are good, and ready to forgive, And abundant in mercy to all those who call upon You" (Psalm 86:5).

"He has not dealt with us according to our sins, Nor punished us according to our iniquities. For as the heavens are high above the earth, So great is His mercy toward those who fear Him; As far as the east is from the west, So far has He removed our transgressions from us" (Psalm 103:10-12).

"Do not grieve the Holy Spirit of God, by whom you were sealed for the day of redemption. Let all bitterness, wrath, anger, clamor, and evil speaking be put away from you, with all malice. And be kind to one another, tenderhearted, forgiving one another, even as God in Christ forgave you" (Ephesians 4:30-32).

Prayers for Stability in Your Children's Relational Lives:

Cultivating Love for Brothers and Sisters. "Beloved, let us love one another, for love is of God; and everyone who loves is born of God and knows God. He who does not love does not know God, for God is love" (1 John 4:7-8).

Trusting God When Troubles Come. "Rebellion is as the sin of witchcraft, And stubbornness is as iniquity and idolatry" (1 Samuel 15:23a).

Loving God's Plan for Their Lives. "I will praise You, for I am fearfully [and] wonderfully made; Marvelous are Your works, And [that] my soul knows very well" (Psalm 139:14).

Waiting for God's Chosen Partner. "Do not be unequally yoked together with unbelievers. For what fellowship has righteousness with lawlessness? And what communion has light with darkness?" (2 Corinthians 6:14).

Additional Prayer Verses:

_____

_____

_____

_____

_____

7. Ibid., p. 163.

THURSDAY: PRAYERS FOR VICTORY

"And do not lead us into temptation, But deliver us from the evil one" (Matthew 6:13a).

"Prayer is a wonderful power placed by Almighty God in the hands of His saints, which may be used to accomplish great purposes and to achieve unusual results."[8]

Note: In John 15:5, Jesus said that without Him, we can do nothing. It is only through abiding in Christ, and His Word, that we can have the power to be victorious in whatever we face. The key to unleashing prayers that God always answers is to have them flowing from a Word-filled life! If you daily put on the whole armor of God, He will give the power to stand against the wiles of the devil (Ephesians 6:11)!

Prayers for Victory.
"Watch and pray, lest you enter into temptation. The spirit indeed is willing, but the flesh is weak" (Matthew 26:41).

"No temptation has overtaken you except such as is common to man; but God is faithful, who will not allow you to be tempted beyond what you are able, but with the temptation will also make the way of escape, that you may be able to bear it" (1 Corinthians 10:13).

"Thanks be to God, who gives us the victory through our Lord Jesus Christ. Therefore, my beloved brethren, be steadfast, immovable, always abounding in the work of the Lord, knowing that your labor is not in vain in the Lord" (1 Corinthians 15:57-58).

"I can do all things through Christ who strengthens me" (Philippians 4:13).

Prayer for Integrity in Your Children's Personal Lives:

Maintaining a Clear Conscience. "The purpose of the commandment is love from a pure heart, [from] a good conscience, and [from] sincere faith" (1 Timothy 1:5).

Learning to Stand Alone. "His divine power has given to us all things that pertain to life and godliness, through the knowledge of Him who called us by glory and virtue" (2 Peter 1:3).

Seeking to Stay Pure in Mind and Body. "Beloved, I beg [you] as sojourners and pilgrims, abstain from fleshly lusts which war against the soul …" (1 Peter 2:11).

Evidencing a Servant's Heart. "Whoever of you desires to be first shall be slave of all. For even the Son of Man did not come to be served, but to serve, and to give His life a ransom for many" (Mark 10:44-45).

Not Becoming Bitter in Trials. "Let all bitterness, wrath, anger, clamor, and evil speaking be put away from you, with all malice. And be kind to one another, tenderhearted, forgiving one another, even as God in Christ forgave you" (Ephesians 4:30-32).

Additional Prayer Verses:

_____

_____

_____

_____

_____

FRIDAY: PRAYERS OF REFLECTION

"For Yours is the kingdom …" (Matthew 6:13b).

"Humility is an indispensable requisite of true prayer. It must be an attribute, a characteristic of prayer. Humility must be in the praying character as light is in the sun. … As a ship is made for the sea, so prayer is made for humility, and so humility is made for prayer."[9]

Note: The word "kingdom" in Matthew 6:9-13 refers to both the future (v. 10) and the present kingdom of God (v. 13). In Luke 17:21, Christ tells us that presently the kingdom of God is within believer's hearts. In other words, wherever the sovereign King of kings is, there is a kingdom, and He is to have complete rule over us. Friday's prayer theme therefore places an emphasis upon examining whether or not we are giving Him first place in our lives. In other words, have you demon-

8. Ibid., p. 179.

9. Ibid., p. 148.

strated vitality in your eternal life this past week so that you can lead your family to do the same?

Prayers of Reflection:

"I, the LORD, search the heart, I test the mind, Even to give every man according to his ways, According to the fruit of his doings" (Jeremiah 17:10).

"Examine me, O LORD, and prove me; Try my mind and my heart" (Psalm 26:2).

"Better to be of a humble spirit with the lowly, Than to divide the spoil with the proud" (Proverbs 16:19).

"A man's pride will bring him low, But the humble in spirit will retain honor" (Proverbs 29:23).

"All of you be submissive to one another, and be clothed with humility, for 'God resists the proud, But gives grace to the humble' " (1 Peter 5:5).

Prayer for Vitality in Your Children's Eternal Lives:

Choosing a Life of Contentment. "I have learned in whatever state I am, to be content: I know how to be abased, and I know how to abound" (Philippians 4:11b-12a).

Choosing a Life of Consecration. "If anyone desires to come after Me, let him deny himself, and take up his cross, and follow Me" (Matthew 16:24).

Choosing a Life of Commitment. "'No one, having put his hand to the plow, and looking back, is fit for the kingdom of God" (Luke 9:62).

Giving a Life Back to the Lord. "Know the God of your father, and serve Him with a loyal heart and with a willing mind; for the LORD searches all hearts and understands all the intent of the thoughts. If you seek Him, He will be found by you; but if you forsake Him, He will cast you off forever" (1 Chronicles 28:9).

Additional Prayer Verses:

_____

_____

_____

_____

_____

SATURDAY: PRAYERS OF PRAISE AND PREPARATION FOR SUNDAY

"... and the power and the glory forever. Amen" (Matthew 6:13b).

"Prayer puts God's work in His hands, and keeps it there. It looks to Him constantly and depends on Him implicitly to further His own cause. Prayer is but faith resting in, acting with, and leaning on and obeying God. This is why God loves it so well, why He puts all power

into its hands, and why He so highly esteems men of prayer. ... [And] giving thanks is the very life of prayer. It is its fragrance and music, its poetry and its crown. Prayer is bringing the desired down so it breaks out into praise and thanksgiving. [10]

Note: To prepare for the Lord's Day services, make sure you've asked God to search your mind and heart to reveal if there is anything displeasing in you (Psalms 26:2). Then, to experience the Lord's presence more fully, ask Him to fill your mind and heart with praise, for God says that He inhabits the praises of His people (Psalm 22:3)!

Prayers of Praise. "Rejoice in the LORD, O you righteous! [For] praise from the upright is beautiful. ... For the word of the LORD [is] right, And all His work [is done] in truth. He loves righteousness and justice; The earth is full of the goodness of the LORD" (Psalm 33:1, 4-5).

"I will bless the LORD at all times; His praise [shall] continually be in my mouth. My soul shall make its boast in the LORD; The humble shall hear [of it] and be glad. Oh, magnify the LORD with me, And let us exalt His name together" (Psalm 34:1-3).

"Oh, sing to the LORD a new song! Sing to the LORD, all the earth. Sing to the LORD, bless His name; Proclaim the good news of His salvation from day to day. Declare His glory among the nations, His wonders among all peoples. For the LORD [is] great and greatly to be praised; He [is] to be feared above all gods. ... Honor and majesty [are] before Him; Strength and beauty [are] His sanctuary" (Psalm 96:1-6).

"Bless the LORD, O my soul; And all that is within me, [bless] His holy name! Bless the LORD, O my soul, And forget not all His benefits" (Psalm 103:1-2).

"Oh, give thanks to the LORD! Call upon His name; Make known His deeds among the peoples! Sing to Him, sing psalms to Him; Talk of all His wondrous works! Glory in His holy name; Let the hearts of those rejoice who seek the LORD! Seek the LORD and His strength; Seek His face evermore! Remember His marvelous works which He has done, His wonders, and the judgments of His mouth ..." (Psalm 105:1-5).

"Praise the LORD! For it is good to sing praises to our God; For it is pleasant, and praise is beautiful" (Psalms 147:1).

"Rejoice always, pray without ceasing, in everything give thanks; for this is the will of God in Christ Jesus for you" (1 Thessalonians 5:16-18).

"Therefore by Him let us continually offer the sacrifice of praise to God, that is, the fruit of our lips, giving thanks to His name" (Hebrews 13:15).

Additional Prayer Verses:

_____

_____

_____

_____

_____

APPENDIX C:
How Should a Believing Parent Respond to a Wayward Child?

One of the greatest challenges in life is raising children. After years of combing through every verse of the Bible dozens of times, I still haven't found the perfect family—a family with a godly dad, a godly mom, and children who are submissive their entire time at home, and grow up to move on into godly marriages and homes. **This just isn't recorded in the Bible.**

What we do find in God's Word are some godly parents who have both godly and ungodly children; we also find some ungodly parents who have all ungodly children, while other ungodly parents end up with some godly children. **There just doesn't seem to be a parenting pattern that always works.**

So what is the answer for us as we parent? When God blesses us with children, He asks us to give them back to Him in dedication. That is what Christ's parents did way back in Luke 2:22. That is also what godly parents have done through the centuries.

But what happens when we dedicate them and they don't turn out as we had hoped and planned? To answer that very relevant question, look with me again at the entire process of child rearing: Christian parenting and our stewardship of the precious lives of our children.

When we as parents present our children in dedication back to the Lord, we are declaring:

"These children belong to You, Lord." Dedication is our public acknowledgement of God's ownership of them (Psalm 127:3). We can then rest in the joyful reality of being stewards of the promises of God's Word. The Bible repeatedly records godly men and women with less than godly children. That is because godliness is a choice; it is an obedient response to the Lord. Godly children can not be made; nor can godliness be forced upon them. They grow that way, by God's grace, with—or sometimes even without—godly parenting.

The bottom line of Scripture is that **God never holds us responsible for how our children turn out—only for how we raised them.**

So let me remind you again of the truths parents affirm when they hold up their precious children to the Lord in dedication of themselves to godly parenting as stewards of their children for the Lord: **I will raise the children God gives me** for His glory; **I will surrender them** back to Him; **I will have His peace** when it is hard, and when they are making their own choices that will shape their future lives; **I will always pray for them,** always love them, and no matter what happens—**I will have God's peace because I gave them to Him**—and raised them for Him as best as I knew how and could do.

Whatever place you are in your parenting—anticipating children, in the midst of raising children, sorrowing over a wayward child, or looking back over wonderful (or not so wonderful) years of parenting—why not go over these dedication truths in your own hearts as parents?

If you have surrendered your children to the Lord already, then reaffirm in your heart these five simple truths: **1. I raised the children You gave me as my very own; 2. I surrendered them** back to You; **3. I will have Your peace** when it is hard, and when they are making their own choices that will shape their future lives; **4. I will always pray for them,** always love them, never give up on them or You; and no matter what happens—**5. I will have Your peace because I gave them to You,** and raised them for You as best as I knew how and could do.

If you are a believing parent, and your child has gone astray from the Lord, **how should you respond to a wayward child?** What comfort is there for parents when this happens? What hope can we have after all the years we loved them, earnestly prayed for them, read God's Word to them, nurtured them in the ways of the Lord, and sought to guide them as best we could?

Here are some truths that comfort our hearts—and the hearts of the many parents we have encouraged over the years:

A Wayward Child . . .

1. A wayward child **is no surprise to God.** Every day of our life (Psalm 139) was written in His book—even the darkest of days!
2. A wayward child **is an opportunity for God to see our response.** Our response is what matters to God most. He is watching and waiting for what we will do, to whom we will turn—and when we turn to Him, our Lord is glorified.
3. A wayward child **drives us to pray** for what we may think is impossible—their return to the Lord and us.
4. A wayward child **opens to us a situation where only God can encourage us** in times like this (I Samuel 30:6b)!
5. A wayward child **fills us with hope** as we remember that God isn't ever through with us as long as we live—and neither is He ever

through with our wayward child.
6. A wayward child **reminds us** we have a perfect heavenly Father as we see our own imperfections reflected by our children.
7. A wayward child **humbles us** as we remember how often we also have failed our children (Psalm 130:3), and failed to respond correctly to our perfect Father.
8. A wayward child **rebukes us** because we expected so much obedience from our imperfect parenting, yet we ourselves gave our heavenly Father such imperfect obedience—even though His parenting was perfect!
9. A wayward child **makes us believe** more and more each day that God is able to do that which we could never do: touch their hearts, soften their hearts, and turn their hearts back to Him (Ezekiel 36:26-27)—and to us.
10. A wayward child **shows us God's never ending grace** as each wave of fear and sorrow rolls over us, but we find our feet firmly planted on the Solid Rock (Psalm 40:1-2)!
11. A wayward child **challenges us to never give up** on him or her. In one of the darkest hours in my job as a dad, I sat with one of my children watching a movie. One line, which was clearly stated twice by Alfred the butler to Master Bruce, will always stay etched in my mind: "So you haven't given up on me yet?" To which the butler answered resoundingly, "NEVER!" I challenge you to say the same in your own heart, to your partner, and by your actions toward a wayward child all your life—**Never will I give up on you, for God will never give up on me!**

I hope that these truths will give you strength when the parenting path gets rough—whether for a moment, or a few weeks or months, or even for the rest of your life. Beloved, God is faithful, so never stop trusting Him—and never cease waiting upon Him! Remember: Faithful prayer, in step with God's plan in His Word, is God's most powerful key to unlock children's hearts as we disciple them for Christ. The battle for our children's souls is won "one prayer at a time"—"Is anything too hard for the Lord? . . ." (Genesis 18:14a)!

APPENDIX D:
Bibliography & Resources Used in this Book

Devotional Books

Bounds, E. M., *A Treasury of Prayer: The Best of E. M. Bounds on Prayer in a Single Volume* (Minneapolis, MN: Bethany House Publishers, 1961).

Cowman, Mrs. Charles E., *Springs in the Valley* (Grand Rapids, MI: Zondervan, 1939).

Cowman, Mrs. Charles E., *Streams in the Desert* (Los Angeles, CA: Cowman Publications, Inc., 1950).

MacDonald, William, *True Discipleship* (Kansas City, KS: Walterick Publishers, 1975).

Taylor, J. Hudson, *Union and Communion* (Minneapolis, MN: Bethany House Publishers, n.d.).

Bible Commentaries

Hendriksen, William, *New Testament Commentary: Galatians and Ephesians* (Grand Rapids, MI: Baker Book House, 1987).

Hendriksen, William, *New Testament Commentary: Philippians* (Phillipsburg, NJ: Presbyterian and Reformed Publishing Co., 1977).

Henry, Matthew, *Matthew Henry's Commentary, Vol. V.- Matthew to John* (McLean, VA: MacDonald Publishing Company).

Lockyer, Herbert, *All the Apostles of the Bible* (Grand Rapids, MI: Zondervan, 1972).

MacArthur, John, *The MacArthur New Testament Commentary: Matthew 10* (Chicago, IL: Moody Press, 1983), electronic edition.

MacArthur, John Jr., *James: The MacArthur New Testament Commentary* (Chicago, IL: Moody Press, 1998), electronic edition.

Wiersbe, Warren W., *The Bible Exposition Commentary: Luke* (Wheaton, IL: Victor Books, 1997).

Wiersbe, Warren W., *The Bible Exposition Commentary: Philippians* (Wheaton, IL: Victor Books, 1985), electronic edition.

Bible Study Tools

Strong, James, *The New Strong's Expanded Exhaustive Concordance of the Bible* (Nashville, TN: Thomas Nelson Publishers, 2001).

MacArthur, John, *The MacArthur Study Bible,* (Nashville, TN: Thomas Nelson, 1997).

Rienecker, Fritz, *A Linguistic Key to the Greek New Testament* (Grand Rapids, MI: Zondervan, 1982).

Tan, Paul Lee, *Encyclopedia of 7,700 Illustrations* (Garland, TX: Bible Communications, Inc., 1996), electronic edition.

Family Life Books

Christenson, Larry, *The Christian Family* (Minneapolis, MN: Bethany Fellowship, Inc., 1974).

DeMoss, Nancy Leigh, *Lies Women Believe: And The Truth That Sets Them Free* (Chicago, IL: Moody Press, 2001).

Drescher, John M., *If I Were Starting My Family Again, Rev.* (USA: Good Books, 1996).

Hughes, R. Kent, *Disciplines of a Godly Man* (Wheaton, IL: Crossway Publishers, 2001).

Lewis, Robert and Hendricks, William, *Rocking the Roles* (Colorado Springs, CO: Navpress, 1991).

Lorang, Dianne, *Keep the Fire Glowing* (Old Tappan, NJ: Fleming H. Revell Company, 1986).

MacArthur, John, *Different by Design* (Wheaton, IL: Victor Books, 1996).

MacArthur, John, *The Fulfilled Family* (Panorama City, CA: Word of Grace Communications, 1985).

Mack, Wayne, *Strengthening Your Marriage* (Phillipsburg, NJ: Presbyterian and Reformed Publishing Co., 1977).

Mayhall, Jack and Carole, *Marriage Takes More Than Love* (Colorado Springs, CO: Navpress, 1978).

Priolo, Lou, *The Heart of Anger* (Amityville, NY: Calvary Press, 1997).

Rosberg, Dr. Gary and Barbara, *The 5 Love Needs of Men and Women* (Wheaton, IL: Tyndale House Publishers, Inc., 2000).

Shedd, Charlie W., *Letters To Philip On How To Treat A Woman* (USA: Revell, 1970).

Wright, H. Norman, *Winning Over Your Emotions* (Eugene, OR: Harvest House Publishers, 1998).

Current Issue Books

Alcorn, Randy, *The Treasure Principle* (Sisters, OR: Multnomah Publishers, 2001).

Glueck, Sheldon and Eleanor, *Unraveling Juvenile Delinquency* (Cambridge, MA: Harvard University Press, 1950).

Holmes, Mrs. C. L., "Little Children, Come to Jesus," *The Children's Hymn Book* (Grand Rapids, MI: The National Union of Christian Schools, 1962).

Livingstone, David, *David Livingstone's Private Journal: 1851-53, ed. 1. Schapera* (London: Chatto & Windus, 1960).

MacArthur, John, *The Vanishing Conscience* (Dallas, TX: Word, 1994).

Postman, Neil, *Amusing Ourselves to Death* (USA: Viking Penguin Inc., 1985).

Reed, Alvin, *Radically Unchurched* (Grand Rapids: Kregel, 2002).

Sanborn, Mark, Paulson, Terry, *Meditations for the Road Warrior.* (Grand Rapids, MI: Baker Books, 1998).

Swenson, Richard A., M.D., *The Overload Syndrome* (Colorado Springs, CO: NAVPRESS, 1998).

Periodicals

Barnett, John, *Discipleship Journal* (Colorado Springs, CO: NavPress), "Are You an Under Rower for Christ?" (Issue 30, November 1985).

Siegel, Dr. Alberta, *Stanford Observer,* (Stanford, CA: Stanford News Service).

Men's Ministry

Eisenman, Tom, *Temptations Men Face* (Downers Grove, IL: Inter Varsity Press, 1990).

Farrar, Steve, *Point Man: How a Man Can Lead a Family* (Portland, OR: Multnomah Press, 1990).

Women's Ministry

Elliot, Elisabeth, *A Chance to Die: The Life and Legacy of Amy Carmichael* (Grand Rapids, MI: Fleming H. Revell, 1987).

Electronic Resources

One of the most moving studies of my life was a ten-year, intensive time in the final book of the Bible— The Revelation. My verse-by-verse devotional commentary entitled "Christ Unveiled in Revelation" is available free of charge online at **www.discoverthebook.org.** Section 8 is called "Exploring Heaven."

Wilkerson, David, "A Manifestation of Jesus" (New York, NY: Times Square Church E-mail, 7-12-02). **http://www.timessquarechurch.org/**

British Broadcasting Company World News, "Health," 11-02-02. **http://news.bbc.co.uk/2/hi/health/default.stm**

Affluenza http://www.pbs.org/kcts/affluenza/escape/

APPENDIX E:
Additional Resources From
Discover the Book Ministries

*All resources, books, MP3 CDs and DVDs are available online at **www.dtbm.org**.*
*A daily devotional e-mail called **E-news** is available free of charge. Sign up on the website.*
*To order, write us at: **BFM Books/TBC, 5838 South Sheridan, Tulsa, OK 74145***
*or simply e-mail us at: **WFF@dtbm.org***

GENESIS: From the Garden to Glory *(Audio MP3 CD)*

Want to understand dinosaurs and cavemen? Study Genesis 1-5! Want to grasp the events of the Flood and the Lost World? Study Genesis 6-8! Want to see where you and every other nationality on earth originated? Learn the secrets of Genesis 9-11! In these 36 fascinating audio MP3 lessons, six colorful slide shows, and nearly 300 pages of footnoted research, you can get a lifetime of study on where we all came from—and where we all are headed!

*Order online at: **www.dtbm.org** | ISBN: 0-9763314-6-2 | $15.00*

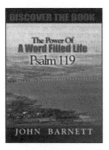

PSALM 119: The Power of a Word Filled Life *(Audio MP3 CD)*

Would you like to know how to unleash the power of God's Word into your everyday life? Learn the disciplines of a godly life: Scripture reading, Spirit-filled living, stewardship, supplication, and suffering. Study the Old Testament keys to meditation and memorization. Our God of New Beginnings created us for great works for His glory. God therefore wants to write Himself across the pages of each of our lives. How is He doing in yours? This CD contains 36 practical, biblical lessons in both MP3 audio files and printable, individual PDF lesson files. You can listen to, and/or print the lessons for use in Sunday schools, home Bible studies, or personal study.

*Order online at: **www.dtbm.org** | ISBN: 0-9763314-8-9 | $15.00*

REVELATION: From Now to Forever *(Audio MP3 CD)*

Revelation is the ending to the greatest Book ever written. This final Word from God explains all you need to know to understand His ordained events from now until forever. Revelation is the place to go— If you are intrigued by prophecy, if you enjoy discovering new truths, and most of all, if you want to know as much as possible about the Lord Jesus Christ. You will see Him gloriously unveiled in all 22 chapters of this amazing book! This CD contains 52 practical, biblical lessons in both MP3 audio files and printable, individual PDF lesson files. You can listen to, and/or print the lessons for use in Sunday schools, home Bible studies, or personal study.

*Order online at: **www.dtbm.org** | ISBN: 0-9763314-7-0 | $15.00*

The Miracle Israel: God's Sign of End Times *(Audio MP3 CD)*

Wars are simmering in the Middle East. Globalism is spreading so fast we can't keep up with all the advancements. Terrorism has shown us how quickly we can be brought to our knees as a nation. And each day news headlines read like chapter titles in those old scrolls written by Hebrew prophets in Jerusalem long ago. Are you up to speed with what God has mapped out for the future? what's next on His time table? 28 Audio Lessons (about 24 Hours of audio messages) plus over 300 pages of printabe lessons in Adobe PDF format!

Order online at: **www.dtbm.org** | *ISBN: 0-9763314-3-8* | *$15.00*

Learn the Old Testament in 24 Hours *(Audio MP3 CD)*

Although mastery of God's Word is the task of a lifetime, this intense 24-hour study will offer you a strategic grasp of the spiritual applications the 39 Old Testament books can have on your everyday life! This single CD represents over 600 hours of study and careful research in dozens of primary sources over a 2-year period. It contains 42 individual teaching messages plus approximately 500 pages of study guides that correspond to the messages (footnotes and references included).

Order online at: **www.dtbm.org** | *ISBN: 0-9763314-5-4* | *$15.00*

JOHN: Abiding in Christ My Vine *(Audio MP3 CD)*

What matters most in life is that which will survive our earthly pilgrimage, as is clearly seen in John 15. This series leads you to the feet of the One we need to know, the One we need to hear, and the One who alone can make us ready for the greatest day of our lives! You will be introduced to the Vinedresser—the heavenly Father who is always watching over each of us. This CD contains 51 practical, biblical lessons in both MP3 audio files and printable individual PDF files. You can listen to and/or print the lessons for use in Sunday schools, home Bible studies, or personal study.

Order online at: **www.dtbm.org** | *ISBN: 0-9763314-1-1* | *$15.00*

The Joy of a Word Filled Family *(Audio MP3 CD)*

*Listen to the messages that produced the book: The Joy of a Word Filled Family. **The Bible presents the oldest parenting manual on earth—Deuteronomy 6. In those verses we find the foundation for the blessings of a Word-filled family. This CD contains 51 practical, biblical lessons in both MP3 audio files and printable, individual PDF files. You can listen to and/or print the lessons for use in Sunday schools, home Bible studies, or personal study.*

Order online at: **www.dtbm.org** | *ISBN: 0-9763314-2-X* | *$15.00*

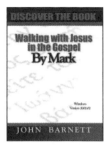

MARK: Walking with Jesus (Audio MP3 CD)

The Gospel by Mark reads like a "shooting script" for an action movie. Mark's Gospel represents the Apostle Peter's recounting of the greatest story ever told. If you will let him, Mark will help you see, feel and experience what it was like to have God in a body— right here on earth. This CD contains 51 practical, biblical lessons in both MP3 audio files and printable, individual PDF files. You can listen to and/or print the lessons for use in Sunday schools, home Bible studies, or personal study.

Order online at: **www.dtbm.org** | ISBN: 0-9763314-4-6 | $15.00

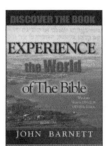

Experience the World of the Bible (Audio MP3 CD)

The more you understand "the Land of the Book," the more you can gain insights into "the Book"—God's Word—the Bible. For the past 20-plus years, John Barnett has been teaching believers from all over the USA from "the Book" in "the Land." On devotional study tours over the past two decades, he has taught over 2500 that God's Word is our textbook, the actual sites are our classroom, and the Spirit of God is our teacher. And now, those actual lessons taught on site in "the land of the Book," are available in audio, print, and slide form—all on one CD!

Order online at: **www.dtbm.org** | ISBN: 0-9763314-9-7 | $15.00

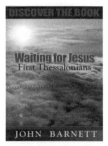

FIRST THESSALONIANS: Waiting for Jesus (Audio MP3 CD)

Paul stopped in the ancient Roman city of Thessalonica for three to six weeks—and turned the world upside down! What type of message changes people in such a way that they go through life all the way to their grave convinced that Jesus is coming again? Pastor John expounds God's Word and explains this life changing ministry Paul had to the Thessalonian people.

If you want a good dose of 1st Century, no nonsense, holy living that looks for Jesus to come back TODAY—then you need to study this "FIRST THESSALONIANS: Waiting for Jesus" series.

Order online at: **www.dtbm.org** | ISBN: 0-9764868-1-4 | $15.00

JAMES: Authentic Christian Living (Audio MP3 CD)

The Book of James was the first New Testament epistle. James the writer, was the first New Testament pastor of a local church—he was also Christ's earthly brother. With the most unique perspective of any writer God used to pen a New Testament book. James takes us to the heart of the life we are to live in Christ: confession of sin; prayer; wealth; resisting temptation; patience; judging; sub-mission; worldliness; the origin of strife; joy in trials; genuine salvation... just to name a few topics! This MP3 CD contains 36 audio MP3 files, plus 36 Word files of each message's outline and text, and a 180 page printable study guide that is in both Word and PDF formats.

Order online at: **www.dtbm.org** | ISBN: 0-9764868-0-6 | $15.00

FINDING HOPE FOR THE END OF DAYS:
The Majesty of Jesus (Chapter 1) *(Audio MP3 CD)*
Feel John's lonely, forsaken, and painful exile on Patmos. See John's face-to-face meeting with the Risen Christ breathe hope into his life and ours. What Christ did—He still does. What John needed—we still need. What Jesus said—we still hear! Find living hope for the end of days in the majesty of Jesus as He is today. There are nine (9) MP3 messages plus the vivid record of Christ's ministry through the eyes of Peter, and by the pen of Mark, in the series entitled MARK: Walking with Jesus through the Gospels (32 messages).

Order online at: **www.dtbm.org** | *ISBN: 0-9764868-2-2* | *$15.00*

FINDING HOPE FOR THE END OF DAYS:
The Message of Jesus (Chapters 2-3) *(Audio MP3 CD)*
Across the pages of history, Christ's messages to the 7 churches of Asia Minor whisper words of hope to us who face the same struggles in different forms. Find living hope for the end of days in the message Jesus gives to us. These eight (8) messages plus the fascinating site-lecture tour of the biblical world explains the historical and geographical insights into God's Word in the Stones of God's Truth series (22 lessons) and the Experience the World of the Bible lectures with slides and photos (14 messages).

Order online at: **www.dtbm.org** | *ISBN: 0-9764868-3-0* | *$15.00*

FINDING HOPE FOR THE END OF DAYS:
The Glory of Jesus in Revelation (Chapters 4-5) *(Audio MP3 CD)*
Get in step with God, join the saints and angels—feel the majesty of worshiping the Lamb. Find living hope for the end of days in the worship of Jesus we share in today. These five (5) messages are a complete semester of biblical worship. The Strategic Grasp of the Bible series (5 lessons) explains Christ in Old Testament ceremonies, sacrifices, symbols, and types—as well as the significance of the Tabernacle. There is also a careful study of the life of Moses (9 lessons).

Order online at: **www.dtbm.org** | *ISBN: 0-9764868-4-9* | *$15.00*

FINDING HOPE FOR THE END OF DAYS:
The Return of the Real King (Chapters 6-9, 16, 19) *(Audio MP3 CD)*
Watch as the long withheld wrath of God breaks out. Find living hope for the end of days in the Return of the Real King—Jesus. These six (6) messages are a graphic look at how Christ's description of the Tribulation is casting its shadow across our world today. Join in the expectant hope of the early church—and wait for Jesus as we go on a careful verse-by-verse journey through Matthew 24 and 1st Thessalonians—looking for Christ's return! This CD also contains the Hoof Beats of the Apocalypse Horsemen series (6 messages), and the What's Next and Prophetic Conference 2005 lectures (28 messages).

Order online at: **www.dtbm.org** | *ISBN: 0-9764868-5-7* | *$15.00*

FINDING HOPE FOR THE END OF DAYS:
The Mystery of Jesus *(Chapters 10-15)* *(Audio MP3 CD)*
Ponder the mysteries of God's plan in conquering back the Father's world. Find living hope for the end of days in the mysteries Jesus reveals. These six (6) lessons show that the Jewish people are God's sign to planet earth—that He keeps His Word! No people have ever been hunted down and targeted for destruction as long and as fiercely as the Israelites. And yet they survive, remaining a visible miracle. Also in the Miracle of Israel (16 messages) we see God's plan for them—past, present, and future in this 16 part lecture series.

Order online at: **www.dtbm.org** | *ISBN: 0-9764868-6-5* | *$15.00*

FINDING HOPE FOR THE END OF DAYS:
Discover the True Bride of Jesus *(Chapter 17)* *(Audio MP3 CD)*
Remember, we who love Jesus are also engaged to be married to Him. In this chapter we see the stark contrast between the false harlot of religion and the true bride of faith in Christ. Find living hope for the end of days in meeting the true bride Christ has redeemed. These six (6) lessons are an in-depth study of the question, "What is the Gospel?" plus the Master's Message series (24 messages), a study of all four Gospels and the book of Acts. This message of Jesus, as it is called, is what we should KNOW, what we should BELIEVE, what we should LIVE, and what we should SHARE!

Order online at: **www.dtbm.org** | *ISBN: 0-9764868-7-3* | *$15.00*

FINDING HOPE FOR THE END OF DAYS:
True Wealth Is in Jesus *(Chapter 18)* *(Audio MP3 CD)*
As Christ reveals the coming meltdown of human civilization, He shows us our real worth is found in what we would have left after we lost health, wealth, prosperity, possessions, and power. Find living hope for the end of days in the true riches Christ gives in these six (6) messages, a study on the modern plague of busyness called Resting In God (8 messages), the Hungering for God series (4 messages), and the Good Heart series (23 messages) on Bible study, the spiritual disciplines, and devotion to Christ.

Order online at: **www.dtbm.org** | *ISBN: 0-9764868-8-1* | *$15.00*

FINDING HOPE FOR THE END OF DAYS:
The Mansions of Jesus in Revelation *(Chapters 20-22)* *(Audio MP3 CD)*
Wait until you see what God has planned for us. Discover the triumph of Jesus as He vanquishes the devil (20:1-10) and renews the earth. Discover the last word of Jesus damning the rebels (20:11-15) as the Judge. Discover the honeymoon of Jesus unveiling paradise for His bride (21:1-8). Discover the wonders of Jesus revealing paradise to His bride. (21:9-27) Discover the extravagance of Jesus offering salvation to all that come to Him (22). Discover the experience of Jesus opening and closing the Revelation of Himself (1-22).

Order online at: **www.dtbm.org** | *ISBN: 0-9764868-9-X* | *$15.00*

Christ Our Refuage

THE SAFEST SPOT IN THE UNIVERSE *(Audio MP3 CD)*

Matthew 24 contains many specific events that would signal the end of days for life on planet earth as it has been for the past several thousand years. Each of the prophetic signs Christ and His apostles gave are specific and not vague. This study is an in-depth look at Christ's precise, clear, specific predictions. You may be startled. Every one of the signs Christ gave are present in your world today. You are the first generation in all of history to experience these trends, these signs—all at once! Includes XX MP3 messages plus the corresponding lessons and study guides for each.

Order online at: **www.dtbm.org** | *ISBN: 1-933561-00-9* | *$15.00*

What's Next for Planet Earth?

THE PROMISES AND PROPHECIES OF CHRIST IN MATTHEW 24 *(Audio MP3 CD)*

When Israel entered the Promised Land, God gave them a constant reminder of His salvation. A strategically placed group of six cities called the Cities of Refuge. One of the most beautiful, the most powerful, the most amazing pictures of Jesus Christ is tucked away in one of those back corners of the Scriptures. Jesus offers to each of us to be a refuge when we are unclean, a refuge when we are weary, a refuge when we are homeless, a refuge when we are helpless, a refuge when we are hopeless, and a refuge when we are tempted. Includes XX MP3 messages plus the corresponding lessons and study guides for each.

Order online at: **www.dtbm.org** | *ISBN: 1-933561-01-7* | *$15.00*

INDEXES:
Biography, Topic Summary, Scripture Passages & Hymns

Scripture Passages

Hymns